GREAT
BRITISH
EDITORIAL

GREAT BRITISH EDITORIAL

Published by
Index Book, S.L.
Consell de Cent 160 local 3
08015 Barcelona
Tel: +34 934545547
Fax: +34 934548438
Email: ib@indexbook.com
http://www.indexbook.com

Copyright © Index Book, S.L. 2008

Publisher
Sylvie Estrada

Concept and Art Direction
emeyele®
Illa de cuba 6 bjs.
08870 Sitges-Barcelona
Tel: +34 938113227
Fax: +34 938113228
Email: estudio@emeyele.com
http://www.emeyele.com

Design
Laura Armet, Javier Fernández (emeyele®)

Coordination
Javier Fernández (emeyele®)

ISBN: 978-84-96774-34-6

BY AIR MAIL
par avion

Royal Mail

Alexander Boxill
Unit 1
Providence Yard
Ezra street
London E2 7RJ
+44 (0)20 7729 0875
www.alexanderboxill.com

SPAIN

8

Icon Magazine
Client Media Ten *Design* Alexander Boxill *Year* 2003-present
Icon is a rigorously designed, accessible and insightful monthly publication on architecture and design. Since its first issue in 2003 we've won many awards, including magazine of the year (twice), best architectural journalist and best critic at the International Building Press awards, and best designed business-to-business magazine and best use of typography at the Magazine Design Awards.

ARCHITECTURE + DESIGN

ISSUE 041 NOVEMBER 2006 £4.50

icon

MONTHLY MAGAZINE OF THE YEAR

THE NEW TABOO-BREAKERS
DESIGN IS EVIL

FredriksonStallard
Timorous Beasties
Peter Zumthor
Rebuilding Beirut
Venice Architecture Biennale
London's design week

icon

issue 019 january 2005 £3.95

architecture + design

studio job

tokyo's recession chic:

exquisite architecure by
ito, kuma, aoki and sejima
+
the world's most hedonistic
design festival

scottish parliament,
finished at last
orgatec
what is design?

plus latest projects by un studio, van lieshout and klein dytham

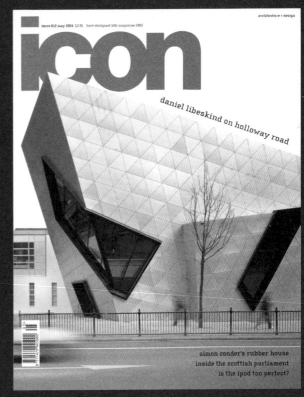

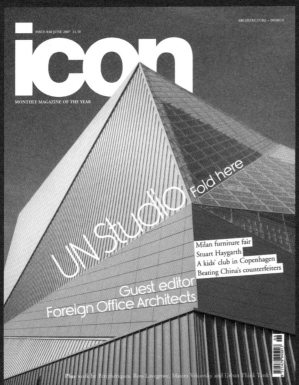

WORDS DANIEL WEST
PORTRAITS ANNIE COLLINGE

Gareth Pugh

is frowning sternly past the camera. Slumped on a knackered-looking chair surrounded by cigarette butts and overfull bags of textile scraps, his intensity is both absurd and unsettling.

Fashion is all about adoption, and Pugh is seemingly adept at that. Aside from today's RADA-worthy sesh here, his clothes, if you can call some of them that, are equally melodramatic. Spectacularly voluminous turtles and catwalk shows that are monochromatic charades have made Pugh the 24-year-old darling of British fashion.

At the photographer shoots her last frame, Pugh snaps into another mode, stepping ↗

words Kieran Long
portrait Rienke Elander

jaime hayon

has been in many different tribes. From his teenage years as a skateboarder in San Diego, to his time at design school in Madrid and his stint at Benetton's Fabrica design institute, he has found himself in league with groups of talented people.

We're sat across a desk from one another in Hayon's Barcelona studio, and he is showing me pictures of his colleagues at Fabrica, where he headed the design department between 1997 and 2004. "This guy is one of the best artists in Japan," he says, before moving on to point to a series of other faces. "He's working for Alexander McQueen, he's a very good designer in Japan, he has a successful design studio working for Foscarini, he's an art director in Costa Rica and she's working for Miyake." Pointing at the final portrait, he says "And she's a secretary. She didn't do too much," as if to define this no-call of success.

Hayon has emerged in the last year as one of Spain's fastest rising industrial designers, having ↗

Marsh View House, Norfolk, by Lynch Architects
words Kieran Long
photographs Sue Barr

it is stories

that distinguish architecture from building.

The architectural theorist Beatriz Colomina writes that contrary to the myth, Daedalus was not the first architect – he built the labyrinth but did not understand its structure. Ariadne, however, interpreted it, with the help of a conceptual device (a ball of string), and thus should be conferred the title. Architecture is a critical and interpretative act as we conceive of it today.

Patrick Lynch is a 33-year-old architect whose career so far has been conducted very much on his own terms. His work is concerned with narrative in a way that is intellectually ambitious, producing architecture that is strange yet familiar, implying rather than describing a genius loci. Marsh View, a new house for an artist in Norfolk, is his biggest project yet, embodying concerns enumerated in his 2001 essay 'Measuring, matter and memory'. In this he wrote: 'The enjoyment and difficulty [of designing] resides in the tension between what you know, can see and control and what you can only glimpse, sense, sniff, barely hear. I'm sure that the way these shadows take up residence in a design project is, in some ways, entirely reasonable. Nonetheless, they resist direct description." For the American novelist John Barth, the problem of space is the impossibility of constructing original narrative. The hero of his short story Lost in the Funhouse ends up being damned to 'construct funhouses for others and be their secret operator – though he would rather be among the lovers for whom funhouses are designed". Lynch explores narrative and sensory data to provide a way out of this postmodern loop.

After studying in Lyon and Liverpool, Lynch studied an MPhil at Cambridge University under ↴

right the view through the studio space with the doors flung away. The exterior spaces are conceived as outdoor rooms

"For whom is the funhouse fun? Perhaps for lovers" John Barth, Lost in the Funhouse, 1968

Jacob van Rijs

Natalie de Vries

Winy Maas

m

vr dv

words Kieran Long
portrait David Levene

"How can you beat them?" asks Winy Maas of MVRDV rhetorically. He is setting out the battleground of contemporary architecture like a general plotting the response to an invasion. "We have to compete with quite heavy opponents," he continues. "New Urbanism in the US is highly politicised and very successful, and there's the retro architecture in Europe which is like an oil spill going over the European landscape." Maas is the oldest and most talkative of the three partners of the Dutch architecture practice. To my right sits the calmer, more pragmatic Jacob van Rijs, looking a bit like an intelligent Knud van Nistelrooy, to my left is the diminutive, bobbed Natalie de Vries.

We are sat in the warehouse building that MVRDV occupies in Rotterdam, discussing how the practice's work has developed from being a junior member of the Superdutch generation of the mid-1990s to working in several countries around the world. But Maas and the other two partners are striking by their willingness to fight battles on a large, even epic, scale rather than just concentrate on individual buildings. As well as construction projects, their work includes polemical exhibitions, films, software and books, all of which make MVRDV as much a research organization as an architecture practice. Climate change, land use, economics, agriculture, energy production and the property market are the parameters of MVRDV's work – to them, there is no limit to the architect's area of responsibility and enquiry, and their own view of interest seems infinitely broad.

MVRDV (the name is an acronym of Maas, van Rijs and de Vries) was founded in 1991 after the partners ↴

012

WORDS KIERAN LONG
ILLUSTRATIONS CECILIA LINDGREN

I am in Shanghai drinking and chatting with a bunch of European designers and journalists. Chinese gallerist Pearl Lam has invited us all here to make connections — between East and West, and between art and design.

Coinciding with the opening of the Shanghai Biennale in September, the event is part of a marketing push for contemporary Chinese cultural output, and a PR exercise in raising the profile of design in China. It's a strange experience, being in the country we are told will be the future of the global economy, yet with the same people you could speak to in Milan, London or any number of other furniture fairs.

The immaculate Lam has three spaces in Shanghai, but spends much of her time in London. She has a vested interest in making connections between Eastern and Western creative cultures, and has invited not just designers but other big players in the effort to connect China with the rest of the cultural world. Philip Dodd, former head of London's Institute of Contemporary Arts and now chair of the Made in China agency, is here, as are curators from London's Victoria & Albert Museum and the Pompidou in Paris, and probably the most prominent collector of Chinese art in the world, the Swiss Uli Sigg.

WORDS ANNA BATES
PORTRAITS RICHARD NICHOLSON

"Everything is like I wanted," says

Piet

Eek

putting his hands behin

Hein

his head. "I have my team, I have my place. I don't have to travel a lot. I don't have to talk too much. I just design. I do what I want." ✦

BY AIR MAIL
par avion

Royal Mail

Aloof Design
5 Fisher Street
Lewes
East Sussex
BN7 2DG
+44 1273 470887
www.aloofdesign.com

Barcelona
España

A

Royal Mail

POSTAGE   PAID   UK
29/03/07   £1.02   BN7
2907   2-1714145-1

Bajos

Aloof Design
5 Fisher Street
Lewes
East Sussex
BN7 2DG
+44 1273 470887
· aloofdesign.com

Georgina Goodman promotional campaigns
Client Georgina Goodman *Design* Sam Aloof, Andrew Scrase, Jon Hodkinson *Year* 2004-2005
Printed promotional campaigns for Georgina Goodman, couture & ready-to-wear shoe designer. Four consecutive seasons, from SS04 to AW05.

018

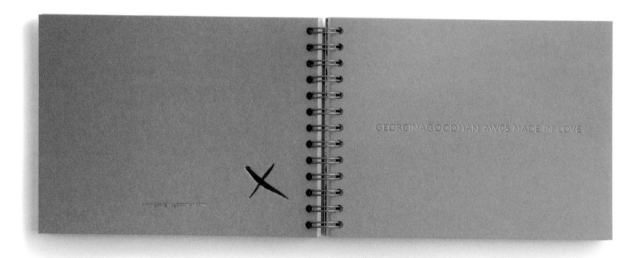

'A love story'

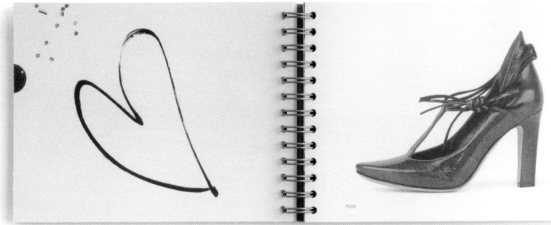

Nola

Nola

Tinsel

Slipper 8

To My heart

020

GEORGINA GOODMAN AW05 MADE IN LOVE

GOODMAN AW05 MADE IN LOVE

GEORGINAGOODMAN SS04

Zita Elze promotional campaign
Client Zita Elze Flowers *Design* Sam Aloof, Andrew Scrase, Jon Hodkinson *Year* 2006
Promotional campaign for London florist culminating in design, photography and production of "Painting with flowers" book and accompanying mailer.

026

ZITA ELZE

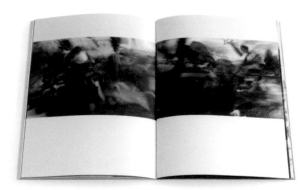

ALAN
AXIS GI
9 SILVE
MANC

Axis Graphic Design Limited
9 Silverdale Road,
Manchester M21 0SH
England
www.axisgraphicdesign.co.uk

Furthermore…'a book of proposals'
Client Further a Field *Design* Alan Ward, Axis Graphic Design *Year* 2004
A collection of artist proposals for a housing development in Liverpool.

Furth
'a book of proposals'
ermo

Building on previous projects we want all the artists who have worked at Sheil Park to submit 'a proposal for a publication of ideas'. We would like the publication to explore and reveal each artist's thinking processes. The publication will accommodate as broad a range of material as possible. We would like artists to include any peripheral material that they think appropriate. Practically, proposals will need to be completed by end of April 2004. The publication will be completed for the Liverpool Biennial, September 2004… …Between now and April it is possible to stay on site in Linosa Close by arrangement. In the longer term, based on proposals submitted, our intention is to commission one or more of these up to a maximum budget of £60,000 (for all commissions).

furtherafield.org.uk

re …

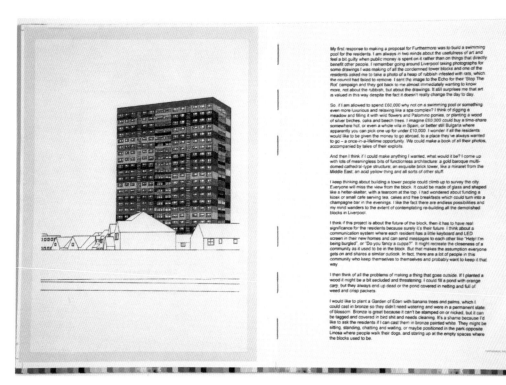

My first response to making a proposal for Furthermore was to build a swimming pool for the residents. I am always in two minds about the usefulness of art and feel a bit guilty when public money is spent on it rather than on things that directly benefit other people. I remember going around Liverpool taking photographs for some drawings I was making of all the condemned tower blocks and one of the residents asked me to take a photo of a heap of rubbish infested with rats, which the council had failed to remove. I sent the image to the Echo for their 'Stop The Rot' campaign and they got back to me almost immediately wanting to know more, not about the drawings, but about the rubbish. It still surprises me that art is valued in this way despite the fact it doesn't really change the day to day.

So, if I am allowed to spend £60,000 why not on a swimming pool or something even more luxurious and relaxing like a spa complex? I think of digging a meadow and filling it with wild flowers and Palomino ponies, or planting a wood of silver birches, oaks and beech trees. I imagine £60,000 could buy a time-share somewhere hot, or even a whole villa in Spain, or better still Bulgaria where apparently you can pick one up for under £10,000. I wonder if all the residents would like to be given the money to go abroad, to a place they've always wanted to go – a once-in-a-lifetime opportunity. We could make a book of all their photos, accompanied by tales of their exploits.

And then I think if I could make anything I wanted, what would it be? I come up with lots of meaningless bits of functionless architecture: a gold baroque multi-domed cathedral-type structure, an exquisite brick tower, like a minaret from the Middle East, an acid yellow thing and all sorts of other stuff.

I keep thinking about building a tower people could climb up to survey the city. Everyone will miss the view from the block. It could be made of glass and shaped like a helter-skelter, with a tearoom at the top. I had wondered about funding a kiosk or small cafe serving tea, cakes and free breakfasts which could turn into a champagne bar in the evenings. I like the fact there are endless possibilities and my mind wanders to the extent of contemplating re-building all the demolished blocks in Liverpool.

I think if this project is about the future of the block, then it has to have real significance for the residents because surely it's their future. I think about a communication system where each resident has a little keyboard and LED screen in their new homes and can send messages to each other like "Help! I'm being burgled", or "Do you fancy a cuppa?". It might recreate the closeness of a community as it used to be in the block. But that makes the assumption everyone gets on and shares a similar outlook. In fact, there are a lot of people in this community who keep themselves to themselves and probably want to keep it that way.

I then think of all the problems of making a thing that goes outside. If I planted a wood it might be a bit secluded and threatening. I could fill a pond with orange carp, but they always end up dead or the pond covered in netting and full of weed and crisp packets.

I would like to plant a Garden of Eden with banana trees and palms, which I could cast in bronze so they didn't need watering and were in a permanent state of blossom. Bronze is great because it can't be stamped on or nicked, but it can be tagged and covered in bird shit and needs cleaning. It's a shame because I'd like to ask the residents if I can cast them in bronze painted white. They might be sitting, standing, chatting and waiting, or maybe positioned in the park opposite Linosa where people walk their dogs, and staring up at the empty spaces where the blocks used to be.

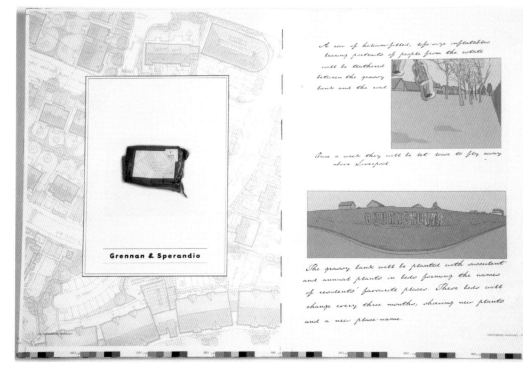

Grennan & Sperandio

A row of helium-filled, life-size inflatable leaving portraits of people from the estate will be tethered between the grassy bank and the road

Once a week they will be let loose to fly away above Liverpool

The grassy bank will be planted with succulent and annual plants in beds forming the names of residents' favourite places. These beds will change every three months, showing new plants and a new place-name.

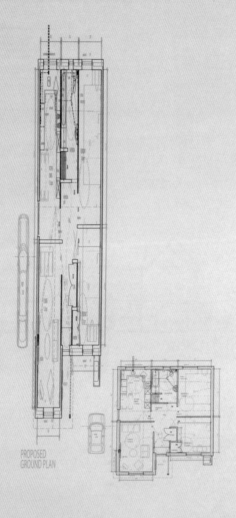

PROPOSED
GROUND PLAN

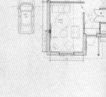

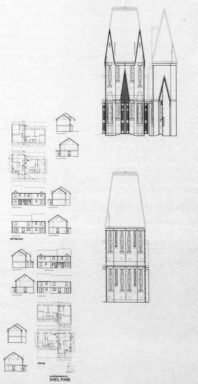

GABLE ELEVATION

SHEIL PARK

SHEIL PARK

@ title: furthermore craftprint / axis graphic design ltd.   section 4 inner/outer

Bureau of the Centre for the Study of Surrealism and its Legacy
Client Book Works / The Manchester Museum *Design* Alan Ward, Axis Graphic Design *Year* 2005
A book accompanying the artist installation by Mark Dion at The Manchester Museum, Manchester.

038

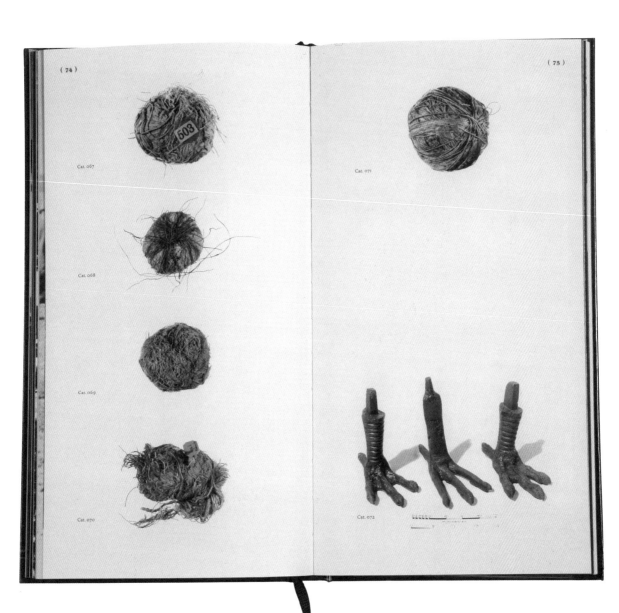

Cat. 067

Cat. 068

Cat. 069

Cat. 070

Cat. 071

Cat. 072

Cat. 012

CHAPTER II
_____

Department of Zoology

+44 (0)20
7422 9181
bbsaunders
.com

7 Plough Yard
London
E 2A 3LP

en

c/.

bajos

BB/Saunders
7 Plough Yard
London
EC2A 3LP
+44 (0) 20 7422 9181
www.bbsaunders.com

centrefold
2

Centrefold

Client Self-initiated *Design* BB/Saunders *Year* 2006

Centrefold is a self-initiated, self-published studio project. Originally conceived as a selling tool for a photographer, it developed into an ongoing project with other contributors. The publication is designed as a series of unbound, interleaved pages working sequentially.
The unbound format allows each centrefold to be removed and exist independently.

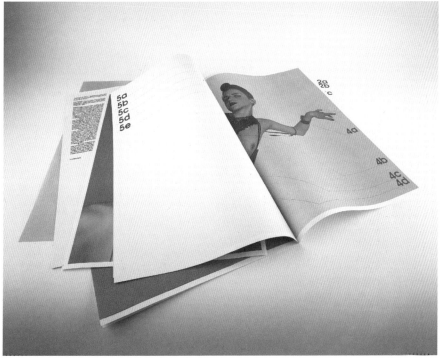

Rankin

Client Rankin Photography *Design* BB/Saunders *Year* 2005

Fashion photographer Rankin commissioned us to create a showcase for his work that would enhance his reputation within the commercial marketplace. We used UV throughout to create a high-gloss luxurious feel. No text was printed, it was knocked out of the varnish.

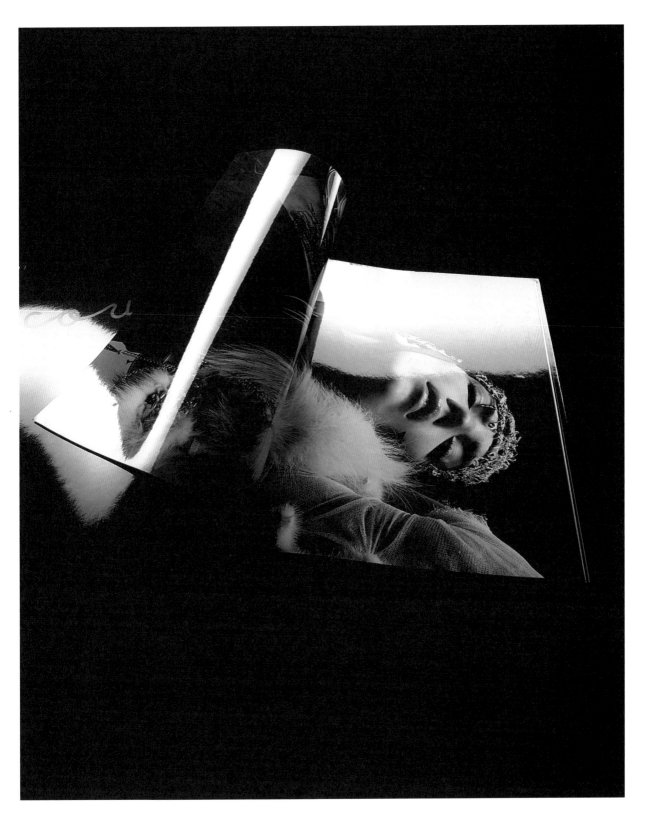

Blueprint
6-14 Underwood Street
London , N1 7JQ
+44 (0) 20 7490 0049
www.blueprintmagazine.co.uk

C/ ̶ ̶ ̶ ̶ ̶ ̶, 28, BAJOS
̶ ̶ ̶TGES
BARCELONA, SPAIN

083

BLUEPRINT

THE MAGAZINE FOR LEADING ARCHITECTS AND DESIGNERS

6-14 UNDERWOOD STREET
LONDON, N1 7JQ

Blueprint redesign

Client Blueprint magazine *Design* Patrick Myles, Kieran Gardner *Year* 2006

The redesign and relaunch of Blueprint magazine took place in June and July 2006. Our publishers wished to reconnect with the magazine's original intention which was to show the best of architecture and design to a predominantly professional community. Although the magazine was a market leader in this respect, rival publications now stood beside it at the newsstand. The publishers wished to preserve the architectural and design focus but retain an intelligent, critical edge. The design had to reflect this.

BLUEPRINT

THE MAGAZINE FOR LEADING ARCHITECTS AND DESIGNERS

January 2007 £4.75

250

THE ARCHITECT AND HER PHOTOGRAPHER

ZAHA
HADID
AND
HELENE
BINET
MORITZ
WALDEMEYER
ARNOLD
SCHWARTZMAN
+ WIN A TRIP TO NEW ZEALAND

Lynch Architects is about to join an exclusive handful of architects invited to design installations for the Ideal Home Show. *Jaffer Kolb* reports

A need to revitalise, a proclaimed commitment to sustainability, and the need for a relatively safe architecture practice have led the Daily Mail Ideal Home Show to commission London-based Lynch Architects to design a large scale installation for this year's show.

The Ideal Home Show was established in 1908 by the Daily Mail, and has a long history of showcasing homewares with a mix of new technologies and popular products. The exhibition has always acted as an index for domestic culture, bursting with new products during boom-times and showing off the finest bomb shelters during war years.

While each year speculative builders construct a mock-village, only a handful of established architects have been asked to design installations in the past: in 1929, RA Duncan exhibited a modernist home; in 1934 Wells Coates showed the Sunspan House, and in 1956 Alison and Peter Smithson's House of the Future was unveiled. 'What's involving architects in this year's show is the whole issue of sustainability,' says Deborah Sugg

Ryan, whose book The Ideal Home Through the Twentieth Century provides a comprehensive history of the exhibition. This may be true in part, as the exhibition has advertised the sustainable features of the design such as energy efficiency and the ability to plug in photovoltaic panels.

Lynch Architects is not primarily known for environmental friendliness, however. According to Patrick Lynch, disappointment over last year's attendance figures was another reason that DMG World Media, the show's organiser, sought a high-profile installation this year. Lynch Architects, which has earned recognition as talented young architects from The Guardian, the Architects' Journal, BD and Wallpaper*, should attract new visitors based on its credit alone.

While it may be well known in architecture and design circles, however, Lynch Architects is not so experimental as to compromise the middle-class respectability of the Ideal Home Show. Past work includes residences, office projects, and a community centre. Future projects are also within established lexicons of

Below: A model of the show homes created by Lynch Architects for the Daily Mail Ideal Home show, running from 9 March to 1 April at Earl's Court. Clockwise from bottom right: suburban, urban and rural houses

form and material, and given that it works intelligently in a new vernacular, synthetic materials and parametrically generated objects are unlikely to abound.

The firm was contacted by Michael Franks, chief operating officer and head of exhibitions at DMG World Media, who liked Lynch's emphasis on building social spaces, an approach to sustainability that emphasises

THE PRACTICE EXPLORED THE ISSUES OF DESIGNING PRIVATE HOUSES IN A SOCIAL SPACE

community over environmental concerns. The designers began looking at their own residential projects, concluding that the planning system in London encouraged anti-social, defensible spaces. These issues are successfully addressed in rural, urban, and suburban houses all designed sympathetically for the show. Lynch restricts himself to planning codes and residential typologies, working within

the parameters of zoning to explore the theoretical issues of designing private houses in a social space.

The urban residence, which comes from a design for the Cricklewood regeneration project masterplanned by Allies and Morrison, uses a traditional Georgian terraced house as its model. A recycled composite wood frame can be adapted to the requirements of a site, and a brick facing provides a material link to the type.

When the houses are built together they form common outdoor spaces. Similarly, the firm attempted to design out the potential for isolation in rural living. 'Rather than a box you can lock down, we created a parallelogram to fragment the space,' says Lynch.

This shape is meant to encourage flows between inside and out, and between residences where there is a cluster. For the suburban house, the architects focused on the development of irregular brownfield sites. The flexible design is massed around a central courtyard and the first floor is skewed to intersect with the surrounding area.

PAPER CITY JAMES WINES

Fresh from the Venice Architecture Biennale opening celebrations in September, the New York-based artist and environmental designer, James Wines, drew his future vision of the city for Blueprint: 'post-global warming, adaptive reuse of existing buildings at sea level'.

This city on stilts fits with Wines's current investigations into the use of information and ecology to push the definition of green design. But it also has the characteristic sense of storytelling that Wines is best known for.

Having founded the design firm SITE in 1970, Wines went on to build the renowned BEST stores in several cities around the US. The most famous of these was in Houston, Texas. A drawing of its iconic crumbling brick facade recently appeared in the Barbican's exhibition Future City.

Wines continues to investigate the overlap between sculpture, architecture and environment in his soon-to-be-completed pavilion for the Fondazione Pietro Rossini in Briosco, Italy.
www.siteenvirodesign.com

Post global warming - Adaptive re-use of existing buildings at sea level

SITE J·W Sept '06

OPENING SHOT
GEERT GOIRIS

This is La Soucoupe, The Saucer, a sports stadium in Saint-Nazaire in the Pays de la Loire region of France. It was designed by the architectural practice Vissuzaine, Longuet et Rivière and completed in 1962. The picture was taken by the Belgian photographer Geert Goiris while on a tour of the town with French sculptor Vincent Lamouroux.

Goiris has photographed other bold avant-garde projects throughout Europe, with post-war Soviet Union architecture featuring prominently in his portfolio. Architecture is only part of his interest. Goiris captures elemental forms – be they buildings, explosions, or animals – whose stillness is threatened in some way. In April an exhibition of his work is being held at the Galerie Catherine Bastide in Brussels.

SUPERBIA THE CASE FOR SUBURBS

FOR DECADES THEY WERE
DECRIED AS VULGAR AND
LACKING IN COMMUNITY. BUT
THE GROWTH OF THE SUBURBS
SHOWS A POSITIVE CULTURAL
SHIFT IN A WORLD WHERE OLD
DIVISIONS BETWEEN TOWN AND
COUNTRY NO LONGER APPLY,
ARGUES **JAMES HEARTFIELD**

ILLUSTRATION BY MILES COLE

'New homes spread like so much detritus discarded across thousands of hectares of southern England … the nowhere lands of the Thames Gateway… Hundreds of thousands of new homes: red-tiled, uPVC-windowed, developers' junk… An England 100% England free.' Architectural critic Jonathan Glancey, imagining the year 2020, gave vent to his hatred of suburbia, and the nowhere people of the Thames Gateway, the M11 corridor and Milton Keynes.

The real growth in the suburbs took place between 1920 and 1939, when housebuilding averaged at 300,000 homes a year, with a peak of 350,000 in 1936. All in all, four million homes were built between the wars, nine-tenths of them in newly developed or existing suburbs – Becontree to the east of London, Kirkby near Liverpool, Longbridge on the outskirts of Birmingham.

Reaction to this fantastic expansion of human civilisation was brutal. Architect Clough Williams-Ellis, a founder of the Council for the Protection of Rural England, published an alarmist tract, England and the Octopus, in which he set out his dread of suburbia. Williams-Ellis's judgment endures to this day in the many pronouncements of the CPRE; and in the views of people like Tristram Hunt, who detest the 'nefarious breed of suburbia, which came to swamp inter-war Britain'.

The journalist Ian Nairn wrote of 'the

annihilation of the site, the steamrollering of all individuality of place to one uniform and mediocre pattern'. At the end of the century, Nairn's anxieties were not realised. Britain's green spaces are, thanks to the retreat of the plough, even more extensive than they were in 1955, but the anxieties are, if anything even greater.

No doubt many people remember glum childhoods and stultifying moralism in the suburbs. But inner cities and countryside can be stultifying too. In his book Sprawl, Robert Bruegmann makes the point that every town was once a suburb. Put another way, decrying the suburbs is just a rhetorical device for decrying modernity and change.

The case against the suburbs reads like a case against most of us. The suburbs – usually creeping or sprawling suburbs – are generally defined against other populations that are in decline: the elegised country folk or, lately, the abandoned inner-city dwellers. In this rhetoric, the contrasting population is invoked not for any of its original characteristics, but to serve to show the shortcomings of suburbia. The qualities that intellectuals moan of in the suburbs – vulgarity and a lack of community and spirituality – are the qualities that they find missing in society at large. 'Suburbia' is just a shorthand for 'anywhere' in these screeds.

Is the belief that new suburbs are uncultured really justified? Simon Gunn and Rachel Bell think that 'the pace at which the associational life of the suburbs grew was vigorous'. Their study of the suburbs near Morden, south London found that the Stoneleigh Residents Association grew in membership from 600 in 1936 to 1,400 in 1939, and 'a whole gamut of activities and organisations was set up under its auspices: whist drives, dances, cricket club, motoring club, cycling club, an orchestra and choral society'.

Critic John Carey makes the case that the suburbs are far from uncultured, producing such talents as the poets Stevie Smith, Philip Larkin and even John Betjeman – one could add film-maker John Boorman, and angry young man John Osborne. Anti-suburban snobs derided 'Essex Girls' in the Eighties, but they ought to include actresses Helen Mirren, Maggie Smith and Sheila Hancock, singers Sade and Alison Moyet, commentators Germaine Greer and Julie Burchill in their list. Indeed one might stretch the point to say that much of the criticism of suburbia was consumed by a largely suburban audience.

The growth of the suburbs coincides with a growth in the cultural life of the population, whether measured in newspaper readership, library membership, the growth of new media like radio and television, or the expansion of education. The »

THE GROWTH OF THE SUBURBS COINCIDES WITH A GROWTH IN THE CULTURAL LIFE OF THE POPULATION, WHETHER MEASURED IN NEWSPAPER READERSHIP, THE GROWTH OF NEW MEDIA LIKE RADIO AND TELEVISION, OR THE EXPANSION OF EDUCATION

Right: The Nelson-Atkins Museum of Art in Kansas City, Missouri. The glass skin is low-iron, which will cut out ultraviolet rays

Far right top: The glass is sandblasted on the inside layer to prevent reflections

Far right bottom: A sculpted detail from the interior

project, we had an advantage because we did eight weeks' worth of work in four.'

Two years ago, Li, who has been with the firm since 2000, moved back to his home city, Beijing, to open Holl's satellite office and oversee its two China projects, the Nanjing Museum of Art and Architecture, a privately funded museum, and Linked Hybrid, a 110,000 sq m mixed-use development located just outside Beijing's first ring road, not far from the Forbidden City. While the Nanjing museum is on hold, Linked Hybrid is in construction. 'It's bigger than all of our completed projects to date,' says Holl. The Vanke Center in Shenzhen, which the firm won in an invited competition in November, is even larger, at 186,000 sq m. Linked Hybrid and the Vanke Center are similar in that both are mixed-use commercial developments, with strong, cubic volumes linked and floating above their sites, bringing a sense of urbanity to their respective locales.

In the case of Linked Hybrid, it was Holl who convinced the developer to alter the original programme, which called simply for 800 apartments in eight towers. The architect proposed introducing other uses, such as open spaces and a ground-floor cinema, as well as retail and restaurants dispersed along upper-level bridges that linked the towers. The number of apartments shrunk to 750, but the developers accepted the trade-off. 'Can you imagine doing that in the US, totally changing a developer's programme and convincing him to give over part of his project to public uses?' asks Holl. 'We were lucky to have this ideal client, who would let us try out things that we couldn't elsewhere.' In a country where luxury housing is equated to gated communities, Holl's impulse – to make the massive development a part of the city, instead of being set apart from it – is admirable.

Also, both projects are propelling Holl's practice deeper into the realm of sustainable architecture. Linked Hybrid has garnered publicity all over China and beyond for its 660 geothermal wells and on-site grey-water treatment facility, which will irrigate the project's landscape and supply the toilets. The Vanke Center, which encompasses offices, a hotel and condominiums, will also be eco-friendly, and both are already being seen as positive development models in a country confronting dire ecological circumstances.

While Holl isn't exactly known as a green architect, many previous projects apply sustainable principles, such as Simmons Hall dormitory at MIT (1999–2002), whose deeply inset waffle-pattern windows shade out summer sun while allowing low-angled winter sun to heat the building. His Whitney water treatment plant and park features a sod-roofed shed and landscaped grounds that mirror the filtration process. The Swiss Embassy residence also features a green roof and a number of passive solar measures, such as expanding its southern exposure and using skylights. As a Swiss government construction, the house had to meet Minergie, the nation's strict green building standard.

Still, Holl doesn't trumpet the green aspects of his projects. 'For me, there are many issues in architecture that are important,' he says. 'Sustainability is one of them, but if it comes to it, I wouldn't sacrifice the architecture.

'At this stage of my career, it's about ideal commissions – projects that have social, environmental and urban aspects – because these are aspects that can live on, and mean that a project can have a significant long-term contribution to a place,' he continues. This interest has driven the firm towards institutional work

such as museums, campus buildings, and other works that fulfil a public role. 'I've turned down projects because their contexts weren't urban enough,' says Holl, noting that size and budget isn't a factor in determining which projects the firm will pursue. (The firm wins most of its projects through invited competitions.)

The most recent news in Holl's office is that the Knut Hamsen Museum, a project he designed in 1994, has been resurrected. Located above the Arctic Circle, near the village where the contentious Norwegian writer grew up, the project was suspended due to controversies over its site and lack of funding. Holl was sanguine about the news. 'You know, this is the sixth or seventh time this has happened to me – having a dead project pulled out of a drawer years later,' he says, listing Pratt and the College of Architecture at the University of Minnesota as other instances.

When his projects are resurrected, Holl has never been tempted to tweak their designs. 'I've always believed that architecture should be completely rooted in its programme and site, unfazed by fashion,' he says. 'In a way, the Knut Hamsen museum proves my philosophy, that if the concept is strong, it will be timeless' ∎

Below: Section of the Linked Hybrid project in Beijing – a massive piece of work for Holl, the development is heated by geothermal wells

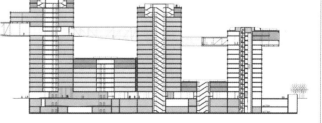

STEVEN HOLL ARCHITECTS

AS ARCHITECTURE BECOMES AN
INCREASINGLY GLOBAL MARKET, MOST
AMERICAN DESIGNERS HAVE BEEN CAUGHT
ON THE BACK FOOT AS THEIR EUROPEAN
COUNTERPARTS HAVE SEIZED THE WORLD
STAGE. AS **CATHY LANG HO** DISCOVERS, AT
LEAST ONE AMERICAN ARCHITECT IS MORE
THAN CAPABLE OF HOLDING HIS OWN IN
THE INTERNATIONAL SPOTLIGHT
MAIN IMAGE: CHRISTIAN RICHTER

Of late, American institutions and developers are infatuated with foreign architects – Richard Rogers has become the architect of choice for museums in major American cities from New York to Atlanta to San Francisco to Dallas, while Santiago Calatrava, Rem Koolhaas, Herzog & De Meuron, Zaha Hadid and many others have all scored juicy commissions that must leave home-grown talent feeling a little bit envious, to say the least. While the globalisation of the architecture profession, like all others, is inevitable, the US clearly has a trade deficit, exporting far less architectural talent than it's importing. New York–based Steven Holl, however, is among the few American architects who enjoy a high level of overseas appeal. At the moment, his 49-person firm has 16 active projects, 11 of them abroad.

In fact, Holl's career was kick-started by foreign work, most notably the Kiasma Museum of Contemporary Art in Helsinki (1992-98), a job won by competition that transformed his three-person studio (which he established in 1977) into a 10-person practice nearly overnight. Two other early overseas projects, the large-scale housing projects at Fukuoka (1989-91) and Makuhari (1992-96), both in Japan, boosted his international reputation while, until fairly recently, his built American work remained dominated by houses. In the past few years, however, his firm has seen the completion of institutional projects in the US that might change the idea that his most significant works are abroad.

In September 2005, Holl's design of Higgins Hall, the expansion of the Pratt Institute's School

The School of Art and Art History at the University of Iowa

Below: The Art School is a collage, departing from Holl's usual use of elemental form

Right: The central communal stair that anchors the variety of interior spaces.

FOR ME THERE ARE MANY IMPORTANT ISSUES IN ARCHITECTURE. SUSTAINABILITY IS ONE OF THEM – BUT IF IT COMES TO IT, I WON'T SACRIFICE THE ARCHITECTURE

of Architecture in New York, was completed, and one year later, the School of Art and Art History at the University of Iowa in Iowa City was inaugurated. Also last autumn, the firm completed the residence at the Swiss Embassy in Washington, DC, and next month his largest and highest-profile US work to date – the addition and renovation of the Nelson-Atkins Museum of Art in Kansas City, Missouri – will open its doors. These projects have already earned top honours from the American architectural establishment: earlier this year, the national AIA bestowed an Honor Award to the Iowa project, as did the AIA's New York chapter.

Among Holl's recent projects, the Iowa School of Art stands out because it departs from his usual vocabulary, which favours tightly composed, monolithic forms. He begins every project by water-colouring initial concepts. Holl likens his Iowa work to Picasso's Cubist guitar – and it's true: a bird's-eye view reveals a rough assemblage of disparate pieces. The building still addresses Holl's obsession with 'porosity' by providing clear sight-lines from the campus through its ground-floor lobby to a wooden pond-front deck. It's sheltered by the project's most dramatic feature – a 7.6m-long cantilevered rectangular box that holds the library (engineered by Guy Nordenson) – but the arrangement of the building's various parts verges

on haphazard. Holl describes the process of assigning functions to spaces as improvisational, a liberty he allowed himself given the nature of the building's use, by artists-in-training. As firm partner Li Hu, who led the project for two years, puts it: 'The building is very readable from the outside; the different spaces, such as the library, classrooms and offices, each have their own form, which radiate around a central communal stair.'

Materially, the building is rough and ready: the structure and most of its cladding is CorTen steel, which has a reddish tone referencing the brick of the nearby, original art school building. The CorTen the architects specified – which is an alloy of steel, copper, chromium and nickel that weathers to an even redder hue – is exposed inside and out, as are other building materials, including concrete piers supporting the cantilever, and concrete-plank flooring (hollow-cored to house the electrical and mechanical systems, eliminating the need for duct-work). The 6,500 sq m project had a budget of $16m (£8m), but the architects brought it in at $14.5m (£7.2m). Choosing robust materials and leaving them unfinished was the correct decision, assuming that the building's users – art students – subject it to extensive wear and tear.

The building is a distant (though clear) cousin to the refined Nelson-Atkins, a 15, 232 sq m

Below: Each type of interior has its own lighting condition – offices feature Holl's favoured milky, channel glass

expansion and 23,225 sq m renovation distilled into five individual buildings, or 'lenses' as Holl likes to call them, cascading down the museum's sloped site. Glowing and irregular, the buildings appear like Jolly Ranchers at various stages of dissolve. Holl's characteristically deft dealing with mass and light reaches its apogee here: the 'lenses' animate the museum's sprawling landscape, giving shape to sculpture gardens nestled between them and funnelling light into linked, subterranean galleries. As in other projects (such as Kiasma and Iowa), Holl chose channel glass for cladding, a material that transmits a diffuse light and can be sculpted into curved forms. In the case of the Nelson-Atkins, the glass had to undergo extensive wind testing, so Munich-based Lamberts custom-made tempered channel glass, which also allowed taller spans.

The next major phase of firm's evolution hinges on China, in more ways than one. Not only are the firm's largest projects based there, but the office that Holl opened in Beijing is bringing a new level of efficiency to the practice. 'It's the ideal arrangement because we are 12 hours apart,' he enthuses. 'We can work all day on something in New York and then fax or email everything to Beijing [where Li heads a staff of 14], and they can pick up the work. It's like ping-pong. For the Vanke »

Above: Design for the centre dedicated to the contentious Norwegian author Knut Hamsen. 'Life isn't all clean,' says Holl. 'It has some messy corners.'

GILE

c/ Jesús
088
Barce

Carter Wong Tomlin
29 Brook Mews North
London, W2 3BW
www.carterwongtomlin.com

FRAG

a, Spain

Four Works
Client Ivory Press *Design* Phil Carter, Nicola Taylor *Year* 2005
A book comprising the work of four artists and the making of their individual works of art/ books.

Eduardo Chillida

Richard Long

Anthony Caro

Anish Kapoor

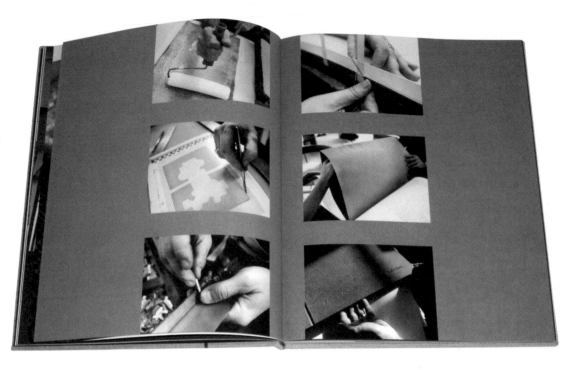

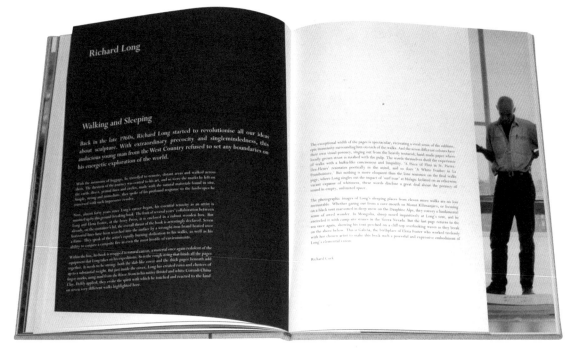

Richard Long

Walking and Sleeping

Back in the late 1960s, Richard Long started to revolutionise all our ideas about sculpture. With extraordinary precocity and singlemindedness, this audacious young man from the West Country refused to set any boundaries on his energetic exploration of the world.

With the minimum of baggage, he travelled to remote, distant areas and walked across them. The duration of the journey was central to his art, and so were the marks he left on the earth. Direct, primal lines and circles, made with the natural materials found in situ. Simply, strong and immediate, they spoke of his profound response to the landscapes he traversed with such impressive resolve.

Now, almost forty years since Long's career began, his essential tenacity as an artist is summed up by this ground-breaking book. The fruit of several years' collaboration between Long and Elena Foster, at the Ivory Press, it is enclosed in a robust wooden box. But already, on the container's lid, the overall thrust of the book is arrestingly declared. Seven horizontal lines have been scratched into the surface by a wrought-iron brand heated over a flame. They speak of the artist's equally burning dedication to his walks, as well as his ability to conjure a campsite fire in even the most hostile of environments.

Within the box, the book is wrapped in natural canvas, a material once again redolent of the equipment that Long takes on his expeditions. So is the rough string that binds all the pages together. It needs to be strong: both the slab-like cover and the thick pages beneath add up to a substantial weight. But just inside the cover, Long has created rows and clusters of finger marks, using mud from the River Avon in his native Bristol and white Cornish China Clay. Deftly applied, they evoke the spirit with which he touched and reacted to the land on seven very different walks highlighted here.

The exceptional width of the pages is spectacular, recreating a vivid sense of the sublime, epic immensity surrounding him on each of the walks. And the seven different colours have their own visual potency, singing out from the heavily textured, hand-made paper where locally grown straw is meshed with the pulp. The words themselves thrill the experience of walks with a haiku-like concreteness and limpidity. 'A Piece of Flint in St. Pierre-Des-Fleurs' resonate poetically in the mind, and so does 'A White Feather in La Frambioniere.' But nothing is more eloquent than the line sentence on the final walks page, where Long singles out the impact of 'surf zone' at Malaga. Isolated on an otherwise vacant expanse of whiteness, these words disclose a great deal about the potency of sound in empty, unlimited space.

The photographic images of Long's sleeping places from eleven more walks are no less memorable. Whether gazing out from a cave-mouth on Mount Kilimanjaro, or focusing on a black tent marooned in deep snow on the Dauphiné Alps, they convey a fundamental sense of awed wonder. In Mongolia, sheep moved inquisitively at Long's tent, and he encircled it with camp-site stones in the Sierra Nevada. But the last page returns to the sea once again, showing his tent perched on a cliff-top overlooking waves as they break on the shore below. This is Galicia, the birthplace of Elena Foster who worked tirelessly with her chosen artist to make this book such a powerful and expressive embodiment of Long's elemental vision.

Richard Cork

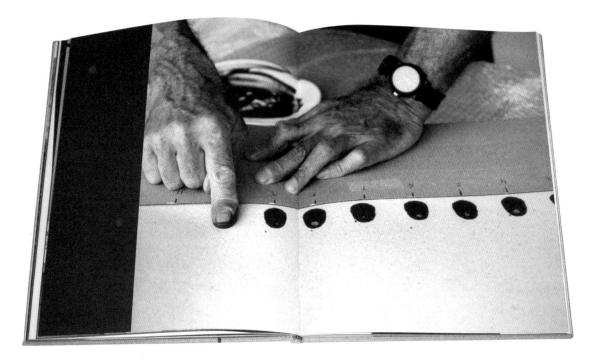

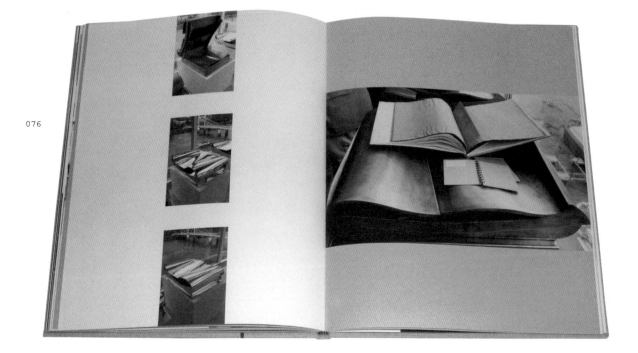

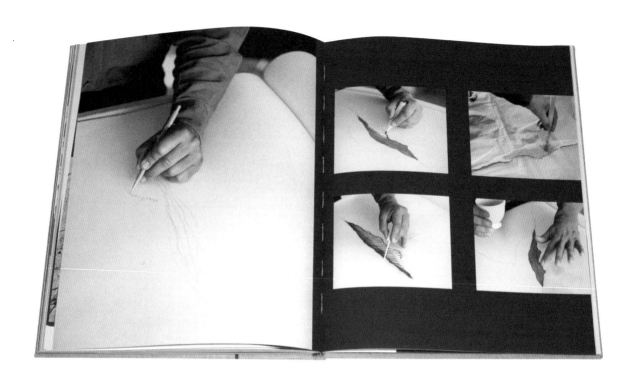

CHK DESIGN LTD 8 FLITCROFT STREET LOND

e le

c/ ba

088 es

air

CHK Design
8 Flitcroft Street
London WC2H 8 DL
+44 (0)20 7836 2007
www.chkdesign.com

Royal Mail
POSTAGE PAID UK
28/02/07 £1.99 WC1V
4010 4-2054206-1

BY AIR MAIL
par avion
Royal Mail

WC2H 8DL

S

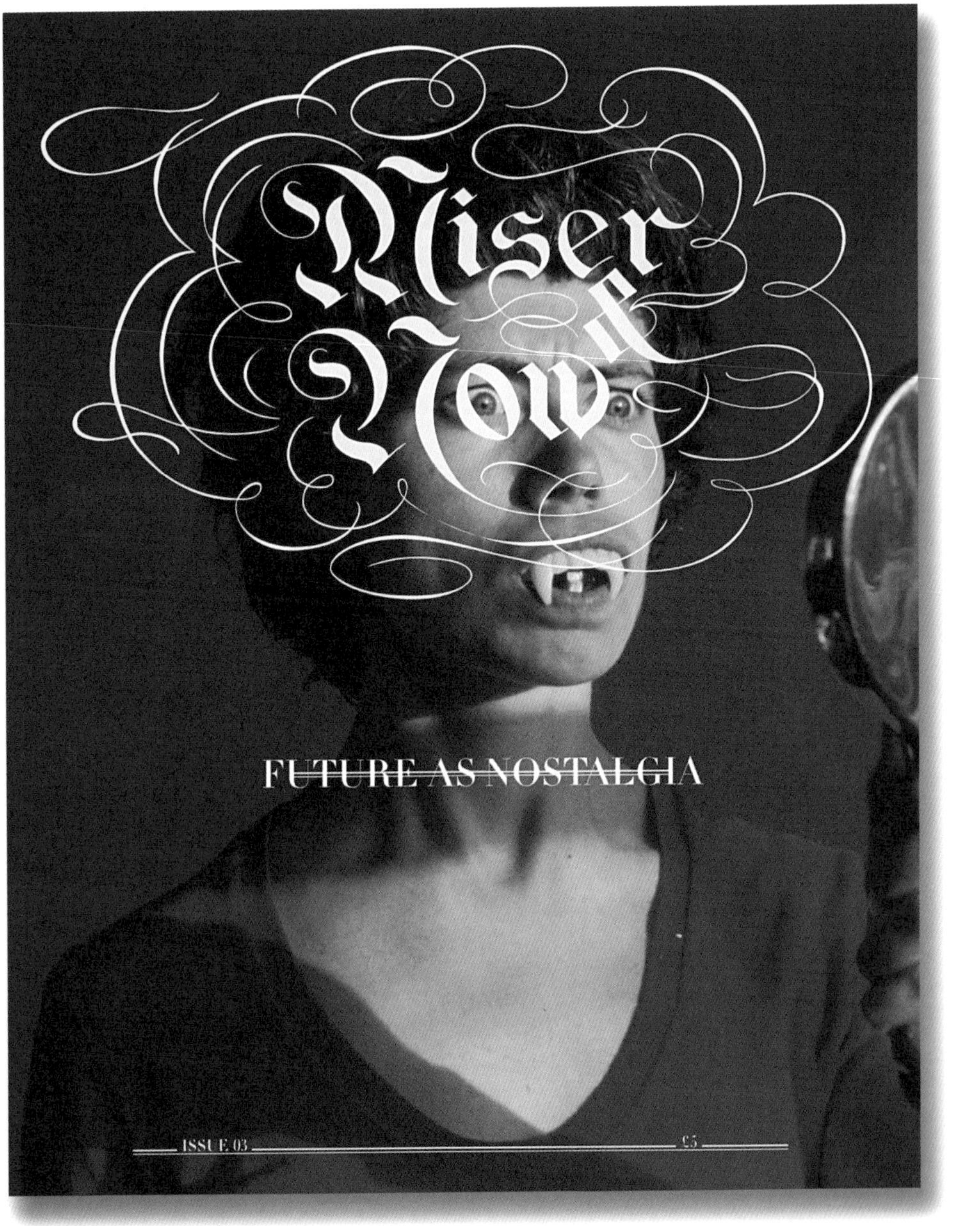

Miser & Now

FUTURE AS NOSTALGIA

£5

Miser & Now

ISSUE FIVE
PLEASURE
FIVE POUNDS

QUARTERLY · ART · MUSIC · DESIGN · FICTION · ESSAYS
MISER&NOW EIGHT — £5 · €8 · $10

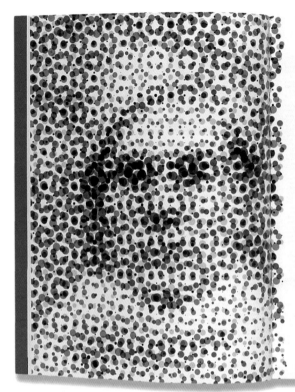

ART AND POLITICS

ROGER · COOK

THE LOVE THAT DARES TO SPEAK ITS NAME

Democratic Dandyism

or the

Aesthetics

of

Self-Invention

Pavilion Museum, Montreal, 1773, British Museum

Miser & Now
PLEASURE

[...]
we owe
to Brummell
the
philosophical
inductions
by which
we have
demonstrated
how much
elegant life
is tied to
the perfection
of all
human
society.

Honoré de Balzac

Miser & Now
PLEASURE

AN INTER VIEW WITH JIMMY EDGAR

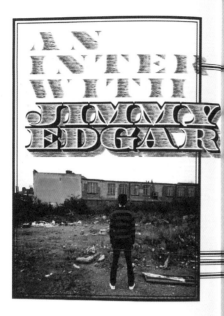

A bona fide teen prodigy, Detroit's *Jimmy Edgar* began fooling around with analogue tape recorders as a precocious nine year-old, making 'pitch-bended tape loops, cut edits and noise tracks, just by messing with the technical parts'. Lessons in classical percussion and dalliances with jazz drums and the Saxophone followed, while a voracious appetite for records had him ingesting everything from Brazilian bossa nova to Stockhausen via Goth rock and throwaway pop. It took the subsequent discovery of Detroit techno, '80s hip hop and New York street beat to focus the fledgling maestro's eclectic zeal, thus setting in motion the most meteoric of recent Motor City music careers.

Instantly – astonishingly – adopted by Detroit's techno aristocracy, Edgar was performing at Michigan raves with internationally celebrated DJ likes Juan Atkins and Derrick May when he was just 15, and by the time of his house-rocking appearance at 2003's Detroit Electronic Music Festival was confirmed as that perennial oxymoron – an underground star. Indeed, such was the excitement during Edgar's set that even the venue security got swept up in the euphoria, resulting in the improbable sight of uniformed Detroit cops getting down to jiggy R&B electronics.

Those same r'n'b electronics had already found their way onto 12" vinyl courtesy of one-off releases on specialist labels like Isophlux and Poker Flat, all of which helped disseminate Edgar's burgeoning talent – the extravagantly diversionary pseudonym Kristuit Salu vs Morris Nightingale ('my dual alter ego' as Edgar puts it) notwithstanding. In early 2002 Miami's Merck label heard his tracks and immediately optioned his first full-length album, My Mines I.

After a subsequent low-key release on Dutch label audio.nl – under yet another alias, Michaux – Edgar signed exclusively to London's puckishly innovative Warp imprint in late 2003. His first Warp release, the terpsichorean Access Rhythm EP, finally bore his given name and further alerted critical ears. A full-length album Bounce, Make, Model followed in summer '04; a judicious amalgam of speedster hip hop, cut'n'paste beats and jazz-flirting electros that induced sheaves of critical hyperbole.

Still only 20, Edgar is full of plans, interspersing his heady musical activities with detours into fashion, design and photography. In fact, he's practically bursting with creative energy – albeit in a willowy, discretely pierced, Marlboro-smoking sort of way. And, affable and articulate to a fault, he's also apparently wise beyond his years.

A SENSE OF THE TACT: ZURICH, BERLIN & LONDON

ROGER COOK

Sense, matter forming itself, form making itself firm: exaction and separation of a tact. With sense, one must have: the tact not to touch it too much. One must have the sense or the tact: the same thing. — Jean-Luc Nancy, *Touching*, *The Sense of the World*, p. 6

It is tact rather than tactics that guide the best contemporary art as well as the best thinking and writing about it. Tactics is fooling through representation, conscious calculation; tact by sense mnemonics: choice, reflexive sense, 'sense-sensing itself'-sense.' Tact is a sense of spacing and touch that has to do with relation, intimate relation: between the interiority of subjective experience and its fold with the outside; with the other, to how the other – the 'I as another' – receives it, is touched by it.'

Miss Camille Chaموnica (Zürich Suite, Migros Museum Zürich of 24–6, 26, 2006) is an inheritor of this self-reflexive tradition in the arts in France that stretches back to the nineteenth century symbolist tradition where much is suggested by what is half-glimpsed or hidden. One can say that this modern embrace a feminine mystique that is part of a continuing and only less necessary cultural need for a becoming that Gilles Deleuze and Felix Guattari called 'becoming-woman' that finds through-lines the nineteenth century and became a pressing need after the war and the gender dimorphic rapid acts the later more gender reflexive period of the 1960s, and into the 1970s, when Chaumonica first entered the field as a cultural product. Slight of build and sensitive as to his 'Intrigences' he

seems to have been instinctively drawn to the tincture of the particular genealogy whilst a student at Camberwell School of Art.

This is why the ambiguity of the threshold and the fold figure so predominantly in his work: the sharply-fold between sense and signification, presence and absence, representation and abstraction, frame and function, craft and art, public and domestic space, and, a dandy's understanding of the ambivalent inter-relation between public and private culture. Understanding of these tact relations has now been honed over more than three decades of work; a referral to fall down on either side of these divides, a dwelling on the edge, a desire to be always situated in the middle. We are always in the midst of things, the philosopher tells us. "One never commences; one never has a tabula rasa; one slips in, enters in the middle; one takes up or lays down rhythms."

Pendulum (1984-2006): the pendulum swings, laying down its persistent rhythm.

Time present and time past,
Are both perhaps present in time future,
And time future contained in time past.

These famous lines from the beginning of T.S. Eliot's *Burnt Norton* succinctly convey the overlapping temporalities that are so central to this work; historical archiving, revisions, restorations and reverberations, the eternal return that is never the same, always full of potential for change.

The past is duration: the present is actualisation; the future is eternal return. But within all three, constitutive of them, is difference. Difference in kind constitutes duration. Actualised difference constitutes the present. The return of difference constitutes the future.

Miss Camille Chaumonica, *Blower Suite* 2004-2005, *Malted 100 Hel ChGel Forewood CK Kable and Arena in Dear and Pepin Acel Kable and Powell 100 Hele of Kable and Dello, 51 Tele, 51 40 10,000 Colorma 100, Brompton*

MEN

*An installation at **Triple Candy**, New York City*

AD Architectural Magazine
Client John Wiley & Sons *Design* Christian Küsters *Year* 2000
Redesign for the UK's oldest architectural magazine. The main point was to make it more relevant to architects working today.

088

AD

4dspace:
Interactive Architecture

Mediating Devices for a Social Statement:

Tobi Schneidler

Interactive Architect

German architect Tobi Schneidler, with his team at the Smart Studio of the Interactive Institute in Stockholm, Sweden, integrates interactive media and network technologies within spatial environments. Here, he explains to Lucy Bullivant how, for him, information technology is not merely hardware or software, but an essential tool that can create 'mediating devices for a social statement'.

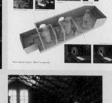

Tobi Schneidler is an architect who fuses digital media and physical space. He sees interactive media and network technologies as key ingredients in a new design, thinking about connected, real-world spaces. A German-born Architectural Association graduate, he directs projects at the Smart Studio of the Interactive Institute in Stockholm, a multidisciplinary research institute specialising in digital media. The Smart Studio creates tangible media expressions from a mix of art, technology and science in the form of interdisciplinary projects, generating new questions and reflections. These are disseminated mainly as international exhibitions, though some permanent and provocative installations have already been made as, under Schneidler's leadership, the technocratic vision is supplanted by one that is culturally and socially driven.

The design question is not one of shaping the increasingly ubiquitous technology to insert. Far more important is how these emerging possibilities will inform new cultures of dwelling as well as social relationships, and thereby the

ACTIVE NARRATIVES

The archive at the Fonds Régional d'Art Contemporain du Centre (FRAC Centre), Orléans, France, houses an outstanding collection of experimental architectural models and drawings from the 1950s, 1960s and 1970s. Marie-Ange Brayer has worked closely with the archive for many years and is now its director. Here, she draws out some examples from the collection to describe how the emergence of 'narrative' in 1960s and 1970s Europe, and then in the US, transformed the architectural project from the singular representation of form into a multidimensional shared script for action.

COMPUTING WITHOUT COMPUTERS

John Frazer trained as an architect in London and at Cambridge during the 1960s and 1970s. He identified at the very earliest stages of their development how the processing power of computers might assist the design process, and then tried to imagine the effects of this on the role of the architect, the client/user and the environment. For 30 years he has confronted this issue with tireless enthusiasm through teaching, researching and designing. Here, he presents a very personal rough guide to where he has been, with a thought for where he thinks we are at now.

AUTO - DESTRUCTIVE ART

architecture principe

1 LA FONCTION OBLIQUE

THE LISTENING POST

Ben Rubin and Mark Hansen

A collaborative visual and sonic artwork drawing on research into Internet chatrooms and forums, the Listening Post harnesses the energy of virtual conversation and converts fragments into an evocative experience. Lucy Bullivant discusses with its American creators the making of the Listening Post, which has been exhibited at the Brooklyn Academy of Music, Next Wave Festival (2001), the Whitney Museum of American Art, New York (2002), MIT List Visual Arts Center and La Villette, Paris (2004).

Artist Ben Rubin and statistician Mark Hansen first encountered the work of one another when they took part in the Arts in Multimedia programme staged by the Brooklyn Academy of Music and Lucent Technologies in 1999/2000, which brought together artists and scientists. Rubin is a sound designer and multimedia artist whose installations and performance works have been exhibited internationally. His firm, Ear Studio (www.earstudio.com) established in 1993 and based in Bowery in New York City, provides design, consulting and technical production services to architects, museums, artists, producers and performers, and he has frequently collaborated with Laurie Anderson and Diller + Scofidio,

among others. Hansen works for the Statistics and Data Mining Research Department of Bell Laboratories.

It was after this meeting, involving research into data sonification, that the duo evolved a joint project – Listening Post, an installation that visualises and sonalises fragments from the vast range of conversations being carried on in thousands of Internet chatrooms, bulletin boards and other public forums. The project stems from Rubin's particular interest in translating data into sound. The texts are read by a voice synthesiser and simultaneously displayed across a suspended grid of more than 200 small electronic screens.

Listening Post is a visual and sonic response to the content, magnitude and immediacy of virtual communication. It works its way through a series of six

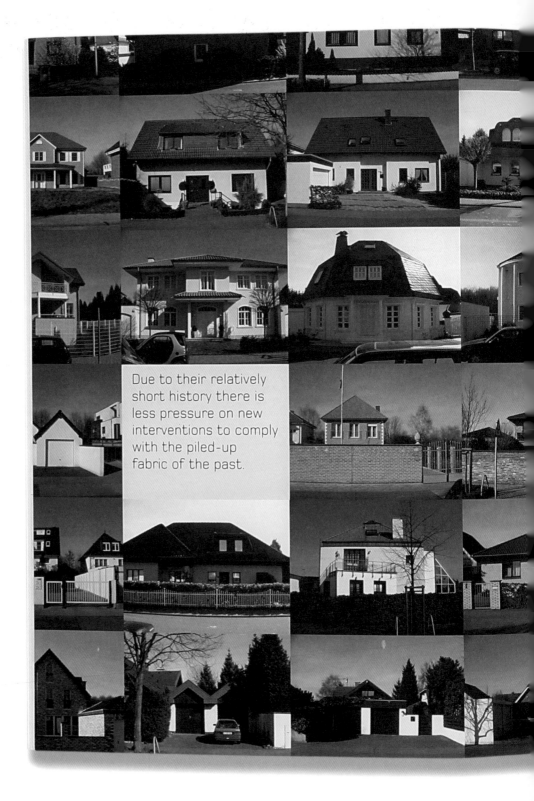

Due to their relatively short history there is less pressure on new interventions to comply with the piled-up fabric of the past.

If cities – in Europe at least – seem to be predominantly defined by their historic cores, suburbia can be regarded as determined by what is to come. Due to their relatively short history there is less pressure on new interventions to comply with the piled-up fabric of the past. In fact, since its inception suburbia has been afforded a blank screen for projecting people's hopes and desires: it is the promise of a new beginning that lures city dwellers away from town centres and the negative side-effects of industrialisation and city-living, such as pollution and urban congestion. This ecology of projection has forever been at work in suburbia, no matter how absurd the results. Yet if architecture would accept this psychological predisposition it could be used as a strategic hinge to get a grip on suburbia and possibly impact on its paradigm.

The Potential of Unbuilt Space

Exploring this ecology of projection is a central concern of the architectural projects assembled in this issue. Common to all of them is the pioneering spirit that characterised the quasi-utopian mind-set of suburbia. All project scenarios onto the situation in order to encourage lifestyles (in the broadest sense of the word) that are partly informed by existing living patterns. A constitutive element common to all of them is the conscious decision to use the unbuilt, rather than the built, fabric as the main tool of intervention. In fact, if architecture generally fails to implement itself in suburbia,

this may be due to its fatal inclination to focus its efforts almost exclusively on the figure of the house or, more precisely, the single-family house.

The projects featured in this issue, however, try to move the focus of the intervention to the ground: the unbuilt space between and around the houses. In suburbia this space is most often treated as a mere infrastructural facility, its sole purpose to give access to the private realm of the houses, which gets all the attention of the private dweller. But the projects here take a complementary stance: they try to turn the (volumetrically speaking) negative space of the street into a (programmatically speaking) positive space of suburban life. Hence established boundaries between public and private are renegotiated as previously underused spaces are proposed for collective use, and public space, previously the blind spot of suburbia, becomes the site of its most relevant future development.

The longing for identity, so over-present in countless built manifestations in the private realm of suburbia, is redirected and granted gratification in the public realm, discovering, again, a new world, but with the difference that this world has been there all the time, albeit apparently unnoticed. Much like Jourdain, in Molière's play *The Bourgeois Gentleman*, who, on being asked by his philosophy master whether he wished to write a love letter to the lady of his choice in verse or prose, learns with excitement that prose is the name applied to the way he speaks, . so that 'for the past forty years I have been speaking in prose without knowing it!', there is a chance that suburbia will eventually discover that it has been surrounded by public space all the time – also without knowing it. ∆

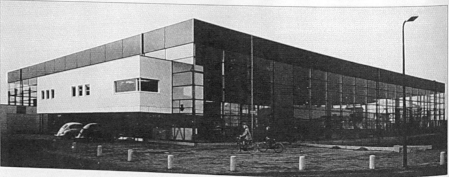

Below Matter-of-fact Modernism, bicycles and Volkswagen beetles. Van Klingeren's multipurpose activity centre at Dronten, the Netherlands, in 1969.

THE AGORA AT DRONTEN

Rarely has a single building represented and fostered so completely the notion of public realm by serving its public first before drawing attention to itself. **James Madge** finds the Agora at Dronten, in the Netherlands, one such triumph. Through analysing Martin Pawley's review of the building in △D in 1969, Madge wonders if it could only have been built in the Netherlands and whether we in the UK will ever learn.

In its July 1969 issue, △D devoted five pages to the De Meerpaal multipurpose centre at Dronten, which had been completed some two years previously to the design of architect/engineer F van Klingeren. This was Van Klingeren's first opportunity to develop the solution of a building type for which there was widespread enthusiasm in the Netherlands during the 1960s and into the 1970s. Visual coverage of the centre stressed the variety of sporting, recreational and cultural activities the building was able to accommodate, and its relaxed, open-ended and democratic response to the needs of its users. However, the text, written by Martin Pawley, called into question the validity not only of this, but of all similarly motivated projects the objective of which Pawley describes as a 'grass-roots-reactivated public realm'.

Recognising, on the one hand, that the so-called Agora at Dronten exemplifies almost to perfection the aspirations implicit in buildings of this type, Pawley has felt himself obliged, nevertheless, to pour very cold water over those aspirations and those buildings, assuring his readers that 'by the year 2000 it [the Agora] will either have suffered a complete change of use, or have been demolished in the course of redevelopment', and that 'I consider it to be already out of date.' His arguments are summarised under the following headings: (a) Increased leisure time? You must be joking, (b) Media privatise, they do not publicise, (c) Life is catching up with art, and (d) The public realm is not safe any more. Under each he wants to show that the ills of Western capitalist culture lie beyond the reach of architectural good intentions.

The first argument is founded in an economic view by which those who are not engaged in productive manufacture at globally competitive rates of pay must sooner or later succumb to mass unemployment 'or revolutionary paralysis'; that increased moonlighting, merely to retain his present economic position, will be the fate of the European worker, and that projections of an automated, work-free future are spurious. In the Western Europe of the 21st century, where almost the only thing successfully manufactured is economic reality itself, the impression of greater leisure, supported by a massive leisure industry, must seem, for many people (including, one would suspect, those who live at Dronten) convincing enough: if there is a meaningful distinction between mass unemployment and extended leisure, then capital has evidently found ways to disguise it. Productive labour can be purchased wherever it is, for the time being, cheapest, but it is upon a perpetually expanding access to the means of consumption that modern economies are now, critically, seen to depend.

That 'the media' (Pawley acknowledges his debt to the ideas of Marshall McLuhan) may be seen as contributory – if not decisive – in the dissolution of the public realm, might be more self-evident in 2004 than it was in 1969; since Pawley wrote, the Internet and the mobile phone might be said to have effectively despatialised even the social realm. Curiously, on the

Copy Fanzine
London
info@copymagazine.org
www.copymagazine.org

PAJOS

Client Self-initiated project *Design* Julie Aveline, Sarah Owens *Year* 2005-2007
Copy is possibly the world's only fanzine about contemporary design culture. It incorporates articles and reviews about design,
art, architecture, music, fashion... observations, manifestos, challenges... and, of course, copies, fakes and oddities.

C.OPY

DESIGN
REPRESEN
TATION
VIRTUAL
TERRITORY
BRANDS
SURREALISM

2

2ᵉ Année. – June 2006

Made "live" at the Hayward Gallery, London, in a surrealist context, this
second edition of COPY will drag you to virtual places, fictional territories
and borderlines; branding, design and representation; doubles and fakes;
authenticity and new realism. Sarah, Julie and The Grandmas strike back.
Photocopier has been hacked. PIRATES are on board. Black and White
is their banner. "Push the green button", their motto. Never forget it is
your COPY-RIGHT and duty.

LONDON   www.copymagazine.org

100

CORP

3rd Year. – March 2007

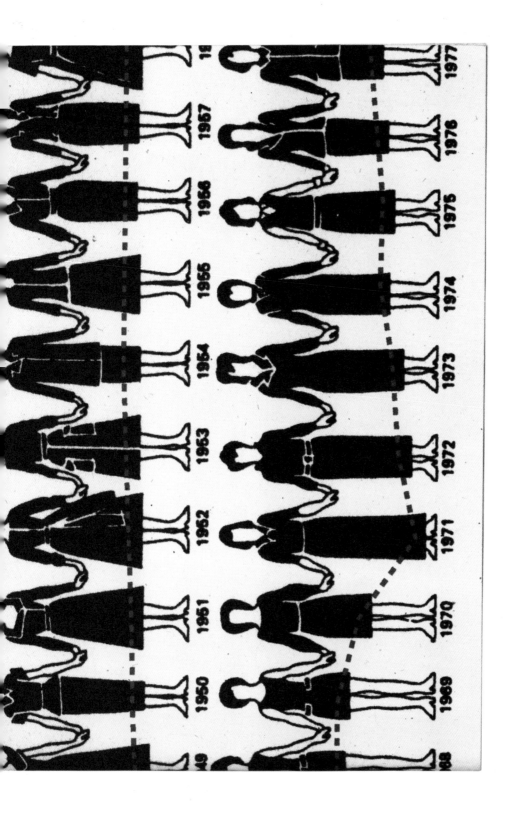

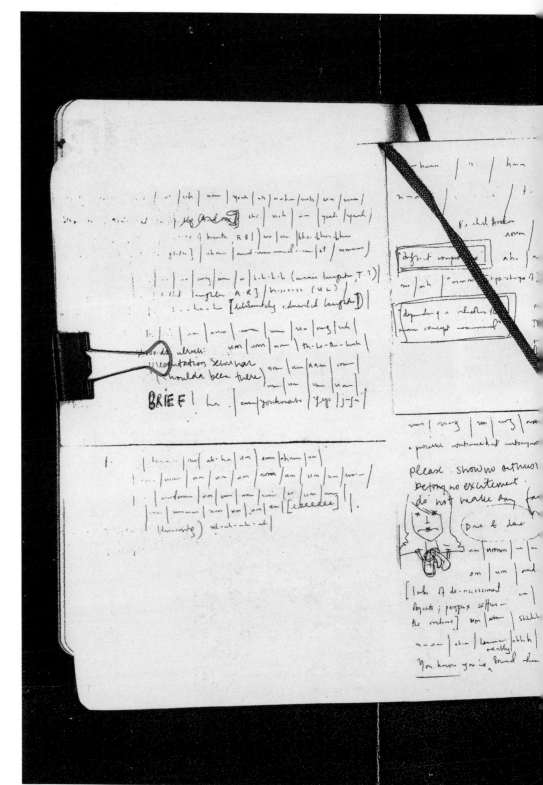

Swift's Guide to Ingenious Conversation (updated)

3.50 pm

[Grunt, KF] / Yeah…yeah / hmm…hmm…hmm / -/ hmm…hmm…hmm / yeah / hie-hummn / n… / hmm…hmm…hmm / ur / urgrhhh / u-um / s…o…o / t-t / (…) [spiralling hands] / (…) / aoum / aoum / aoum / aoum / am / i-t-t / ahr / aoum / um / aoum / ur / um / ai-h / ur / uh / ["mmm" shaped lips, TG] / airr / um / uh / uh / uh / uhr / aoum / urm / aoum / urm / urrm / aoum / urm / urg / um / urg / aughr / um / umm / [loud "ing" tone, K-DP] / urm…yeah / &um / yaah / a-a… / um / hmmm / aoum / um / aoum / [sharp intake of breath, RB] / uar / umm / uo / ur / ur /um / um / umn / um / uh / um / urgh / um / urg / um / urg / …& / um / urmm / um / um / um / um / um / um / urggh / I-I / om / um / …and… / um / urg… / um / om / arrg / um / um / um / um /um / urhg-um / um / urg-um / um / oum / slllhhh [slight intake of breath, RB] / um / aoum / ur / u-um / ah'm / hmmmnnnn / ahhh… / eeh / um / um / um / um / uh / uh / um / [stomach growl, ET] / yeah… yeah… yeah / ah / uh / urm / yeah / uh / uuhnm / urh / um / urm / ehr / urh / w- / yeah / yeah / bu- / t- / hmmm / [intake of breath, RB] / ur / um / hher-hher-hher [plus assorted polite laughter] / uhmn / and-um- l-um / et / ummn / uh / urh/ um / urh / um / ur / urg / eum / er / h!-h!-h!-h! [manic laughter, TG] / um / ur-ur-ur / um / ha-ha-ha-ha ["getting the smart joke" laughter] / um / um / um / andte / urmrm / um / aum / urm / umm / umm / um / urg / uh / um / urm / urm / th-he-th-huh / urm / urm / aam / erm / um / um / um / um / emr / youknowso / yep / j-ja / uh-hmm / hmmm / hmmn / ur / ah-ha / um / arm / aham / um / um / um / ummn / urm / um / um / um / aoum / um / um / um / ur- / um / um/ um / um / urdmm / um / um /um /um / er / um / um / u- / um / um / um / ummm / um / um / um / um / [spiralling hands] / uh-hu-uh-hu .

6.01 pm

[Joint Study Day- History of Design, Curating Contemporary Art and Conservation: transcript of non-verbal utterances.]

- Elaine Tierney

Richard Swift Interview

Richard Swift is a man out of time. His double album 'Walking Without Effort/The Novelist' exists somewhere between genres; he effortlessly straddles a musical fence with one foot dangling in the green pastures of folksy croon-land, the other trailing sleepily through the dusky waters of early jazz. 'The Novelist' sounds like something you'd put on while dragging on a tired cigarette in your oldest silk negligee, contemplating the sepia-tinted first half of the twentieth century. And so, to find out if he actually recorded on a dusty gramophone or just mixed it all on his MAC, COPY tracked him down for an i-chat. Read on to find out what Dick thinks of photocopying, Prince and being dubbed a 'postmodern troubadour'.

AIM IM with Richard Swift <richards****t77@aol.com>

08:58 am

PhC: Hello!

RS: hello

PhC: yay! generally i don't trust technology that much but this was a very good idea

RS: indeed

PhC: so...dick, huh? thanks for letting me in the club. i've been calling you richard this whole time.

RS: that's fine. life is a joke.

PhC: you mean your name is a joke?

RS: no / i mean LIFE IS A JOKE and it's funny to make people call you dick / keeps me beat

PhC: right on. if i were a william I would make people call me willy.

RS: how about PETER?

PhC: i was going to say that but it just seemed silly. i read your online bio. you aren't really related to jonathan swift are you? that's too weird. weird...and awesome!!!!

RS: yes i am / he's like my 5th great uncle

he may have been gay / so he didn't have kids

PhC: right on with the historical gossip! alright. let's get it rolling.

how long have you been composing songs?

RS: since childhood really / but i've been writing songs for/with other people since i was 17 or 18 / not seriously until the last 4 or 5 years maybe

PhC: the theme of this is 'photocopying', what cha think?

RS: how do i fit in?

PhC: i see your work as a type of musical pastiche (well done, natch). putting together different sounds, things that sound a little familiar, but doing it in a new way

RS: that's interesting / i love the look of photocopies

PhC: me too! plus- face/butt on the photocopier is always a good time

RS: yes

PhC: can you share some musical influences?

RS: right right. influences: um...white noise...tomorrow...margo guryan...the kinks...os mutantes...e.l.o....lee perry...king tubby...sly and the family stone...the united states of america...can...mcdonald & giles...etc

PhC: i have a secret elo addiction

RS: right on. no secrets

RS: i admit...i'm just discovering prince

PhC: whoa...just discovering? Please. he has a song to fit every (bizarre and surreal sexual) moment of your life. plus he wears purple high heels

RS: the later stuff is amazing...i'm thinking about doing "paisley park". I mean early stuff/stoner.

PhC: looking at your influences, i wouldn't say that they are necessarily represented in your album, at least not in 'the novelist', which really seems more...wait. what's this stoner business? you smoking the cheeba?

HOT	NOT	HOT	NOT
Angelina Jolie	Jennifer Aniston	CATHOLIC SCHOOL ♥♥ GIRLS	PROTESTANT WORK ETHIC $$$
CAIN	ABEL...	DOCTORS	VETS
Captain Hook	Peter Pan	TEA	COFFEE
Pocketbooks	Panstick	Pink Wafers	'Nice' biscuits
"piano man"	JOOLS HOLLAND	AFFECTATION	SALT OF THE EARTH
Dolly Parton → COPY	Ed Norton → ARC	DIAMOND HEIST	RIPPED-OFF CAR STEREO
LEVITATING ALICE BANDS	WALKING WHITE DREADS	felice della rovere	lucrecia borgia
— Dr Tanya's House of Tiny Tearaways —	— Celebrity Love Island —	SPACE TRAVEL	TIME TRAVEL
GEORGE ELIOT	T.S. ELIOT	"Nail Polish"	"Nail Varnish"
Silk steamed stockings	American Tan Tights	HOME MADE ///	HAND MADE ///
CASSETTE MIX TAPES	IPOD	a pleasant drive in the countryside	gumball 3000
History of Design	History of Art	PIRATES	COASTGUARDS
HIGH-TOPS	LOW-TOPS	BUSES	TUBE
OLD-SCHOOL SLOANES	BOHO SLOANES	sharapova	kournikova
Brian Sewell	Waldemar Januarek	Old man pubs	Martini Bars
PALE & INTERESTING	FAKE BAKED	Cartoon "T"	Animation "A"
Middle-Class	Working-Class	Heartbreaking	Heartbroken
WHITNEY	BEYONCÉ *	BUTT → ASS	
VICAR'S TEA PARTY *	LATE NIGHT POKER	BUTT → FACE	
ORGAN GRINDER'S MONKEY	PG CHIMPS	"MR. WHIPPY"	'HÄGEN DAAZ' !!!
HR INVESTMENT BANKING	PR MANAGEMENT CONSULTANCY	...	
Moral High Ground	Low morals	Dostoyevsky	Kafka
		cheddar	brie
		HANSEL	GRETEL
		Croquet	Cricket
		PETER USTINOV	DAVID SUCHET

HARRY	WILLIAM
Chicken Jalfrezi	Chicken Korma
Terry Wogan	Cat Deeley
SECOND-HAND	VINTAGE
BABYCHAM ✳✳✳	CRISTAL
Cecil Beaton	Evelyn Waugh
Richard Dawkins	Stephen Hawkins
REGIONAL	ESTUARY
Being a bad WINNER	Being a good LOSER
CLUEDO	MONOPOLY
ENGLISH SEASIDE	FRENCH RIVIERA
Country	Western
LIVING FAST	DYING YOUNG
PILOTS	PILATES
C U L8r	Spelling, punctuation and grammar
30	18
Taxidermy	Taxi drivers
FLORENCE	TALLINN
VULGAR RICHES	UNDERSTATED WEALTH
NIGHT TO REMEMBER	TIME TO FORGET
Short and sweet	Long-winded
V Poetry IN DIESEL	V Poverty IN DIESEL
MILK w/ 2 SUGARS	SKINNY LATTE
DEAD ICONS	FALLEN IDOLS
Mountains	Molehills
MAN OF THE WORLD	MAN OF THE PEOPLE
BAD HABITS	GIVING UP

-HOT-	-NOT-
CAMILLA	DIANA
mapping Academic Arms	stalking PhD hump
Necrophilia	Paedophilia
BIG BUSH UNDER THE RADAR	BRAZILIAN OVER EXPOSED
Flamingoes BEEF EATERS	Pigeons SWISS GUARDS
GUIDE DOGS	DAVID BLUNKETT
"Please"	"Thank You"
WHAT GOES ON TOUR, STAYS ON TOUR	MONOGAMY
Benedict XVI	John Paul II
TOP SECRET	YESTERDAY'S NEWS
Lovers	Haters
DERRING-DO	STAYING IN
Victorian perverts	Victorian poets
KIP	NAPOLEON
HYPERBOLE	MODESTY
Z 130 ml	ZED 125 ml
Summer of ♥♥♥ Love	Winter of our Discontent
SCANDAL	TRUTHS
SHELLSUITS Responsible Citizens	NATURAL FIBERS Hippies
ANALOG	DIGITAL
OBVIOUS	SUBTLE
MARRYING MONEY =ALIEN=	WORKING TO SUPPORT YOURSELF =PREDATOR=

>Made in China:

Challenges of contemporary Chinese design

Based on an interview with Dr. Xiyang Yuan, Head of the Design Theory Department, Associate Professor and Deputy Dean of the Design College in the Nanjing Arts Institute, China.

Dr. Yuan is currently residing in London as a British Academy research fellow, hosted by the RCA and SOAS, researching the influence of Aubrey Beardsley on Chinese graphic design and illustration between 1919-1937.

It was my great good fortune to find myself sitting next to Dr. Yuan on an Easy Jet flight from Tallinn, Estonia, where the RCA History of Design had just concluded a confusing negotiation of group identity as bear-sausage eating tourists and architectural critics, tinged with a dash of 19th century anthropologist's panache. Airplane small-talk led to a more profound discussion about globalization and national identity in design. This naturally strengthened my agoraphobic tendencies which lead me to believe that whatever I look for is usually not more than a tube ride from the studio apartment I call home.

According to Dr. Yuan, these are formative years for
the identity of contemporary Chinese design. With the
upcoming Olympic Games in Beijing in 2008 and the
Chinese Design exhibition planned at the V&A for the
same year (followed by the 2010 World Expo in Shanghai)
design will play an important part in forming an up-
to-date image of contemporary China. CAFA (Central
Academy of Fine Art) in Beijing has formed a special
centre devoted entirely to Design for the Olympic
Games and Domus has devoted an edition to the Chinese
architecture for the Olympics. For Yuan, this spells a
long-awaited shift in the design-manufacture dynamics
of China, a place which has been for the past 20 years
described as 'the workshop of the world'.

The question of Chinese design identity is practical and
theoretical at the same time—a synergy which seems
to characterize much of the turbulent history of design
education in China. Nanjing, or 'South Capital' (Beijing
is 'North Capital'), has been home the Institute since
1957. Established in 1912, the oldest art and design
higher education facility in China has undergone, and
indeed still is undergoing, profound and telling changes.

Unlike many design schools around the world which
were modelled after the Bauhaus and Ulm, mention
of these schools was banned in China during the cultural
revolution. In the 1950's, the Institute offered courses
in fine art, decorative art, music and craft and design.
It was only with the political and economic reforms of
the 1980's that a shift in emphasis from art/craft to
design began driving the establishment of an independent design department. In 1995 a Design College was
established within the Institute. The Department of
History and Theory of Art and Craft, still associated with
ideas of the Arts and Crafts Movement in England and

Nutsoid.

These are carrot sticks of the type which DO NOT contain nuts.

Shay said... Shocking!!!

3:46 PM
copy team said... When you really start thinking about it, the fact that a bag of carrots says "nut-free" just makes you think about all the stuff it doesn't say it doesn't contain. maybe it contains bugs, and maybe its got sheep piss on it, and maybe its radioactive? who knows??? we only know it doesn't contain nuts. Is it suitable for vegetarians? And does it have gluten? have these carrots been cloned? do they contain arsenic or hemlock or some kind of poison? how can I be sure if these "carrots" CONTAIN carrots or this is just clever branding like Orange, which contains no oranges or nuts but little micro chips and ringtones. its just too chaotic. must rest... n.

9:31 AM
copy team said... well... now after eating these orange sticks and thinking about sheep's piss... i think I'm feeling sick. well, at least I can assure you they weren't carrots. or at least didn't taste like them. s.

12:55 PM
copy team said... I guess the role of packaging in England is more important than in other parts of the world... packages here really tell you what it is you are eating, unlike in other places where the package information is cross referenced with the experience of the taste and smell of the food. so, if you got a bag which says "carrots" in Israel for example, and they tasted like carrots, then you know that's what they are. but if the bag says carrots, but they taste like tomatoes, then you know they got the labels mixed. but here, taste is really only implied through visual stimulus. so, instead of buying a cheese because you like the smell and you know you like goat-cheese, you buy a cheese that tells you it had a "mild, nutty, creamy flavour". then you eat it, and it has no flavour, but you say "hmm...its quite creamy and nutty...quite mild". or you buy custard (ew) and it says "a rich creme anglaise with fresh cream and Madagascar vanilla" and you eat this pale yellow slop and you say "hmm...its quite rich and fresh, creamy, and you can really taste the natural vanilla". i wonder what would happen if they began writing bad stuff, or bizarre stuff like "Carrots: for a mild

hallucinogenic effect, in which you will see pink elephants, Lucy in the sky with a smoky, tangy, chutney flavour", or "BEANS: with a nauseating aftertaste which will leave your intestines in turmoil all night long". n.

1:57 PM

ibergus said... the power of advertising. stephen butler leacock, a *canadian* humorist, said that "advertising may be described as the science of arresting the human intelligence long enough to get money from it." what surprises me is that there is no "cholesterol free" and, as you wrote, "suitable for vegetarians" labels besides the "nut free" one.

2:41 PM

copy team said... Knowing Tesco, there probably IS a "suitable for vegetarians" label on every single one of their products, including toilet tissue. It might just be on the other side of the package (!!)

8:18 PM

copy team said... lacto-ovo friendly toilet paper - i see a new winning product! also, organic toilet paper, gluten free toilet paper, and fair trade toilet paper ...why not try them all! coming up: Miso flavoured toilet paper in red, white and brown. your butt has never been so pampered!

8:40 PM

copy team said... oh.. and of course, cholesterol free toilet paper, sugar free toilet paper (for diabetics), fat free and low carb toilet paper, and in the new sensations range, hand-cooked chutney and Jamaican lime flavoured toilet paper.

8:43 PM

copy team said... when you think about it, the world of toilet paper really has not been developed enough... how about hand-pressed toilet paper, Japanese rice toilet paper, large-sizes toilet paper...

8:45 PM

copy team said... anti-bacterial toilet paper, anti-allergy toilet paper, KIDS toilet paper, (then obviously girls, then boys), Disney toilet paper (that may exist actually)...

8:47 PM

copy team said... Elite women's toilet paper aka. the "ladies toilette papier" with French Etoile wallpaper ornaments.

11:01 AM

copy team said... And then also plebeian toilet paper with Old Bailey testimony statement: "i was minding my own business when suddenly a gentleman and lady approached me... pointing her ladyship, marked that I had stolen her toilette papier of one shilling and three pence. And I tell you, I had never so much as laid a finger on any toilette papier, for I am a good protestant and a poor housemaid and no French wine will pass my lips."

112

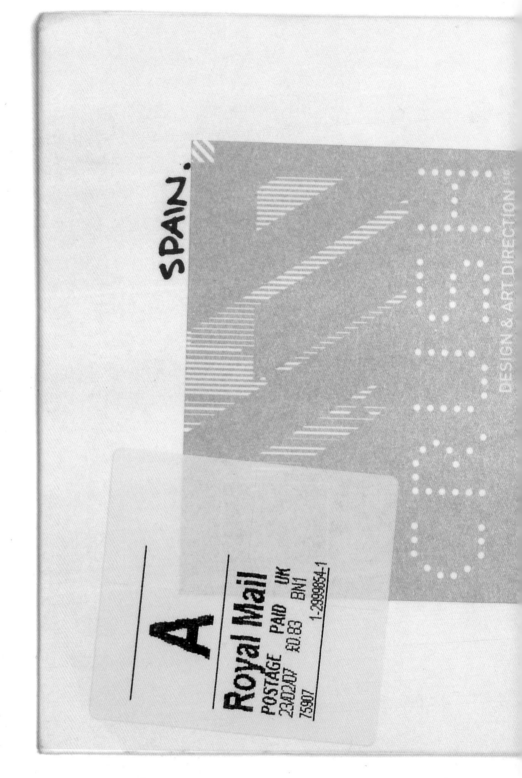

SPAIN.

A

Royal Mail
POSTAGE   PAID   UK
23/02/07   £0.83   BN1
75907   1-2999054-1

Crush
6 Gloucester Street
Brighton, BN1 4EW
+44 (0) 1273 606 058
www.crushed.co.uk
info@crushed.co.uk

Faber & Faber Seasonal Catalogues
Client Faber & Faber *Design* Chris Pelling *Year* 2007
Design, Art Direction and Illustration of two catalogues to promote Faber & Faber's new titles.

New Books From Faber
July – December 2007

Poetry

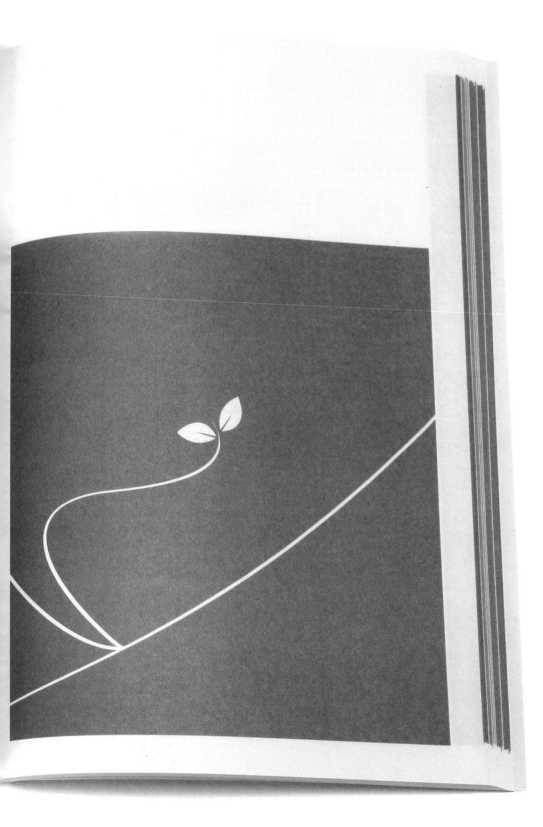

THE DARK STUFF
NICK KENT

• Paperback • 448pp • £9.99 • 19th April 2007
• UK and Commonwealth excluding Canada • 0 571 23271 X • 978 0 571 23271 0

A modern classic, unavailable in the UK for the last few years, and a superb addition to Faber's growing pop-culture list, **The Dark Stuff** stands alongside Jon Savage's **England's Dreaming** and Lester Bangs's **Psychotic Reactions and Carburetor Dung** as one of the essential collections of writing on rock music.

In **The Dark Stuff** Nick Kent profiles many of the most gifted and self-destructive talents in rock history. From Brian Wilson to Syd Barrett, the Rolling Stones to Neil Young, Iggy Pop to Lou Reed, he offers intimate portraits that are unimaginable in the world of today's market-driven music business. Including previously unpublished material on Johnny Cash, Sly Stone and Phil Spector, this edition will introduce a new generation to the art of one of the most brilliant and notorious journalists of his field.

In 2002 Nick Kent was presented with the NME God Like Genius award for his 30-year career as a rock writer. He is a contributor to the *Guardian*, the *Times*, *Literature*, *Mojo* and *Q* and is currently working on an all new collection of **The Dark Stuff** to publish in 2008.

'A superb interviewer. . . . He conveys the acne and ecstasy of the adolescent spirit of rock to perfection.' *Guardian*

'I could tell you stories about Nick Kent that would uncurl the hair in your afro.' Morrissey (*Tot*)

'[A] genius wordsmith, Kent is a man who has lived rock 'n' roll to the full . . . . **The Dark Stuff** is a mighty tome, containing some of the best music journalism ever written.' *Spectator*

POET TO POET | **D. H. LAWRENCE**
SELECTED BY TOM PAULIN

• Paperback • 96pp • £3.99 • 5th April 2007
• World all languages • 0 571 23451 7 • 978 0 571 23451 2

Tom Paulin has published eight collections of poetry as well as a *Selected Poems 1972–1990*, two major anthologies, two versions of Greek drama and several critical works, including *The Day-Star of Liberty: William Hazlitt's Radical Style* and, most recently, *Crusoe's Secret*.

David Herbert Lawrence was born in Nottinghamshire in 1885. His first book of verse, **Love Poems and Others**, appeared in 1913. This was followed by **Amores** (1916), **Look! We Have Come Through** (1917), **New Poems** (1918), **Bay** (1919), **Tortoises** (1921), **Birds, Beasts and Flowers** (1923) and **Pansies** (1929). His **Collected Poems** appeared in 1928 and **Last Poems** was published posthumously in 1932. D. H. Lawrence died of tuberculosis in Venice in 1930.

POET TO POET | **GEOFFREY CHAUCER**
SELECTED BY BERNARD O'DONOGHUE

• Paperback • 128pp • £3.99 • 5th April 2007
• World all languages • 0 571 23069 3 • 978 0 571 23069 5

Bernard O'Donoghue was born in Cullen, Co. Cork in 1945. He is a Fellow of Wadham College, Oxford, where he teaches Medieval English. He has published four collections of poetry, *The Weakness* (1991), *Gunpowder*, *Here Nor There* (1999) and *Outliving* (2003).

Geoffrey Chaucer (c.1343–1400) was a diplomat, customs controller and knight of the shire and author of *Troilus and Criseyde* and *The Canterbury Tales*.

POET TO POET | **ALEXANDER POPE**
SELECTED BY PETER PORTER

• Paperback • 128pp • £3.99 • 5th April 2007
• World all languages • 0 571 23070 7 • 978 0 571 23070 9

Peter Porter was born in Brisbane and has lived in England since the early 1950s. His *Collected Poems* appeared in 1983.

Alexander Pope (1688–1744) was an essayist, critic, satirist, poet and translator. He published **An Essay on Criticism** in 1711 and republished version of **The Rape of the Lock** in 1714. His **Collected Works** were published in 1717 and he successfully translated the **Iliad** and the **Odyssey** into English. **The Dunciad** (1728), one of his most famous works, was a vicious satire on dullness featuring many of his contemporaries.

JOHN CLARE
SELECTED BY PAUL FARLEY
POET TO POET

• Paperback • 96pp • £3.99 • 5th April 2007
• World English language • 0 571 22463 4 • 978 0 571 22463 0

John Clare (1793–1864), the 'peasant poet', worked as an agricultural labourer in Northamptonshire until a deterioration in his mental health saw him committed to an asylum. He published four volumes of verse, including **Poems, Descriptive of Rural Life and Scenery** (1820) and **The Shepherd's Calendar** (1827).

Paul Farley's first collection, **The Boy from the Chemist is Here to See You**, won a Forward prize and a Somerset Maugham award. His second collection, **The Ice Age**, was a Poetry Book Society Choice and received the Whitbread Poetry Award in 2002. A third collection will appear from Picador in 2006.

THOM GUNN
SELECTED BY AUGUST KLEINZAHLER
POET TO POET

• Paperback • 96pp • £3.99 • 5th April 2007
• World English language • 0 571 23069 3 • 978 0 571 23069 5

Thom Gunn (1929–2004) was educated at Cambridge University, and had his first collection of poems, **Fighting Terms**, published while still an undergraduate. He moved to North California in 1954 and taught in American universities until his death. His last collection was **Boss Cupid** (2000).

August Kleinzahler was born in Jersey City in 1949. He is the author of ten collections of poems, most recently **The Strange Hours Travelers Keep** and **Green Sees Things in Waves**. He lives in San Francisco.

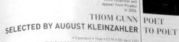

JOHN DONNE
SELECTED BY PAUL MULDOON
POET TO POET

• Paperback • 96pp • £3.99 • 5th April 2007
• World all languages • 0 571 23089 X • 978 0 571 23089 1

John Donne (1572–1631) forfeited his Parliamentary seat and was briefly imprisoned when his secret marriage to Ann More was discovered in 1601. He spent the subsequent decade in poverty, trying to rehabilitate his reputation. He entered the Church in 1615, and became Dean of St Paul's. His first volume of poetry was published posthumously in 1633.

Paul Muldoon was born in County Armagh in 1951. His first collection was New Weather (1973). Since 1987 he has lived in the United States, where he is the Howard G. B. Clark Professor in the Humanities at Princeton University. From 1999 to 2004 he was Professor of Poetry at Oxford University.

Faber and Faber
3 Queen Square
London, WC1N 3AU

www.faber.co.uk

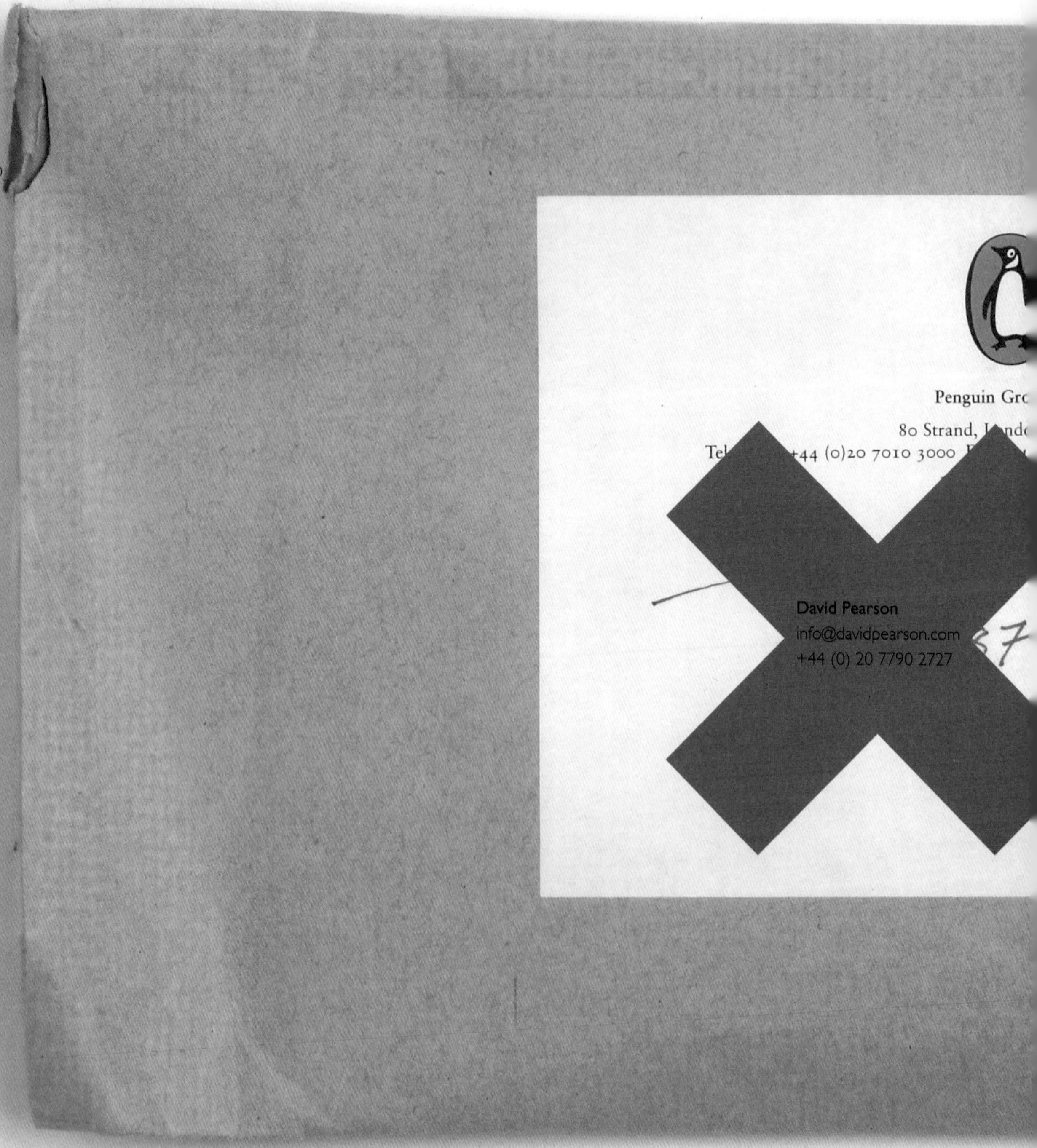

120

Penguin Gro

80 Strand, London

Tel: +44 (0)20 7010 3000

David Pearson
info@davidpearson.com
+44 (0) 20 7790 2727

cc : 110024
7010 6060 www.penguin.com
,28, Bajos
Sitges
PRIORITAIRE
En cas de non remise
Prière de retourner à
POSTFACH 2001
36243 Niederaula
ALLEMAGNE
Deutsche Post
Port payé
60544 Frankfurt
ALLEMAGNE
Brief /Luftpost

Each of the Penguin series is a repackaging of backlist titles. Designed specifically to set them apart from other editions currently in print.

122

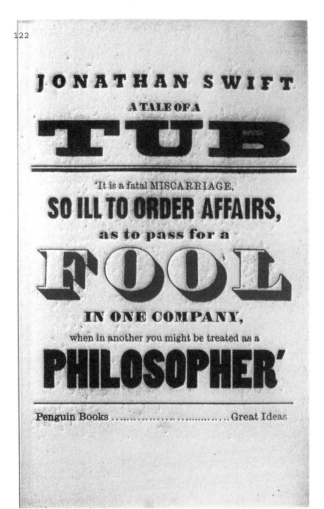

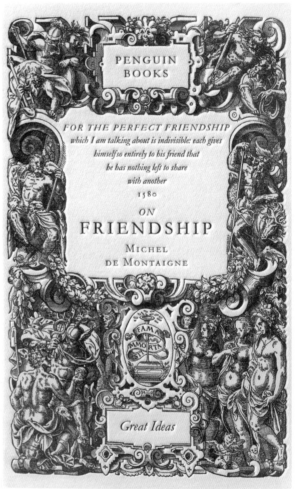

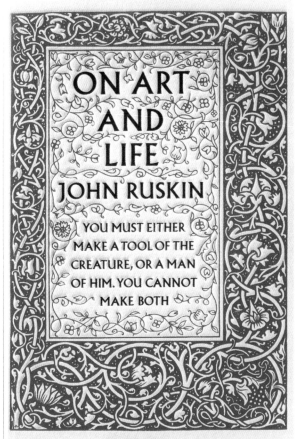

ON ART
AND
LIFE
JOHN RUSKIN

YOU MUST EITHER
MAKE A TOOL OF THE
CREATURE, OR A MAN
OF HIM. YOU CANNOT
MAKE BOTH

PENGUIN BOOKS
GREAT IDEAS

Let the ruling classes tremble at a Communistic revolution.
The proletarians have nothing to lose but their chains.
They have a world to win.
Working men of all countries, Unite!
The Communist Manifesto
Karl Marx & Friedrich Engels

Penguin Books Great Ideas

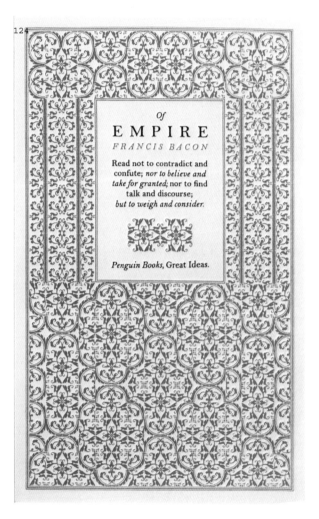

Of

EMPIRE
FRANCIS BACON

Read not to contradict and
confute; *nor to believe and
take for granted;* nor to find
talk and discourse;
but to weigh and consider.

Penguin Books, Great Ideas.

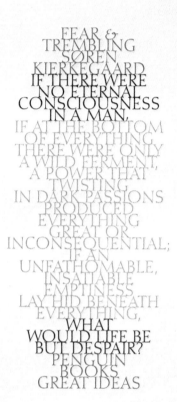

FEAR &
TREMBLING
SØREN
KIERKEGAARD
IF THERE WERE
NO ETERNAL
CONSCIOUSNESS
IN A MAN,
IF AT THE BOTTOM
OF EVERYTHING
THERE WERE ONLY
A WILD FERMENT,
A POWER THAT
TWISTING
IN DARK PASSIONS
PRODUCED
EVERYTHING
GREAT OR
INCONSEQUENTIAL;
IF AN
UNFATHOMABLE,
INSATIABLE
EMPTINESS
LAY HID BENEATH
EVERYTHING,
WHAT
WOULD LIFE BE
BUT DESPAIR?
PENGUIN
BOOKS
GREAT IDEAS

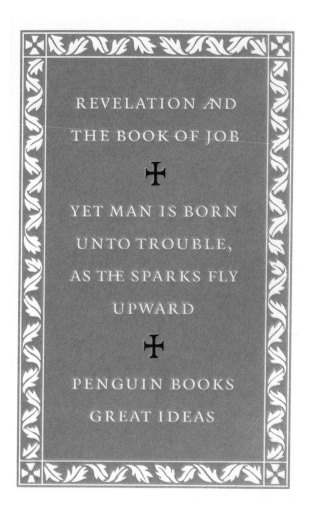

REVELATION AND

THE BOOK OF JOB

✠

YET MAN IS BORN

UNTO TROUBLE,

AS THE SPARKS FLY

UPWARD

✠

PENGUIN BOOKS

GREAT IDEAS

There is but one truly serious philosophical problem and that is suicide

Albert Camus *The Myth of Sisyphus*

Penguin Books Great Ideas

Great Journeys
Client Penguin Group *Design* David Pearson (Illustrations by Victoria Sawdown) *Year* 2007
Repackaging of backlist titles. Designed specifically to set them apart from other editions currently in print.

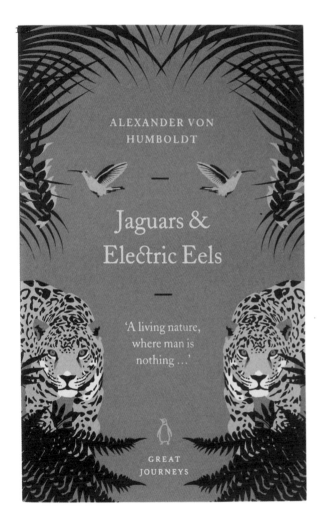

JAMES COOK

Hunt for
the Southern
Continent

—

'Farther than any
man has been
before me ...'

GREAT
JOURNEYS

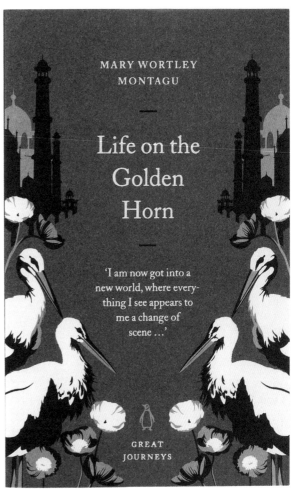

MARY WORTLEY
MONTAGU

—

Life on the
Golden
Horn

—

'I am now got into a
new world, where every-
thing I see appears to
me a change of
scene ...'

GREAT
JOURNEYS

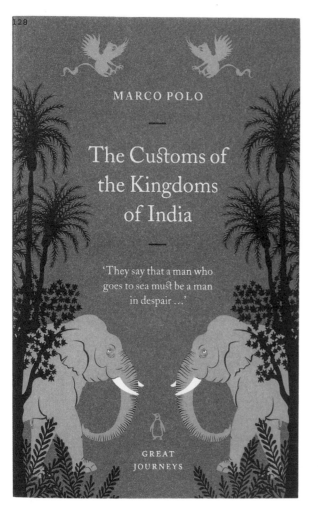

MARCO POLO

—

The Customs of
the Kingdoms
of India

—

'They say that a man who
goes to sea must be a man
in despair …'

GREAT
JOURNEYS

WILLIAM DAMPIER

—

Piracy,
Turtles &
Flying Foxes

—

'Our feet were blistered
and our thighs stripped
with wading through
so many rivers …'

GREAT
JOURNEYS

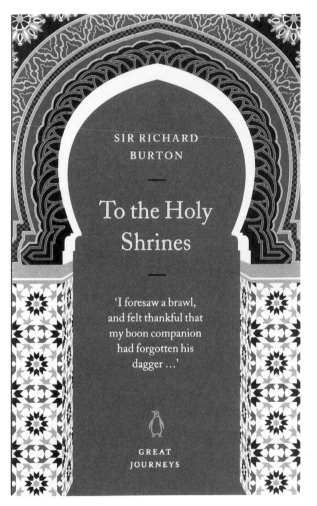

SIR RICHARD
BURTON

—

To the Holy
Shrines

—

'I foresaw a brawl,
and felt thankful that
my boon companion
had forgotten his
dagger …'

GREAT
JOURNEYS

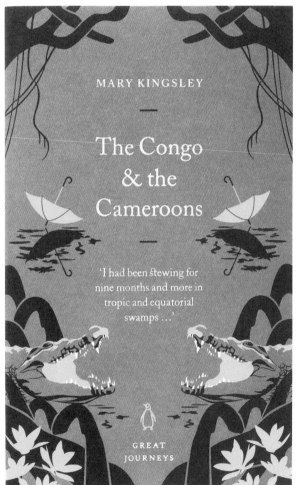

MARY KINGSLEY

—

The Congo
& the
Cameroons

—

'I had been stewing for
nine months and more in
tropic and equatorial
swamps …'

GREAT
JOURNEYS

Popular Classics

Client Penguin Group ***Design*** David Pearson ***Year*** 2007

Repackaging of backlist titles. Designed specifically to set them apart from other editions currently in print.

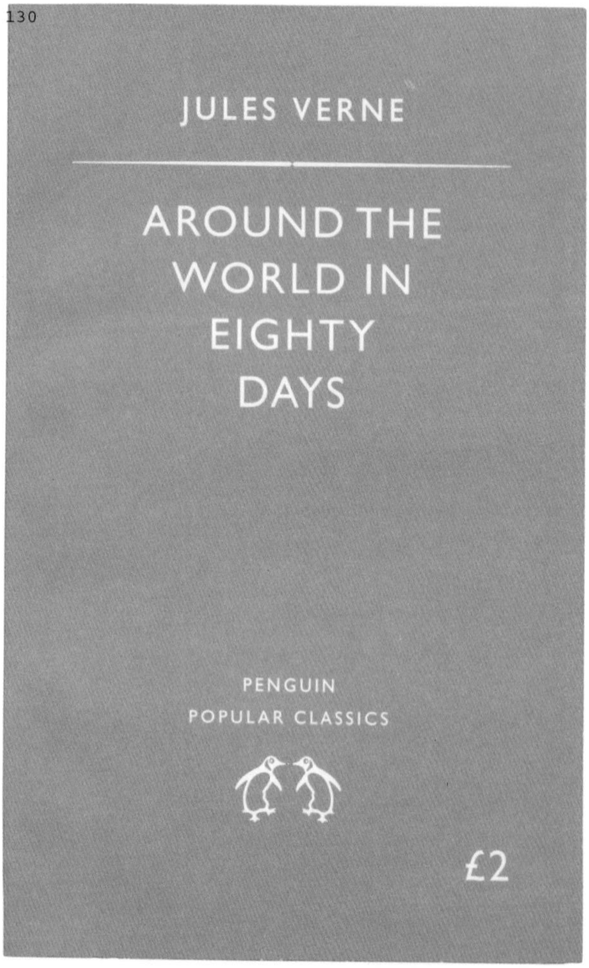
JULES VERNE
AROUND THE WORLD IN EIGHTY DAYS
PENGUIN
POPULAR CLASSICS
£2

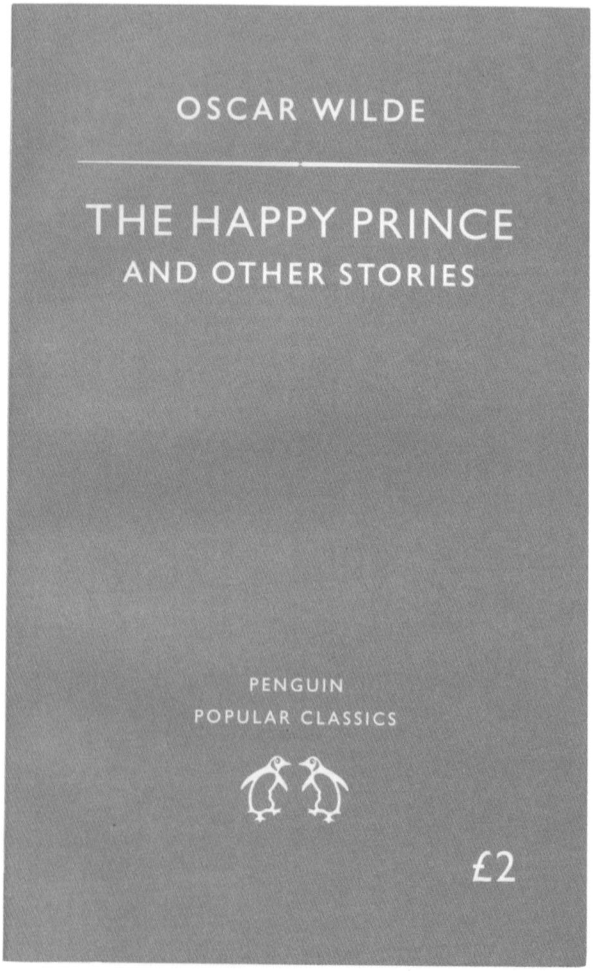
OSCAR WILDE
THE HAPPY PRINCE
AND OTHER STORIES
PENGUIN
POPULAR CLASSICS
£2

JEROME K. JEROME

THREE MEN IN
A BOAT

PENGUIN
POPULAR CLASSICS

£2

ROBERT LOUIS STEVENSON

TREASURE ISLAND

PENGUIN
POPULAR CLASSICS

£2

132

VAIKOM MUHAMMAD
BASHEER

*Grand-père avait
un éléphant*

z

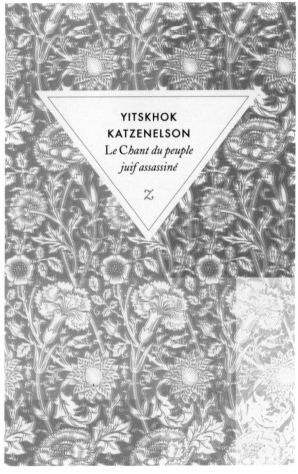

YITSKHOK
KATZENELSON

*Le Chant du peuple
juif assassiné*

z

ZULMA

Pierre Albert-Birot (1876–1967), sculpteur, peintre, fondateur de la revue *SIC*, se consacre uniquement à l'écriture à partir de 1918.

Mon ami Kronos, inédit à ce jour, réjouira les amateurs du langage subtilement pris au piège du pur plaisir littéraire.

Couverture : David Pearson

ZULMA

9 782843 044076

8,50 € Diffusion Seuil

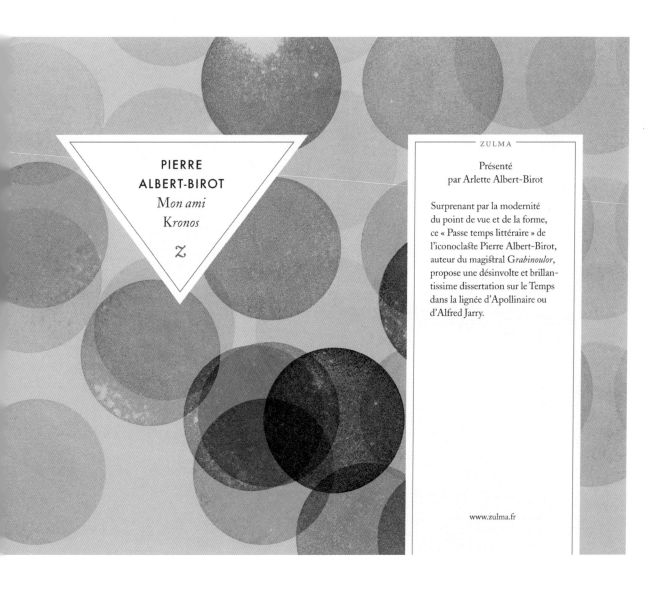

PIERRE
ALBERT-BIROT

Mon ami
Kronos

Z

ZULMA

Présenté
par Arlette Albert-Birot

Surprenant par la modernité
du point de vue et de la forme,
ce « Passe temps littéraire » de
l'iconoclaste Pierre Albert-Birot,
auteur du magiſtral *Grabinoulor*,
propose une désinvolte et brillan-
tissime dissertation sur le Temps
dans la lignée d'Apollinaire ou
d'Alfred Jarry.

www.zulma.fr

ZOYÂ PIRZÂD

*Comme tous les
après-midi*

Z

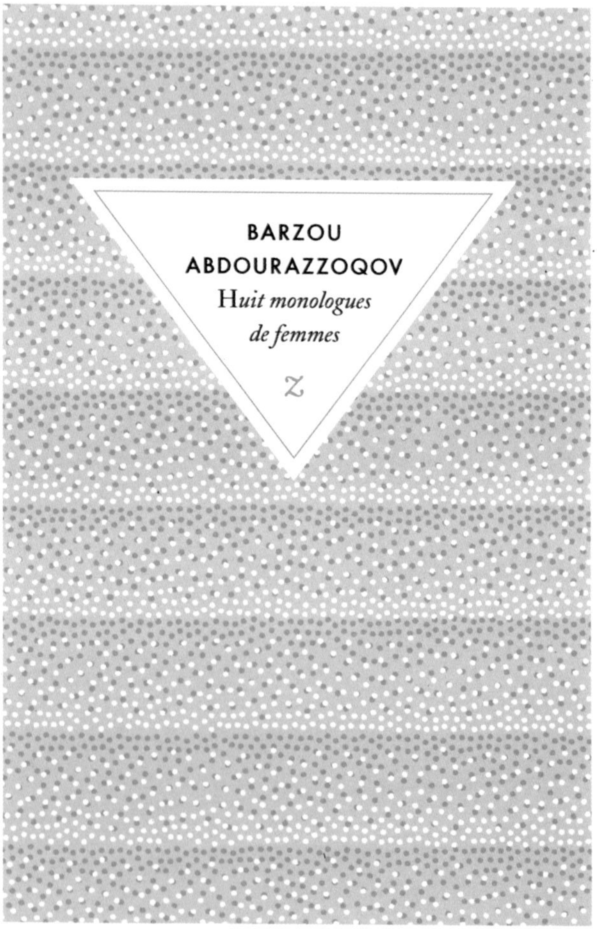

BARZOU
ABDOURAZZOQOV

*Huit monologues
de femmes*

Z

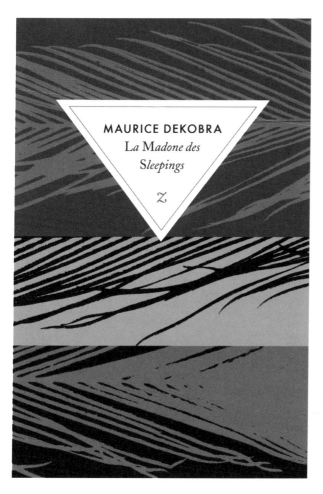

MAURICE DEKOBRA

La Madone des Sleepings

Z

LEE SEUNG-U

La vie rêvée des plantes

Z

ZULMA

Yitskhok Katzenelson est né
en 1886 en Biélorussie dans une
famille de lettrés. Dès 1904, il
publia ses poèmes à Varsovie,
où parurent la plupart de ses
œuvres. En 1910, il reprit l'école
paternelle qu'il dirigea jusqu'en
1939. Entre-temps, il voyagea
en Europe, en Palestine et en
Amérique.

Il vécut et lutta trois années
dans le ghetto de Varsovie,
bientôt anéanti par les nazis.
Interné ensuite au camp pour
« personnalités » de Vittel, il
futdéporté en avril 1944 à
Auschwitz où il fut gazé dès
son arrivée.

Couverture : David Pearson

ZULMA

9 782843 044083

9,50 € Diffusion Seuil

**YITSKHOK
KATZENELSON**

*Le Chant du peuple
juif assassiné*

z

ZULMA

Traduit du yiddish
par Batia Baum

Présenté par Rachel Ertel

Écrit en yiddish en 1943 dans le
camp de Vittel et miraculeuse-
ment sauvé, *le Chant du peuple
juif assassiné* est un témoignage
unique sur la barbarie nazie et le
ghetto de Varsovie. C'est aussi
et surtout un chef-d'œuvre ab-
solu qui interpellera à jamais
les générations futures par sa
beauté littéraire comme par sa
bouleversante humanité.

www.zulma.fr

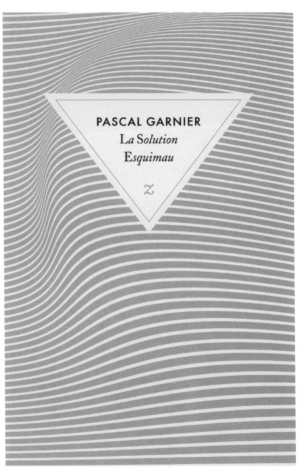

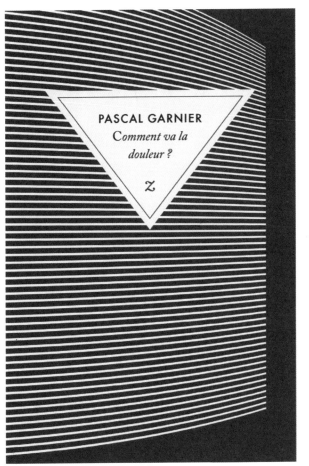

PASCAL GARNIER

*Comment va la
douleur ?*

Z

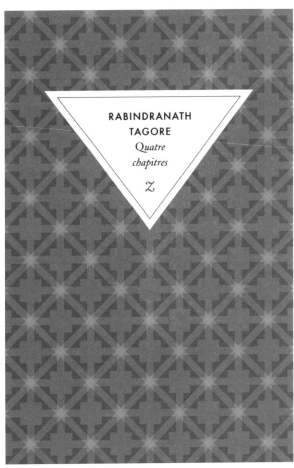

RABINDRANATH
TAGORE

*Quatre
chapitres*

Z

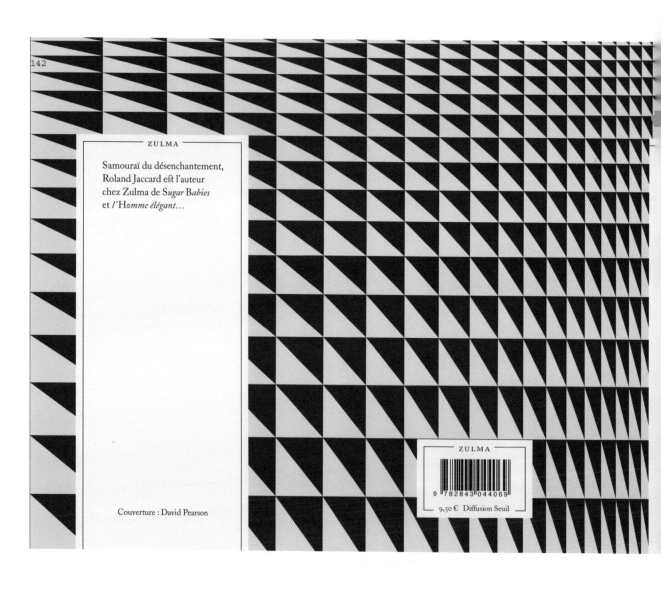

ZULMA

Samouraï du désenchantement,
Roland Jaccard est l'auteur
chez Zulma de *Sugar Babies*
et *l'Homme élégant*…

Couverture : David Pearson

ZULMA

9,50 € Diffusion Seuil

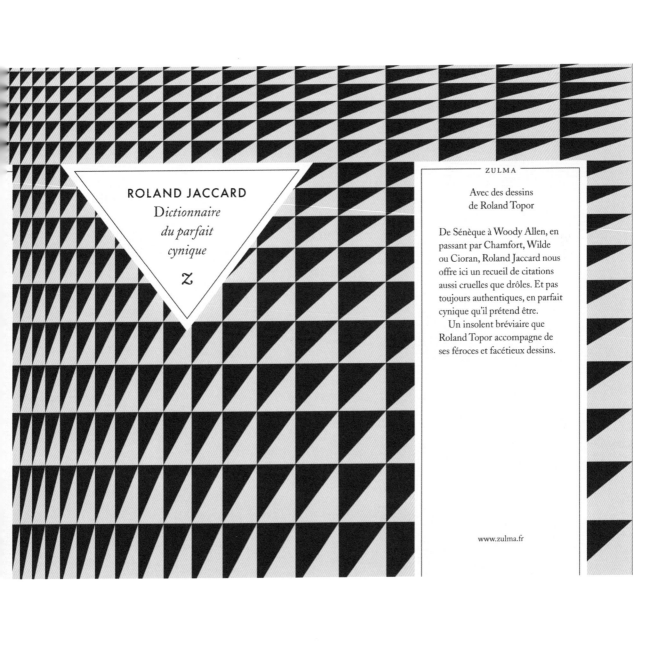

ROLAND JACCARD

*Dictionnaire
du parfait
cynique*

Z

ZULMA

Avec des dessins
de Roland Topor

De Sénèque à Woody Allen, en
passant par Chamfort, Wilde
ou Cioran, Roland Jaccard nous
offre ici un recueil de citations
aussi cruelles que drôles. Et pas
toujours authentiques, en parfait
cynique qu'il prétend être.
    Un insolent bréviaire que
Roland Topor accompagne de
ses féroces et facétieux dessins.

www.zulma.fr

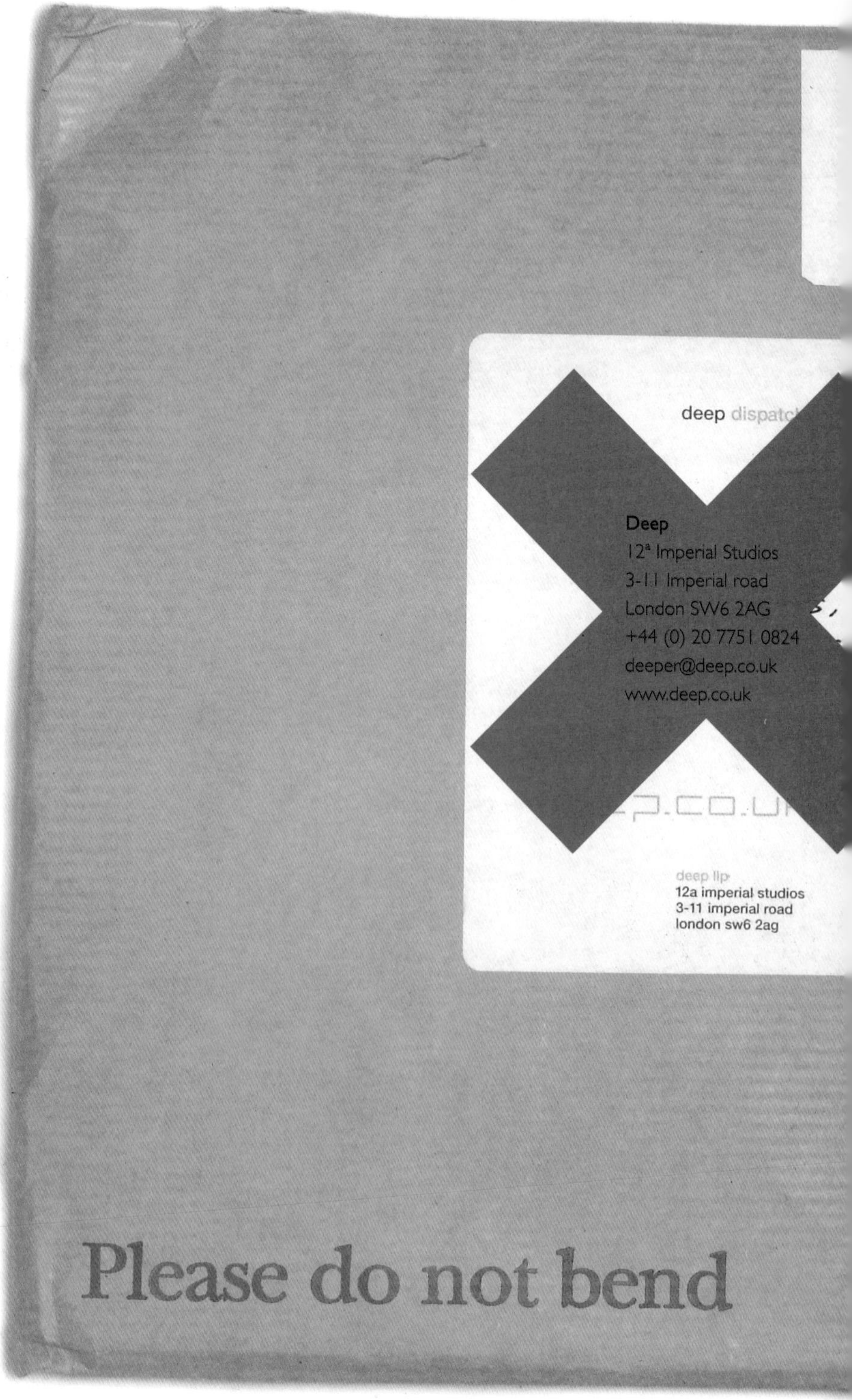

144

deep dispatch

Deep
12ª Imperial Studios
3-11 Imperial road
London SW6 2AG
+44 (0) 20 7751 0824
deeper@deep.co.uk
www.deep.co.uk

ep.co.uk

deep lip
12a imperial studios
3-11 imperial road
london sw6 2ag

Please do not bend

deep.co.uk
graphic & internet design

1
01
16
99
00
35

LONDON
10.04.07
SW8

GREAT BRITAIN
POSTAGE PAID

0179

PB 456130

NANDER .

BAJOS

S

contact
+44 (0) 20 7751 0824
+44 (0) 20 7751 0826
+44 (0) 20 7751 0823

internet
www.deep.co.uk
e: deeper@deep.co.uk
isdn: +44 (0) 20 7751 0981

Ritz Magazine
Client The Ritz Club London / Spafax Publishing *Design* Grant Bowden *Year* 2006-2007
Bi-monthly customer magazine.

146

RITZ

RITZ LONDON MAGAZINE | SUMMER 2006 | ISSUE 14

carousel

0.36.37

Carousel
A Nouvre Film by
Rcier Fine Jewellery
Words Alice B-B
Images Peter Marsh

Oscar Sculpey
wears Clark Foster
brooch, bracelet by
Rcic Fine Jewellery

coehlo.

Portrait: Paulo Coelho

For anyone for whom words like 'inspirational' or 'life-enhancing' start alarm bells clanging in the back of their mind, meeting Paulo Coelho is a daunting prospect. He is an ex-hippy and a former pop lyricist, but today he is a writer whose books - The Alchemist, for instance, or his latest novel The Zahir - sell in their millions across more than 150 countries. One has been made into a computer game, another into a film. Whatever language you speak - whichever one of 56 at the last count, to be precise - this man is a best-seller. For many of his readers, though, he is much more than just another international publishing phenomenon: for them, he is a guru, a leader in the one true path, a guide to spiritual enlightenment.

And he looks the part, which is slightly off-putting - the suave good looks, the crisp suit of an American fundamentalist preacher, the mildly detached interest with which he looks at you, and the occasional slightly portentous pronouncements. "Being a writer is sharing your view through books," is one of his aphorisms. He has the ease of a successful hypnotist, perhaps, or a very expensive New York therapist. It is disturbingly like meeting some sort of holy man - but I don't happen to buy into the magic, and before we have even sat down, I am starting to wonder whether this meeting was a good idea.

Con-men look like that too, I think, sourly.

It would be understandable if all the adulation had turned his head. After all, it's not only his misty-eyed acolytes who treat him with such reverence - the hard-nosed publishing executives who are standing round also speak in the slightly hushed tones they reserve for authors who can earn them millions of pounds with a single book. When he speaks to them, he has the easy assurance of a man who knows that, whatever he wants, someone will

be found to fetch it for him. And what's more, his success isn't measured only in five-pound notes and dollar bills - Coelho collects literary honours and awards like ambitious bankers collect cocktail party invitations.

He has slightly less exalted admirers as well - apart from his official website, there are several unofficial ones, where Coelho fans enthuse about his writings and what his books mean to them. Their views tend to be adoring rather than critical. It would be tempting to use the word 'groupies', except that their passions seem to be strictly spiritual.

So it's a relief, and a bit of a surprise, when I ask him what he makes of all the adulation. How comfortable is he with his role as therapist to the world? His first reply, reassuringly down to earth, is a very un-gurulike snort. And when he enlarges on this, he leaves no doubt about how he feels. "This is a big misunderstanding. My readers may say my books change their lives, but other books change people's lives as well," he says.

"People don't follow me like a religion - that's just newspaper talk, and it's not my cup of tea. Maybe my books can be a help, but people have to take responsibility for their own lives."

I make a grudging mental apology for having been so grumpy and suspicious. But what is it about his books, then? What do they offer his readers? Is there a sort of facile optimism in what he writes that makes it so attractive to people who don't feel easy with their own lives?

"It's not up to me to judge how people classify my books. Why are they a worldwide success? I don't know," he says, picking an invisible speck of dust off his immaculate cream suit. "I certainly don't see myself as praising optimism, but I am a person who has hopes. To be cynical is easy, but it means you are not committed to anything."

Ouch! I hope that reference to cynicism is just a coincidence, but I catch myself wondering guiltily whether he might just have been reading my mind a few moments ago.

Andy Tsoyke
Dominatrix Johnes

ROAD CHEF

030.31

alchemist

Portrait of Paulo Coelho
Words: Andy Taylor
Image: Paulo Coelho

Ritz
Magazine

Title
Toro! Toro! Toro!

Inside Story
Bullfighting

¡TORO!

Y ou may be a would-be Ernest Hemingway, an aficionado of the corrida with a fine appreciation of every sweep of the matador's cape; you may be a first-time tourist, with brightly-flowered shorts and a tendency to put your hands in front of your eyes at the moment of truth, as the bull sinks to its knees; or you may be an animal rights campaigner with a solemn expression and a detailed knowledge of the statistics of a sport that kills an estimated 30,000 bulls a year in Spain alone.

But one thing is certain: not many people are indifferent to the bullfight.

Bullfighting, they say, traces its history in Spain back to the 18th century, with the establishment of the strict three-part structure in which the bull is taunted, weakened, and then killed. Or, depending on whom you ask, further back than that, to 1133 AD, when King Alfonso VIII celebrated his coronation with what was then claimed to be the first bullfight on Spanish soil. Or back further, to Roman times. Or further still, back some 4,000 years to the wall paintings of Knossos, in Crete, which show men and women grabbing the horns of a charging bull, and vaulting over it.

So bullfighting has a history – but so, too, does the opposition to it. In the 16th century, Pope Pius V was so shocked at the slaughter that he formally banned the sport – a decision which the people treated with contempt. They ignored the Papal edict, and Pius's successor in the Vatican, Gregory XIII, had no choice but to rescind the decree. "The bullfights are in the blood of the Spanish people," declared the mystic cleric Fray Luis de Leon more than 400 years ago, and it still is. But the opposition, largely from outside Spain, continues to snap at the heels of the enthusiasts. Groups like People for the Ethical treatment of Animals and Fight Against Animal Cruelty in Europe still campaign against bullfighting with some success – two years ago, the city of Barcelona responded to a 250,000 petition by voting to ban the corrida.

But what is it that the Spanish people love and the protesters loathe with such passion? Former matador Mario Carrion, who fought bulls in Spain, France, Portugal, and several Latin American countries, describes it as "a type of dramatic ballet dance with death". It is, he says, not a sport but an art – and an art in which the artist puts his own body on the line. He should know – he was seriously gored twelve times in his career. "As he would in dancing, the bullfighter must control his movements maintaining the rhythm, not of music, but of danger. On stage, a faux-pas means an interruption of artistic flow; in the bullfighting arena, a mistake could mean the death of the star of this drama," he says.

But that description makes the bullfight sound like something that happens in a theatre, before a dinner-jacketed and tiara-ed audience that might slip away for cocktails and a brief chat in the interval. It conveys nothing of the smell of sawdust, blood, and sweat, none of the mounting excitement, none of the passion that marks the corrida.

**Blood, Sweat
and Tears**

Words
Shane Stitt

Images
Iain Crockart

4260

bloodsweat

Design Holborn
123 Aberdeen House
22-24 Highbury Grove
London, N5 2EA
+44 (0) 20 7288 7200
www.designholborn.co.uk

ROYAL MAIL
111
17 JAN 2008
6 - 15
MOUNT PLEAS...

48

BY AIR MAIL
par avion
Royal Mail

S SALA

BAJOS

GES

Next Level Magazine
Client Next Level *Design* Jesse Holborn *Year* 2006
Independent Art, Photography and Issues publication. Each issue is centred around a theme, which is then explored by new and established artists
and writers in collaboration with Next Level, to produce their own personal interpretations.

NextLevel

Art / Photography / Ideas / # 10

£12.95

WO
MEN

Trevor Forrest
Recent Days

FLO REN CI A

Artist: Florencia Durante
Writers: Alejandra Aguado, Paul Kilsby and Alexandra MacGilp
Light Actions

PK: Photography has many histories. One insists that photography is, by its very nature, transparent and objective, relaying images of the world without inflection. In this history the camera is understood as a machine and photography as mechanical. In another, rather less familiar history, photography is understood as essentially magical and its images have about them something uncanny and spectral.

AM: It is light that makes photography possible, but in Durante's work it is photography that allows us to perceive light. Photography is the result of light's aggressive trace on a surface. In her practice, Durante makes explicit how the process of photography functions. The action of light on film is fetishised in a kind of 'mise en abîme'.

AA: Light is always a spectre and a sign, and as such, it is never still. It is always pointing at something different than itself, referencing another being, allowing it to appear for us and ready to flicker away.

Light comes 'encapsulated' (that's how we know it), as if reinforcing its elusive nature, its ungraspable self can't be made visible if it is not contained.

PK: Just as Roentgen's discovery of X-rays in 1895 showed what the eye cannot see, there were many who believed that the photograph might 'see' in special, privileged ways beyond normal sight and that the photographer might

claim visionary gifts. There is, for example, a wonderful photograph dating from 1900 of the Symbolist Frederick Holland Day in his darkroom, his trays of chemicals laid out on the floor and wearing a long dark cloak, looking for all the world like a magician rather than a laboratory technician. Other equally famous thinkers believed passionately that photography should be understood as an essentially visionary medium: witness August Strindberg's 'celestographs' and Arthur Conan Doyle's vigorous defence of spiritualist and fairy photography.

In Florencia Durante's photographs I feel I am being shown something that is both spectral and, bafflingly, ordinary.

AM: In the series *Enveloped*, an old man, Durante's uncle Ross, portrayed as sensitively as in a Ghirlandaio painting, sits on a chair in a white room. Light becomes increasingly kinetic, performing around the sitter with playful energy. He is variously embraced, absorbed and wrapped up by this luminous, frantic light. His figure glows out of a line of light. These are mesmerising images, but are they joyous or menacing? Is he experiencing the rapture of an ascension or an assumption? Light scribbles, doodles over him until he resembles a Giacometti drawing. His silhouette is illuminated like a protector who has self-immolated.

AA: Florencia Durante plays the magician and lets light dissolve, stretch, expand without

Text: Anselm Franke

Stunned Man / Trilogy of Failure Part 2
2004
3-channel film installation
Shot on Super 16mm
Loop 33 min
Film still

JULIAN ROSEFELDT

TRILOGY OF FAILURE

Julian Rosefeldt's work investigates the rituals, structures, and absurdities of everyday life. It bears witness to a rationalising view from a distance and a precise gift of observation akin to the objectifying methods of the natural sciences. The investigation is a persistent articulation and extrapolation of both unconscious and well-known stereotypes and routines of everyday life. In terms of content, the result of this rationalising investigation can be classified in two categories. For one, Rosefeldt exposes nonsensical and absurd elements in the logical and logistical processes of everyday life: he discovers irrationality within rationality. For another, he designs the opposite scenario: in authentic, irrational human expression, he emphasises the serial, mechanical and automatic elements. His work thus centres on the paradoxical image of society as an organic machine.

Julian Rosefeldt's early work was marked by the rationalising answer to this paradoxical image. The attempt to understand society as an image machine can be summarised in the question: "how does it work, what is its structure?". It calls for an archaeology, which determines the cement between the individual devices that make up the machine: what is it that keeps the individual parts together, if it is obviously not an "inner tie", unless God were a machine? In the academic discourse of recent years, this question has been discussed not least in the shape of visual culture criticism, in which the production of cultural meaning appears as "glue" (of the brand "meaning", "significance" or "emotion") between basically autonomous data, devices, technologies, and layouts. Around the turn of the millennium, there appeared indeed a sudden and unfamiliar identity between academic discourse in culture or media criticism and artistic practice, which took an archaeological approach to the media.

As in the case of a number of artists, this interest was reflected in Julian Rosefeldt's compilation and structuring of found materials for Global Soap (2000) he compiled hundreds of excerpts from daily soaps worldwide, which he catalogued, as in an atlas, according to topoi, solemn formulas and standardised gestures.

The result of Global Soap is not lacking in a certain humour – precisely because it exhibits the mechanical reproduction of emotions, of stereotypes. Yet this humour remains subordinate to the academic interest, which advances the compilation as an object of study and piece of evidence.

Julian Rosefeldt's focus has hardly changed in recent years, but his artistic methods have. From an academic collector and organiser, he has developed into a director who works with characters – stereotyped social groups at first, then individual characters. These steps reflect the shift in focus within this media-archaeological postulate: it is not meaning that is the organic element in culture, the glue which fits the data and devices of the cultural machine together.

Instead, it is the mechanical element, which breaks into the dynamics of life, culture and meaning, structures them and thus gradually submits them to its regime. By reversing the critical gesture, humour has come into its own in critical discourse – humour, they say, brings a certain truth to light. The truth of humour, however, differs from the truth of critical discourse. The truth of humour is not static or unreal, but dynamic, temporary, affirmative, and invulnerable. The Latin root of the word literally means moist, liquid, and it is hardly far-fetched to set this meaning against the media-archaeological metaphor of glue.

According to Henri Bergson's theories on the mechanical elements which encrust life, humour is to laugh about both the stereotypical and the non-conformist, and therefore social, behaviour of others. This postulate is confirmed by the tradition of clowns and comedians, in particular by the "kings of comedy", by inventing characters such as Charlie Chaplin and Buster Keaton. In their early time, we become witness to a repeated, mechanical ritual of bodily failure. The humour of these films originates not so much in the plot, namely a failure to come to grips with certain situations. Even before the plot

BY AIR MAIL
par avion
Royal Mail

Eat Sleep Work/Play
332 Kingsland Road
London E8 4 DA
+44 (0) 79 5065 8097
www.eatsleepworkplay.com

From

Eat Sleep Work/Play

332 Kingsland Road
London E8 4DA
Unted Kingdom

AX

Royal Mail

POSTAGE   PAID   UK
15/01/08 £5.39 E8
102002   2-5029023-1

E YELE

, 28, BAJOS

TGES

ONA, SPAIN

Royal Mail®
airsure®

| PRIORITY |
| MAIL |

 **Exprès**

DELIVERY CONFIRMATION

LY 1995 8390 3GB   No sig req

LY 1995 8390 3GB   No sig req

LY 1995 8390 3GB

Scan   No Signature

Central Saint Martins Degree Show Book

Client London University of the Arts *Design* Antoine Choussat & Zamir Antonio, David Lane, Stephen Osman *Year* 2006

Visitors are given mini-stabilo highlighter pens and are invited to highlight names on the cover as they evolve throughout the show. Everyone's work was photographed in one day on a constant frame of 1×1,5m, with each of the 161 students given only 5 minutes to lay out their compositions.

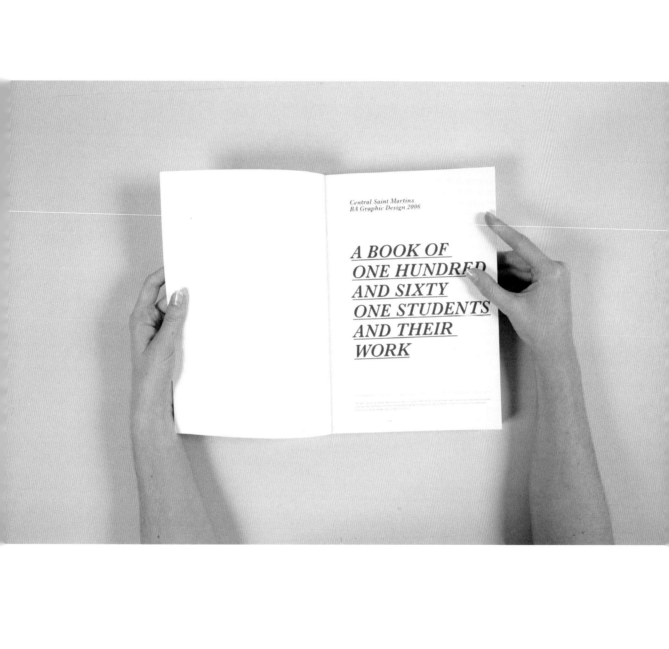

Central Saint Martins
BA Graphic Design 2006

A BOOK OF
ONE HUNDRED
AND SIXTY
ONE STUDENTS
AND THEIR
WORK

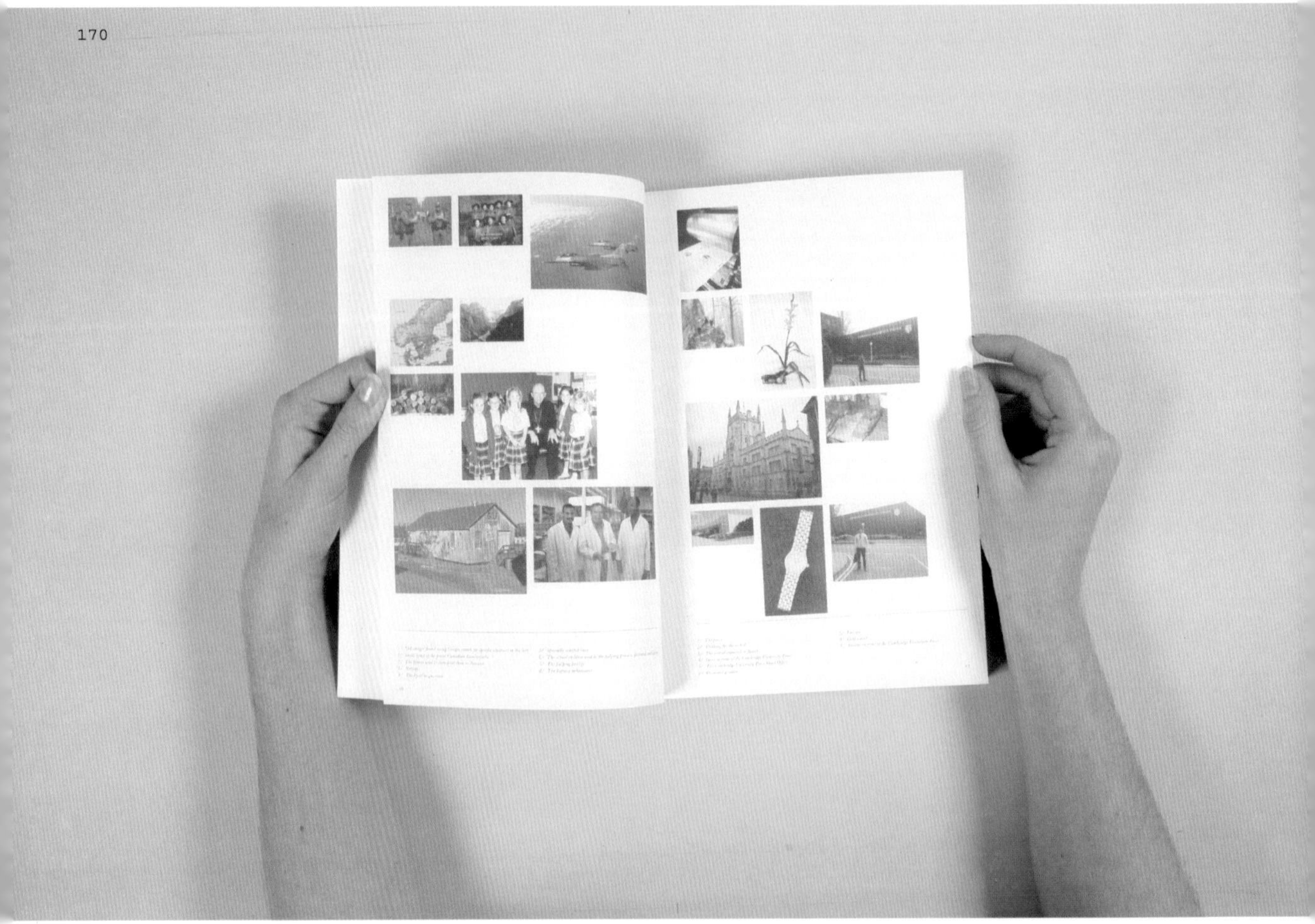

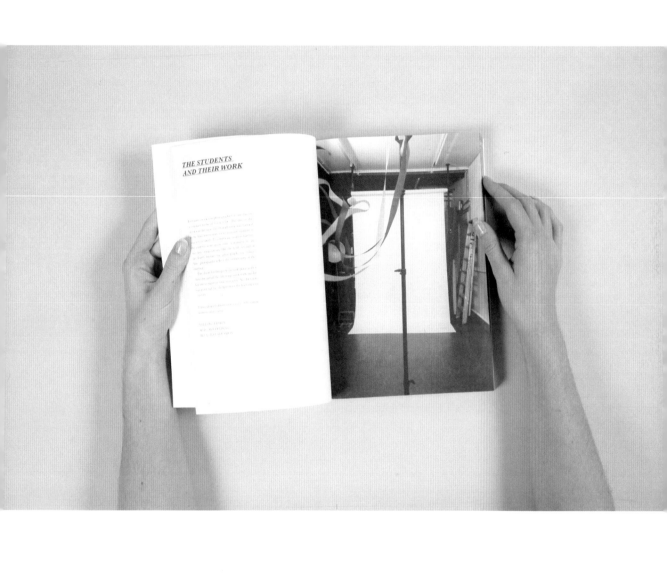

David Lane

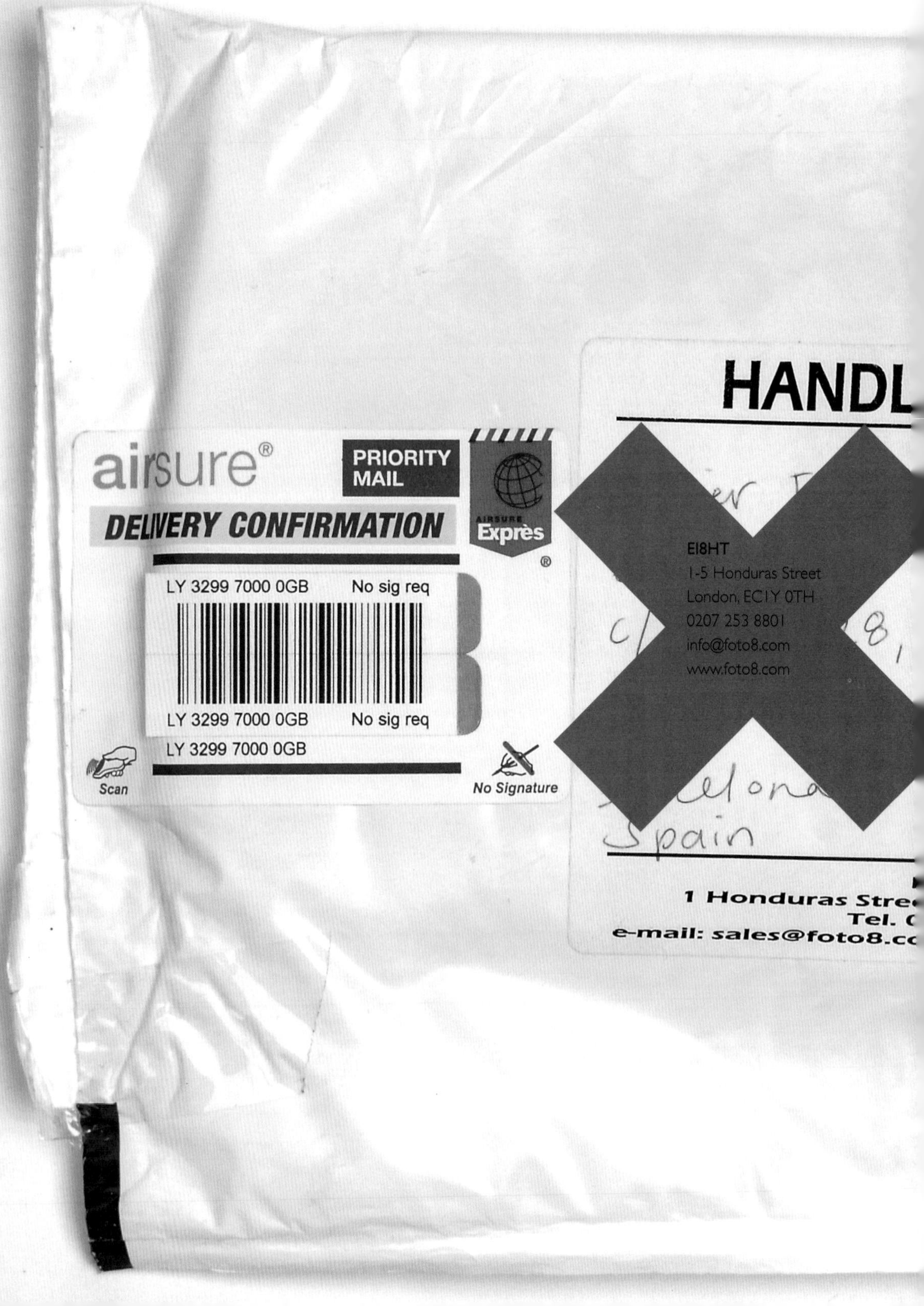

airsure®

PRIORITY MAIL

DELIVERY CONFIRMATION

AIRSURE
Exprès
®

| LY 3299 7000 0GB | No sig req |

LY 3299 7000 0GB | No sig req

Scan

LY 3299 7000 0GB

No Signature

HANDL

EI8HT
1-5 Honduras Street
London, EC1Y 0TH
0207 253 8801
info@foto8.com
www.foto8.com

c/

81

lona

Spain

1 Honduras Stree
Tel. 0
e-mail: sales@foto8.co

AX

Royal Mail
POSTAGE PAID UK
20/03/07 £5.53 EC1V
28003 6-2321601-1

SMALL
PKT

WITH CARE

les

ajos

to 8 Ltd
London, EC1Y 0TH, UK
)7 253 8801
web: www.foto8.com

Client Foto8 *Design* Phil Evans, Rob Kester *Year* 2006-2007
Photography magazine. The photographs are the primary focus, always taking into account the sense of relating a narrative through the images.

178

8

EI8HT PHOTOJOURNALISM

INDUSTRY

EI8HT PHOTOJOURNALISM V5N2 SEPT 06

VOL.5 NO.2 SEPT 2006 £10 WWW.FOTO8.COM

EI8HT PHOTOJOURNALISM

4TH BIRTHDAY EDITION

ENGLAND FEATURES
GRIME   SURVIVAL PROGRAMMES   BAGHDAD GARAGE
THE LAST WITCH   ALLOTMENTS
WORLD FEATURES
NIGERIA   103RD STREET   ACID ATTACKS   PIPELINE   GENERALS
COLUMNISTS
TIM MINOGUE   JOHN O'FARRELL   DAVID PRATT   JOHN VIDAL
INTERVIEW
SUSAN MEISELAS
BOOK REVIEWS   RESOURCES
VOL.5 NO.1   JUNE 2006   £8   WWW.FOTO8.COM

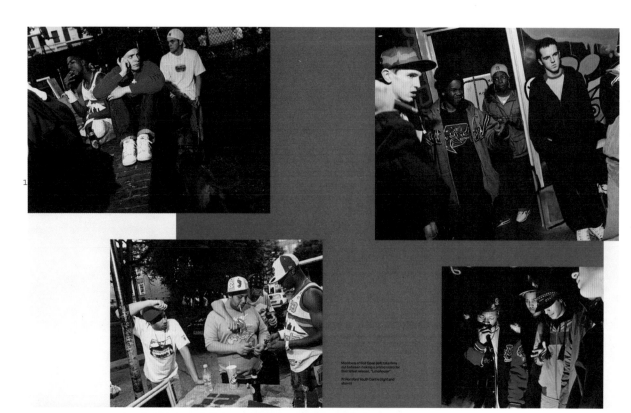

Members of Roll Deep (left) take time
out between making a promo video for
their latest release, "Lifehouse"

At Romford Youth Centre (right and
above)

1

Grime
Ewen Spencer

There is a certain threshold photographers rarely cross, probably because it requires a kind of collapse into something. It creates an intimacy that's difficult to sustain and only won by patience and return. It's a condition of agreed privilege, changing the way we see our subjects and influencing what they are willing to reveal to us. It is hard earned.

It's sometimes suggested that our youth is without politics, as less young people than ever before choose to vote. Ewen Spencer acknowledges dynamic, aware and pressured lives, played out against what is unmistakably urban London. High walls and fenced courts, whitewashed brick window frames. Monotony. Youths exchange drugs and smoke. Drug-smoke threads through this series – even the youngest subjects exhale clouds of weed or pinch damp spliffs. Fingers roll skins, update mobiles or grip beer bottles.

Yet, for all such drama, the photographs do not seem sensational, opportunist or accusing. Rather they appear accurate and exhilarating. There is little despair, none of the sense of implosion found, for example, in the juvenile gang work of Joseph Rodriguez. Spencer's depiction of the Grime/Garage music scene in London is unsettling in its energy. It relates something of the richness that comes to photographers willing to negotiate such an involvement. His are revealing images – detailed, tough and agile, emphasising the kinship of young groups as they record, perform and hang out.

Spencer employs colour and strategic repetition, and purposefully so. Waves of youths recur, communing, sharing microphones and dope, listening, watching. It's an insular community, and he couldn't be closer, mapping routines as bodies flow to the edge of busy frames.

Ewen Spencer's work is built around a vital moment of self-expression. Its very simple, occasionally solemn, a moment that's been echoed in many forms through recent decades. It was there in doo-wop. It's still found in the best examples of bluegrass, when musicians build their sound, guiding the mood of the room as they lean with reverence towards a microphone; a sound like a single voice expanding, exorcising, before a diminished returning to the shadows. And Spencer holds many shadows, each part of a chiaroscuro technique achieved by his off-camera flash. This is not a narration towards collapse. Nothing is threatened or in crisis. These young people are dignified, entirely immersed in their music, in each other, and in life **8**
Ken Grant

This work will form part of the exhibition 10 Years of British Youth Culture at Lazarides Gallery, 8 Greek Street, London, from 18 June

Recording an MC "battle" (above) for a
DVD, Lord of the Decks. Many of these
battles take place by last minute
invitation – the MCs have no rehearsal
or multiple takes in front of the camera.
If a rhyme sounds familiar or preconceived the MC will be ridiculed by
those present – these moments
inevitably make their way to the final
cut. The DVDs hold a cult status and sell
in their thousands, worldwide

MC Fumin (right) in Walthamstow

Salt

Salt Flat
Caroll Taveras

Bolivia's dazzling Salar de Uyuni is the brightest spot on earth visible from space. The Surrealist painters were captivated by the hallucinatory quality of the light on the great salt desert, where all that is solid melts into the thin Andean air.

This vertiginous landscape, its ecology unchanged for centuries, offers work to the inhabitants of the Altiplano and holiday memories to moneyed tourists from across the globe. Against the blinding backdrop of azure sky, workers painstakingly scrape salt from vast lakes that evaporated thousands of years ago, most of which is consumed in Bolivia. Holidaymakers stay the night in the hotel built entirely from salt blocks. 8

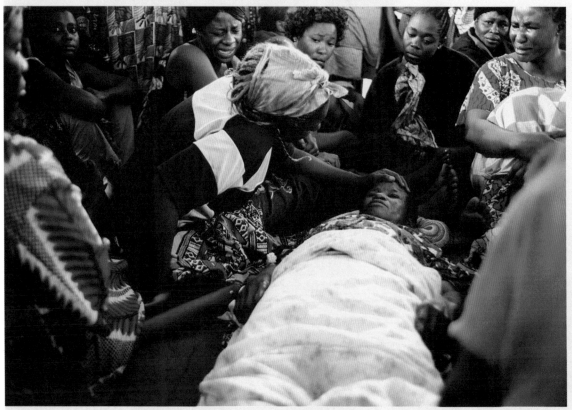

Mystery train: (facing page, clockwise from top). Leaping off the train before it pulls into the station

Isabelle N (left) is on her way back from Kindu where she just got married in her hometown of Lubumbashi. She had to buy a ticket from the military who took over the compartment

A man who has been doing business during the whole train ride counts his money

This woman died on the train. Now her family watches over the body

A man drinks "cinq cents", a small bottle of palm alcohol named after its price. Passengers drink a lot of it during the endless hours of waiting when the train runs out of fuel

Hats pulled down (this page, top right) members of the Presidential Guard, who are travelling on the train pose anonymously

When the train derails, passengers clear the creeping vegetation which has overgrown the track

At dusk on the roof of the train, at the Kitanda station. After four days of stranded with no fuel, help arrives

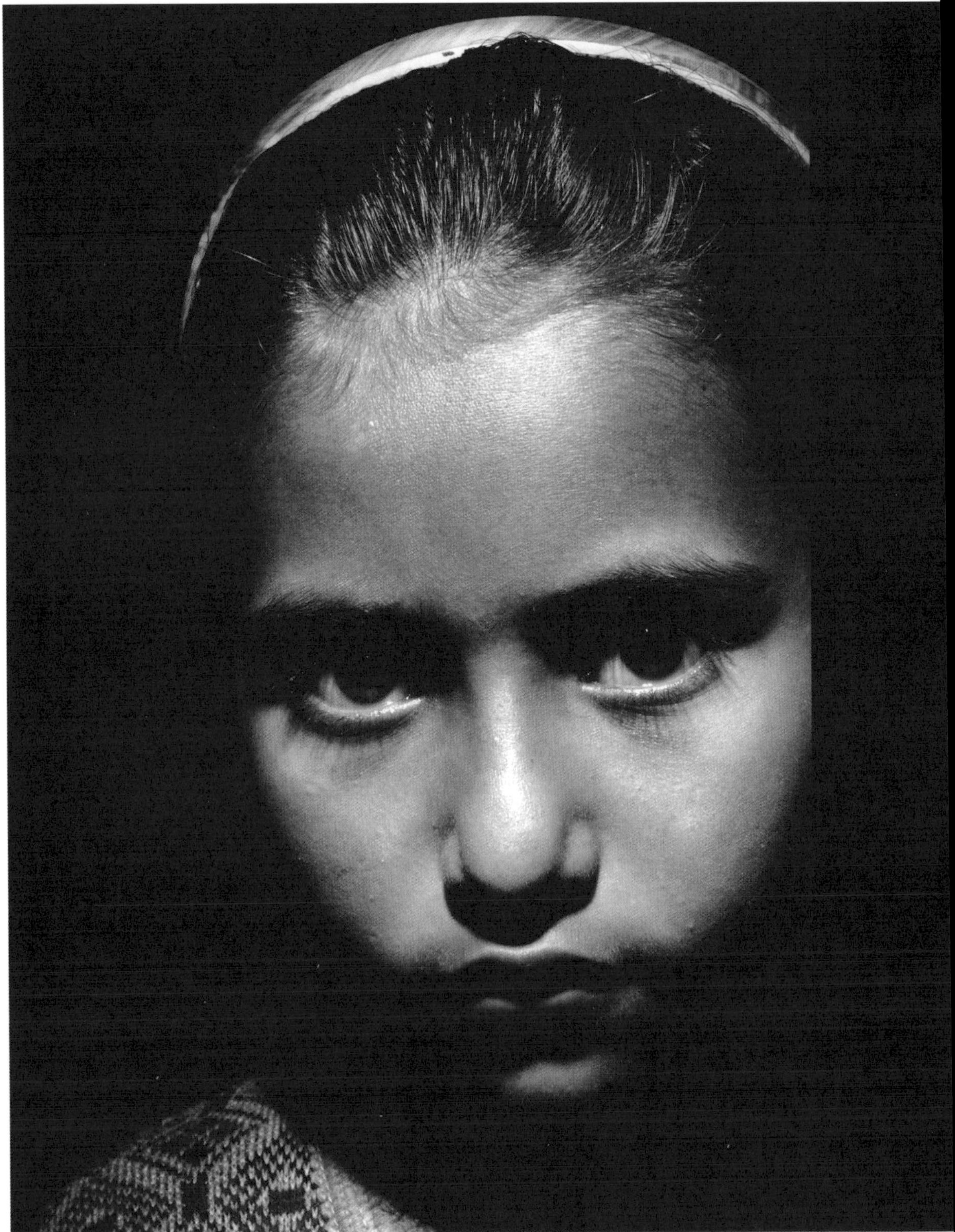

188

Great Britain
Recommandé

Royal Mail

signedfor
international

R

RI 9303 8177 5GB   Sig req

RI 9303 8177 5GB   Sig req

RI 9303 8177 5GB

PRIORITY HANDLING & REGISTERED DELIVERY

www.emmi.co.uk

A

Royal Mail

POSTAGE   PAID   UK

26/03/07   £4.60   E8

102002   2-4338967-1

ail

c/ Je

08870 S

Barcel

SPA

EMMI
Studio 17
310 Kingsland Road
E(4DB London
+44 77 5200 1311
hello@emmi.co.uk
www.emmi.co.uk

Artist Portfolio

Client Elsa Salonen *Design* Emmi Salonen *Year* 2007

A portfolio for a Finnish fine artist who does painting and video installations, based in Bologna, Italy.

190

when judie
was forced
to be
her own
background

technique	an audio-video installation with four images projected onto four plexiglasses
year of production	2006
duration	7 minutes, 39 seconds
dimensions	app. 130cm x 400cm these dimensions worked out as the minimal size of the wall that is needed to project the work. the size of every piece of plexiglas is 82cm x 56cm.
installation materials	a projector, two speakers, a dvd player, four pieces of plexiglas.

con
–
the serie
of five

technique	an audio-video performance/installation
year of production	2006 - 2007
duration	35 minutes, 37 seconds
dimensions	entire room
materials	performance: 3 videos with a musician/ installation: 5 videos with the audio registration from the performances

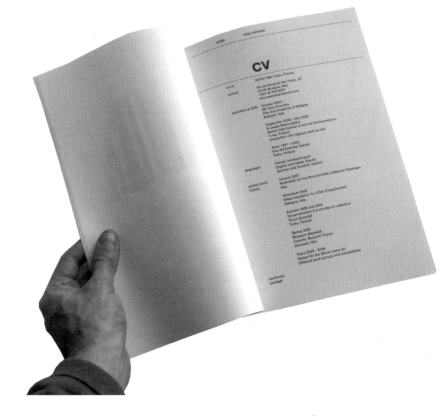

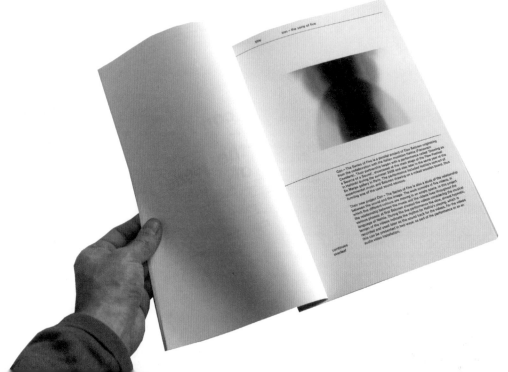

con

a serie
of five

—

elsa saloner
2006

Studio Catalogue
Client Self-promotional *Design* Emmi Salonen *Year* 2006
Self-promotion item for the studio, featuring latest work and press in an easily updatable style.

HELLO

This is a showcase
of selected works
and words from a
graphic designer
and an illustrator,
Tomi Salonen.

If you like what
you see, have any
enquiries, would like
to commission work,
need a quote or just
want to chat, please
get in touch.

35 FRAGMENTS

Client: University of Westminster (UK)

Item: Degree show catalogue

BOOK DESIGN

BROCHURES

Client: Phaidon Publishing, designed while at karlssonwilker inc. [New York, USA]

Item: A book on retail architecture

CASE STUDY 1

Brief:
End of year catalogue for Contemporary Media Course at the University of Westminster, London, UK. Not everyone had pieces of work ready to showcase by the time of going to print but others had stunning photography. How to show the work of 80 students without giving any one person more coverage than another?

Solution:
Full colour images of student work displayed on the folding front and back cover, double sided, with page numbers only. Inside pages have contact details and project information on one colour blue paper. This way the publication is visually cohesive and emphasises the equality of the group.

35 FRAGMENTS

Client: University of Westminster (UK)
Item: Degree show catalogue

Item: Overall corporate identity

198

Great Britain
Recommandé
signedfor
international

RI 8790 1155 1GB   Sig req

RI 8790 1155 1GB   Sig req

RI 8790 1155 1GB

PRIORITY HANDLING & REGISTERED DELIVERY

FL@33, 59 Briton St
London EC1M 5UN, UK

Royal Mail
POSTAGE   PAID   UK
04/05/07   £4.69   EC1M
55003   7-2041517-1

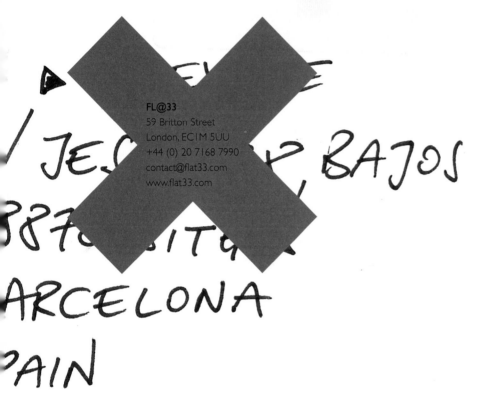

FL@33
59 Britton Street
London, EC1M 5UU
+44 (0) 20 7168 7990
contact@flat33.com
www.flat33.com

/ JE... BAJOS

?87... ...ITY

ARCELONA

?AIN

RI 8210 6583 4GB

Client Laurence King Publishing *Design* Agathe Jacquillat & Tomi Vollauschek *Year* 2006
The book cover has a special finishing with spot uv highlights and sexy black flock.

202

Drusilla Cole is senior lecturer and course
director of BA (Hons) Surface Design at
the University of the Arts, London. She is
the author of *1000 Patterns*.

For our current catalogue please contact:

Laurence King Publishing Ltd
e-mail: enquiries@laurenceking.co.uk
www.laurenceking.co.uk

Printed in China

£19.95

ISBN 1-85669-505-0

90000

9 781856 695053

www.laurenceking.co.uk

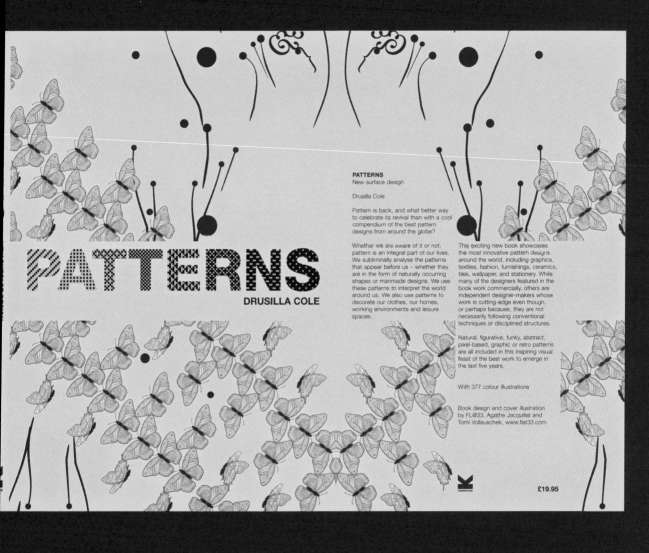

PATTERNS

PATTERNS
New surface design

Drusilla Cole

Pattern is back, and what better way to celebrate its revival than with a cool compendium of the best pattern designs from around the globe?

Whether we are aware of it or not, pattern is an integral part of our lives. We subliminally analyse the patterns that appear before us – whether they are in the form of naturally occurring shapes or manmade designs. We use these patterns to interpret the world around us. We also use patterns to decorate our clothes, our homes, working environments and leisure spaces.

This exciting new book showcases the most innovative pattern designs around the world, including graphics, textiles, fashion, furnishings, ceramics, tiles, wallpaper, and stationery. While many of the designers featured in the book work commercially, others are independent designer-makers whose work is cutting-edge even though, or perhaps because, they are not necessarily following conventional techniques or disciplined structures.

Natural, figurative, funky, abstract, pixel-based, graphic or retro patterns are all included in this inspiring visual feast of the best work to emerge in the last five years.

With 377 colour illustrations

Book design and cover illustration by FL@33, Agathe Jacquillat and Tomi Vollauschek, www.flat33.com

PATTERNS

DRUSILLA COLE

£19.95

ACKNOWLEDGEMENTS

I would like to extend my heartfelt thanks to all the contributing artists and designers who have made this project possible by donating their artwork so freely and helpfully.

I have really enjoyed doing the project and it has been a real privilege to have been able to view all the lovely colours and patterns you sent me. I also very much enjoyed reading the comments, which were most enlightening and inspiring.

Many thanks, too, to Helen Evans and Susie May at Laurence King Publishing, Tomi and Agathe at FL@33, and Caroline McNamara for all their help and support.

Dru Cole

CONTENTS

CONVERSATIONAL PATTERNS

'Art, by its nature, will always come up with surprises, and deals not so much with specifics or with directions, as with overall patterns that must always be free to fall in fresh and unexplored directions.'

Robert Butts

Conversational patterns are sometimes referred to as novelty prints and contain images of objects or situations. In these designs the artists' inspirations are not always immediately apparent until examined closely. For example, one series of wallpapers has been based on the song lyrics of Edith Piaf[1]. Other artists' designs are based on books[2], films[3] or even landscapes[4]. Some patterns in this section tell a story without words[5] or promote a point of view[6]. Also included here are patterns which contain repeating units of motifs which are similar but which differ sufficiently to give visual interest[7]. The inspiration for these motifs can be natural[8] or man-made[9] in origin. Occasionally, a designer uses the human form as a design element[10], or combines people with fantasy figures[11] and backgrounds[12].

[1] p.40
[2] p.13, p.57 (top)
[3] p.22 (left), p.56
[4] pp.54–55
[5] p.14 (bottom), p.50 (top)
[6] p.25, pp.38–39 (bottom)
[7] p.10, p.23
[8] p.32 (right)
[9] pp.96–97
[10] p.43, p.52 (top left)
[11] p.46 (bottom)
[12] p.44

RETRO PATTERNS

"As is often the case in retro fashion, historical accuracy is somewhat beside the point."

New York Times

Retro patterns are designs that are inspired by, or that seek to emulate, a previous era's style. They achieve this by using a combination of its characteristic colours and motifs[1] or by referencing illustrative styles of the period[2]. Designs that include icons of the period[3] naturally evoke the epoch, as do patterns that emulate art movements such as Op Art[4] or Pop Art[5] and designs that pay homage to an artist from a previous era[6]. Also included are designs that appear to capture the distinguishing mood of a period[7] or that use a retrospective style of colouring and technique[8].

GEOMETRIC PATTERNS

"Pattern is both uplifting and calming to live with. It reflects the repetition found in nature and creates inspiring spaces."

Dominic Crinson

Geometric patterns are nonrepresentational patterns that have been arranged into an ordered or regular repeat. Some of these designs have an entirely mathematical basis[1] and almost all have an underlying invisible geometric grid upon which the pattern is constructed[2]. Several of the designs have a regular structure, which the artists then deliberately interrupt[3] to achieve an asymmetrical balance to their patterns. A few of the artists do not use a formal arrangement at all for their designs[4], but still manage to attain a geometric look. Digital techniques are particularly successful in constructing regular patterns[5], which are then digitally printed[6] or screenprinted[7]. Texture serves to soften the rigid outlines of geometric designs, especially when a soft fabric such as felt is manipulated into a design[8] or when plastics are incorporated into a weave[9].

Trans-form Magazine
Client Self-initiated *Design* Agathe Jacquillat & Tomi Vollauschek *Year* 2001
This large scale magazine is exploring the magic of urban sculptures which appear and disappear in the cities we are living in.
Tower cranes which are lifting, transporting, re-constructing, drawing, cutting, performing and 'trans-forming' are usually unnoticed by the public's eye.

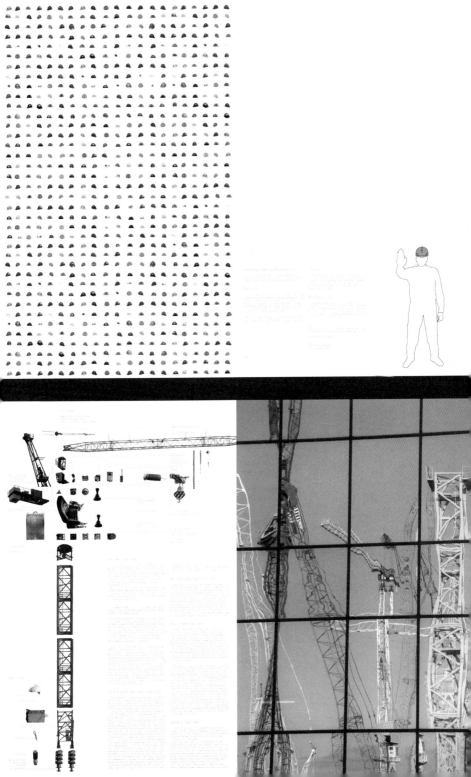

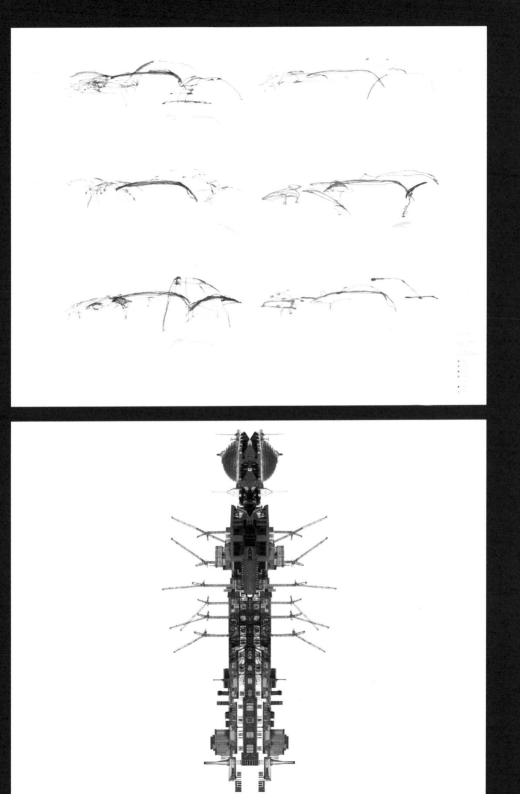

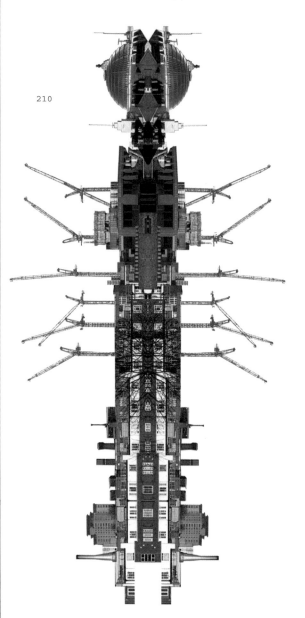

Tolleno Isoptera Aedificatio

Tolleno Phyllomorp

aciniata Aedificatio

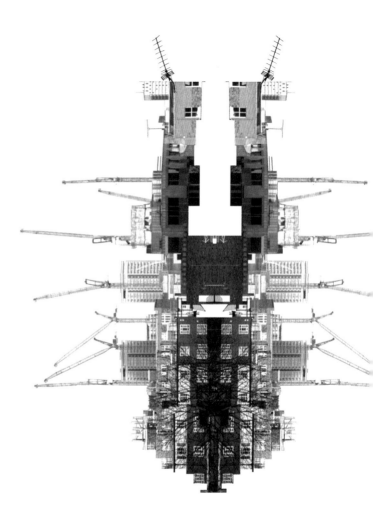

Tolleno Pollyphylla Fullo Aedificatio

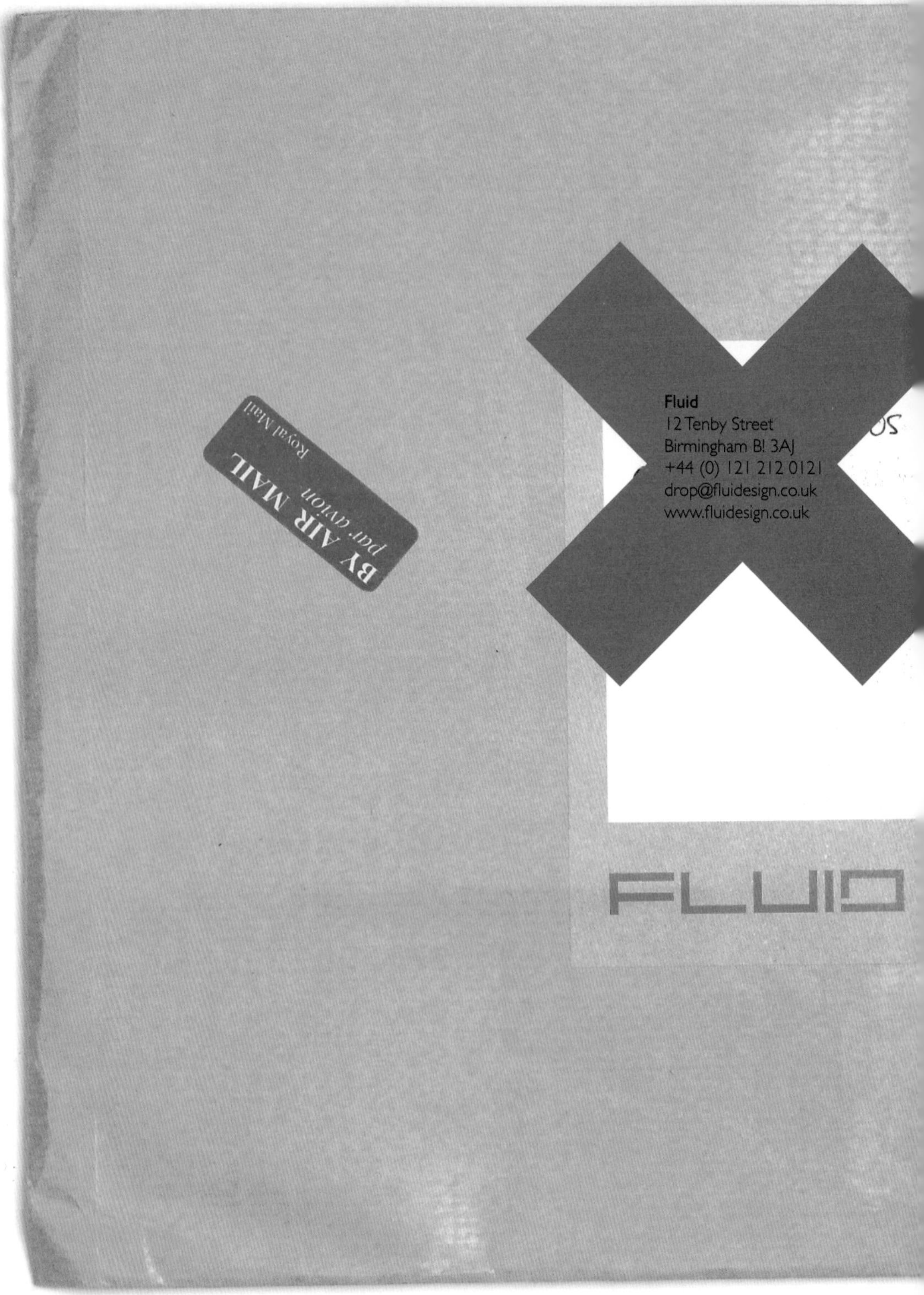

BY AIR MAIL
par avion
Royal Mail

Fluid
12 Tenby Street
Birmingham B! 3AJ
+44 (0) 121 212 0121
drop@fluidesign.co.uk
www.fluidesign.co.uk

FLUID

A

Royal Mail
POSTAGE   PAID   UK
19/03/07   £4.83   B18
413201   5-2797858-1

Great Britain
Recommandé

Royal Mail signedfor
international

R

RI 7227 7457 6GB   Sig req

RI 7227 7457 6GB   Sig req

RI 7227 7457 6GB
PRIORITY HANDLING & REGISTERED DELIVERY

d Studios, 12 Tenby Street, Birmingham B1 3AJ
+44 (0)121 212 0121. Fax: +44 (0)121 212 0202
ail: drop@fluidesign.co.uk. www.fluidesign.co.uk

Architecture Week Performance Programme

Client Fierce Earth ***Design*** Paul Whittaker ***Year*** 2006

Performane programme booklet and event branding.

FURTHER INFORMATION:
WWW.FIERCETV.CO.UK
WWW.ARCHITECTUREWEEK.ORG.UK

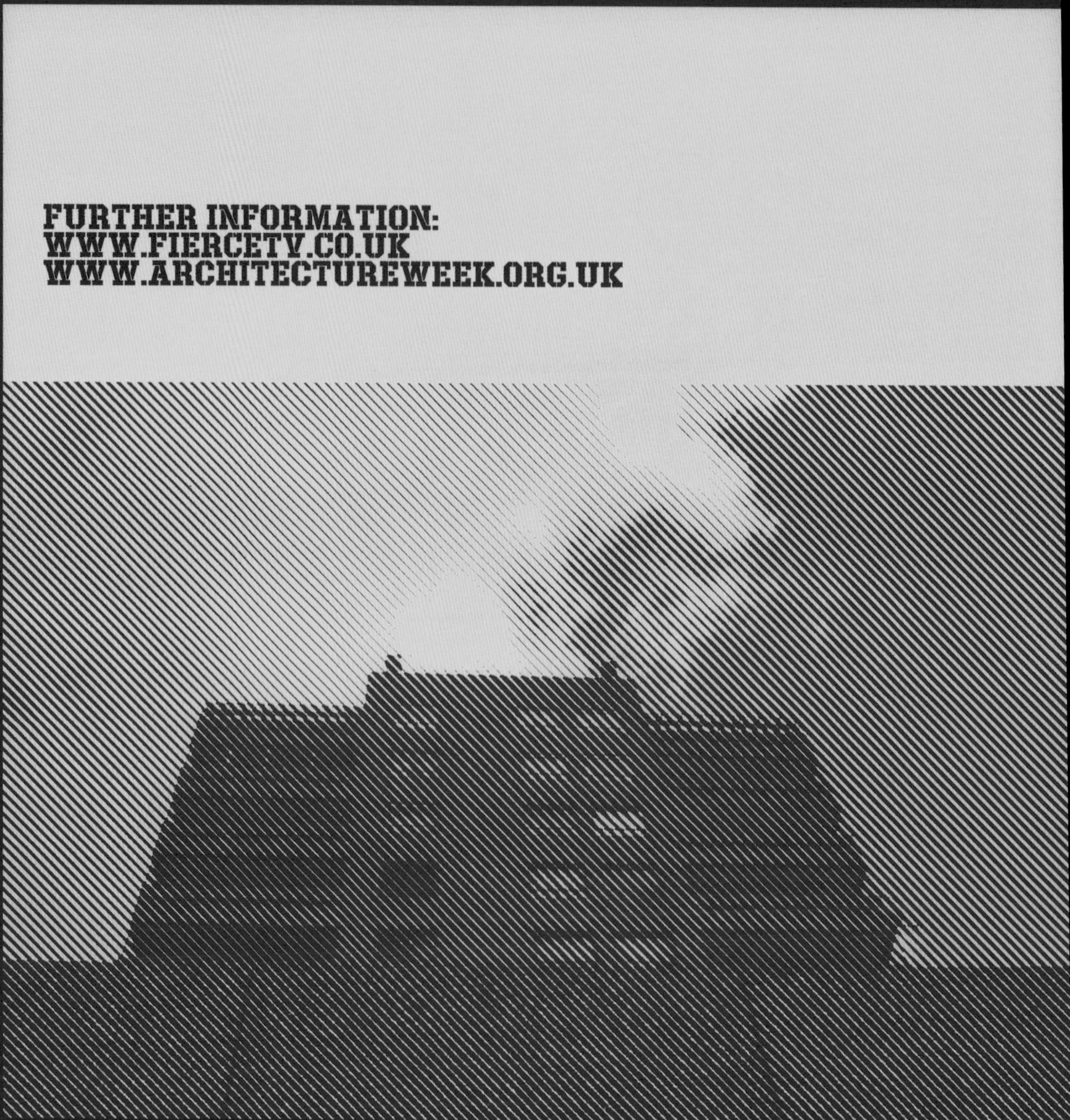

FIERCE
ARCHITECTURE WEEK:
FILM, PERFORMANCE & TOURS
16-25 JUNE 2006

Image Credits
Architecture / Glenn Howells Architects
Film / BFI Stills

Name
Glenn Howells

Company
Glenn Howells Architects

Location
UK

DR STRANGELOVE
OR: HOW I LEARNED TO STOP WORRYING AND LOVE THE BOMB
Director: Stanley Kubrick / 1964 / 93 mins / Rating: PG

Wednesday 21st June / 6.30pm
Fort Dunlop, Fort Parkway (A47)

Glenn Howells is the founding director of Glenn Howells Architects and established the practice in 1990. Glenn led the practice to win several major design competitions and awards for a diverse range of building types including residential, commercial, urban regeneration, education and arts projects. He has an overview of all aspects of the practice and regularly reviews all projects during design, development and construction stages.

With offices in Birmingham and London, Glenn has a strong track record in delivering innovative high quality projects throughout the UK and is currently working on design development projects for international projects. Current schemes include The Rotunda, Birmingham; Lime Street Gateway, Liverpool; Savill Garden, new visitor centre in Windsor Great Park; Westgate Development, Rotherham (CABE Design Champion) and West Bar, Sheffield.

Glenn is a committee member of CABE's design reviews (Commission for the Built Environment), a member of the RIBA Awards Group, chair of MADE (Midlands Architecture to the Designed Environment) and also deputy chair of the IKON Gallery in Birmingham. He has recently been appointed as an advisor to Bradford Centre for Regeneration. In the academic field, he is a visiting lecturer and tutor at universities throughout the UK and is an external examiner at the University of Nottingham.

For further information visit
www.glennhowells.co.uk

Black comedy where a fanatical U.S. General orders his bombers to attack the U.S.S.R., forcing the U.S. President to call a desperate meeting with his advisors, that include the mysterious mastermind named Dr Strangelove, a wheelchair-bound German scientist with obvious Nazi proclivities.

"I chose Kubrick's Dr Strangelove for the reason that it is a perfectly realised film where the filmmaker is in possession of a unique visual craftsmanship. Stanley Kubrick was an accomplished photographer before he became a filmmaker and his craft-based approach lends his films a sort of accidental beauty that is not at all self conscious in the way Wim Wenders films make you aware of their beautiful thin care. Over 40 years he made 13 feature films and this level of dedication and commitment to each project is there in very single frame. Although his films are technically accomplished they are not architecture as you might expect. If anything his touch is light. There was a freedom in his films that allowed him

to explore subjects as the more you watch them the more you get out of them. The other significant thing about the film was that it woke up a whole generation to what was really going on. My parents generation had been told the story but we could actually light and with a nuclear war. Artists like Kubrick and Bob Dylan made people realise that the hypothesis of Mutually Assured Destruction acting as a deterrent to war was absurd. For a film to be a catalyst for turning public feeling against the military and against what both governments were peddling was amazing.

Kubrick's films work because at one level they are incredibly simple, there is the danger in any creative art form of guilding the lily and looking everything overly self-conscious. My approach to architecture is a craft based, not abstract but an empirical journey about the process of making, all our buildings are derived from the fun, pain and joy of learning how to craft them as well as

possible. I'm not suggesting you could conceive my work to Kubrick but I do find his approach inspiring.

In Medieval times the architect was the master craftsman, the master builder who knew the most about putting a building together. He built a cathedral and it fell over he would use more stone. Architecture has evolved out of an empirical process. The Architect as celebrity has emerged out of Modernism. The ability to communicate with the media has greatly contributed to the rise of the starchitect phenomenon. Whilst the media focus is generating an enormous amount of interest, maybe architecture is out as people expect visual stimulation - our eyes are very very tired. This is not a necessarily bad thing. However as Kubrick was so acutely aware, human folly and vanity built into our spaces will be our downfall. The future in architecture is about creating great spaces and buildings and that is more important than fashionable journalism."

Image Credits
Architecture / Richard James Lander
Film / Film Stills

THE
THIRD MAN
Director: Carol Reed / UK / 1949 / 104 mins / Rating: PG

Monday 19th June / 6.30pm
The Custard Factory Theatre

Name
Lord Norman Foster

Company
Foster and Partners

Location
UK

Born in Manchester in 1935, Norman Foster received his architectural training at Manchester University School of Architecture, which he entered at age 21, and at Yale University.

Foster and Partners shows an uncompromising exploration of technological innovations and ideas. The firm's work also shows a dedication to architectural detailing and craftsmanship. Foster and Partners has studios in London, Berlin, and Hong Kong, employing some 500 people.

Projects include Singapore's Supreme Court (2006), The Sage Gateshead (2004), London's Swiss Re HQ (2004), Great Court at The British Museum (2000), Hong Kong International Airport (1998), The Reichstag, New German Parliament in Berlin (1999) and the Sainsbury Centre for Visual Arts at University of East Anglia in Norwich (1978). Forthcoming work includes Beijing Airport, National Arena Scotland and Moscow City Towers.

Foster was awarded the RIBA Royal Gold Medal in 1983, and in 1990 the RIBA Trustees Medal was awarded for the Willis Faber Dumas building. He was knighted in 1990, received the Gold Medal of the AIA in 1994, appointed to the Order of Merit in 1997 and, in 1999, received the Pritzker Architecture Prize and was created a life peer. In 2000, he was voted the Most Admired Living Architect.

For further information visit
www.fosterandpartners.com

An American pulp writer chases the elusive shadow of Welles' quintessential underground man Harry Lime. He reaches a friend in a black market racket in the rubble-strewn sector of post war Vienna. Based on Graham Greene's tale about graft, disillusion, corruption and betrayal.

"The Third Man is the best British war ever made. The story was based on a clever tale simply evoked in one sentence by novelist Graham Greene. 'I saw a man walking down the Strand, whose funeral I had only recently attended.'

Set in Vienna, beautifully shot by Robert Krasker in atmospheric black and white, and accompanied throughout by the insistent, haunting zither music of Anton Karas. Carol Reed's deliberately unsettling, canted camera angles, forced perspectives and distorted wide-angled lens shots exaggerate and distort the ruined and fractured landscape.

Combined with a tour de force performance in the other principal character of the film, a few sentences Reed, a cleverly ambiguous no man's land of empty streets, cemeteries, and control places that even-once beneath the schizoid control even beneath the dark above is an uneasy certainty. Harry Lime, it seems, has become one with the nightmarish place.

The Third Man works as a mystery because you can smell the sewers, the fear and the betrayal. The question Reed puts to us is this: What is Martins looking for? As Martins searches for his loved weird characters cross his path and help flesh out this bizarre world - their wolfish Viennese faces bearing testimony to an unspeakable truth.

There are two extraordinary sequences in this film that use architecture to perpetuate the narrative. The first, in a showdown between Lime and Martins takes place on a slow revolving

ferris wheel as an almost dreamed foreground. As Martins and Lime debate, Reed zeros up the shots, inside from outside, to convey the dissimulation that by now has reached dizzying proportions. Diagonal lines suggest a world without an axis and a culture of conspiracy where no one can be trusted. The other notable scene takes place during the finale where Lime is chased through labyrinthine sewers. These beautifully photographed chiaroscuro scenes bear a striking resemblance to the famous prison etchings of 18th century artist Giovanni Battista Piranesi, spaces that seem to go nowhere and everywhere at the same time.

Film and Architecture emerge as comparative with Reed's framing of perpetual structures such as volume and by their particular emphasis, somehow ignoring the haunting presence of Lime as a mythical shadow who looms large over the pathetic daily lives of ordinary people."

OTHER
EVENTS
Fierce Architecture Week: Film, Performance & Tours

Event
Why?

Performed by
Gravity and Levity

Location
Fort Dunlop, Fort Parkway

Date / Time / Entry
16 June / 7pm / Free
(as part of the national opening night for Architecture Week)

Providing a spectacularly riveting for Architecture Week 'Why?' is an aerial dance duet for 3 dancers suspended horizontally on single-ply harnesses against the side of Birmingham's landmark Fort Dunlop building. Choreographed by Tim Walkeer, with original music composed by Ben Park, 'Why?' asks questions about the inevitable downsides and faces of life celebrated. Power and despair are juxtaposed with ease and surrender. 'Why?' is performed by Lindsey Butcher and Lee Clayden of the Gravity & Levity company. This intriguing work is made and performed by some of the UK's best exponents of contemporary performance.

Gravity & Levity was set up in 2004 by performer and director Lindsey Butcher to develop the creation of expressive potential of aerial dance. 'Why?' is part of a 'Taking Flight', a series of events (including new work and films) which explore the multi-dimensionality and possibilities of performance sites.

An exhilarating live event with Total Theatre.

The 'Why?' designers reinterpreting 'Why?' places a chair and Clayden in harnesses against a wall. In the first section they are apart, yet aching attuned. In the second half, flanked by Ben Park's excellent score, for rumbling percussion now punctuated amongst the one-two-beaten, the new and lyrical against one another in a quasi-weightless ballet of clambolism support, Donald Hutera, The Times.

For further information, visit www.gravitylevity.net

Wings Credits
Architecture / Lawrence Rose
Film / Bay Entertainment

WINGS
OF DESIRE
Director: Wim Wenders / Germany / 1987 / 88 mins / Subtitled / Rating: PG

Tuesday 20th June / 8pm
The Custard Factory Theatre

Name
Adam Caruso

Company
Caruso St John

Location
UK

Born in 1962, Adam studied architecture at McGill University in Montreal. After working for Florian Beigel and Arup Associates, he established his own practice with Peter St John in 1990. Caruso St John has gained an international reputation for excellence in designing contemporary projects in the public realm, plus a particular love known for the New Art Gallery Walsall. The £21m building, which houses temporary exhibitions and a large permanent collection, alongside extensive educational facilities, opened to wide public acclaim in 2000 and has won numerous awards. Since the completion of the New Art Gallery, the practice has worked for many institutional and private clients in the museums and galleries sector, including the new Gagosian Gallery in Kings Cross and the Victoria and Albert Museum of the Museum of Childhood to Bethnal Green.

In 2004 they were approached to design a new Centre for Contemporary Art in Nottingham,

which is due for completion in 2008. Based in a former factory in east London, Caruso St John is working on a wide range of projects, including schools, housing, office buildings and public spaces, recent commissions include a Kids Centre for Culture in Alençon, Switzerland and a large housing development near Bordeaux, in France.

For further information, visit www.carusostjohn.com

Angels roam invisibly through Berlin, watching over human frailty and listening to human thoughts. Angel Damiel falls in love with a lonely trapeze artist prompting a desire to become mortal.

I have always loved film. I love how a true darkness of the auditorium you can and the American manner of John Ford, the intense romantic world of one of Wim Wenders, Michael Landau, or the omnipresence of a sublime primordial force that lurks in those deep green jewels of darkness The Look of the Eagle. These atmospheric settings undercut and anticipate the sheer awe of their characters. When they work, films are affecting, your ways being is changed to a usual way. However, I am hesitance; a pulsating film too literally with architecture. The partaking to a film active works in the same way as architecture provides a framework for real life - in a way all good films have something to say about architecture.

Architecture and film both tell us we are we and enfold the world around us and to see it's perverse in more ways to inspired by this when you can make architecture about reality.

In our early days, coming out from our Fort London studio Peter and I gravitated towards a ariele that made a one too visual radar and aesthetic value anomaly the choice of contemporary life. In the photography of Lee Friedlander, the art of Robert Smithson and the films of Wim Wenders we saw nature filled with powerful and possibility.

In his 1987 film Wings of Desire, Wim Wenders' meditation takes a divided Berlin. The no-man's land that traversed the path of the wall is depicted as a sort of desert, and arid largely empty but capable of sustaining an aura of emotional life. Bruno Ganz's melancholy angel has to choose between his state of grace and his love for Solveig Dommartin's circus trapeze artist,

We cast, described a Berlin-era trouper, as the city in translation of gross flowers and nature coming through the cracks will be war and forgot

Wenders later described how in the very nature of the divided Berlin he found the city's defining quality. In the city as centrifuge, this was the peaceful calm, the eye of the hurricane. A great tranquility erupted in the squares, and suddenly rabbits and hares appeared, and even our elephant could move about there. Children played, there were those berries, paths, and it was possible to lose the city in the background a felt an open factory look.

Two years after the film's release Berlin had a Utopian not so different from the angel's, and the powers that be simultaneously rejected the difficult beauty of Wenders' city.

BY AIR MAIL
par avion

Royal Mail

Form
47 Tabernacle Street
London EC2A 4AA
+44 (0) 20 7014 1430
studio@form.uk.com
www.form.uk.com

SMALL PAC

Form®

47 Tabernacle Street
London EC2A 4AA, UK

Telephone: +44 (0)20 7014 1430
Fax: +44 (0)20 7014 1431
ISDN: +44 (0)20 7014 1432

Email: studio@form.uk.com
Web: www.form.uk.com

The first in a series of leflets discussing investment in the arts.

The statistics to support the essays were brought alive with colourful illustrations which are revealed when the text spreads are opened out.

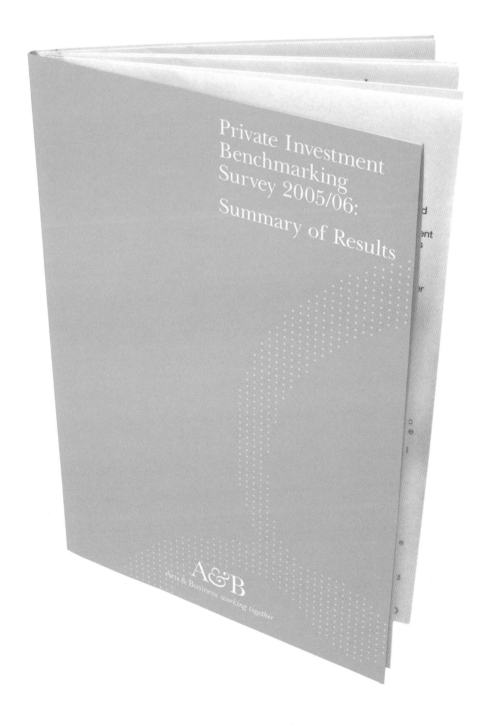

Arts & Business aspires to be the world's most successful & widespread people support the arts & the arts inspire business people, because good business & great art together create a richer society.

Introduction

Colin Tweedy, Chief Executive of Arts & Business, writes...

Thirty years ago, when A&B was founded, the amount of business investment in the arts stood at £600,000. In 2005/06 the figure for private sector support of the arts reached £529.5 million, with business investment accounting for £153.4 million of this amount. Every year A&B works to produce the most comprehensive and detailed survey ever produced on private sector support of the arts. Compared to thirty years ago the level of data and detail is astonishing. A&B's new figures reveal that there is more money going into the arts in this country from the private sector than ever before.

Many cultural commentators speak of a cultural renaissance and offer a compelling snapshot of higher quality creative work, better access and bigger and more diverse audiences. I sense that our sector is in good health and we have both sustained investment from the public and private to thank for this. Yet some feel uncertain of the future, through a fear that public investment in the arts could cool. The Treasury is deliberating the next comprehensive spending review and many predict that the best to hope for is a flat real settlement, signalling the end to recent good times.

We know that business wants to support a healthy, dynamic sector. If public money dips, some arts bodies may chase private income harder and meet with success, but overall the lifeblood and vibrancy of the arts will suffer. Businesses will look elsewhere. The best formula maybe a simple one — if political parties believe in the arts and invest in the arts, then businesses will believe in the arts and invest in them.

It is good business to invest in the arts, it brings business rewards and helps the UK maintain its creative edge. The Treasury has calculated that within 10 years, the creative and knowledge economy will be 50% of the UK economy. The causal relationship between a healthy arts environment and a dynamic creative economy is becoming accepted, and A&B has a clear role in strengthening and advocating this relationship.

There are many stories to tell from these figures and what will inform the strategic intent of A&B going forward. We know what we have to do. There are still arts organisations struggling to balance budgets, seemingly unable to secure private investment. We all need to find the resources, and ideas to bring in additional private investment into the arts. We must ensure that this figure decreases as the future health of the arts in the UK and thus society's well-being depends on the success of this work.

With the economy still strong, why have business investment figures fallen in real terms? Is this a minor blip, or part of a downward drift? I sense a blip, but either way A&B needs to take the level of investment up to a new level. I believe that London 2012 and the build up to the 2012 Olympic and Paralympic Games are an unmissable opportunity for the arts. The 2012 Games will give us the spark and the once in a generation opportunity to showcase its creativity and heritage. By involving the arts, the business of games we can ensure we energise the cultural sector and leave a real [...]

This is only one measure of A&B's effectiveness. We know we have had a bigger impact. From contributing almost £4 million of value through our professional development programmes to being the world renown authority on this work.

Thirty years from now, two constants will remain — the need to create art and the desire to appreciate it. The artist also faces the challenges of finding support for that work and the roll call of artists should have a complimentary roster of patrons.

A&B's quality is that we can make this happen efficiently. But we can never be complacent as only 8% of arts organisations show private investment representing more than 50% of their income. Arts & Business cannot assume we have all the answers. [...] aspire to higher standards of [...] service. We owe it to our many [...] in their interests.

extrapolated results

Arts & Business UK Analysis

Funding Decentralisation in the UK Cultural Sector

Cultural organisations in the UK have traditionally relied on public subsidies and earned income (e.g. ticket sales) to support their activities. In the past thirty years, private investment from businesses, individuals and trusts and foundations has become a reliable and indispensable funding option for a significant part of the UK cultural sector. In 2005/06, the private sector invested £529.5 million in culture, 2.2% more than in 2004/05 after taking inflation into account. This level of private investment compares favourably to the main public funders of culture in the UK. For instance, Arts Council England receives close to £410 million in parliamentary grant-in-aid and distributes over £150 million from National Lottery Funding. Similarly, the Scottish Arts Council distributed close to £60 million in 2005/06. This places businesses, individuals and trust & foundations as key players in the cultural funding landscape.

The impact of this source of funding is evidenced by the strong synergy developed between the private sector and small and emerging cultural organisations. Whilst private investment in 2005/06 amounted to more than 10.5% of total turnover of organisations surveyed, it represented the total income of organisations with a turnover of £100,000 or less. In a separate poll amongst cultural organisations in the UK conducted by A&B [...] that 83% of these organisations [...] had their audiences limited if [...] received private investment.

Headline Results

Business cash sponsorship experienced no growth in real terms in 2005/06. All other components of business investment experienced a significant decrease. This trend can be partly explained by the growing competition for corporate donations and sponsorships from other charitable causes and the appeal of other sponsorable events such as sports and TV shows. For instance, broadcasting amounted to only 3% of the business sponsorship market in the nineties. By 2003, broadcasting accounted for a quarter of total sponsorship in the UK. Furthermore, businesses have become more strategic in the way they distribute funding for charitable causes, aligning their own charitable activities closely to the government's social agenda.

A&B has always promoted more strategic relationships between businesses and the cultural sector. For close to 20 years, we have promoted, advocated and brokered formal employee volunteering partnerships between top managers and directors of UK companies and cultural organisations. These partnerships take the form of mentoring relationships, involvement in consultancy projects and participation in the board of directors of UK cultural organisations. For the first time this year, A&B valued the in-kind contribution these employees make to the UK cultural sector. In 2005/06, their involvement amounted to a sizable £3.9 million in time and expertise. Most of this support came from the legal, financial and business services sectors. ▸

Open out for Headline Results chart ↻

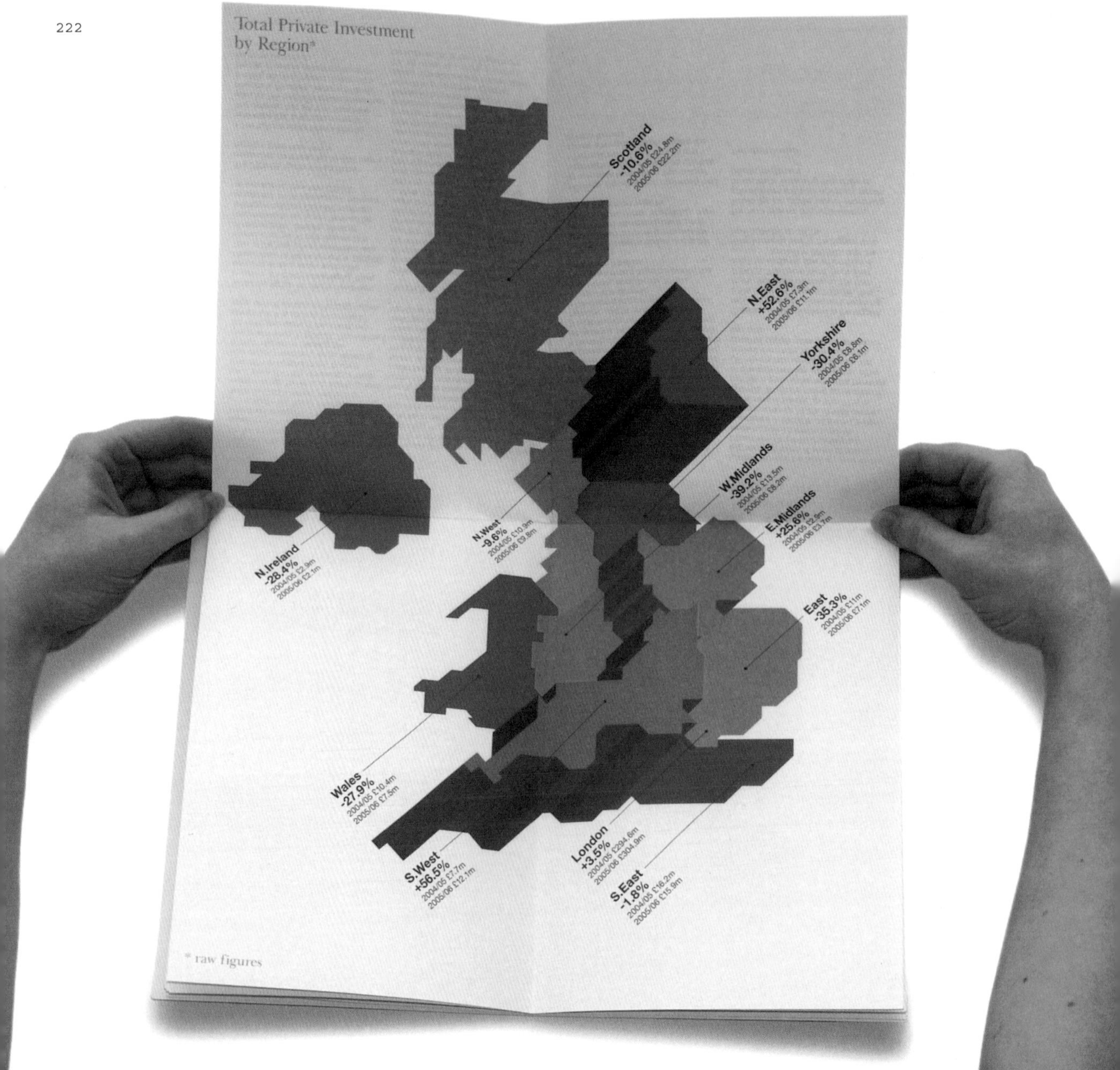

Total Private Investment by Region*

Scotland
-10.6%
2004/05 £24.8m
2005/06 £22.2m

N.East
+52.6%
2004/05 £7.3m
2005/06 £11m

Yorkshire
-30.4%
2004/05 £8.5m
2005/06 £5.9m

W.Midlands
-39.2%
2004/05 £13.5m
2005/06 £8.2m

E.Midlands
+25.6%
2004/05 £2.9m
2005/06 £3.7m

East
-35.3%
2004/05 £11m
2005/06 £7.1m

N.Ireland
-28.4%
2004/05 £2.9m
2005/06 £2.1m

N.West
-9.8%
2004/05 £10.9m
2005/06 £9.8m

Wales
-27.9%
2004/05 £10.4m
2005/06 £7.5m

S.West
+56.5%
2004/05 £7.7m
2005/06 £12.1m

London
+3.5%
2004/05 £294.6m
2005/06 £304.9m

S.East
-1.8%
2004/05 £16.2m
2005/06 £15.9m

* raw figures

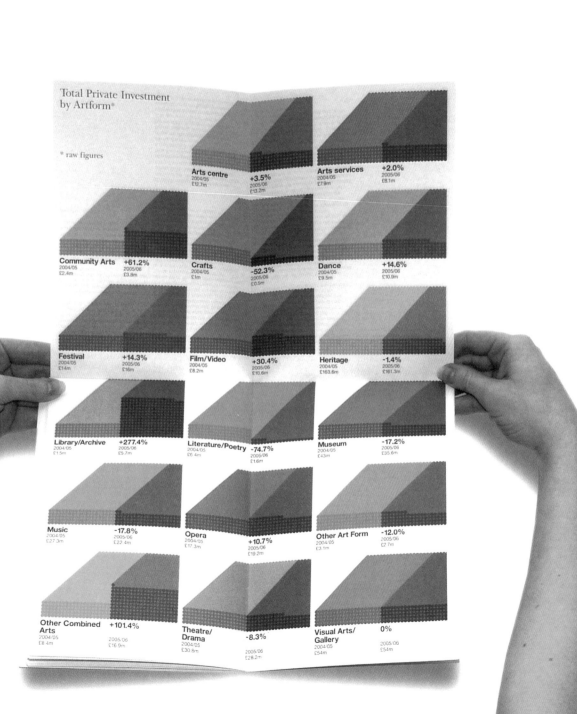

Total Private Investment
by Artform*

* raw figures

Arts centre **+3.5%**
2004/05 2005/06
£12.7m £13.2m

Arts services **+2.0%**
2004/05 2005/06
£7.9m £8.1m

Community Arts **+61.2%**
2004/05 2005/06
£2.4m £3.8m

Crafts **-52.3%**
2004/05 2005/06
£1m £0.5m

Dance **+14.6%**
2004/05 2005/06
£9.5m £10.9m

Festival **+14.3%**
2004/05 2005/06
£14m £16m

Film/Video **+30.4%**
2004/05 2005/06
£8.2m £10.6m

Heritage **-1.4%**
2004/05 2005/06
£163.6m £161.3m

Library/Archive **+277.4%**
2004/05 2005/06
£1.5m £5.7m

Literature/Poetry **-74.7%**
2004/05 2005/06
£6.4m £1.6m

Museum **-17.2%**
2004/05 2005/06
£43m £35.6m

Music **-17.8%**
2004/05 2005/06
£27.3m £22.4m

Opera **+10.7%**
2004/05 2005/06
£17.3m £19.2m

Other Art Form **-12.0%**
2004/05 2005/06
£3.1m £2.7m

Other Combined Arts **+101.4%**
2004/05 2005/06
£8.4m £16.9m

Theatre/Drama **-8.3%**
2004/05 2005/06
£30.8m £28.2m

Visual Arts/Gallery **0%**
2004/05 2005/06
£54m £54m

Global Warming: The last chance for change
Client Dakini Books *Design* Paula Benson, Andy Harvey, Paul West *Year* 2006
320 page hardback book outlining the issues around global warming.

224

"How much longer must we sit by and watch an increasing number of unusual natural disasters unfold before we realise that something is amiss? The small island countries warned more than a dozen years ago that there would be an increased frequency and intensity of storms and other adverse weather events as a consequence of global warming. In a sense they have served as mankind's early warning system... the canaries in the coal mines. Is anyone listening?"

Tuvalu can be seen sinking in 2006 at the entrance of the Cook Islands. He was one of the parties to a 1995 application by Tuvalu at the Climate Change Conference.

'If there is anything at all we can assume about the shape our fragile world is taking it is that the condition of the air we breathe, the water we drink and the land we live on will all get worse if human rapaciousness continues to go unchecked.

'A big chunk of the responsibility for containing the plague driving our polluted and populous planet towards peril rests with industry and business. Balancing the imperatives of creating jobs and selling products and services with the absolute necessity of protecting and regenerating what remains of the natural environment is an onerous challenge. That it can be done is beyond doubt, but this is a task requiring a commitment to ideals more than bottom lines, to the good earth rather than profiteering.'

In line with modern environmental thinking there is nothing in Tata's anxiety about the future that implies a reduced quality of life; in fact, the opposite. The company's plan is that both the existing generation and the next can enjoy this rich world, rather than watch powerless as climate change takes hold. As we can see in the final chapters of this book communities across continents are already making painless changes to wean themselves off fossil fuels for cooking, heating and lighting, and provide themselves with a clean water supply and sanitation. As they do so they improve their own quality of life. In the manufacturing sector the race is on to exploit clean technologies and create new industries and thousands of jobs. In older industries for example car manufacturing the competition is focused on finding ways to mass-produce vehicles that do not rely only on oil for propulsion. But much more needs to be done, and quickly.

With international political leadership still going far too slowly to solve the problem, it is up to committed individuals at city and community level to make the difference. Increasingly it is clear that personal choices need to be made about how we could each lead our lives to reduce our carbon footprint. It is not always easy while the world is still hell bent on an unsustainable path, but every day new products and new opportunities appear for individuals to help change the world.

The size of the problem is frightening but there is still time, just.

Left, top: Deserts can bury villages as the sand dunes move across the country like waves on the incoming tide. Here in Mauritania the women of Ujomawre drag a giant net to the top of the encroaching dunes to try and hold back the Sahara desert from smothering their homes and fields.

Left, bottom: The rapid retreat of the Gurschen Glacier in the Andermatt region of Switzerland led the ski resort to cover ice with a specially made fleece at the start of the 2005 summer in a bid to cut the rate of melting by blocking out the ultraviolet rays of the sun. The thinning of the glacier has meant that the resort, which attracts 250,000 visitors annually, has had to build a larger ramp each year to get skiers to the slopes. The 4,800 sq metre fleece is designed to cut ice loss by 75%. The alpine glaciers are losing an average 7% of their mass each year threatening many of the ski resorts with bankruptcy.

The Kyoto Protocol

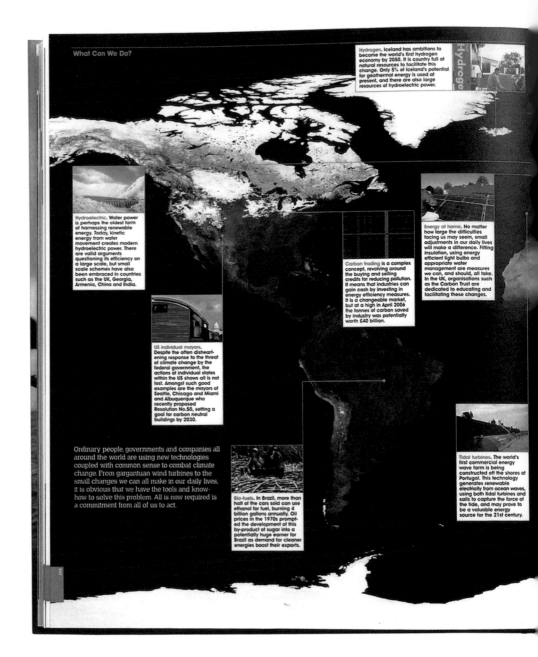

Hydrogen. Iceland has ambitions to become the world's first hydrogen economy by 2050. It is country full of natural resources to facilitate this change. Only 5% of Iceland's potential for geothermal energy is used at present, and there are also large resources of hydroelectric power.

Hydrogen

Hydroelectric. Water power is perhaps the oldest form of harnessing renewable energy. Today, kinetic energy from water movement creates modern hydroelectric power. There are valid arguments questioning its efficiency on a large scale, but small scale schemes have also been embraced in countries such as the UK, Georgia, Armenia, China and India.

Carbon trading is a complex concept, revolving around the buying and selling credits for reducing pollution. It means that industries can gain cash by investing in energy efficiency measures. It is a changeable market, but at a high in April 2006 the tonnes of carbon saved by industry was potentially worth £40 billion.

Energy at home. No matter how large the difficulties facing us may seem, small adjustments in our daily lives will make a difference. Fitting insulation, using energy efficient light bulbs and appropriate water management are measures we can, and should, all take. In the UK, organisations such as the Carbon Trust are dedicated to educating and facilitating these changes.

US individual mayors. Despite the often disheartening response to the threat of climate change by the federal government, the actions of individual states within the US shows all is not lost. Amongst such good examples are the mayors of Seattle, Chicago and Miami and Albuquerque who recently proposed Resolution No.50, setting a goal for carbon neutral buildings by 2030.

Ordinary people, governments and companies all around the world are using new technologies coupled with common sense to combat climate change. From gargantuan wind turbines to the small changes we can all make in our daily lives, it is obvious that we have the tools and know-how to solve this problem. All is now required is a commitment from all of us to act.

Bio-fuels. In Brazil, more than half of the cars sold can use ethanol for fuel, burning 4 billion gallons annually. Oil prices in the 1970s prompted the development of this by-product of sugar into a potentially huge earner for Brazil as demand for cleaner energies boost their exports.

Tidal turbines. The world's first commercial energy wave farm is being constructed off the shores of Portugal. This technology generates renewable electricity from ocean waves, using both tidal turbines and sails to capture the force of the tide, and may prove to be a valuable energy source for the 21st century.

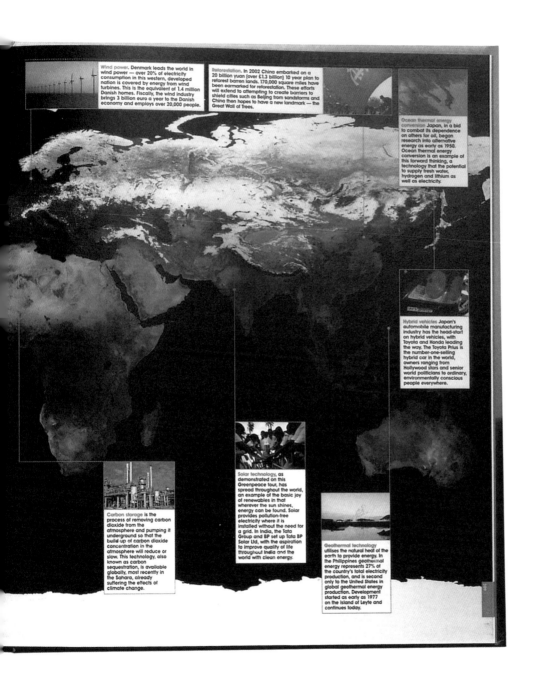

Wind power. Denmark leads the world in wind power — over 20% of electricity consumption in this western, developed nation is covered by energy from wind turbines. This is the equivalent of 1.4 million Danish homes. Fiscally, the wind industry brings 3 billion euro a year to the Danish economy and employs over 20,000 people.

Reforestation. In 2002 China embarked on a 20 billion yuan (over £1.3 billion) 10 year plan to reforest barren lands. 170,000 square miles have been earmarked for reforestation. These efforts will extend to attempting to create barriers to shield cities such as Beijing from sandstorms and China then hopes to have a new landmark — the Great Wall of Trees.

Ocean thermal energy conversion Japan, in a bid to combat its dependence on others for oil, began research into alternative energy as early as 1950. Ocean thermal energy conversion is an example of this forward thinking, a technology that the potential to supply fresh water, hydrogen and lithium as well as electricity.

Hybrid vehicles Japan's automobile manufacturing industry has the head-start on hybrid vehicles, with Toyota and Honda leading the way. The Toyota Prius is the number-one-selling hybrid car in the world, owners ranging from Hollywood stars and senior world politicians to ordinary, environmentally conscious people everywhere.

Carbon storage is the process of removing carbon dioxide from the atmosphere and pumping it underground so that the build-up of carbon dioxide concentration in the atmosphere will reduce or slow. This technology, also known as carbon sequestration, is available globally, most recently in the Sahara, already suffering the effects of climate change.

Solar technology, as demonstrated on this Greenpeace tour, has spread throughout the world, an example of the basic joy of renewables in that wherever the sun shines, energy can be found. Solar provides pollution-free electricity where it is installed without the need for a grid. In India, the Tata Group and BP set up Tata BP Solar Ltd, with the aspiration to improve quality of life throughout India and the world with clean energy.

Geothermal technology utilises the natural heat of the earth to provide energy. In the Philippines geothermal energy represents 27% of the country's total electricity production, and is second only to the United States in global geothermal energy production. Development started as early as 1977 on the island of Leyte and continues today.

228

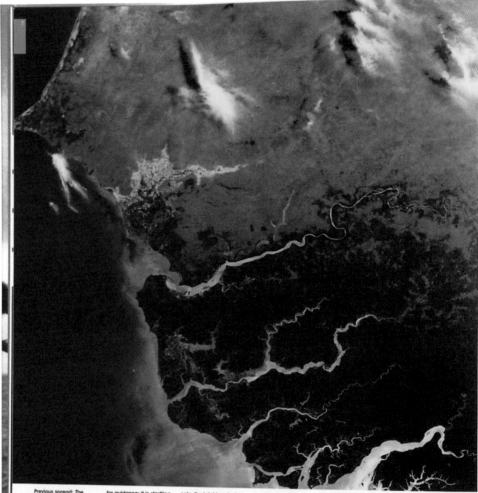

Previous spread: The permanent bright lights of Earth seen from space. This remarkable image constructed from satellite photographs shows the most urbanised areas of the planet, but not necessarily the most populated. Compare China and India with western Europe. The outlines of a world map have been superimposed for guidance; it is startling how many centres of population are on the coast, and are vulnerable to sea level rise. It is clear that the United States, Europe and Japan are using large amounts of electricity for lighting cities at night. It is a sobering thought that most of the light comes from the burning of fossil fuels. Two lines on the map are of note, the bright squiggle in eastern North Africa shows the concentration of population along the Nile, and across Russia, the light marks the route of the Trans-Siberia railway from Moscow to Vladivostok. Dark areas are the great deserts in Africa, Arabia, Australia, Mongolia, China and the United States, and the mountainous areas of the Himalayas. Although Iceland can be seen, Greenland and Antarctica remain dark.

Above: It is surprising how much of what is happening to natural systems on Earth can be monitored from space. This picture covers the transition zone between the desert and savannah in the north of Africa and the tropical vegetation further south. Clearly seen is the discharge into the sea of sediment via the river system along the west coast. This is the result of soil erosion, partly caused by overgrazing and the loss of vegetation. A series of images over time can keep track of changes and pinpoint where intensification of land use is causing problems and action is needed on the ground to halt the erosion.

Above: The Sahara desert will spread north and leap the Mediterranean, according to scientists studying climate change. This may sound fantastic but, as this picture taken on November 14th, 2004 shows, vast clouds of dust can be carried out over the sea from North Africa. This image shows Libya in the centre and Tunisia top left. Much of the dust fell in Europe over several days as a large weather system whipped up gale force winds which affected Algeria, Italy and as far north as Albania. Arid conditions in southern Spain, Portugal, Italy and Greece were already causing concern before the prolonged drought and heat wave in 2005. All four countries are vulnerable to climate change, which will in this region bring extra heat and prolonged droughts. Because of the deteriorating conditions these southern European states have all joined the UN's Desertification Convention.

230

2002   2003   2004

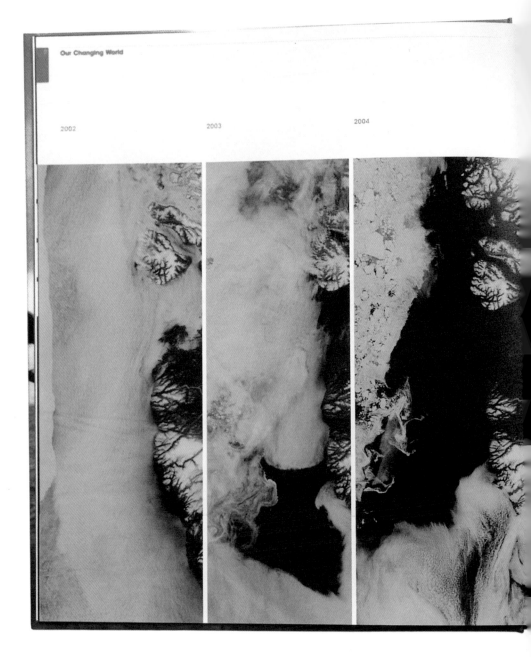

Climate change is the most important issue of the 21st century. The global economy, and civilisation itself, may collapse unless greenhouse gas emissions are controlled. Already global warming touches every part of the planet and people everywhere are affected in their daily lives.

Changing weather patterns and the need to adapt to new conditions will dominate policy as the earth's temperature and sea levels continue to rise.

Scientists believe that time is already very short — there may be as little as 15 years to prevent irreversible climate change. Yet politicians, who have been made aware of the dangers, continue to act as though it were some far off threat. As carbon dioxide builds up in the atmosphere at an ever faster rate, leaders of nations talk about the need for more talks to discuss how to solve the problem.

This book looks at the key issues. The science, the politics, what is happening in today's threatened world and what (if anything) can be done. It is extraordinary how many people still do not understand the danger the planet is in. The information is available to anyone who cares to investigate, and so there are some who believe that most of the developed world is in denial. They pick as an example the people who drive fashionable four-wheel-drive cars and take cheap flights to holiday homes. They are the same people who at the same time make incredible efforts to give their children the best education and start in life, on the assumption that life will be much the same in 50 years. It won't be. In Europe governments are worrying about pensions because of an ageing population. They are exhorting 30-year-olds to start planning for their pensions. These young people, at least those who know about climate change and the economic havoc it will cause to the "safest" of our financial institutions, just laugh. They are almost certainly right to do so. For those who are in any doubt that climate change is real and happening now, this book explains the issues. It explores other related environmental problems, which are made worse

by climate change. Reducing poverty, improving water resources and sanitation, cutting air pollution, controlling tropical diseases and saving species from extinction are all important. Add to that the need to increase food production to feed an ever rising population, on what will soon be significantly smaller land masses, and you will see the difficulty.

The pictures show the changes that are already obvious. Photographs from space document disappearing ice, forests and the dust storms from enlarging deserts. To bring this down to the particular there are pictures of creatures in the wild which are already disappearing and may be extinct in the lifetime of our children — or at least kept alive only in zoos because their natural habitat has disappeared. Polar bears are a good example.

But while it may be sad to lose these, and numerous other less majestic creatures, their fate is only an illustration of what may happen to much of the human race. Sea level rise is going to wipe out the homes of millions of people. Already islands in the Indian and Pacific oceans are being evacuated because of rising waters. People are having to abandon homes their forebears have lived in for thousands of years. They are being made uninhabitable by saline intrusion into water supplies and high tides overtopping their islands. Other island countries, like the Maldives, have begun fortifying some islands as "safe havens" against the sea. How long will they last?

That is only the beginning. The small island states, the idyllic palm-fringed islands of the holiday brochures, are home to a few million people. But in Bangladesh 15 million live less than a metre above sea level, in India there are another 8 million. These are the people with

Hat-Trick
3rd Floor
3 Morocco Street
London SE1 3HB
+44(0) 20 7403 8926
info@hat-trickdesign.co.uk
www.hat-trickdesign.co.uk

Bajos

hat-trick

Client Self promotional *Design* Jim Sutherland, David Kimpton, Gareth Howat, Jamie Ellul *Year* 2002
Spurred by our company name, this is a self promotional photographic book about the power of three.

Tate Modern, London

Trafalgar Square, London

Tuileries Gardens, Paris

The Beach, Brighton

Palace Pier, Brighton

London Zoo, London

AIR MAIL

HDR Visual Communication
Bradbourne House
East Malling
Kent ME19 6DZ
+44 (0)1732 875 200
mail@hdr-online.com
www.hdr-online.com

rcelon

Spain

bajos

Baseline Magazine #49

Client Bradbourne Publishing Ltd. *Design* Paul Arnot, Jo Lewis, Amish Shah, Hans D. Reichert *Year* 2006
International typographics magazine. Published quarterly in UK.

240

the GREAT SOCIETY blows
another mind...

The goal is:
1. To find life
2. To perceive its pulsation
3. To establish lawfulness in life
Herbert Matter, 1930–31

baseline

international typographics magazine   No.49 2006

Printed in England   UK £13.00   US $18.95

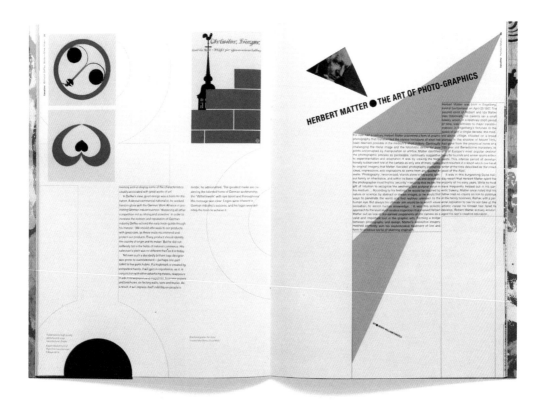

HERBERT MATTER ● THE ART OF PHOTO-GRAPHICS

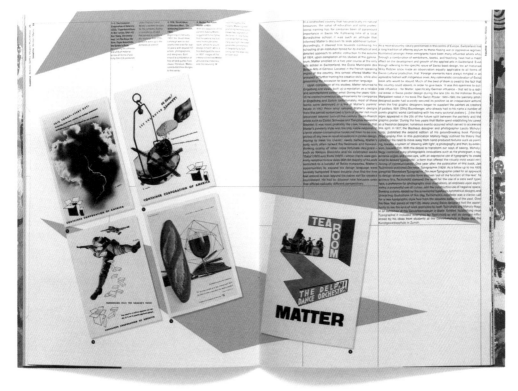

244

Matter foresaw the potential of the liberated camera. No longer solely dependent on subjects external to the lens, Matter transcended the established mechanical processes of the medium to realize what Bauhaus member Laszlo Moholy-Nagy termed the 'optical truth' of the photographic eye.

Exposed to the work of many artists – amongst whom numbered several he would later come to know on both a personal and professional level, such as Alexander Calder and Alberto Giacometti – and movements – such as Surrealism and Constructivism – Paris was an intoxicating mixture of radical visions and new ideas. Matter's time at the Académie Moderne and later working at the typographic foundry

individual's 'emotional capacity'. For Matter this engendered an openness to diverse ways of seeing that would mark his creative life. Over the coming years he would see fit to utilize the forms of sculpture, painting, architecture, and film as acceptable means through which to realize his particular vision. It was a spirit of exploration and invention that also gave birth to Matter's approach to photography. Witnessing the photograms, solarised imagery, and montages manufactured by such pioneers as Man Ray and Maurice Tabard,

matter

Deberny and Peignot were crucial in equipping him with the necessary means and expertise through which to realize his own response to these new methods of representation. While also developing his typographic and design skills, it was at Deberny and Peignot that Matter eagerly sought opportunities to experiment in the medium of photography. The manner in which he pursued this dictated that he would utilize the camera as a means of expression, as an opportunity to crystallize and develop all the competing ideas and movements of modern art and design he had studied in depth. Shaped by one of the most intensely experimental periods in the history of modernism, Matter would spend a lifetime continually testing and challenging the creative parameters of this, his favourite medium.

Charged with this 'New Vision', Matter returned to Switzerland in 1932. There, in just a few short years, he produced what are widely regarded as some of the most celebrated posters in the history of design. Commissioned by the Swiss National Tourist Office, his groundbreaking works such as 'Pontresina' and 'All Roads Lead to Switzerland' further illustrated his new found awareness of the formal elements of photography. No longer working with discrete isolated images, he now composed the photograph in such a way that it came to function as a single element in the totality of a graphic design. It was an approach where all the different components could be integrated across the same plane, achieving an elegant cohesive simplicity. It was a time when Matter abandoned perspective, wishing 'to work on a flat surface where I have strict control and manipulation at all times'. Montage met this need. It would serve to inform his life long approach to photography and define a greater part of his creative work over the coming years. It was his 'security'.

The creative force that had compelled Matter to journey to Paris was certain to surface again with his return to his homeland. This small country could never sustain his insatiable yearning to continually 'renew himself' and 'receive other influences'. Subsequently, in 1935 he set out for America. It was a departure that came at the midpoint of an exodus of designers who were abandoning Europe's troubled shores throughout the 30s for the relative freedoms of the US. While Paris and Berlin had occupied the centre of progressive arts and design during the 20s and 30s, New York was to become the creative hub of artistic invention during the 40s and 50s. For émigré designers like Will Burtin, America provided the 'conditions which made the continuation of studies possible: people less biased by narrow interpretations of tradition; devotion to high productivity; a great industrial apparatus.' Without catching his breath, during his first few weeks in the city Matter gathered up all his Swiss posters, pamphlets, and magazine covers and descended on the offices of art directors, galleries, and publishers.

Alongside fellow émigrés such as Herbert Bayer, Leo Lionni, and Joseph Binder, Matter would use his innovative experiments with image and type to effect a wholesale transformation of American advertising, corporate identity, magazines, and poster art. His was always a wide-ranging vision. Unencumbered by preconceived notions of how the image in design should be treated, his photographs leapt from page to billboard, exhibition to trade fair, mural to film. In a culture ever eager to renew itself, this multifaceted approach became a much sought after commodity.

Whether Herbert Matter saw this exhibition is unknown. It is certain, however, that he studied these books and they certainly played a decisive role in the development of his own ideas. What is clear is that he was living and working through a period in Swiss art and design history when major transformations were taking place. Individual designers such as Ernst Keller, Johannes Handschin, Walter Cyliax, and at a later date, Max Bill, began to produce works that abandoned the accoutrements and embellishments of the artist-designed poster. They neglected what Tschichold labelled the 'line' of the artist' and chose an 'anonymity in the elements' of text, image, and space. The outcome were works of great clarity where 'every part of the text relates to every other part by a definite, logical relationship of emphasis and value, predetermined by content.' While the impact of these works were significant, it would be disingenuous, however, to say their arrival was unforeseen. In many ways the groundwork had already been laid over the previous two decades. The modern art movements of Cubism and Futurism had already paved the way for a reassessment of the traditional language of artistic expression and the classical representation of the human form. Creating works that questioned the artifice of trompe l'oeil perspective, they explored two-dimensional geometric space through fractured objects, figures, and abstractions, combined with an examination of the ability of colour to express pure sensation and emotion. One of the key figures of the modern arts who reached beyond the fine art tradition to affect a seismic shift in the graphic arts was Fernand Léger (1881–1955). According to the design historian Philip B Meggs, in Léger's Cubist paintings 'his almost pictographic simplifications of the human figure and objects were a major inspiration for modernist pictorial graphics that became the major thrust of the revived poster art of the 1920s. Léger's flat planes of colour, urban motifs, and the hard-edged precision of his machine forms helped define the modern design sensibility after World War I.' Léger's influence on post-war arts and design was further advanced when, in 1924, he began teaching at the Académie Moderne in Paris with Amédée Ozenfant.

Herbert Matter seemed blessed with an uncanny ability to locate the engines of artistic innovation central to 20th century visual culture. As such, his unique vision was fashioned by, and became part of, some of the most influential movements in modern art and design. Thus, when just 20 years old Matter left home to seek out the source of the exhilarating array of ideas that were just then beginning to cascade across his native soil. This journey led him to the modernist wellspring of Paris in the late 1920s. It was here that he discovered a time and place where art had become an indistinguishable part of everyday life, where architectural constructions such as Le Corbusier's 'Villa La Roche' (1925), or posters like Cassandre's 'Étoile du Nord' (1927), conveyed ideals of beauty that had evolved from their intended function, not applied as an ornamental afterthought. It was a climate of radical new visions, where Matter's involvement with the avant-garde sparked an intense desire for progress and innovation that would never diminish. He enrolled at the Académie Moderne in 1928. Here he entered a sphere of influence where artists were transgressing the narrow limits of their established disciplines and in the process generating exciting new forms. Indicative of the times, one of the central tenets of this school was to cultivate the disregard for traditional hierarchies of art history and technique. For Léger, a work's value lay 'in its own worth', where it was 'not possible to establish a sole criterion', but rather depended on

6. 'Ballet of the A, B, C's or The Crafty Linotyper', by Percy Seitlen. Layout by Herbert Matter, *PM/AD*, November, 1941.
In a spirit similar to the children's books fashioned by Kurt Schwitters, this layout by Matter looks to employ typography as source material from which to construct a magical dream-like story. Perfectly in harmony with Seitlen's words Matter's design transmits its excitement through a range of graphic elements including yellow lines, circles and oversize letters.

7. *Portfolio*, No 3, 1951. Designed by Alexey Brodovitch.
For an article upon the work of Alexander Calder in the final issue of this ground breaking magazine, Brodovitch utilized strips from Matter's film on the artist's work entitled 'Works of Calder' (1951). Matter's working relationship with Calder had begun in 1937 when he photographed his work for an exhibition at the Pierre Matisse gallery in New York

8. 'The Architectural Centre', *New Pencil Points* magazine, July, 1943.
This design introducing the Architectural Centre in Los Angeles begins with a loose montage contrasting natural forms with those of the built environment. It then proceeds to highlight examples of organic design and finally concludes with the grid-like structures of skyscrapers

12. *Fortune* magazine, October 1943.
Matter's ability to use darkroom manipulation to achieve broad vivid colours and contrasting textures is evidenced in this dazzling cover design. Detailing the accuracy of new ball bearings, Matter's use of overprinting, photograms, and geometric shapes creates the impression that the bearings are actually spinning on the page

13. *Graphis*, No 212, 1980–81.
As this cover design reveals, Matter continually tested the boundaries of the possible in photography. For those touched by his work, his influence persisted throughout their lives. As one-time Matter student John Cohen noted 'some people didn't always see what he was saying...for me he was one of the most exciting teachers I've had'

In the following years magazines such as *Vogue*, *Harper's Bazaar*, and *House & Garden* all called on Matter's versatile treatment of photographic material to associate the fresh 'look' of the avant-garde with their publications. Numbered among these working relationships were also some of the most celebrated artistic and cultural figures of the modern age, who shared more sincerely the philosophical roots of Matter's work: Alberto Giacometti, Alexander Calder, Edward Steichen, Jackson Pollock, Charles and Ray Eames, and R Buckminister Fuller. Working with these individuals Matter continually confirmed a true renaissance spirit, aspiring to equal their lofty achievements by incessantly seeking out new avenues to enrich his own capacity and flair. In just under a single decade, Herbert Matter demonstrated a pioneering attitude to design that served to set his work apart from many of his fellow émigrés. In a short space of time, art directors, editors, and corporations quickly realized how Matter could generate works that would connect their products and layouts with all that was modern and fresh in contemporary art and design. His skill lay in an ability to assimilate corporate logos, slogans, or formats into works that were always uniquely his own. Displaying an acute awareness for the interaction of image and design, 'Matter's responsibility to the photograph is not merely artistic', as one commentator noted, 'it is social in some sense, this concern for the "home" in which it will live.' In his exhaustive attention to detail, Matter would home in on the nucleus of a design problem and in solving it generate an unexpected and original response. It was a unique ability perfectly encapsulated by the words of James Johnson Sweeney when he said:

'Matter is an artist in his field. But there are several such. A researcher, however, who is both artist and technician is rare. This is Matter's importance. He respects the achievements of the leaders in "straight" photography. Still his basic aim is to expand the frontiers of pictorial expression. And in this realization of it he combines for us the photographer, artist, and explorer.'

'A tall stoop-shouldered man', the critic D J Ebin noted in 1954, 'Matter is a gymnast among photographers...he nimbly walks astride the two worlds of art and commerce. Rarer still, this modest-mannered Swiss-born confectioner's son has introduced the lessons and vigour of modern art into the camera image. Today, seasoned and self-assured, he continues to ask of himself: What is a photograph and who is Matter?' It speaks of the continuing relevance of Matter's work today, that this proposition remains unresolved. Through inventive and graceful designs orchestrated via a singular vision, the timeless virtuosity of Matter's groundbreaking works continue to fascinate and absorb, decades after their realization.

graphis 212

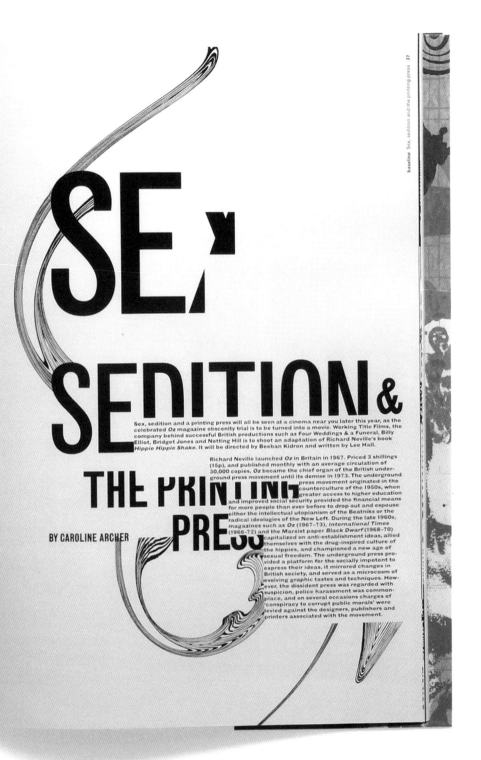

SEX

SEDITION &

THE PRINTING PRESS

BY CAROLINE ARCHER

Sex, sedition and a printing press will all be seen at a cinema near you later this year, as the celebrated *Oz* magazine obscenity trial is to be turned into a movie. Working Title Films, the company behind successful British productions such as Four Weddings & a Funeral, Billy Elliot, Bridget Jones and Notting Hill is to shoot an adaptation of Richard Neville's book *Hippie Hippie Shake*. It will be directed by Beeban Kidron and written by Lee Hall.

Richard Neville launched *Oz* in Britain in 1967. Priced 3 shillings (15p), and published monthly with an average circulation of 30,000 copies, *Oz* became the chief organ of the British underground press movement until its demise in 1973. The underground press movement originated in the counterculture of the 1950s, when greater access to higher education and improved social security provided the financial means for more people than ever before to drop out and espouse either the intellectual utopianism of the Beatniks or the radical ideologies of the New Left. During the late 1960s, magazines such as *Oz* (1967–73), *International Times* (1966–72) and the Marxist paper *Black Dwarf* (1968–70) capitalized on anti-establishment ideas, allied themselves with the drug-inspired culture of the hippies, and championed a new age of sexual freedom. The underground press provided a platform for the socially impotent to express their ideas, it mirrored changes in British society, and served as a microcosm of evolving graphic tastes and techniques. However, the dissident press was regarded with suspicion, police harassment was commonplace, and on several occasions charges of 'conspiracy to corrupt public morals' were levied against the designers, publishers and printers associated with the movement.

250

Hemisphere
Binks Building 30-32
Thomas Street
Northern Quarter
Manchester M4 1ER
+44 (0)161 907 3730
www.hemispheredmc.com

Binks Building, 30:32 Thomas Street, Northern Qua

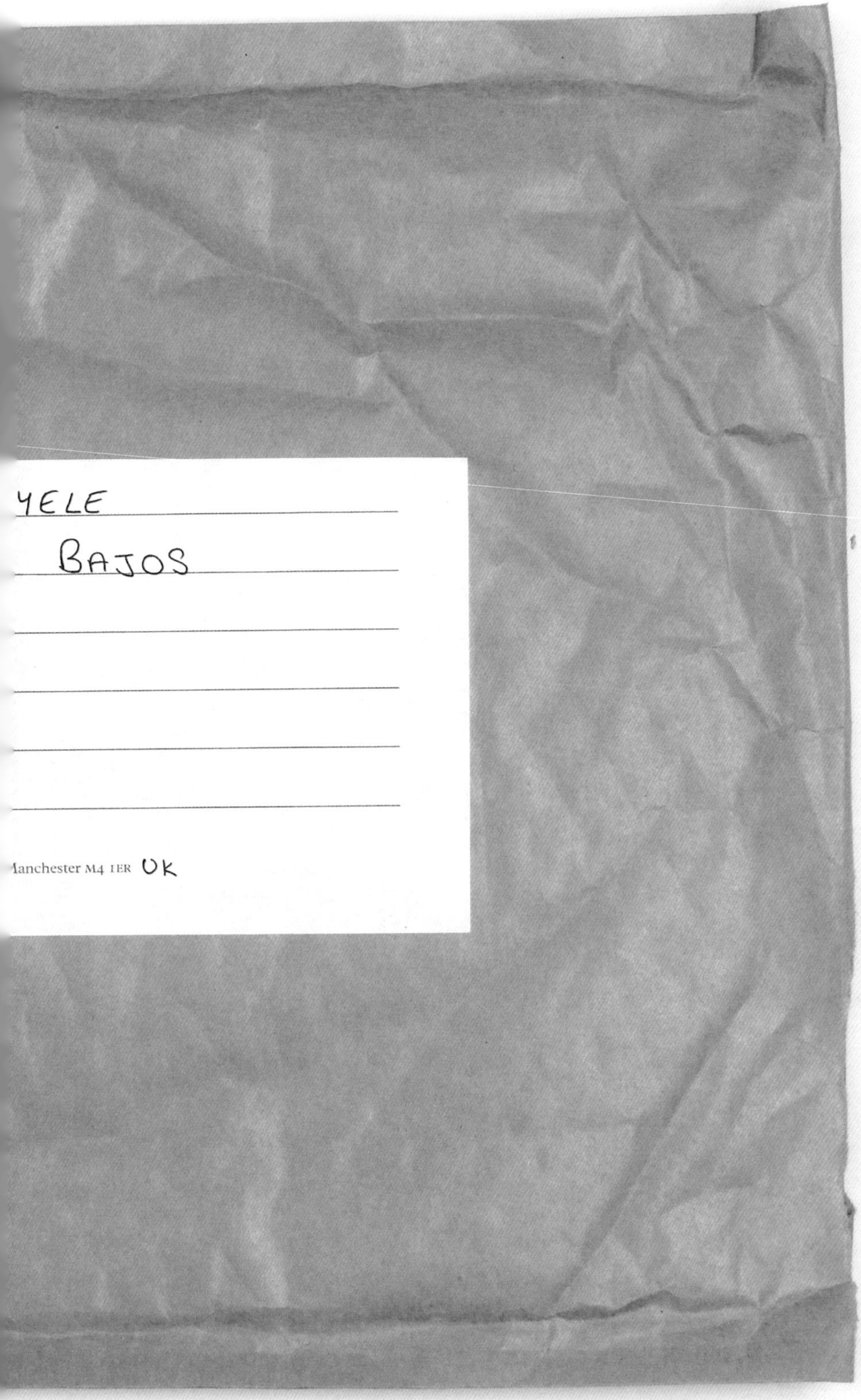

YELE

BAJOS

Manchester M4 1ER UK

From margins to mainstream
Client Sustainability Nothwest *Design* Grant Windridge / Hemisphere *Year* 2002
64pp + soft cover, 110x170mm perfect bound book, printed using fully recycled stock, Three spot colour (red + two blacks).
A pocketable Annual Report. A series of essays on sustainable development in the Northwest of England illustrated by lateral,
sometimes provocative studio photography. The recycled stock gives it an 'already lived in' old paperback feel.

252

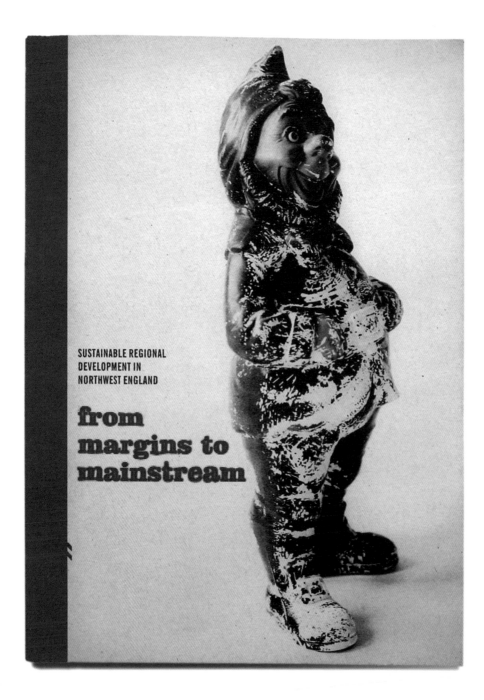

the hard sell

Sustainability Northwest (SNW) has always had communications at the heart of its strategic approach. This is because sustainable development is largely about convincing individuals or groups of individuals to make some sort of change in their behaviour. Convincing people to change their behaviour means entering into a dialogue with them about what they need to change and how they can effect that change to the benefit of all concerned.

SNW has had a communications strategy in operation for some years. This was drawn up with the help of, and in consultation with, a number of marketing and public relations experts from its private sector partners. The communications strategy was also informed by three of the region's largest PR agencies.

In essence, for SNW, communicating sustainability is about:
1) Addressing communications first and not last;
2) Knowing who your audience is;
3) Understanding how to speak to that audience;
4) Professional presentation that turns heads; and
5) Understanding which marketing 'channels' are most effective.

"We must engender an awareness throughout enterprises of all types that a sustainable approach to their business not only makes good strategic sense but, wisely managed, makes good economic sense too."

Justin McCracken, Regional Director, The Environment Agency

The study's endorsement of the environmental technologies sector helped the Northwest Development Agency, leading environmental technology companies and SNW to establish the environmental technologies cluster, **Envirolink North West.**

Now formally launched and with former SNW Operations Director Jackie Seddon as Chief Executive, Envirolink will maximise the market opportunities for the sector.

Environmental technologies are amongst our most vital of economic sectors. They build on **the strengths we want to enhance and grow** most within the region: innovation and technology; higher-education linkages; business incubation and skills development. Importantly, the products stemming from strong support of the environmental technologies sector are also amongst our most exportable.

The second factor in making environmental technologies a key growth sector for the region is that in addressing directly, through product and process innovation, problems like contaminated land, energy use, the need to increase renewable energy sources, waste minimisation and management and waste water treatment, **these areas of business can contribute directly towards the improvement of our region's environmental quality.**

It is within the region that Envirolink will address itself first. Already events have been held to promote our region's environmental technology companies to other industrial sectors within the region. At present the region spends billions of pounds on environmental technologies and services but the vast majority of this business goes outside the region; this needs to change.

Envirolink has conducted a **sector mapping** exercise, has put a strong partnership together to promote the sector and held a formal launch in March 2001. The Northwest cluster has also helped to shape the new national sectoral forum.

Key weblinks
Envirolink: www.envirolink.co.uk
Enworks: www.enworks.com
photo of business advisor courtesy of Enworks/Groundwork North West
Biofuel pellets supplied by Martin Steel at Envirofuels

Space to inspire
Client Groundwork North West *Design* Mat Bend / Hemisphere *Year* 2004
A document recording a community environment programme in East Manchester.
Published to a very tight production timescale, photographer Len Grant shot all photographs in January, design happened in a fraught seven days using a pre-determined grid and the book was delivered for its launch in mid February.

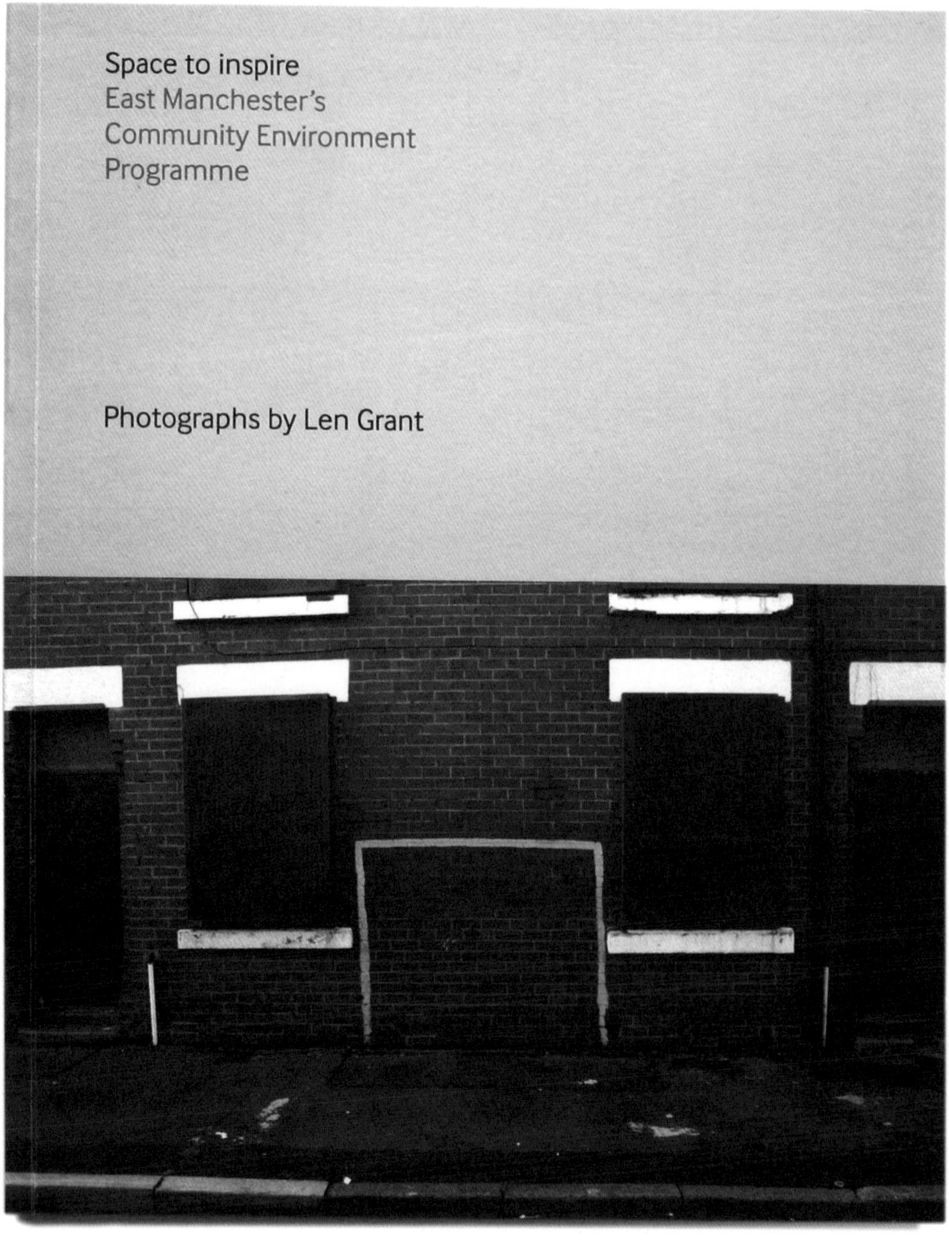

Space to inspire
East Manchester's
Community Environment
Programme

Photographs by Len Grant

East Manchester's Community Environment Programme

"It used to be a dogs' toilet," explains Maria Scott, describing the patch of former wasteland behind her house. "Now it's fantastic, I can't get my kids to come in, even in the rain." When you talk to residents in East Manchester they sum up the impact of environmental improvements very succinctly.

Maria Scott is one of thousands of residents who have been involved in East Manchester's Community Environment Programme over the past four years. In Maria's case, she has been one of the driving forces behind a project that has seen a croft behind rows of terraced houses transformed into a community garden.

The open space had become the domain of drug-users, joyriders and fly-tippers. A place of fear, literally, a few metres from residents' back doors. "We basically didn't go out. The only time we went out was to put the bins outs. Kids didn't go out because if they fell over they would need a hospital visit there was that much glass about."

Over the past three years, the project has helped recreate a sense of community, uniting neighbours who previously had little or no contact and enabling residents to tackle wider issues such as crime and nuisance behaviour. For Maria, working together is vital: "It's much easier to tackle a problem as a group, rather than as an individual. You are not alone."

Maria Scott (opposite)
Maria's back yard now borders
New Century Family Garden,
an enclosed community space
surrounded by 36 terraced
houses. Maria is helping residents
in neighbouring streets develop
similar projects.

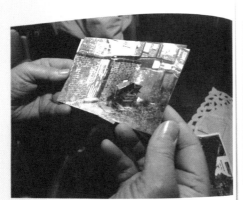

Alan Hutchinson and Alan Davies
have been volunteering with other
residents to help create Jubilee
Gardens, a secure community
space behind their terraced street

"It's made a hell of a difference. It's a secure environment now. Margaret doesn't have to be cutting away at a Borneo jungle to put the washing out, it's great. And in the summertime we can get out there and have a few tinnies."

Alan Davies

A way of life

Client Len Grant, Photographer *Design* Grant Windridge / Hemisphere *Year* 1999

Photographer Len Grant's personal project recording portraits from the UK funeral trade in words and images.

The photographs were given as much room to breathe as possible in this layout, supported by text playfully used with a simple four column grid.

portraits from the funeral trade

a way of life

photographs by Len Grant

introduction by Blake Morrison

gravedigger

Each plot is three and a half feet apart. You get your boards, lay them down, mark it out. Once you've marked it out you just cut around it and dig down keeping within the template you've made. Every time you dig down a foot or so you put a pair of boards in. You have what we call 'stays' at the foot and at the head. We put six pairs of boards in and then put a 'shape' at the bottom. It's a hole a couple of feet deep where the coffin goes. There are no boards in the shape which would get in the way. Once the coffin is in and the service over we just fill it in.

We go down about six foot. Years ago it used to be deeper. Family graves used to be for about six or eight because families were a lot bigger then. Now they're just dug for a maximum of four coffins so we don't have to dig them crazy like my dad used to. He'd dig them fifteen or twenty feet deep, with a winch at the top to bring the buckets of earth up. Those days are gone, thankfully.

We use mechanical diggers now, as well as digging by hand. Mainly the new ones get done by the machine. It's awkward if there's a headstone at either end and you can't get a machine on, so that's when it has to be dug by hand.

People just think we dig a hole but we do a lot really. As well as digging new graves, opening old ones and filling them, we do turfing, building walls, sanding jobs, emptying baskets, marking out the plots for the next set of graves, anything that's got to be done really. There's more to it than people think.

With this job you're moving around, never in the same place. You get about a bit, that's what I like about it really. I hate working inside. I did it when I first left school. I just couldn't do it now.

I try not to mention what I do. People have strange ideas. My wife takes great pleasure in telling people just to wind me up. Most of them are intrigued. They think it's macabre but they'll always ask questions. They ask whether I've seen anything, dead bodies and that. It's very strange what people think. They think you see dead bodies and all you see is a box.

People say, 'I can't do it, I'd be dead upset.' But I just look at it that we're digging a hole and putting a box in it. I try not to think about what's in the box anyway. It's one of those things, it doesn't faze me.

There's not a chance I'm being buried. I've already got an idea of what I want when I'm cremated. I'm having nothing mentioned about God and there are certain songs I'm having played going in and coming out and my ashes are going to Manchester City's football ground. I'm not sure whether they still scatter ashes at Maine Road, they used to. If they don't I've got this deal with my mum that she'll go in the stands and start throwing them about and hope the wind doesn't blow them back into people's faces. So I'd still get them on there somehow.

REVD HAZEL ADDY
CHAPLAIN

When an elderly person dies that's the easy funeral. 'They've had a good innings,' people say. It's the natural order of things. But my involvement is generally with the unnatural order of things.

I've been doing funerals of people who've died of Aids for about ten years at least.

In that time I've seen the same people turning up for funeral after funeral after funeral, and you can look at them and know that some time down the line they're going to be next.

Most recently there appear to be an awful lot of younger men now who are infected. To me, and this is more to do with how I've changed, they look like boys, and that has struck me very forcefully lately.

hospital chaplain

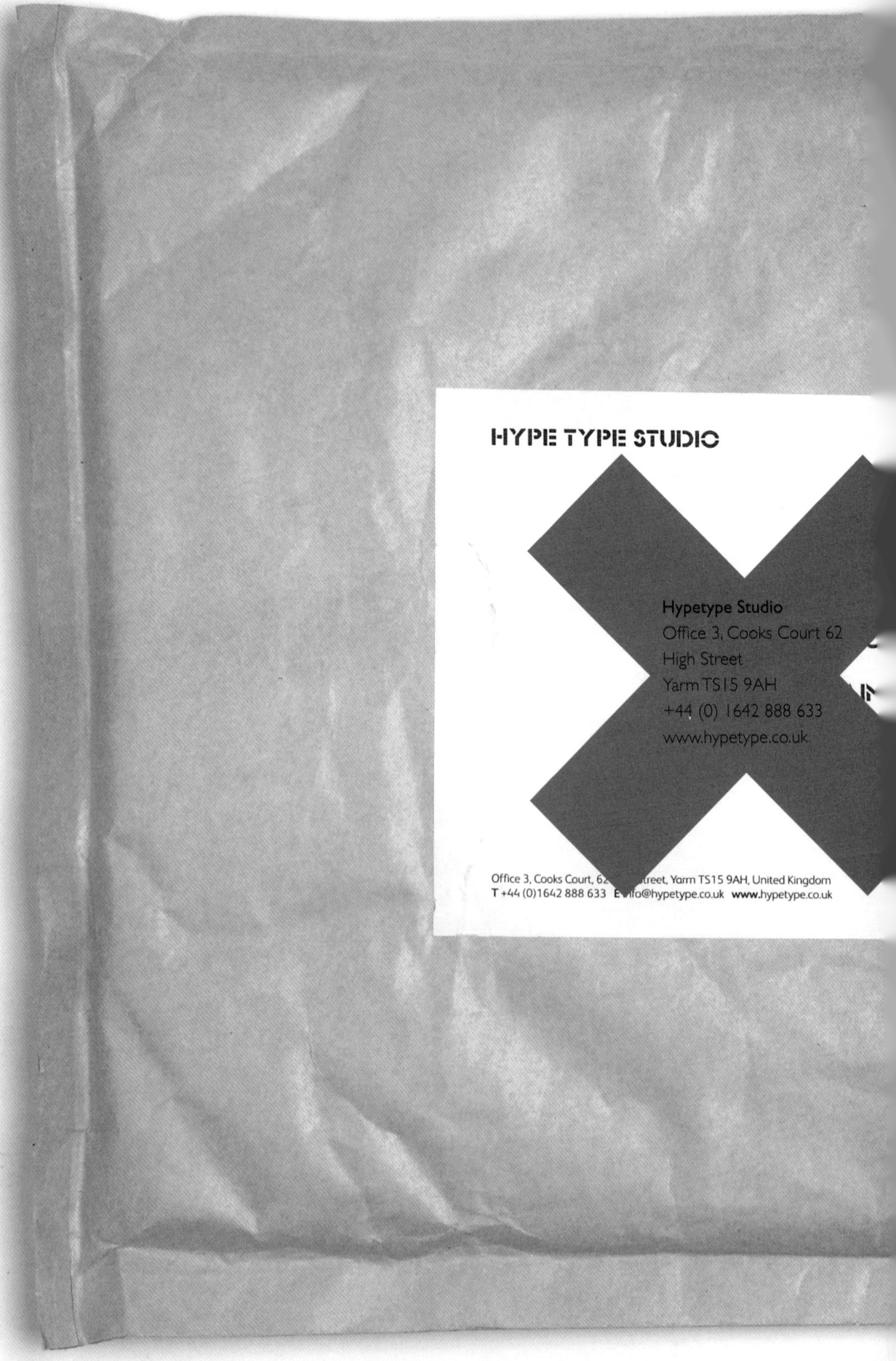

HYPE TYPE STUDIO

Hypetype Studio
Office 3, Cooks Court 62
High Street
Yarm TS15 9AH
+44 (0) 1642 888 633
www.hypetype.co.uk

Office 3, Cooks Court, 62 High Street, Yarm TS15 9AH, United Kingdom
T +44 (0)1642 888 633 **E** info@hypetype.co.uk **www.**hypetype.co.uk

A

Royal Mail
POSTAGE PAID UK
12/03/07 £5.12 TS15
241327 4-2125070-1

P. PAPER

Andy Howell Book
Client Paul Hutchison, Andy Howell *Design* Paul Hutchison *Year* 2006
Artist monograph.

WARNING
The U.S. SURGEON GENERAL has determined that the contents of this package are hazardous to our society's health, because **these products promote creativity and individuality** at a young age. Furthermore, prolonged use of this unacceptable activity will result in devastating amounts of enjoyment for all those concerned.

The New Deal *By Skaters, For Skaters*

Andy All of us on Schmitt Stix wanted to do our next company—we were always talking about it. Chris Miller kept going to Paul and saying, "Let's split up from Vision and start our own thing." But Paul wouldn't buy it and Chris couldn't wait around. He bailed and started Planet Earth and subsequently launched Rhythm, Adio, and Hawk Shoes. Steve Douglas, Ed Templeton, and I, along with some of the other guys on the team, knew that was the last straw. He was our best skater. It was at the Del Mar Street Contest when everything went down, the one where Tony Hawk won and gave his trophy to Hensley because Matt [?] he blew everybody's doors in that contest.

Steve Douglas We were in a Denny's at this Del Mar hotel. Chris Miller had just left, and Paul was about to go to Europe the next morning. So I said to Andy, "It's time to do something, and I've got a plan." The relationship between Paul and Brad Dorfman was horrendous. We were the second class citizen company. Brad [?] worked all the trash shoes and already met a guy from NHS who said, "When you're ready, we'll back you." Turns out, Paul had actually known this all along. So we basically all stormed this and said, "We're starting a new company, and if you don't agree, we're leaving." I'd just come back from the U.K. and my friends over there had a span called The New Deal, so I was wearing their T-shirt and had the sticker on my board. That name just seemed to fit. We wanted a new deal!

We went back to the hotel, all happy, then John and Steve, who was on the next room down, came and and looked at me and said, "You Schmitt guys look you too happy. Why are you all leaving?" Steve Notie just left, mmm." He looked at me in my T-shirt and said, "If you're going to leave Vision and start a new company called New Deal." It was three minutes after we'd decided to do just that—I was totally shocked! So I said, "No no no, Paul's got no balls, he won't do that." My heart was beating—we had to keep it quiet!

By the time we got back to the room, Andy was already sketching our New Deal logo on a napkin. Paul came in and said, "As long as we're not a victim and not bland and we don't make coffee, we're okay." He'd gone in, and already researched the name to see if we could use it. So we said, "That's our first art, here's our first logo!" And Paul's words became the tag line in the bottom of the ad.

Andy Ed Templeton, the godsend Dreams and I went to this grocery store across the street, and I bought a set of crayons and a chisel-drawing pad. We went back to the hotel room, and I drew this New Deal logo that same night—totally in crayon. Everybody was stoked, and I thought, "It's messy. It looks like kids did it, and it's perfect for a skateboard company made by skaters." At the time every board graphic out there was hyper-realistic skills and each 90% graphic design. Then by professional artists. It was nothing we gave a shit about.

Paul Schmitt My success was shared in research and development, not marketing, so if I hadn't let go of Schmitt Stix's creativity wouldn't have had the success I had.

I let go, took Andy's lead, image and marketing-wise, and Steve's lead in terms of the drive to build a team.

Andy Paul got put between a rock and hard place and finally had to give in, but luckily, he'd secretly built his own woodshop. He's lost it to turbo away for about two or three years and it was his R&D lab where he was developing new concepts and resids and basically innovating boards through the '80s. When he got pushed over the edge by all of us, he broke his contracts and together we started New Deal, and since we now already had our own custom woodshop, we could make all our own boards. That's how he'd earned the nickname "Professor Schmitt" in the '80s. He'd started off as an apprentice boat maker and then turned his attention to boards, not boats. He was the mad scientist of skateboarding, constantly innovating.

Johnny Schillereff, President, Element Skateboards Launching this new, punk-rock start-up company was a super ballsy move, especially for Paul Schmitt. If there was anybody who took a massive risk, it was the guy who had a company called "Schmitt Stix," decided to not call it that any more and leave his name behind for a corporation to use if they wanted, and start New Deal instead.

Steve Douglas It was a great time, really creative, we used to camp out at Paul's house in Costa Mesa, secretly doing this company. We had to keep it quiet because we were still getting our checks from Vision.

Andy I was living in this garage, sleeping on an old mattress, freezing at night, stayed there for five months as we created the company. We did it all just sitting at the kitchen table creating the graphics and the logo. I gave New Deal a very do-it-yourself vibe with hand drawn logos and black and white ads, with simple two blocks. I used a spilt color of yellow, and that became the company color. The cartoon-style graphics were basically all the stuff that my friends and I were graffitiing on walls in Atlanta. It was a total brand. Whenever we got sick of working, we'd go out with a camera and film footage for a promo video, to launch the whole thing.

Shepard Fairey New Deal helped push skateboarding forward from the skulls and slick graphics-driven and brought in an urban aesthetic that befit its street skating. Everything went from tent skating and backyard suburban culture—all mellow jackets and mohawks—to a new culture of railings and steps and hip-hop and graffiti.

Andy There weren't many companies solely created by people who lived and breathed skateboarding. We had a perfect unit, the on all creative fronts—board graphics, ads, promo videos, clothing design, overall creative direction—Steve Douglas managing the team and acting as the general company visionary, and

New Deal Box, 1990.
When we started New Deal and I was creating all the graphics and the look and feel for the company, I was obsessed with customizing everything. My friends and I in Atlanta were drawing lots of graffiti-styled characters and I decided to create a box design for New Deal that had the style of a kid bombing the New Deal Logo on a wall. One side would catch him in the act, and the other side would show the wall after he had finished the tag and split the scene. I had drawn a series of spraycans with the New Deal tag on them, and I incorporated them into the design. And of course I added in my trademark sunsuit on the low top as a warning to anyone who dared open it. By the time the box was released, New Deal owned the bright yellow color we were using in our ads, so the box became this glowing beacon, and shop owners could see us coming when the UPS man came to make the drops.

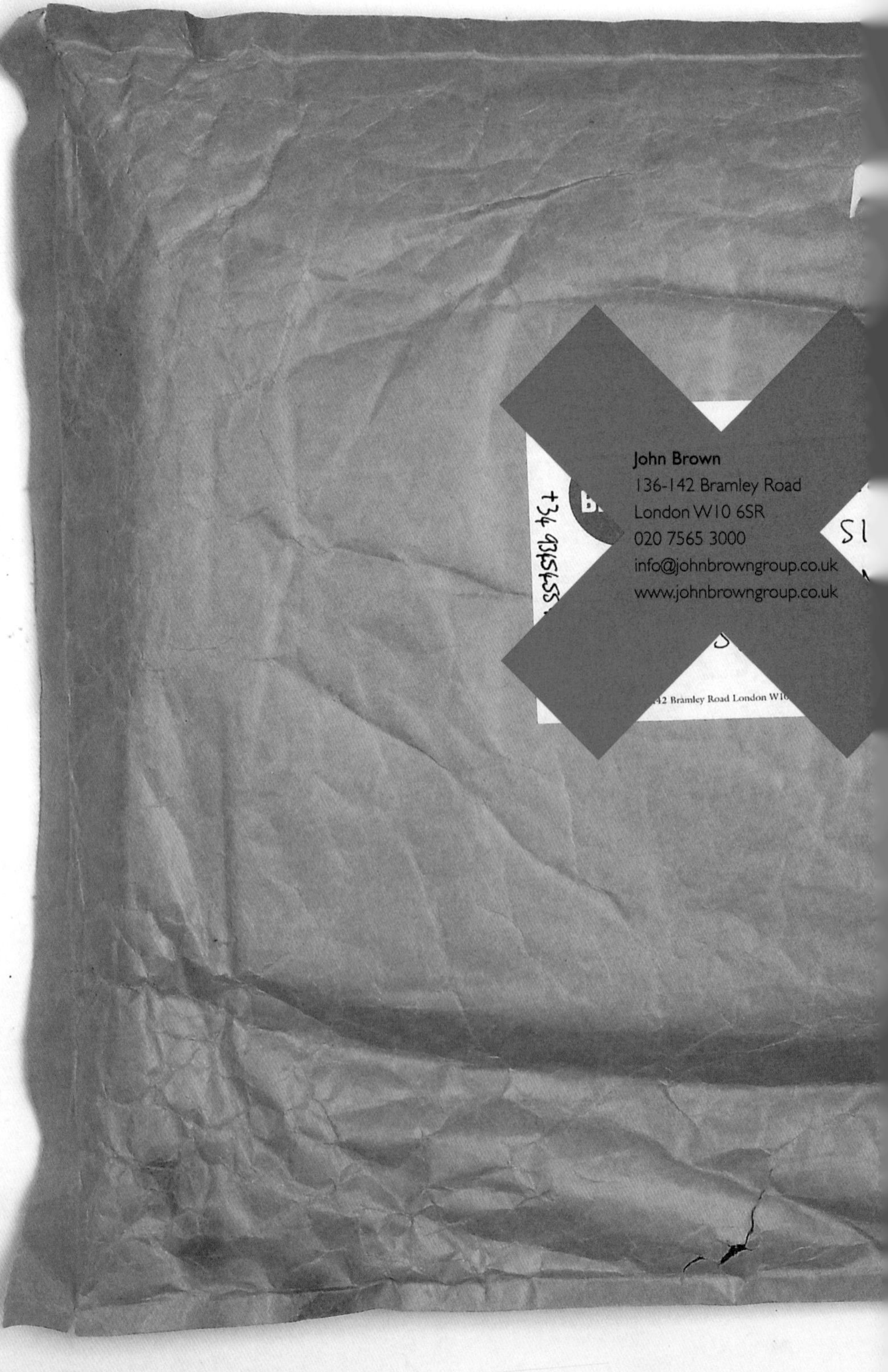

John Brown
136-142 Bramley Road
London W10 6SR
020 7565 3000
info@johnbrowngroup.co.uk
www.johnbrowngroup.co.uk

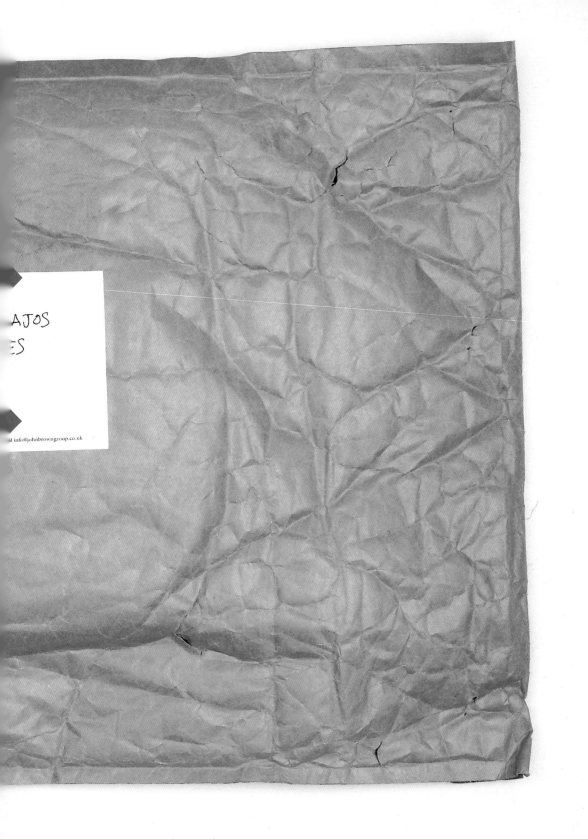

AJOS
ES

info@johnbrowngroup.co.uk

First Edition
Spring 2007

33

THE
AWARD
WINNING

THOUGHTS

1-33 BRAVE HEARTS, DIASPORA,
HEAVEN AND HELL, SERIOUS WONGA,
MAPPING ADVANTAGE, BANGING THE GONG

BDO Stoy Hayward

19.

MICRO-FINANCE: EDUCATING THE YOOF OF TODAY

The sight of a political party getting down with the kids is always embarrassing, but few initiatives have been quite so cringe-making as the Tories' recent 'Sort it!' campaign, which invited youths to 'Take the tosser test', 'See the tosser inside' and, most alarmingly, 'Look at what my tosser did'.

The terminology might be, em, unfortunate. But the campaign's aim of teaching young people basic money-management skills are timely enough. The past 30 years have seen a revolution in personal finance, yet vast swathes of the public remain at the mercy of an often unscrupulous industry. The Parepak Christmas hamper debacle was shocking not just for the misery it caused, but for the fact that so many customers fell for the sales proposition: no interest was paid on their money; and subsequent investigation has shown you could buy the contents of a £90 hamper for under £50 in a supermarket. Even the most basic savings account looks munificent by comparison.

In a laudable effort to bridge this knowledge gulf, from 2008, personal finance will be included in the National Curriculum. But can't you already feel the tedium of the lessons? Teaching children the dangers of debt and the importance of saving is all very well, but it's rather like making them eat a diet consisting of steamed greens.

To truly awaken an interest in finance, they will surely need added spice: an introduction to the real drama of markets. Reality TV shows such as *The Apprentice* may have sharpened appetites, but there's nothing like watching a stock pick soar – or fall – to get a feel for how investment works.

> *'The Tories' recent 'Sort it!' campaign: 'Take the tosser test!'; 'See the tosser inside'; "Look at what my tosser did'*

20.

CARBON: THE 21ST-CENTURY CURRENCY?

Hot air, hot profits

"Repent, for the end of the world is nigh!" seemed to be the basic message of Sir Nicholas Stern's report on climate change, which presented a compelling case for immediate action to avoid catastrophe. Stern's prescriptions sounded like an invitation to governments to play god, so you might have expected the markets to make more of a fuss. Not a bit of it. It was all music to the ears of City players, who reckon the climate-change

market is worth some £90bn and that London – the acknowledged centre of carbon trading (the business of buying and selling output credits and permits) – is poised to clean up. Indeed, with record funds already pouring into green energy funds, some warn of a bubble comparable to the tech bust.

No pain, no gain

There is a widespread consensus that the profit motive is the most realistic means to achieve lower emissions, but it would be wrong to assume the transition will be painless. City traders might be expecting a further bonanza in credit trading when compulsory emission limits are placed on companies, but for large manufacturers, the shift is going to be tough. Moreover, the market itself is far from immune to sudden jolts. Carbon prices, which depend on the scarcity of emission licences, crashed last year when European governments kowtowed to corporate demands to issue more.

Come the revolution...

Some argue the market will become fully mature only with 'personal carbon trading'. The blueprint says every adult Briton will be set a quota of about five tonnes of CO2 p.a. (a return flight to NYC – approx. 1.5 tonnes). If you exceed your limit, you'll be able to buy more credits at market price; unwanted credits can be sold at profit. "I suspect it will be hugely popular, a national game," suggests Polly Toynbee. "It tickles parts of the psyche that like to trade and bargain."

21.

COMPETITIVE PHILANTHROPY

2006 will go down as the year in which giving got serious, heralding a return to a golden age of philanthropy not seen since the days of Peabody, Rockefeller and Carnegie. Warren Buffet's gift of £30bn to the Gates Foundation was merely a high point in what is fast becoming the billionaire's competitive sport of choice. There's even a new word to describe it: 'Billanthropy' (after Mr Gates, not 'billion') – the emphasis being on professional management and return on investment.

What's behind the shift? The key seems to be the swelling ranks of the nouveau riche. People who make their own money feel less of a duty to pass it on to succeeding generations than those who have inherited it. The modern rich take their cue from Buffet's memorable line that he didn't want his wealth to end up with "the lucky sperm club". They are searching for a more meaningful legacy.

Not everyone's happy. With donations in the US alone exceeding £250bn in 2005, the largesse of the super-rich far exceeds anything formal bodies such as the UN can scrape together. Critics argue that the wellbeing of the less fortunate now lies in the hands of a few capricious billionaires. Moreover, some detect an increasingly cynical bent. Sir Richard Branson's pledge to channel some £3bn to a new green venture, Virgin Fuels, was hailed as a stellar example of super-philanthropy. But trying to make money is hardly the same as giving it away.

No matter. Whatever the motivation – be it vanity or the desire to get one up on the Joneses – few would deny that the competitive approach to 'giving while living' is bringing new dynamism, money and skills. Today's 'venture philanthropists made their fortunes by being "strategic, analytical and forward-thinking," says Nigel Harris of New Philanthropy Capital. "They want to use the same part of their brain when they give." What's not to like?

22.

NAME OR SHAME

In the old days, giving a name to a business was remarkably easy: you simply followed the example of HJ Heinz and used your own. The subsequent history of corporate names tells its own story.

By the **1990s**, pseudo-classical names had become all the rage

Then, the internet caused lower-case and capital-letter havoc

1920–1950: gravitas was deemed the primary consideration

INDUSTRIAL BUSINESS MACHINES

National Cash Register

Imperial Chemical Industries

1950–1980: go-go names to reflect new consumer trends, making good use of abbreviation

NABSCO (formerly the National Biscuit Company) **K-TEL** *Ronco* **WAL-MART** (Alan Michael Sugar Trading)

The space age spawned a welter of companies ending in 'tron' **CABLETRON** MEGATRON *On the high street, there was a new trend for exoticism*

French Connection **MONSOON** *1980s: brand names combined shock value with puns*

Knickerbox BODY SHOP **Metalbox** **Carphone** THE Warehouse

Aiwa **ALTRIA** (handy camouflage for Philip Morris cigarettes) *Consignia* (though ditched for a return to the classier Royal Mail)

AVENTIS *diageo* **Corus** **permira** O2AY

MY SPACE *MyTravel* easyJET i soft *Literary references became hip* **QUARK** named after an atomic particle, the word originates from James Joyce's Finnegans Wake

STARBUCKS named after the first mate in Herman Melville's Moby Dick YAHOO from Jonathan Swift's Gulliver's Travels: a person of repulsive appearance *Established companies tried to assert mould-breaking new credentials* **ACCENTURE** formerly Andersen Consulting

Thus formerly Scottish Telecom *Quest* formerly Southern Pacific Telecom *New companies went for eccentricity* **Google** from googol – a huge number (10 to the power of 100)

Red Hat from the woolly hat worn by its techie student founder *2000 onwards: modern trends: Numbers* **160** OVER **90** named to reflect the marketing agency's goal of stirring a reaction 160/90 is a state of heightened blood pressure **180** Europe's fastest growing ad agency

Wholesome simplicity **INNOCENT** **eat** **FRESH** **MOTHER**

For established, global companies, there has been a return to the faceless, non-location-specific acronym **DSG** formerly Dixons **BP** has dropped British Petroleum **ICI** no longer Imperial Chemical Industries **BAE** Systems: no longer British **EDF** no longer Energie de France

And the hottest new thing? According to the experts, we've come full circle: founder names are back.

25.

PRIZES WITH AGENDAS

1 Celebrating the uncelebrated
The Ig Nobel Prizes

These punningly honour whimsical, unusual and frankly weird pieces of academic research – some of which are arguably more beneficial to mankind than the real Nobels.

Recent awards

For medicine: Francis Fesmire, for his report: Termination of Intractable Hiccup with Digital Rectal Massage.

For economics: Gauri Nanda for "inventing an alarm clock that runs away and hides – repeatedly – ensuring that people DO get out of bed, theoretically adding many productive hours to the workday".

2 Improving behaviour
The Ibrahim Prize

Founded in 2006 by telecoms billionaire Mo Ibrahim, this is a $5m annual prize, plus a $200,000 stipend for life, to the African leader demonstrating the greatest commitment to democratic principles and good governance. Some slam the award as an insulting bribe, but, as Ibrahim points out, African leaders do not enjoy the same incentives to leave office (fat directorships etc) as their western counterparts. A case of the ends justifying the means.

3 Pushing frontiers

The Blue Riband: The prize for the fastest transatlantic crossing. Created by shipping companies in the 1860s, it kick-started transatlantic travel and may assume new relevance in a greener world.

The Ansari X Prize: Space-age version of the above. Founded by Iranian-born Anousheh Ansari, the $5m award – for the first manned suborbital space flight funded by private

investors – was won in 2005 by SpaceShipOne. The new $5m X Prize is for the first commercial flight to the moon. It's not rocket science, you know. Oh, wait...

4 Jump-starting markets
The Turner Prize

Founded by the Tate Gallery in London in 1984, the Prize swiftly became the main celebrant of conceptual art: Emin's icky bed, Hirst's pickled shark etc – thereby fuelling a new multi-billion investment boom.

The same might be said of the Brit Awards, which (when on form) spur on the UK music industry; and, to a lesser extent, the Man Booker Prize for contemporary fiction.

5 Making money
Trade awards

A classic money-spinning exercise for the organiser – usually a cash-strapped magazine or trade body. You pay to enter, you pay again if you're short-listed, you pay again for a table at the ceremony, and then for the raffle... meanwhile, sponsor companies pay for the privilege of handing out prizes. Such affairs are a win-win for all concerned. The winners get plaudits; the losers get the message to pull up their socks; countless obscure trade magazines remain in business; everyone has a jolly good night out.

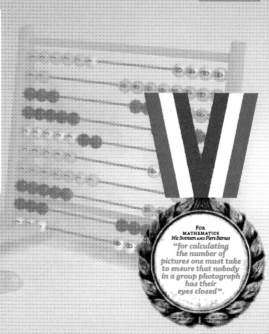

FOR
MATHEMATICS
Nic Svenson and Piers Barnes
"for calculating the number of pictures one must take to ensure that nobody in a group photograph has their eyes closed".

The best-laid plans can go awry

Who would have thought, 18 months ago, that Lord Browne, the 'Sun King' of the oil industry, would have such a disastrous final year at BP? But a fatal explosion in Texas and losses in Alaska dented the oil giant's credibility, leaving Browne exposed as a lame duck. He should trust to posterity: when the current fuss dies down, he'll surely be remembered for engineering an extraordinarily successful decade.

Stagger your departure

That way, you get to pick your successor – an important consideration in any endgame. The retirement of Anthony Bolton, star manager of Britain's largest investment fund, Fidelity Special Solutions, was always going to cause ructions. Bolton softened the blow by splitting the fund in two, allowing his chosen successor, Jorma Korhonen, to establish credibility before the final handover.

Resist the temptation to go out with a bang

Former General Electric CEO Jack Welch had hoped to cap an extraordinarily successful 20-year stint by turning GE into an e-business powerhouse and buying Honeywell International, but the bid failed and he ended up leaving with the shares significantly down.

Take care when deploying the Churchill strategy

"Keep buggering on" was Sir Winston Churchill's motto – and many corporate leaders have followed suit with aplomb – notably Kneart founder, Sebastian Kresge, who recently retired aged 98 due to failing eyesight. But safeguards are critical. Warren Buffett, now in his mid-70s, has no immediate intention of retiring from Berkshire Hathaway – but has briefed the board to engineer his removal on certain signs that he might be losing the plot.

Tony Blair's drawn-out departure from Number 10 has been described as "one of the worst examples of the endgame yet seen in British politics" – but his reluctance to leave reflects a common problem for chief executives: how do you ensure the closing months of your career seal your reputation as a business great? More to the point – how do you avoid cocking it up?

ENDGAMES: THE RULES

Make a clean exit

When you go, make sure you really go. Former Vodafone chief Chris Gent's reputation was not enhanced by his disagreements with his successor, Arun Sarin. Take a leaf from the book of former PM Sir John Major, who announced on leaving office: "When the curtain falls, it is time to get off the stage, and that is what I propose to do," adding cheerfully that he was off to The Oval for lunch.

10.

INDIAN SUMMER:
THE REBIRTH OF NATIVE AMERICA

Little more than a generation ago, the Seminole tribe of Florida lived a precarious life of poverty in the alligator-infested Everglade swamplands. Once known as the 'Unconquerable People', they came close to extinction during the 19th-century American Indian wars.

But the Unconquerables are back – and in style. Last autumn, they beat off formidable competition to acquire the Hard Rock international restaurant chain for $965m. For the Indians, who completed the deal in traditional dress accompanied by a medicine man, the move has huge significance. "Our ancestors sold Manhattan for trinkets," said tribe council member Max Osceola. "We're going to buy Manhattan back, one hamburger at a time."

The Seminoles' Hard Rock triumph marks the first major international deal ever struck by an Indian tribe. But it's unlikely to be the last. Where the Seminoles lead, other tribes follow. In the 1980s, they pioneered the move into offering gambling on their reservations, kick-starting what is now a mighty $20bn, pan-American tribal gaming empire. They are rulemakers in every sense of the word.

"Native America is in the midst of an economic boom," notes the Harvard Project on American Indian Development. "Economic growth has been about three times the US rate since the early 1990s." But the wealth is far from evenly spread: while a few high-profile tribes prosper, hundreds are still struggling to survive.

The upshot has been a series of bitter rows over tribal membership. Ultimately, it boils down to bloodlines: if you can prove the correct lineage, you're quids in; without it, you're stuffed.

33.

FORGIVE YOUR ENEMIES, BUT NEVER FORGET THEIR NAMES.

John Fitzgerald Kennedy

The eleventh in a series of untitled magazines that
inform and inspire discussion about print communication

FEATURING: FHM, Vogue, Australian Women's Weekly, Dhuzhe,
Kung Fu Monthly, Playboy, Wired and Télé magazine

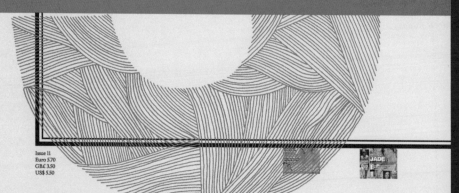

Issue 11
Euro 5.70
GB£ 3.50
US$ 5.50

launched it straightaway in handbag size. It was the first handbag-size magazine here. That was certainly a challenge for me because I also, at the same time as launching that, decided that that would be the first of the Condé Nast titles in the UK to use InDesign instead of QuarkXPress.

Everybody thought I was mad doing that, that we would be gambling enough on a launch as it was, and to complicate matters by introducing new software was even dafter. Luckily, the art director and I knew each other very well, he trusted me, and he ended up being very, very keen on InDesign. Glamour was an absolute runaway success.

Things here at IPC have changed immensely, because the company has made a very definite decision that one of the best ways of growing our business is by launching new magazines, and to launch new magazines and make them successful, you have to be in it for the long term. This is probably about the most exciting publishing company to be with in the UK right now, because we've got massive backing from our American parent company, Time Warner. Since they bought us, they've been very happy with us, and they're giving us loads of money to spend, which is great.

VF   It's great, until you stop making money.

JS   Yes, exactly.

VF   I definitely think you need money. I think it's foolish to start a magazine, put all your energy into a magazine, print it, and it just lasts a couple of issues – just to see how it goes. I think there is an art to making magazines. People know a lot about making magazines, and there are a lot of new things now. I don't know... it depends what you want from it. From IPC's point of view, it's going to be about getting out magazines that make substantial returns, and most publishers would obviously want the same thing. The other end of the scale, there are individuals who are making magazines who aren't doing it for the money at all; they will do everything possible to get one ad in that whole 180-page magazine, just to cover the print costs. It's the passion to make magazines that's driving them. It's that addictive thing of making something a reality, isn't it?

JS   Yes, I know exactly what you mean.

VF   And there are many magazines out there that are probably just covering their costs. They're not the Vogues of this world, but maybe they will be in the future. Maybe that will be more the future of the magazine world. There are magazines like The Face, which for me was one of the most influential magazines of my generation. It got me excited about magazines, and I was passionate about music – yet that magazine would not be the same today. Like we said about Nova, it came back years later, but times have changed, people have

changed, media has changed, television and cinema have changed, and there are a lot more challenges out there. Magazines today have to compete with many other forms of entertainment and information.

JS   The Face was particularly interesting because it almost defined a generation. It said so much about the people who grew up on it, who read it, who were influenced by it. It had a very strong culture about it.

VF   It also had a lot less competition at the time. I go to colleges and talk about magazines today, and the majority of the kids have never heard of The Face. Someone was playing The Beatles on the stereo in the studio earlier today, I think it was 'Hey Jude', and one of the young girls working here, who is maybe 23, said, "Who's this?" You kind of presume that everybody knows about these things, The Face, Nova, i-D, but there are a lot of people out there who don't know any of that.

JS   Yes. I think what we are seeing is that the lifespan of magazines is getting shorter. A magazine does have a lifespan, and once it's got past it, it's a bit pointless trying to keep flogging it. We find that, which is another reason why we're keen to keep launching, because you need things that are coming up while others are going down. Though it doesn't always happen that way. One of our magazines, Country Life, has been published for hundreds of years, and it seems to carry on.

VF   I suppose that doesn't go in and out of fashion.

JS   Yes, exactly.

VF   Fashion is forever changing, and I think things have to evolve. You think that the marketplace is absolutely saturated, and everybody is saying that there is no room for any other magazines, then along comes Wallpaper*. That was some time ago now, but everybody was astounded that it managed to sneak through somehow. How could there be room for that magazine? What is it? It doesn't fit in all the other boxes.

JS   That's what fascinated me about Wallpaper*, it is one of those things that you can't pigeonhole at all.

VF   It just seemed to be the perfect time. If Tyler Brûlé hadn't done it, maybe someone else would have. I worked on the launch of a new magazine called Smith, which was a men's magazine for the intelligent man, which never came to anything because everybody fell out over it. They had seven editors working on it, which was a nightmare.

wavelength. You've got to trust each other, you've got to rely on each other. Each person's role in an editorial team is vital, otherwise they wouldn't be there.

JS   Absolutely.

VF   I know what it's like trying to do a whole 120-page magazine by myself without any editorial team.

JS   That must be quite a challenge. I'd like to have a go at that myself.

VF   It is a challenge, but it's doable, and it makes you appreciate how hard the whole thing is to do. So when you do have a chance to work with a team, and they do good things, you appreciate that. It makes all the difference. In my studio here – we've got 25 people here in Sydney, and 25 in Melbourne – we work on a huge range of projects from designing sound systems, furniture, identities packaging, advertising, magazines and books, and so I'm constantly working with a team. And it doesn't really matter whether it's a magazine or a massive signage project for a new restaurant: that team has to work together with the objective of making the best of the opportunity we've got.

The difference with magazines, or the wonderful thing about magazines, is that they come normally once a month. So you've kind of created this momentum that's never going to go away, unless you're not working on it any more – each month you've got to produce a complete magazine in a relatively short period of time, knowing that you're creating some kind of paper trail. And it's interesting also when you create a magazine, that it tends to go out for a couple of months, or you tend to go to print a couple of months before it's on the newsstand, and when it's out, you're already onto your third issue. I think that you learn from your mistakes by making magazines; you learn to work with people. Success for me as a result of building relationships with that team, and with writers and photographers and printers and repro houses and all those kinds of people. Building a relationship that you can rely on at 12:30 at night when you desperately need an image for a story that's been dropped or changed or whatever. It's a very live, fluid process, and it's really very exciting.

Q: Is excitement important to success?

VF   Absolutely. I have to be passionate and excited about the content. If I'm not interested in the content, I'm not interested in laying it out. It really makes a difference. If the team is just doing it as a job and watching the clock, then it doesn't work, although I've never worked on any magazine that's been like

Jasper Scott
10.30am, King's Reach Tower, London, UK. Former production director of Condé Nast, Jasper Scott has worked on the launches of UK Glamour and the weekly men's magazine Nuts. He is now manufacturing director at IPC Media, which is owned by TimeWarner.

Client Dorling Kindersley *Design* Ian Pierce *Year* 2006

A random encyclopedia for families and children.

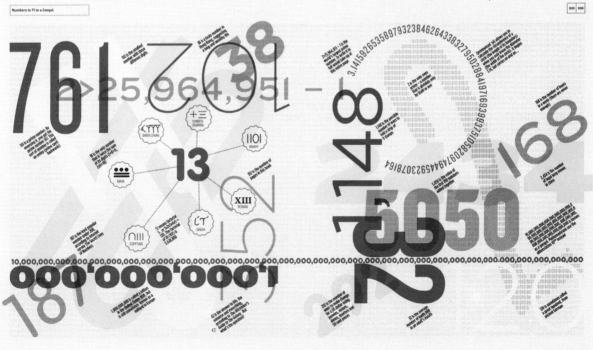

We Love Magazines

Client Editions Mike Koedinger *Design* Jeremy Leslie *Year* 2007

A book about magazines all over the world. Ten variations for the cover, each one with a different illustration on the same background.

274

We
Love
Magazines

We
Love
Magazines

We
Love
Magazines

We
Love
Magazines

276

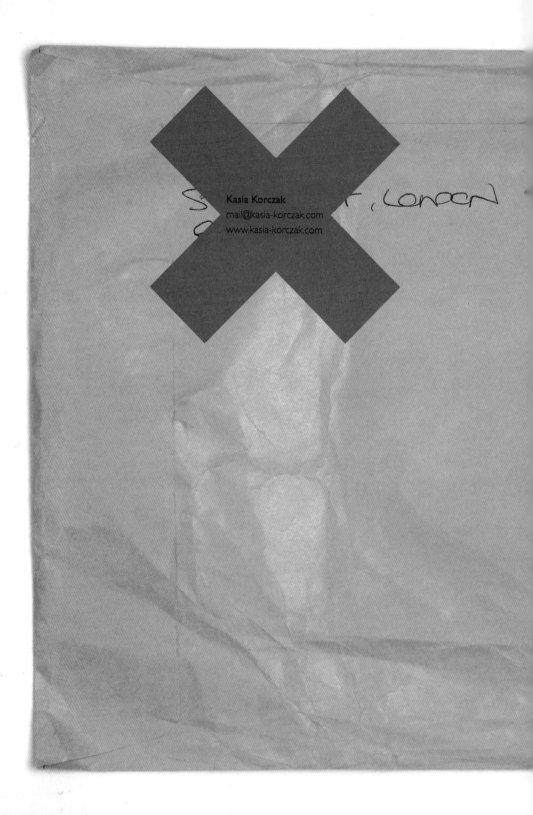

Kasia Korczak
mail@kasia-korczak.com
www.kasia-korczak.com

Cross Magazine
Client Valerio Spada *Design* Kasia Korczak *Year* 2003-2004
Cross is an intimate cultural quarterly that takes a particularly defeatist though no less relenting look at our surroundings.

our stars

Cross

are buffed

When Woyzeck begins to shave his colonel, he does so manically, finishing the job within seconds. The colonel turns around and asks him, "Woyzeck, what on earth am I to do with the extra 10 minutes you've saved me?" *(continued on page 13)*

ISSN 1723-901X

40002

Issue 2
Spring 2004

you can

Cross

me out

The beginning matters little, the end matters less: everything revolves around the middle and the middle is where Cross hopes to plunge itself, its readers, and its contributors. If the beginning or end is where we simply are, then the middle is where we become. It is not by chance that the highest speeds are always in the middle. And if we slow down, do not worry... *(continued on page 19)*

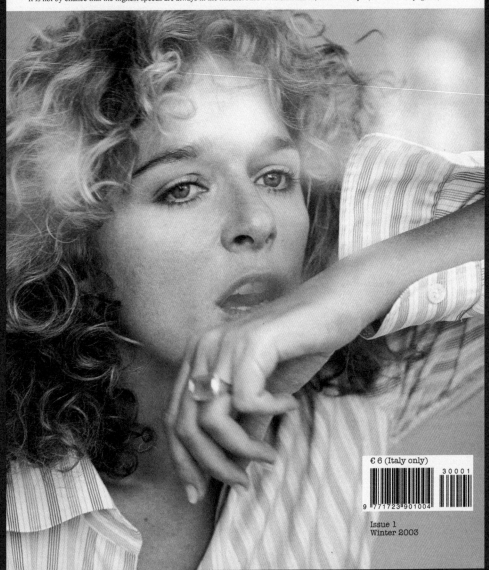

€ 6 (Italy only)

Issue 1
Winter 2003

The canvas
fallen off the Shores

We seek happiness. But we are not without the distraction of carnage and the names we were called on life's playground. We long for a moment of glee, often sweeping ourselves tearfully into a nostalgia we falsely imbue with purity.

The lovely, mesmerizingly-patterned fabrics of Kent Henricksen's work draw us in with their simple pleasure. His use of the traditional medium of embroidery contributes to this innocence. Because of its association with craft, the medium works double-time both to give the visually appealing look Henricksen aims for and also to evoke the unthreatening emotions that many of us have in association with this hobby. Because of their entrenchment in the often intimidating world of museums and galleries, materials more commonly associated with fine art—paint, graphite, pastel—wouldn't nearly have the impact the artist delivers with his needle and thread. It's the familiarity that so cunningly baits us.

For once we're reeled in, Henricksen disrupts our peace with unkind hoods of oppression; shrouded, strange, creepy characters we would rather avoid. But here he has put them smack dab in our utopian garden. He's sticking his tongue out at our futile attempt to cover the world in cheery wallpaper. And no doubt, he is having some fun at our expense; Henricksen surely finds joy in stirring things up. But beneath the fun, beneath the simply strange juxtaposition of naughty and nice, lies the dire seriousness that bespeaks the artist's greater intent. And this is where Henricksen's work gets discomfortingly enticing; once he's disarmed us with cuteness, he lets the big bad wolf in for a feast.

The open-ended narrative begins to unravel. Faced with the hooded beings, we begin to wonder, Who are they? They are so common yet clearly unidentifiable. Are they fearsome Klansmen on the hunt, terrorists out to incite fear, or the burglars who steal our dreams? Are they burqa-clad victims or POWs awaiting torture? In several, only eyes and mouths peak out: Will they sputter ugly hatred or ask for our help? Are they looking for harm or hope? In any case, we are not at peace; we are not happy. Mischievously, successfully, Henricksen has flipped us from naïve wonderland to the daily headlines.

But the colors and the patterns, they're so sweet. Just look at them.

Text: Cherie Louise

At the picnic, Drinking at the picnic, 2004.

It is of utmost importance that **we repeat our mistakes as a reminder** *to those in future generations of the depths of our stupidity.*

A monumental calendar for a monumental déjà-vu.

In 2002, Dmitry Vrubel and Victoria Timofeeva created a limited edition calendar for the Belta Gallery of Contemporary Art in Moscow. With a different facial expression of Russian president Vladmir Putin for each month of the year, the size of the calendar—110 cm x 70 cm—suits the propos of the artists and the atavistic scale of Putin's power like a glove. What most of the Western media failed to mention in blaming Putin's abuse of presidential powers in the run-up to the parliamentary and presidential elections is that Russians' soft spot for unchallenged, monocratic leaders is not a recent phenomenon: it pre-dates communism and goes back as far as the very creation of Russia itself and the rule of Alexander Nevsky.

I have often said that if people are stupid enough to want a certain thing, let them have it. After having spuriously consolidated a hefty majority in the last parliamentary elections and a landslide victory in the recent presidential ones, Putin has very little to stand in his way for the next 4 year term. Maybe, just maybe he is a necessary evil for a country still at odds with its own self-image, its standing in the world, and its hesitant drive towards reform. For, now that his power is unchecked, he has no excuses. The world will be paying very close attention to what he does and does not achieve. In the meanwhile, let us cross our fingers and hope that he does not further betray the very intellectually demanding spirit of his hometown, St. Petersburg, for the ruthlessly self-interested reputation of his adopted hometown, Moscow...

Text: Payam Sharifi

ART AS IN THE PRACTICE OF EVERYDAY LIFE 76 / ART 77

The ESTATE Thief

The intimist who slipped through the back door ...

Stand in front of a Cy Twombly drawing in any major art museum and it won't be five minutes before you hear a museum-goer comment, "My two-year old could do that." The work is unremarkable because it is, ostensibly, neither hard to do nor especially original. Follow the same museum-goer home, and you might watch him take a few snap-shots of his two-year old playing golf on the front lawn, happily documenting the child's accomplishments, birthday parties, senior prom, and family vacations. He is modelling a family legacy in albums of amateur photographs, one to show off to friends and loved ones who will feign interest until it is retired to cardboard boxes in the garage and eventually left to future generations. *Stolen* intercepts this inheritance; its artist, Cyprien Gaillard, is an estate thief.

A collection of photographs stolen from friends, acquaintances, and strangers, Gaillard's recent work openly and shamelessly indulges in the illicit. Theft, we are told, is bad, and in the world of art and ideas, property is hard to keep track of. Stealing feels good, and *Stolen* tickles our fancy for the naughty, the voyeuristic. But the work satisfies more than a wicked appetite—one could easily be

convinced that each photograph was taken by the same well-seasoned contemporary photographer. This imaginary photographer could be complimented on his creative use of reflections and critical references to popular culture, middle-class leisure culture and its relationship to the environment, references systematically overlooked by the collection's original authors. Yet everyone seems to share an eerie collective vision: Mr Amateur Photographer is, like it or not, a part of all of us, and what follows is that in aesthetisizing teenage-rebel theft, Cyprien Gaillard is not stealing from individuals, but rather reclaiming public property—he erases the particulars, re-disciplining the rejected snap-shot by tagging it. Theft and originality are no longer issues. *Stolen* operates in a Robin Hood system of ethics in which artistic pretense is humbled, without the sacrifice of beauty. It is original in its definition, because Gaillard's hijacked estate is not a physical space, nor is it the domain of work of one deceased individual—the living works straddle the unconscious of everyone seeking to preserve memories through images. Our snapshots are in the hands of a vandal and a thief, but we have never looked better.

Text: Victoria Camblin

ART AS IN THE PRACTICE OF EVERYDAY LIFE 34

To The Right Honourable the Lord Viscount Cobham

Photography: James Bby Long

Theme: High Seat
Styling: Timothy Gaydené
Models: Khaled & Elise & Isyor/Chiara Borgen's perdén
Photographic Assistant: Jack Dacor
Thanks: Mike Doyle/Dixon

Never shall I behold a view as breathtaking *as the view I borrowed from you.*

by Heidi Vogels

Deliberately focused on the minutiae that make up our everyday life, Vogels spent one month interviewing models she met through friends or by chance in Barcelona. Her contribution for Cross is an exclusive excerpt of the project, entitled Borrowed View N.1.

"The last place I lived in Barcelona was a beautiful apartment, with Art Nouveau tiles, high ceilings, and very affordable. I rented a room from the owner, as most foreigners do. As a model..."

Each room had double doors. They were open all the time, as if they were escorting you from one space to another. In the heart of the summer, when it was too hot and dry to do anything, you could just sit there and enjoy a sudden cool breeze coming through.

With decorative patterns, lazy afternoons, noisy traffic whistling past your window at night, you never know exactly where you are. The continuity between forms that wrap and unwrap, open and close, serves as a focal point when you enter some place new. It makes the outside as important and definitive as the inside. The synchronicity of life situations, passages or combinations situate the space. And meanwhile we frame,

order and compose to stay on track.

Poetic space, gaze and desire, and a will to migrate define the traveler. Appearances, direct personal presence, like decorations, often are the first expressions to connect with the changing surroundings. In Barcelona, where the beautiful townscape is made up of elements of nature and artifice, life is at its best when spent outdoors. The slow pace, brief encounters and decorative motifs make it a perfect place to search for this narration of daily life, in which different layers of perspective, fiction and objectivity come to the surface.

"The city was completely new to me but when I saw the city from the sky, with the coast and the sea, and the calm of the tides, something got a hold of me. I took a breath and I felt new, somehow."

Wassim / Lebanon
Matías / Argentina

Architectural Association

Client Architectural Association *Design* Kasia Korczak *Year* 2006

Publication for AA showcasing work of the cluster Architectural Urbanism, Social and Political Space program on the theme of scale and/ of engagement. 96 pages, stencil print (by Extrapool, NL), open, hand bound (21 cm x 17/16/15 cm).

284

Presentations 1 & 2: Cover

Presentations 1:

Diploma Unit 10, Diploma Unit 15, MA Landscape & Urbanism, Diploma Unit 2.

A Document

of Scales

Presentations 2:

PhD Programme, Diploma Unit 6, Intermediate Unit 10.

and/of

Engagement

Architectural Urbanism, Social and
Political Space Cluster 2005-2006

Cluster Curators: Katharina Borsi & Shumon Basar
Edited by: Ana Rute Faisca, Christian Parregno,
Christina Papadimitriou, Eleni Axioti, Kirk Wooller,
Marc Britz, Tal Bar, Telemachos Telemachou

Architectural Association School of Architecture

Presentations 1 & 2: Diploma Unit 10, Diploma Unit 15, MA Landscape & Urbanism, Diploma Unit 2, PhD Programme, Diploma Unit 6, Intermediate Unit 10.

Discussion 1 & 2: Andreas Lang, Anna Save de Beaurecueil, Bonnie Chu, Carlos Villeneuva Brandt, Chris Lee, Eduardo Rico, Francesca Hughes, Franklin Lee, Hugo Hinsley, Katharina Borsi, Larry Barth, Lena Tutunjian, Marina Lathouri, Mark Cousins, Shumon Basar, Tim Den Dekker, Yicheng Pean.

Commentaries: Ana Faisca, Christina Papadimitriou, Christian Parreno, Eleni Axioti, Kirk Wooller, Marc Britz, Tal Bar.

Colophon

Architectural Urbanism, Social and
Political Space (AUSP) Cluster
Curators (2005–2006): Katharina Borsi and
Shumon Basar

Editors-in-Chief: Katharina Borsi and
Shumon Basar

Editors: Ana Rute Faisca, Christian
Parreno, Christina Papadimitriou, Eleni
Axioti, Kirk Wooller, Marc Britz, Tal Bar,
Telemachos Telemachou

Graphic Design: Kasia Korczak (Slavs)
www.kasia-korczak.com
at Werkplaats Typografie
www.werkplaatstypografie.org

Copy Editor: Tarsha Finney

Printed at: Extrapool, Nijmegen,
Netherlands

With thanks to Brett Steele, the editorial
team, Kasia Korczak, Belinda Flaherty,
Joana Seguro, Henrik Rothe, Mark Hemel,
our fellow cluster curators, all the
generous participants and those that have
shown engagement with this cluster's
experiments so far.

©authors and editors
No part of this publication may be
reproduced in any manner whatsoever without
written permission from the publisher.

Published by AUSP Cluster at the AA, 2006

Founded in 1847, the AA is the UK's only
independent school of architecture,
offering undergraduate, postgraduate and
research degrees in architecture and
related fields.

For further information visit
www.aaschool.ac.uk

AA School of Architecture
36 Bedford Square
London
WC1B 3ES

The Architectural Association (Inc.)
is a Registered (Educational) Charity
No. 311083 and a Company limited by
guarantee. Registered in England
No. 171402. Registered office as above.

Presentations 1: Diploma Unit 10

Direct Urbanism
by Diploma Unit 10

Diploma Unit 10 is directed by Carlos Villanueva Brandt. Diploma Unit 10 engages
with the political, social, economic and physical forces that control change in the city.
The unit aims to question the factors that make up the current urban condition working
from a process of emersion to a process of insertion between two different working
sites in the city of London, an operative and active one.

Tim Den Dekker and Lewis Kinneir presented a variety of projects
from Diploma 10 that centred around questions of how one urban
scale engages and informs another, how the construction of urban
systems affects the way we interact with one another, and how issues
at an architectural scale may inform how we engage ourselves, as
architects, at an urban scale.

Four primary questions were asked:

1. Can a problem at one scale be solved by a solution at
   another scale?
2. Can urban systems be proportionally enlarged without
   changing how they operate, or do the majority of urban
   systems have an optimum, or maximum, scale?
3. What can we learn from systems that operate on both the
   1:1 and the urban scales, and what makes certain systems or
   processes more effective than others?
4. Which tools are most efficient/palpable for use in
   describing our work, and how do they relate to scale?

The first question was addressed through Alinda's project on
the London borough of Camden, in particular the Kings Cross
Redevelopment, Camden Central Single Regeneration Budget, Camden
Town Redevelopment policy, and community schemes in Somers Town
and West Euston. The project proposed a tram network, spanning 5
boroughs and 16.2 kilometres, to connect areas north and south of
the river. Alinda's thesis aimed to explore how an operative line of
infrastructure can activate the city by asking the question: can a
large-scale urban intervention, like the tram, generate potentials
for design or manipulation for local benefit?

The second question, of whether urban systems can be proportionally
enlarged without changing how they operate, was addressed by a
project that focused on Nine Elms – a neighbourhood in decline,
a wholesale market not running at full potential, and pending large-
scale commercial developments. The project analysed how the concerns
of these various sized groups could be addressed by overlapping
timetables of key activities that not only altered the barriers
between these activities but also highlighted potential areas for new

Discussion I & 2: Andreas Lang, Anna Save de Beaurecueil, Bonnie Chu, Carlos Villanueva Brandt, Chris Lee, Eduardo Rico, Francesca Hughes, Franklin Lee, Hugo Hinsley, Katharina Borsi, Larry Barth, Lena Tutunjian, Marina Lathouri, Mark Cousins, Shumon Basar, Tim Den Dekker, Yicheng Pean.

Commentaries : Ana Faisca, Christina Papadimitriou, Christian Parreno, Eleni Axioti, Kirk Wooller, Marc Britz, Tal Bar.

---

reorganization of the urban territory. Architecture was viewed as an
instrument for change, and the idea of intervening and reforming a
broader milieu started from the dwelling unit.

At first, the definition of the typical dwelling unit was a rational,
scientific procedure that permitted the architect to think of
the dwelling as a place that could be defined statistically, and
therefore, a methodical solution to the question of housing and the
question of the city. Secondly, different dwelling types based on
different size/scale configurations were to allow the individual unit
to be complemented in a coordinated urban settlement, and eventually,
into an urban and regional pattern. It is quite interesting, that
in the second congress of CIAM (International Congresses of Modern
Architecture, Frankfurt, 1929), which had as its theme the dwelling
for minimum existence, only floor plans were used. Here, the plan
sets a normative framework, within which, ideas of the modern city
developed. The typical floor plan was not only a link between the
individual and the collective, but was also seen as a link between
patterns of inhabitation and processes of production of the urban
field. The plan form was of particular significance in involving a
certain arrangement to be realized by precisely defining the location
of different functions, the size, and relative displacement of areas
and programmatic elements.

In these examples the plan is not just a tool for design and
construction of the building, but carries within it, both,
the tenets of architectural theory, and a social model as to how
people can and should carry out their lives. In other words, not
only was the plan to provide the basic infrastructure, but also
a particular living environment, thought of as prototype of the

Presentations 2: PhD Programme

urban future. Thus, the creation of domestic types could be used in
a policy of intervention, the aim of which was to reorganise the
environment in a thoroughly normative way.

The photographic recording of Hannes Meyer's Co-op room is
indicative. It seeks to record and depict elements, which were seen
as essential to the modernization of the family. It is not concerned
with the organization of a unit, but attempts to formulate a new
semiotics of the house. One that transcends the framework of the
traditional household type, and one that represents in iconic form a
new conception in the culture of dwelling.

Later, from the late fifties and sixties on, we have cluster diagrams
to describe a different way of understanding these multiple
relationships between scales of operation and levels of association.
The cluster diagrams by Alison and Peter Smithson describe what
the architects characterized not as objects or entities of forms,
but as operations, forces, or events. It is mostly the creation of
an image, which reveals an understanding of the urban as a system
formed by aggregates of things, events, and activities. They describe
accumulations and proximities of elements of the city that form
focal groups, or, as they called it, points of crystallization at
various scale levels, each level comprising a complete range of

Discussion I & 2: Andreas Lang, Anna Save de Beaurecueil, Bonnie Chu, Carlos Villanueva Brandt, Chris Lee, Eduardo Rico, Francesca Hughes, Franklin Lee, Hugo Hinsley, Katharina Borsi, Larry Barth, Lena Tutunjian, Marina Lathouri, Mark Cousins, Shumon Basar, Tim Den Dekker, Yicheng Pean.

Commentaries : Ana Faisca, Christina Papadimitriou, Christian Parreno, Eleni Axioti, Kirk Wooller, Marc Britz, Tal Bar.

This publication might be seen as a litmus test for the operations of the cluster Architectural Urbanism, Social and Political Space(AUSP). Barely a year old, this cluster-like the strategy of AA clusters in general-is still in a process of defining its mandate and its field of action. Conceived as a mechanism of internal and external communication; a test bed for unlikely collaborations across units and programmes-and ultimately establishing research links towards the "outside"-each cluster by definition must experiment with the scope of its possible activities. The themes that catalyse this publication and our inquiry this year are salient to many units and programmes within the AA. As curators, we have held that AUSP should be driven from the apparent existing activities and interests of the school, and the two discussion sessions presented here were conceived of as promoting this burgeoning dialogue.

The theme for the discussions-"Scales and/of Engagement"-emerged from the 2006 Open Jury sessions, which, for the first time, created a discursive forum that cut across every segment of the AA. It seemed to us that the scalar range of analysis and interventions in our Open Jury session was extremely encompassing: from modelling at "one to one" to the scrutiny of geologically sensitive regions. By focusing on the theme of Scale and/of Engagement, we hoped to orchestrate a fruitful discussion on larger urban questions rather than focusing on the particularities of unit and programme agendas.

We were extremely pleased with the enthusiasm with which everybody accepted our invitations to present and engage in discussion at a very busy time in the academic year. The cross section of the school coming together for discussion seemed unprecedented: Diploma Unit 2, Diploma Unit 10, Diploma Unit 15, Intermediate Unit 10, Landscape & Urbanism, and Histories & Theories each presented their work in light of the given theme. Through the specific presentations a productive discussion about the the of the use-value of terms and approaches was elicited. Consensus was, of course, rarely met. However, the discussion about the notion of communication between units and programmes an questions of "the urban" could be taken as a productive outcome of these disagreements. In terms of language or lexicons, we might have opened as many differences as commonalities across the school. A simplified version may posit that these approaches that take scale as a concept defined by the body and governed by a set of interests deal with an entirely different set of questions than those pedagogies that take scale to be a category already given within urbanism. On the other hand, in the graphic representational and analytical work, one can also discern some potential for interesting overlaps. We hope that this publication begins the desire to stimulate the conditions of productive (dis)agreement. Our objective might not so much lie in the hope of a "common ground," or merely in the discussion of broad themes. Rather, this cluster wishes to further what kind of urban problems-and reactions-we as a school and a culture might fruitfully address with our range of expertises.

A Document of Scales and/of Engagement is organised in three parts. The first section summarises the presentations of the units and programmes. The second part is a transcription of the two subsequent discussions. And the last section contains commentaries by the 2005-06 Histories and Theories students who have generously and engagingly acted as editors and colleagues. Aided by the inventiveness and intelligence of our graphic designer, Kasia Korczak, we hope that this booklet reflects the new nature of the cluster. Paramount to us was a swift turnaround from event to artefact. We have tried to capture the spirit of the statements and the debates without tiring laboriously over perfect verisimilitude. Speed sometimes equates to urgency-as it has here. Any mistakes and errors should thus be seen in the light of this ambition. Our contributors are to be sincerely thanked for stopping on to this maiden voyage with genuine optimism. It has made our job all the more enjoyable and worthwhile. Look out for the follow-up to this document in the beginning of 2007, where the scales and/of engagement will zoom out to consider the contemporary phenomenon of "Cities from Zero" sprouting up in places like Dubai, China and Africa.

Katharina Borsi & Shumon Basar
Cluster Curators

Discussion 1:

Anna Save de Beaurecueil,
Diploma Unit 2

Carlos Villaneuva Brandt,
Diploma Unit 10

Chris Lee, Eduardo Rico,
Diploma Unit 2   Landscape & Urbanism

Francesca Hughes, Franklin Lee,
Diploma Unit 15   Diploma Unit 15

Katharina Borsi, Larry Barth,
Histories & Theories   Housing & Urbanism

Mark Cousins, Tim Den Dekker.
Histories & Theories   Diploma Unit 10

Discussion 2:

Andreas Lang, Bonnie Chu,
Intermediate Unit 10   Intermediate Unit 10

Chris Lee, Hugo Hinsley,
Diploma Unit 6   Housing & Urbanism

Katharina Borsi, Larry Barth,
Histories & Theories   Housing & Urbanism

Lena Tutunjian, Marina Lathouri,
Intermediate Unit 10   Intermediate Unit 10

Mark Cousins, Shumon Basar,
Histories & Theories   Intermediate Unit 9

Yicheng Pean.
Diploma Unit 6

Discussion 2, 14 March 2006, Studio 1, AA

Shumon Basar: I am wondering whether Marina would like to comment on the presentations with respect to a kind of genealogy that you have identified in your presentation. Do you detect within that genealogy any kind of relationship or continuity within the practices that we have seen this afternoon or whether you see something quite different?

Marina Lathouri: Chris, I didn't know exactly how the reference to the plan by Le Corbusier (of Plan Voison) was related to your understanding of typology; whether that was a kind of exhibiting of your understanding of typology or the use of typology as a design device or whether it was something that you were trying to differentiate from?

Chris Lee: What I was pointing to was the mode to look at type. If we look at type as typology as both an object of scrutiny as well as a mode of scrutiny then I think there is an opportunity for the type to slide up in scale or to slide down in scale. The projects show essentially forms of challenging the type and pushing the type towards the scale of the urban plan as a way of development, rather than stopping the development of the type and of the scale of architecture and then proliferating these as modules. Because I think there is a big difference between modulation and modules for instance.

Marina Lathouri: That is what I was also trying to say. Not type as module but typology understood in terms of modulation. That means that type is not something fixed, a form of organization, which is actually to be multiplied and repeated in different scales. But it sets up a kind of a system of organization, which then leads to work that operates at various scales. The problematic question might be this kind of transition from one scale of operation to another scale. Whether the

Contributors

Ana Rute Faisca is a training architect and graduate student in the MA in Histories & Theories of Architecture.

Andreas Lang co-directs Intermediate Unit 10. He is an AA graduate, practicing architect and founding member of the art/architecture collective public works.

Anna Sova de Beaurecueil co-runs Diploma Unit 2 and teaches in media studies programme. She is a practicing architect and co-principal of SUBdV.

Bonnie Chu is an Intermediate Unit 10 student.

Carlos Villanueva Brandt is Unit Master of Diploma Unit 10. Visiting Lecturer/Professor at the Royal College of Art, practicing architect and founding member of NATO.

Christian Parreno is an architect, an artist and graduate student in the MA in Histories & Theories of Architecture.

Christina Papadimitriou is an architect, an archaeologist and graduate student in the MA in Histories & Theories of Architecture.

Christopher Lee is Diploma 6 Unit master. A practicing architect, researcher, writer and lecturer.

Ed McGinn is a Diploma Unit 15 student.

Eduarda Rico is a civil engineer, an MA in Landscape & Urbanism graduate and tutor, researcher and practicing consultant in the UK & Spain.

Eleni Axioti is a structural & civil engineer with practice in disasters emergency respond plans and graduate student in the MA in Histories & Theories of Architecture.

Francisco Hughes co-directs Diploma Unit 15 and has lectured widely. She is a founding member of Hughes Meyer Studio and editor of The Architect: Reconstructing Her Practice (MIT Press: 1996).

Franklin Lee co-runs Diploma Unit 2. He is a practicing architect and co-principal of SUBdV.

Hiromichi Hata is an Intermediate Unit 10 student.

Hugo Hinsley teaches at Housing & Urbanism graduate programme, PhD & Future Practice programmes. He is an architect with experience in housing, community buildings and urban development projects.

John Linares is a Diploma Unit 15 student.

Katharina Borsi is an architect, AA PhD candidate, Histories & Theories AA programme tutor and the AUSP cluster co-curator.

Kirk Wooller is a practicing architect and graduate student in the MA in Histories & Theories of Architecture.

Lawrence Barth is a lecturer an urbanism in the AA's Graduate School (Housing & Urbanism, Landscape Urbanism and PhD programmes) and has written on the themes of politics and critical theory in relation to the urban. He practises as a consultant urbanist.

Lena Tutunjian is an Intermediate Unit 10 student.

Lewis Kinneir is a Diploma Unit 10 student.

Marc Britz is an architect and a scholar graduate student in the MA in Histories & Theories of Architecture.

Dr. Marina Lathouri teaches at the AA Histories & Theories programme and has written and lectured widely. Trained as an architect, she continued her studies at the Berlage Institute and at the Sorbonne.

Mark Cousins is AA's Histories & Theories programme director, Visiting Professor of Architecture at Columbia University, Visiting Professor Designate at the University of Navarre and a founding member of the London Consortium graduate school.

Max Marz is a Diploma Unit 6 student.

Shumon Basar is an Intermediate 9 Unit master, AA summer school co-director, lecturer at Royal College of Art, co-founder of Newsletter and sexymachinery, writer and editor. Shumon co-curates the AUSP cluster.

Tal Bar is a practicing interior designer and graduate student of the MA in Histories & Theories of Architecture.

Tomoa Hasakimata is an Intermediate Unit 10 student.

Telemachos Telemachou is an architect and graduate student in the MA in Histories & Theories of Architecture.

Tim Den Dekker is a Diploma Unit 10 student.

Yichang Paan is a Diploma Unit 6 student.

Commentaries:
Ana Faisca, Christian Parreno, Christina Papadimitriou, Eleni Axioti, Kirk Wooller, Marc Britz, Tal Bar.

analysis. Finally, an essential engagement with architecture usually occurs at the very basic level of the purpose of architecture, which is its 'function'. Although, considering the level of sophistication that design has achieved today, it can often be difficult to answer a simple question like: 'How on earth does the door open?'

A friend of mine recently explained the importance of scripting in contemporary architectural design. 'If you can't script, you can't really do much today!' she said. 'I can't understand scripting, I'm doomed,' I thought! But, during the two sessions of the AUSP meetings (and certainly during the AA Open Jury), this assumption was definitely challenged. A panorama of means and techniques passed in front of our eyes. Architecture either written in parametrical equations or sophisticated words, scripted or not, using emerging nano-technology or wood and plaster, described by poetic films, philosophical texts or scientific diagrams, is something further than its language of analysis or its terminologies. And this part of architecture needs to communicate and engage all.

1. AUSP Session
2. http://en.wikipedia.org/wiki/Jean-François_Lyotard, 25/05/2006

The Story of the (Unwritten) Story of the Pool, part 2
by Kirk Wooller

Circa 1975: Rem Koolhaas writes a story about a floating swimming pool, called 'The Story of the Pool'. An architecture studio project in Russia 1923-anonymous in authorship and embodying a collective desire-the pool was a radical modern design of geometric and ideological purity: architecture for a better world. The students, who both built the pool and were its lifeguards, soon realised that by swimming in unison their combined efforts would propel the pool in the opposite direction. To flee cultural repression the architect/lifeguards decided to make for America. Four decades later the pool reached Manhattan. The New Yorkers, who were attempting to establish Post-Modernism at the time, despised the pool's outdated design and Utopian pretensions. Though the city gave an impromptu reception to recognise their swim to freedom, the locals were more than relieved to see the architect/lifeguards board the pool and continue their journey elsewhere…

Circa 1975: New York City is dead. A loss of nerve over Modernism and the metropolis sees Manhattan floating in an historical pastiche. Meanwhile, as the Pool rounds the tip of Manhattan, a gaggle of students jump onboard.

SPAIN

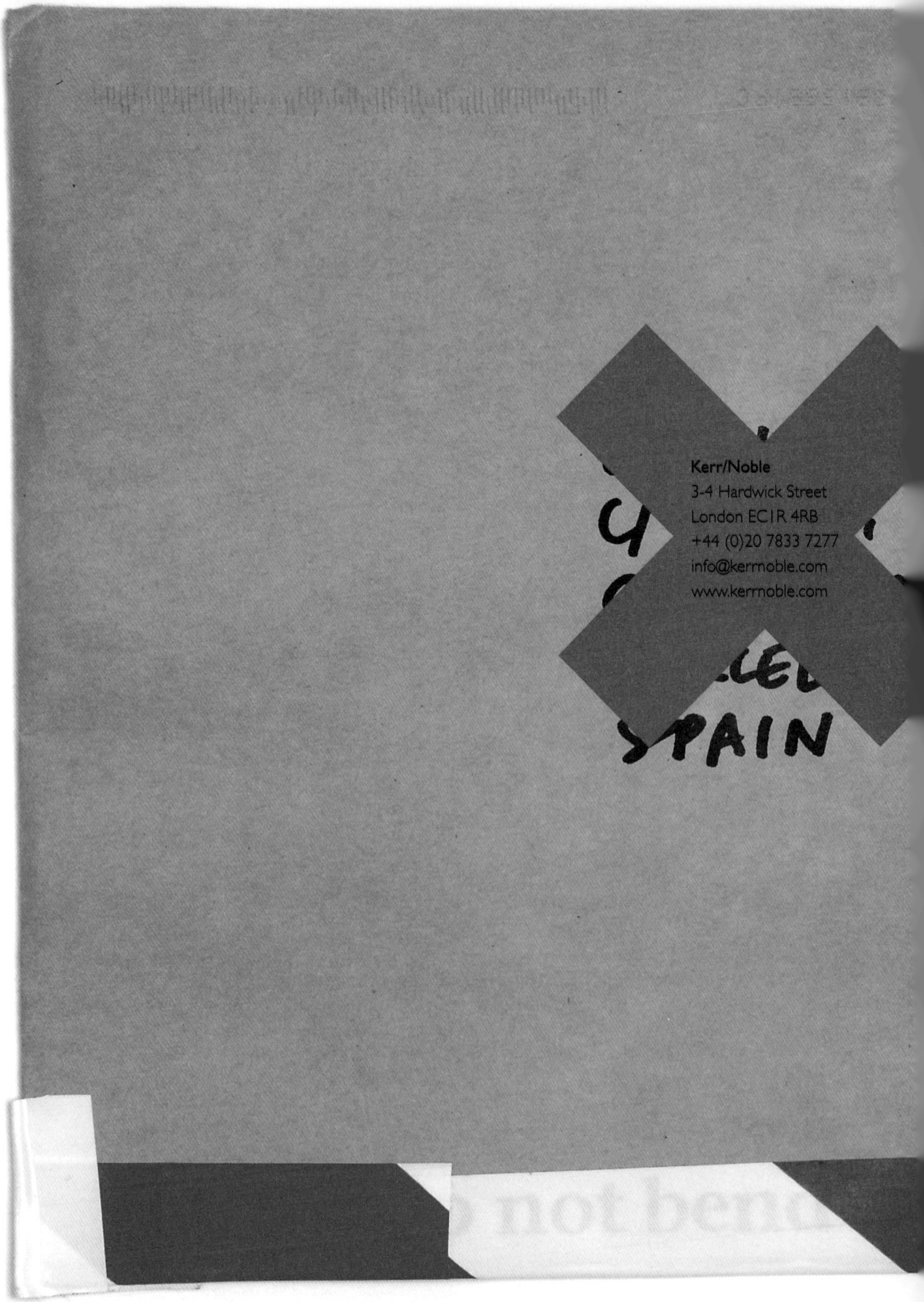

Kerr/Noble
3-4 Hardwick Street
London EC1R 4RB
+44 (0)20 7833 7277
info@kerrnoble.com
www.kerrnoble.com

o not bend

NDEX BOOK)

B, BAJOS

GES

Client Phaidon *Design* Marianne Noble *Year* 2006
Rose Carrarini's simple approach to food, 'No sauce. No garnish. No fuss,' was the key to our design concept.
We wanted to keep it simple and beautiful, complimenting Toby Glanville's photographs and in keeping with the integrity and values of Rose Bakery.

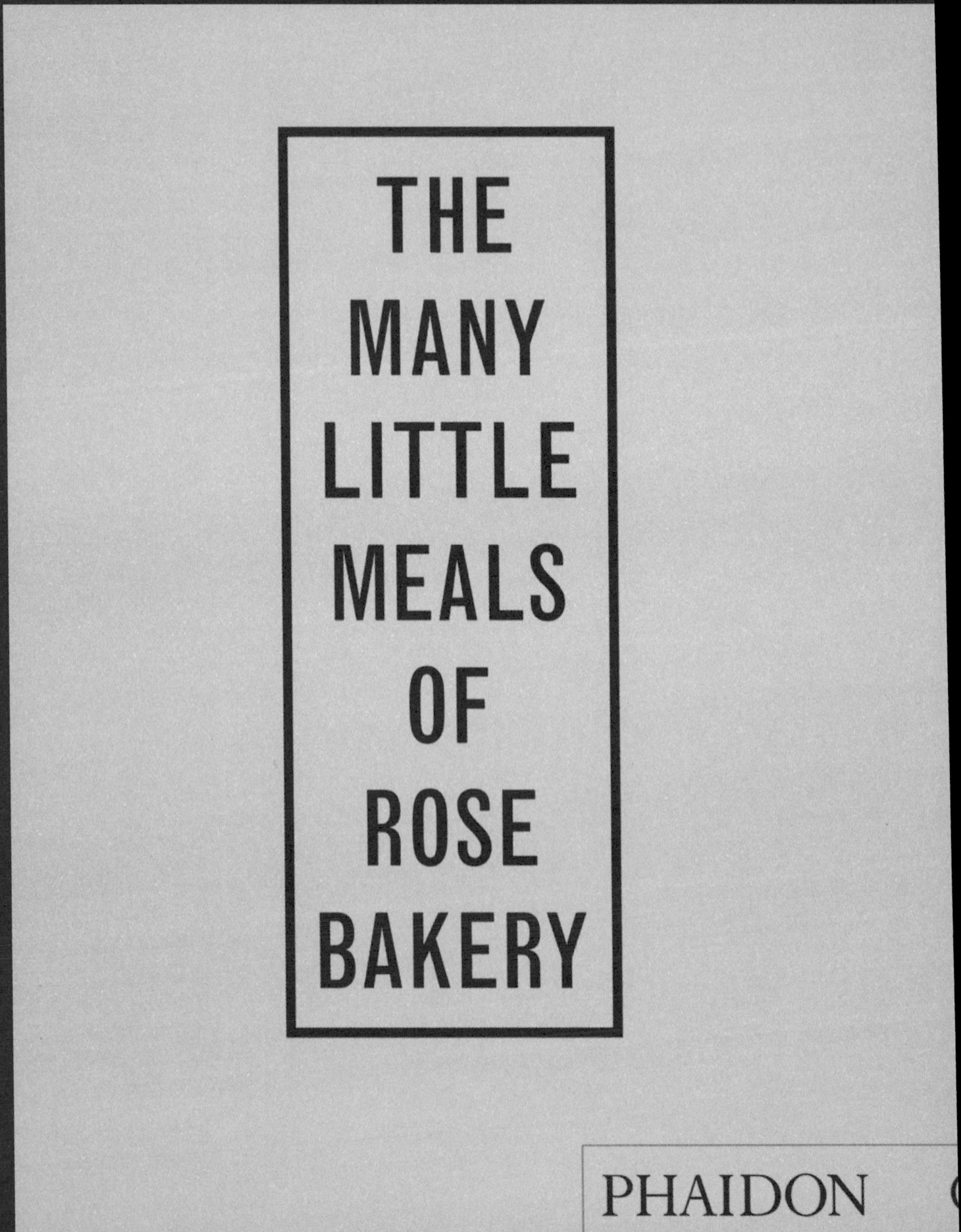

THE
MANY
LITTLE
MEALS
OF
ROSE
BAKERY

PHAIDON

BREAKFAST LUNCH TEA

ROSE BAKERY

PHAIDON

CONTENTS

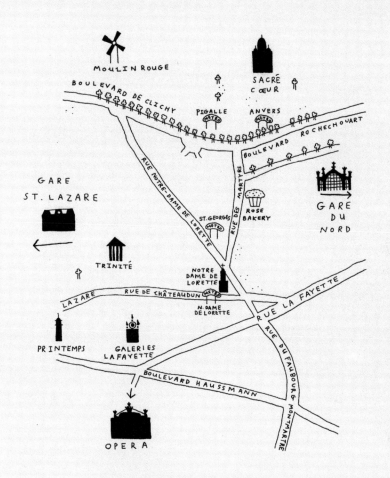

ROSE BAKERY
46, RUE DES MARTYRS
75009 PARIS
01 42 82 12 80

«Breakfast, Lunch, Tea» is the first cookbook
by Rose Carrarini, who co-founded the much-
imitated delicatessen Villandry in London
in 1988, and now serves her signature simple,
fresh and natural food at Rose Bakery, the
Anglo-French bakery and restaurant in Paris.
Rose holds a passionate philosophy that «life
is improved by great food and that great food
can be achieved by everyone.» Simplicity,
freshness and the ability to choose the right
things to cook are the keys to success and,
with Rose's guidance and recipes, perfection
and pleasure are easily attainable.

This book includes recipes for over 100
of Rose Bakery's most popular dishes, from
breakfast staples such as crispy granola to
afternoon treats, including sticky toffee
pudding and carrot cake, as well as soups,
risottos and other dishes perfect for a
light lunch.

OUVERT
9 HEURES

JUICES AND SMOOTHIES

At Rose Bakery our classic freshly squeezed juice is our
Sunrise Juice, which is simply a mixture of pink grapefruit
and oranges (blood oranges when in season) – combined,
their colour reminds us of the sunrise...We also have on
the menu a smoothie, to which we do not add crushed ice
as they usually do in restaurants. So it is pure fruit and
yogurt (or a non-dairy alternative). Of course, you are
welcome to add the ice if you prefer its texture.

CLASSIC BANANA SMOOTHIE

Serves 1
1 banana
1 teaspoon honey
2 tablespoons apple juice
125ml (½ cup) natural (plain) yogurt
or soya (soy) milk

Put all the ingredients in a food processor and
liquidize until smooth and frothy.
Serve immediately.

Variations
• Add a handful of strawberries in season.
• Replace the apple juice with lime juice, the
honey with 1 tablespoon sugar and add a
handful of desiccated (dried) or grated fresh
coconut (grated fresh is better).
• Replace the banana with soft chunks of
mango and add a dash of lime juice to the
apple juice.
• Use any poached fruit and some of its liquid,
especially apricots, instead of the banana and
you won't need the apple juice.
• A popular and different kind of smoothie is
made with rice milk instead of yogurt. You then
add a few chopped dates, a handful of oats and
almonds, and a banana. And so on. If you wish.

LIME, GRAPEFRUIT AND GINGER JUICE

Serves 2
3 tablespoons caster (superfine) sugar, plus
extra to taste
2 tablespoons grated fresh ginger
juice of 2 limes
juice of 2 grapefruit

Put the sugar in a small saucepan with
250ml (1 cup) water and the ginger and simmer
for about 5 minutes.
Take off the heat and allow to infuse and cool.
Strain into a jug and stir in the lime and
grapefruit juices.
The juice should be sweet enough, but add
extra sugar if you wish.

**TOMATO, CELERY AND SPRING ONION
(SCALLION) JUICE**

Serves 2
4 ripe tomatoes, chopped
1 stick celery, chopped
2 spring onions (scallions), chopped
1 tablespoon concentrated tomato purée (paste)
1 teaspoon red or white wine vinegar
salt and pepper

Put all the ingredients in a food processor with
125ml (½ cup) water and liquidize.
Taste and add more salt and pepper if needed.
Strain into two glasses.

CLASSIC BANANA SMOOTHIE

FRUIT

FRESH MIXED FRUIT SALAD
MELON AND GINGER SALAD
COMPÔTE OF APRICOTS AND VANILLA
RHUBARB AND ORANGE
CRÈME ANGLAISE
POACHED PEACHES AND RED FRUITS
FRUIT TABOULÉ

JUICES AND SMOOTHIES

CLASSIC BANANA SMOOTHIE
LIME, GRAPEFRUIT AND GINGER JUICE
TOMATO, CELERY AND SPRING ONION JUICE

CEREALS

SUGAR-FREE GRANOLA
HONEY GRANOLA
RAW MUESLI
TRADITIONAL PORRIDGE

EGGS

PERFECT SCRAMBLED EGGS

PANCAKES

CLASSIC PANCAKES
RICOTTA PANCAKES
GLUTEN-FREE BUCKWHEAT PANCAKES
VEGAN PANCAKES

SCONES

PLAIN SCONES
SULTANA SCONES
BLUEBERRY SCONES
MAPLE SYRUP SCONES
DATE SCONES
CHEDDAR CORNMEAL SCONES

ŒUF À LA COQUE AVEC 'TOAST MARMITE'

RAW MUESLI

We keep this healthy and nourishing dish simple, as it has always been, resisting the temptation to add different fruits. It is just so good as it is, all through the year.

Serves 4
150 g (2 cups) rolled oats, soaked in 250 ml (1 cup) water or apple juice for about 1 hour, or even overnight
125 ml (½ cup) natural (plain) yogurt
1 apple, peeled or unpeeled, grated, plus extra to serve (optional)
2 heaped tablespoons chopped almonds
1 tablespoon wheatgerm
1 tablespoon honey, plus extra to serve (optional)
pinch of ground cinnamon (optional)
1 small handful sultanas (golden raisins)

Mix all the ingredients together, then serve as we do – topped with extra grated apple and a little more honey if desired.
Wonderful. I can't think of a nicer way to start the day!

TRADITIONAL PORRIDGE

At Rose Bakery our staff love eating this with maple syrup and sliced bananas. It's a great, energizing start to a cold winter's day.

Serves 2
75 g (1 cup) rolled oats
pinch of salt

To serve
milk or cream, warmed
honey or brown sugar

Put the oats in a small saucepan with 500 ml (2 cups) water and slowly bring to the boil, stirring all the time.
Turn the heat down immediately, then add the salt – a vital ingredient!
Continue to stir well until the mixture thickens and becomes creamy. This will take anywhere between 5 and 15 minutes.
When you are satisfied that the texture is perfect, pour the porridge into a bowl and serve with warm milk or cream, and honey or brown sugar.

NOA, ONE OF OUR REGULARS

ROSE & JEAN-CHARLES CARRARINI

MERCI
&
THANKYOU

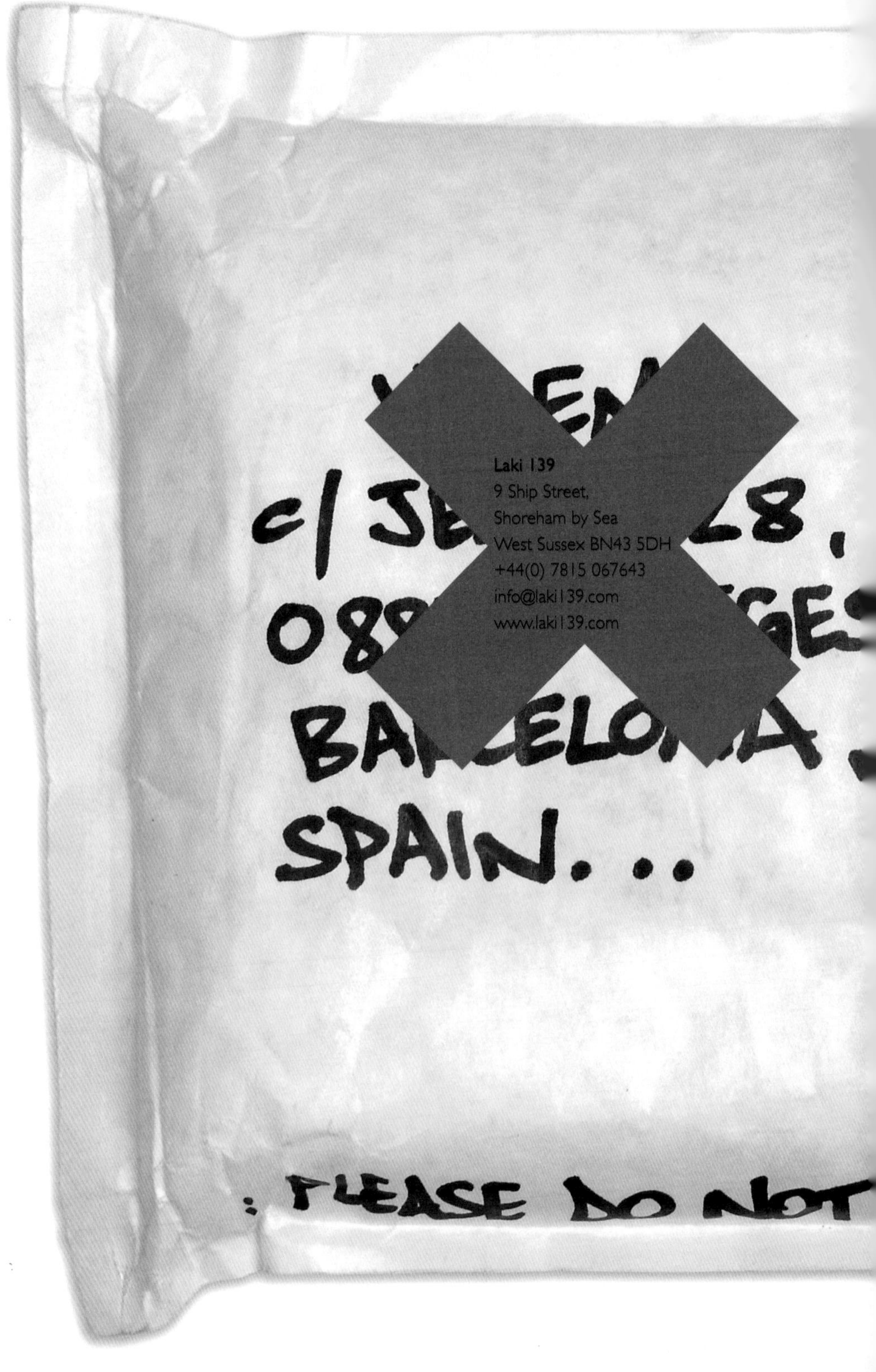

298

c/ JE... 28,
089...
BARCELONA,
SPAIN. ...

: PLEASE DO NOT

Laki 139
9 Ship Street,
Shoreham by Sea
West Sussex BN43 5DH
+44(0) 7815 067643
info@laki139.com
www.laki139.com

ÁJOS.

A

Royal Mail

POSTAGE PAID UK
05/03/07 £7.49 W1T
56009 3-2092207-1

Great Britain
Recommandé

 signedfor
international

R

RI 8821 9740 5GB Sig req

RI 8821 9740 5GB Sig req

RI 8821 9740 5GB

PRIORITY HANDLING & REGISTERED DELIVERY

BEND!!.

Aura Magazine
Client Self initiated *Design* Simon Slater *Year* 2005
This journal is a celebration of graphic communication which has mutated and expanded from the association of traditional graffiti art.
Limited edition of 139 copies for issue one.

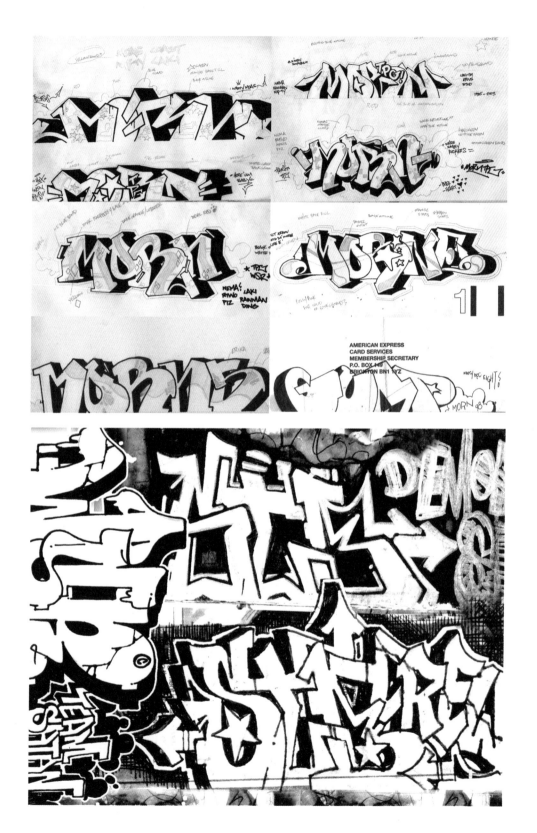

AMERICAN EXPRESS
CARD SERVICES
MEMBERSHIP SECRETARY
P.O. BOX 449
BRIGHTON BN1 1YZ

?   ?   ?   ?

?   ?   ?

?

?   ?   ?

?   ?   ?

HOCK

CHANOIR

?

POCH

?

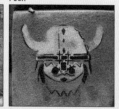

?

?

?

?

?

8

?

?

?, D*FACE, FLYING FORTRESS

?

?

?

?

306

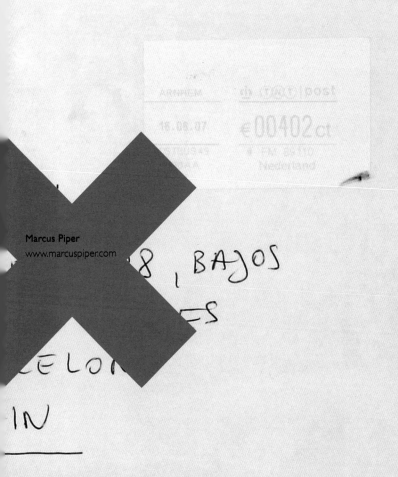

Crafts Magazine covers

Client Crafts Council *Design* Jeremy Leslie *Year* 2006-2007

The concept behind the covers was to bring Craft to the fore of the magazine. Showing what it can be and including Crafts people in the production of the magazine. Each issue we ask a different crafts person to create a cover using the logo and their specific craft. It is a step away from the traditional magazine cover which has become so much the disappointing norm these days.

DAI REES'S
WORLD OF LEATHER

DO IT FOR ME
THE COMMISSIONING
POWERPLAY

BANG OR WHIMPER?
WHEN CRAFT AND
TECHNOLOGY COLLIDE

GLITTERING SURPRISES
JAPANESE JEWELLERY TODAY

WHY **JOHN WARWICKER**
NEVER TIRES OF TYPE

ANYA GALLACCIO'S
WORLD OF MACRAMÉ

NO 204
JANUARY/FEBRUARY 2007
UK: £5.95 | US: $12.50

CRAFTS

THE MAGAZINE FOR CONTEMPORARY CRAFT

MEET THE CRAFTITECTS
BRINGING THE HUMANITY BACK TO BUILDINGS

JANET LEACH
FROM TEXAS TO ST IVES

ALL OVER THE WORLD AND ALL OVER THE SHOP
CRAFT GOES GLOBAL

WHEN JASPER MORRISON LOVES JAPAN

WHEN HANS MET RICHARD
THE BEST OF BRITISH GLASS
DRAWING WITH SCISSORS
POST-MAC POSTER ART
TANYA HARROD: NOSTALGIA HURTS

NO 203
NOVEMBER/DECEMBER 2006
UK: £5.95 | US: $12.50

CRAFTS

THE MAGAZINE FOR CONTEMPORARY CRAFT

A SORT OF REVOLUTION
SIR CHRISTOPHER FRAYLING
ENDS A 30-YEAR DEBATE

THE COVER UP
COLLECTORS FALL IN LOVE
WITH BOOKBINDING

ETTORE SOTTSASS
NIGEL COATES IN PRAISE
OF THE POLYMATH

DUTCH PIRATES
DESIGNS ON CRAFT

FREDRIKSON STALLARD
CROSSING THE
BILLERICAY-MALMO DIVIDE

NO 205
MARCH/APRIL 2007
UK: £5.95 | US: $12.50

9 770306 610029

CRAFTS

THE MAGAZINE FOR CONTEMPORARY CRAFT

GERDA FLÖCKINGER
THE YOUNGEST
80 YEAR OLD IN TOWN

OPPORTUNITY KNOCKS
WHY AUSTRALIAN CRAFT
IS A WIDE OPEN WORLD

GAINSBOROUGH SILKS
THE SUFFOLK MILL THAT CAN'T
STOP MAKING HISTORY

TORD BOONTJE
HEARTS AND DARKNESS

DAVID ADJAYE
ON MUD IN MALI

NO 206
MAY/JUNE 2007
UK: £5.95 | US: $12.50

9 770306 610029   05

312

By air mail
Par avion

John Morgan Studio
Room B.225
MacMillan House, Platform 1
Paddington Station
London W2 1 FT
+44 (0)20 7402 6622
www.morganstudio.co.uk

-8, bajos

tges

SPAIN

Common Worship: Times and Seasons
Client Church House Publishing *Design* John Morgan *Year* 2006
250 × 155mm, 688pp. Hardback with 2 ribbons. The latest in the Common Worship family of resources

Extended Prefaces

M1   *From the First Sunday of Advent until 16 December*

It is indeed right and good to give you thanks and praise,
almighty God and everlasting Father,
through Jesus Christ your Son.
For when he humbled himself to come among us in human flesh,
he fulfilled the plan you formed before the foundation of the world
to open for us the way of salvation.
Confident that your promise will be fulfilled,
we now watch for the day
when Christ our Lord will come again in glory.
And so we join our voices with angels and archangels
and with all the company of heaven
to proclaim your glory
for ever praising you and saying:

M2   *From 17 December until Christmas Eve*

It is indeed right and good to give you thanks and praise,
almighty God and everlasting Father,
through Jesus Christ your Son.
He is the one foretold by all the prophets,
whom the Virgin Mother bore with love beyond all telling.
John the Baptist was his herald
and made him known when at last he came.
In his love Christ fills us with joy
as we prepare to celebrate his birth,
so that when he comes again he may find us watching in prayer,
our hearts filled with wonder and praise.
And so, with angels and archangels,
and with all the company of heaven,
we proclaim your glory,
and join in their unending hymn of praise:

Blessings and Ending

P1   Christ the Sun of Righteousness shine upon you,
scatter the darkness from before your path,
and make you ready to meet him when he comes in glory;
and the blessing …

P2   May God himself, the God of peace,
make you perfect and holy,
and keep you safe and blameless, in spirit, soul and body,
for the coming of our Lord Jesus Christ;
and the blessing …

P3   May God the Father,
who loved the world so much that he sent his only Son,
give you grace to prepare for life eternal.
Amen.

May God the Son,
who comes to us as redeemer and judge,
reveal to you the path from darkness to light.
Amen.

May God the Holy Spirit,
by whose working the Virgin Mary conceived the Christ,
help you bear the fruits of holiness.
Amen.

And the blessing …

P4   May God the Father, judge all-merciful,
make us worthy of a place in his kingdom.
Amen.

May God the Son, coming among us in power,
reveal in our midst the promise of his glory.
Amen.

May God the Holy Spirit make us steadfast in faith,
joyful in hope and constant in love.
Amen.

And the blessing …

P5   Our Lord says, 'I am coming soon.'
Amen. Come, Lord Jesus.

May the Lord, when he comes,
find us watching and waiting.
Amen.

Adv

Instructions for Marking the Easter Candle

A minister brings the Easter Candle to the president, who traces the cross and then the Greek letter *Alpha* (A) above and the Greek letter *Omega* (Ω) below it. The numbers of the current year are marked in the space between the arms of the cross, as in the diagram below.

```
              A
              |
              |
              |
              |
    2         |         0
              |
              |
4 ————————————2————————————5
              |
              |
   [0]        |        [0]
              |
              |
              |
              |
              |
              |
              |
              3
              Ω
```

As the vertical of the cross is traced the president says

Christ, yesterday and today,

As the horizontal is traced the president says

the beginning and the end,

As the Alpha is traced

Alpha

As the Omega is traced

and Omega,

As the first number of the year is traced the president says

all time belongs to him,

As the second number is traced

and all ages;

As the third number is traced

to him be glory and power,

As the fourth number is traced

through every age and for ever.

All   **Amen.**

Five nails or incense studs may then be inserted into the Candle, reminding us of the five wounds of Christ. Each stud is placed in the Candle at the points marked, in the order indicated by the numbers. As each is inserted the president says

```
                    1
               By his holy

    4            2              5
guard us   and glorious   and keep us.
              wounds




                    3
               may Christ
                our Lord
```

The Advent Prose

**Pour down, O heavens, from above,
and let the skies rain down righteousness.**

Turn your fierce anger from us, O Lord,
and remember not our sins for ever.
Your holy cities have become a desert,
Zion a wilderness, Jerusalem a desolation;
our holy and beautiful house,
where our ancestors praised you.

**Pour down, O heavens, from above,
and let the skies rain down righteousness.**

We have sinned and become like one who is unclean;
we have all withered like a leaf,
and our iniquities like the wind have swept us away.
You have hidden your face from us,
and abandoned us to our iniquities.

**Pour down, O heavens, from above,
and let the skies rain down righteousness.**

You are my witnesses, says the Lord,
and my servant whom I have chosen,
that you may know me and believe me.
I myself am the Lord, and none but I can deliver;
what my hand holds, none can snatch away.

**Pour down, O heavens, from above,
and let the skies rain down righteousness.**

Comfort my people, comfort them;
my salvation shall not be delayed.
I have swept your offences away like a cloud;
fear not, for I will save you.
I am the Lord your God, the Holy One of Israel,
your redeemer.

**Pour down, O heavens, from above,
and let the skies rain down righteousness.**

Horst - Platinum

Client Hamiltons Gallery / Jefferies Cowan *Design* John Morgan *Year* 2006
395 x 310mm, 72pp. Cloth bound slipcase. Published to celebrate 100 years of photographer Horst PHorst.
29 reproductions of platinum prints. Four editions with various bindings. Texts by Tom Ford, Andy Cowan and Philippe Garner.

PLATINUM

HORST

JEFFERIES COWAN
2006

Mainbocher Corset, 1939

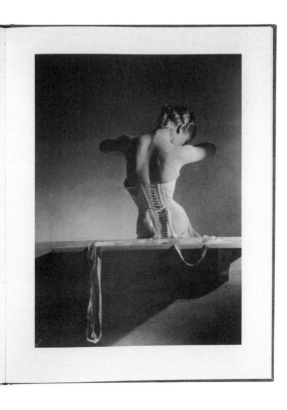

Fall Fashion, 1969

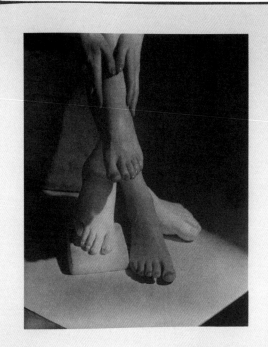

Barefoot Beauty, 1941

322

Lisa as V.O.G.U.E., 1940

Client Invisible University (I.U.) ***Design*** John Morgan *Year* 2006

Tabloid, 24pp. Prospectus for the Invisible University. correct at 07.00, 19th June 2006, 35 Clerkenwell Road, London EC1

Prospectus for the Invisible University
correct at 07.00, 19th June 2006,
35 Clerkenwell Road London EC1

Imagine yourself with a lap-top
on a lawn by a shed,
the screen & your tutor,
the garden is why

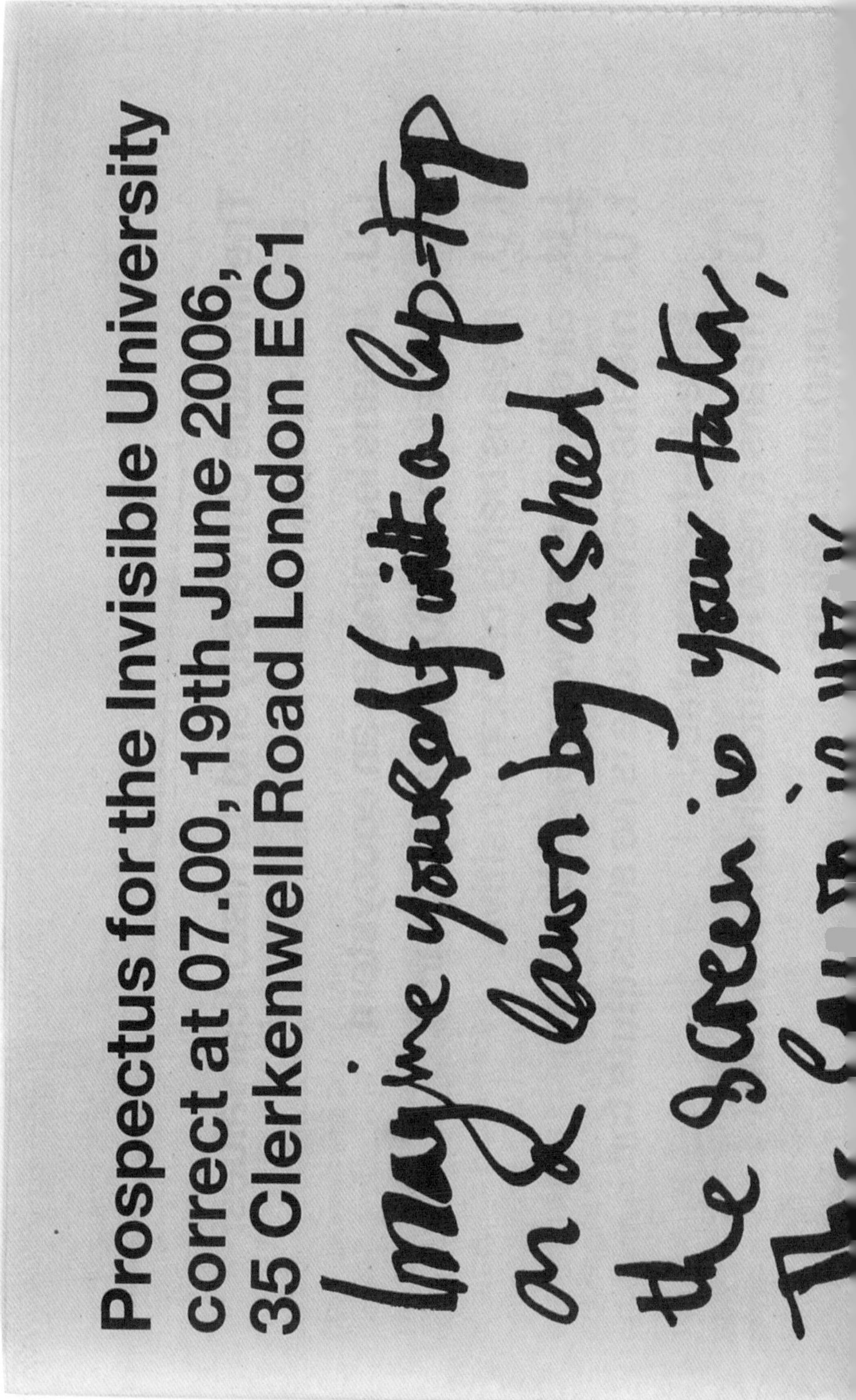

Classrooms and the school your university.

EXP Research into the architecture of the culture and foster of Smaller and faster.

Pastoral: relating to, or associated with shepherds or flocks and herds. Portraying country life, usually in a romantic or idealised form.

Arcadia: a mountainous district in the Peleponnese of Southern Greece. In poetic fantasy it represents a poetic paradise, the home of song loving shepherds.

Arcadian: an idealized peasant or country dweller. Especially in poetry. Simple and poetically rural.

Arcady: an ideal rustic paradise.

Position Description: Distance 7 (IU 1366-001)

Ginogriffiths Architects

    18 lectures
    12 exhibitions
22382 miles of road
  134 suburban housecalls
 2593 photographs
  178 days

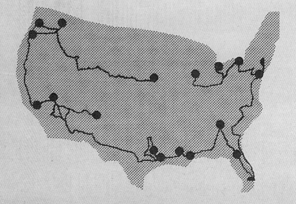

Adjunct professor will teach Distance 7 (IU 1366-001) for the Invisible University during Fall and Spring semester. This course explores the applied principles of transitional exchange in developing a design process by combining the experience of distance with new development in the making of space. These issues are investigated collaboratively and individually in a project with a specific and predominant use, within clearly defined contexts, and in connection to a mass of prevalent public spaces. Classes will meet on Mondays, Wednesdays and Fridays, L.A.W.u.N campus from 6:00-9:10pm.

Hope

Duration: At IU members are enrolled without exception, in perpetuity from the moment of conception. Members are known throughout not as students but as Seers. For their Duration, members are considered to be Amateurs until such time as they think of themselves as professionals.

Extelligence: Membership then lapses until the age of retirement when they are reinstated as Amateurs again. At the onset of death their work is entrusted to the Department of Extelligence. It is here that the Reader Emeritus in Thaumatography, Andrew Holmes, acts as Unco-ordinator of Studies.

Infinite Patience: The only requirements of a full time Seer are infinite patience, an excitable mind imperfectly disciplined by education, a willingness to be exposed to enthusiasm and a belief that we are all looking to a bright new future.

Department of Thaumatography was founded in 1939 by Ernest Dudley Chase who produced the first true thaumatograph, as encylopedic compendium of superlatives describing a broad range of cultural and natural wonders, depicting these phenomena on the Mercator projection.

Walter Hope: On August 9, 1888 Ed Cross and Shorty Harris discovered unusually high levels of thaumasite in the Bullfrog Hills. The men founded the town of Hope close to the gushing spring on land settled by Walter Hope, a Squaman searching for a cache buried by the Jayhawkers in 1849.

Mr Crump Don't Like It: AC Crump, aka Ace, a limner of extraordinary ability arrived in Hope in 1927, having left Memphis under something of a cloud. The occasion being recalled by Frank Stokes in his blues 'Mr Crump Don't Like It'. Ace was the right man at the right time in the right place.

Liming: Thus it was that Ace chanced upon the combination of thaumacite and limning that we now call thaumatography. To accomodate the increasing number of visitors to Hope he designed and built the motel that bears his name, the first of many structures that comprise the Department of Thaumatography.

Crump's Vision: Crump's vision was to create a Beacon of Light in Hope for visiting Seers. The Beacon still remains prominent at the entrance to Ace's original dwelling. It is said that a Seer standing in the aura of the Beacon perceives a white horse, a thaumatrope, travelling through time.

Meeting place type 1: urban pasture / weather sensitive – Summer only NW1 4RY

**What is there to design?
If you start from scratch where
would you start?
What do you need?
Remember –
Time, memory and battery-life.**

Work online from your desk, wherever you decide your desk is going to be today.

Broad-Band-Stand

– Assess meeting place.
– Discuss the wider implications involved in trying
  to conduct a meeting in a public place.
– Look at some historical examples of meetings
  in public places and places designed to meet in.
– Overview of how many and what type of
  spaces there are where it is possible to meet as
  non-consumers.
– Assess the demand for and supply of such locations.

At each meeting there will be a short presentation
(subject connected to venue).
Post-able envelope/notebooks will be provided.

Possible venues:
Airports, Museums, Stations, Sports Centres,
Shopping Centres, Benches, Bus Stops.

VENUE equals SUBJECT

Inaugral spelling seminar organised
by the Word Department. In attendance:
Kevin Shepherd, Jason Griffiths,
David Greene, Samantha Hardingham,
Will McLean, John Morgan, dog, Eddie
Farrell, Victoria Watson, Brian Parsons,
Corrina Till, Graham with beard.

The era of mass media is giving way to personal and participatory media.
Andreas Kluth, Economist 22.04.06

Meeting place type 2: un/propped monument / air-rights clock – 36 months NW1 5RZ

Date	Time
May	18:25
May	20:44
May	08:05
May	17:45
May	09:17
May	07:49
May	09:19
May	18:57
May	09:34
May	16:38
May	17:17
May	09:01
May	20:24
May	11:34
May	14:40
May	14:42
May	14:52
May	18:05
May	21:03
May	21:04
May	21:11
May	21:18
May	21:20
May	08:07
May	09:43
May	11:19
May	20:18
May	09:09
May	20:04
Jun	18:43
Jun	16:09

Date	Time
Jun	20:07
14 Jun	10:23
15 Jun	09:02
17 Jun	08:53
17 Jun	11:06
20 Jun	18:35
21 Jun	08:45
28 Jun	11:15
29 Jun	08:21
1 Jul	18:58
2 Jul	08:07
2 Jul	09:03
4 Jul	20:21
7 Jul	17:20
8 Jul	09:21
13 Jul	12:37
14 Jul	09:03
14 Jul	10:32
14 Jul	10:58
14 Jul	19:43
15 Jul	17:42
15 Jul	17:50
19 Jul	21:28
19 Jul	21:35
21 Jul	23:17
24 Jul	15:47
25 Jul	08:16
25 Jul	08:22
25 Jul	08:44
25 Jul	09:46
27 Jul	09:08
28 Jul	19:46
29 Jul	08:53
29 Jul	08:57
30 Jul	18:06

Provost's office

Meeting place type 4: lost ideas office – 29.12.04: Forest Row, East Sussex 06.06.06 Brisbane, Australia

I.U. Caretaker
IU 管理员

The Caretaker should take care of everything – people, things, places and ideas.
管理员将负责看管一切，包括人、物、地方与创意。

The care of lost, stolen or misused *ideas* is a particular responsibility of the Caretaker.
看护丢失的、被盗的或者误用的创意是管理员特定的职责。

The Caretaker must collect up all lost ideas and maintain a *lost ideas office*.
管理员必须收集所有丢失的创意，同时管理维持一个丢失创意办公室。

Making a mess in the IU will be positively encouraged and rewarded.
在 IU 里，制造混乱将得到积极鼓励并予以奖励。

The Caretaker should dispose of excesses of information before someone thinks it might be useful.
管理员将清理过量的信息，直到有人认为有用。

The Caretaker is required to maintain a tool shed full of equipment for coping with too much information, subduing excessively loud drawings, de-rendering (not make things become into a state?) computer images, a sump pump to drain off excess information.
管理员要维护一个储藏设备的工具房，用于应付过多的信息，控制过量积压的无用绘图，解除计算机图像，像污水泵一样消解过量信息。

The tools will be more powerful than we can yet imagine, concentrating on assisting with comprehensive thinking rather than specialist tasks. Some will be extensions of our minds and fundamentally change the limits of our thinking and imagination. Most of them will take the form of extended phenotypes and act as turbochargers to the brain by compressing future space and time – a form of accelerated evolution.
这些工具的效力远比我们想象的强大，它们主要集中在辅助完成综合思考，而非专项任务。有些是我们思维的延伸扩展，从根本上改变我们思考与想象力的限制。大部分工具将采用延伸表现性的形式，像涡轮增压器一样压缩未来空间与时间，对大脑发挥影响，这既是加速进化的一种方式。

The motto of the Caretaker shall be TAKE CARE
管理员的口号是：请当心。

JHF 2005 SH/DG Nov05

2004/12/29

Dear Professor Greene,

I have read your advertisement for the I.U. with interest and wish to apply for the post of Caretaker and to propose a project to equip the Caretaker's toolshed. I submit a job a description, a project description (1 page A4 as specified + 2 diagrams).

Trusting that I can be of service to your esteemed institution.

Yours truly,

John Frazer

Dear John, you and I know all the words and are familiar with the arcane list day of effects of global view-free technology; too a space geography de-constructed etc...de what we are actually unfamiliar with is what do new programme and visual relationships will look like. You may say who cares, you may pay they will look alike this or that. Can we agree that the consequential environmental effects are unclear? David.

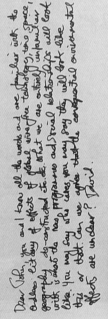

The shortage of more
Cedric Price

The motto of the Caretaker shall be

管理员的口号是

take
care

请当心

NB Studio
4-8 Emerson Street
London SE1 9DU
+44(0)20 7633 9046
mail@nbstudio.co.uk
www.nbstudio.co.uk

4–8 Emerson Street
London SE1 9DU
United Kingdom

T +44 [0]20 7633 9046
mail@nbstudio.co.uk
www.nbstudio.co.uk

ABP Annual Report 2004

Client Associated British Ports *Design* Daniel Lock, Johnny Kelly *Year* 2004

We decided to take an illustrative approach which could show ABP from a different angle. Using axometric illustrations we created a typical port scene which conveyed the complexity of ABP's business activities and sites. This type of illustration allowed for lots of detail so we were able to capture all of the daily comings and goings and present it as an absorbing miniature world. The same style was employed throughout the document to convey bar and pie charts, maps and operational projects which was backed up by tight typography and layout.

334

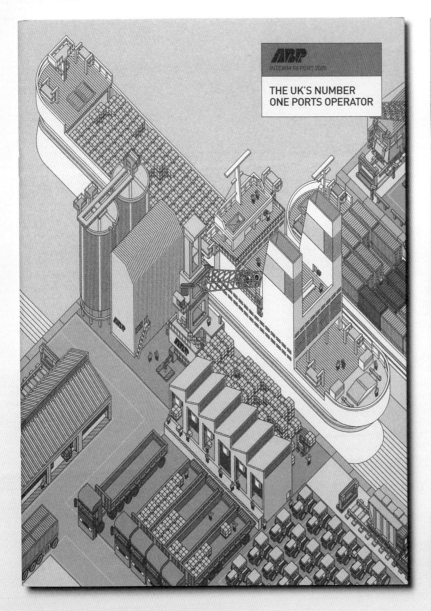

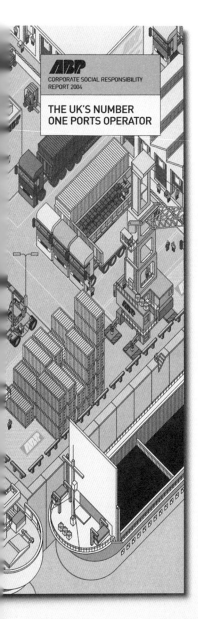

ABP
CORPORATE SOCIAL RESPONSIBILITY
REPORT 2004

THE UK'S NUMBER
ONE PORTS OPERATOR

ABP
ANNUAL REPORT & ACCOUNTS 2004

THE UK'S NUMBER
ONE PORTS OPERATOR

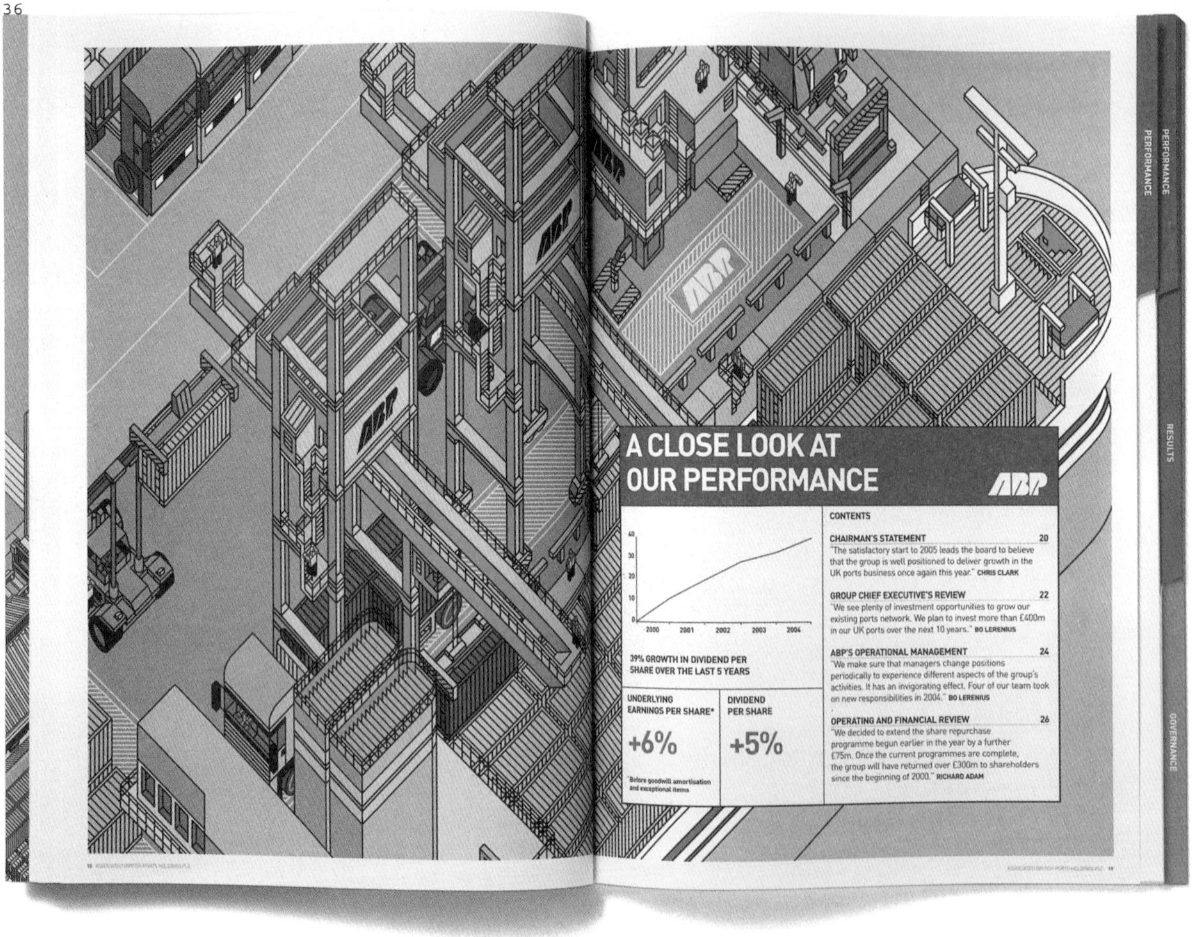

PERFORMANCE
PERFORMANCE
RESULTS
GOVERNANCE
A CLOSE LOOK AT OUR PERFORMANCE
ABP
40
30
20
10
0
2000
2001
2002
2003
2004
39% GROWTH IN DIVIDEND PER SHARE OVER THE LAST 5 YEARS
UNDERLYING EARNINGS PER SHARE*
+6%
*Before goodwill amortisation and exceptional items
DIVIDEND PER SHARE
+5%
CONTENTS
CHAIRMAN'S STATEMENT 20
"The satisfactory start to 2005 leads the board to believe that the group is well positioned to deliver growth in the UK ports business once again this year." CHRIS CLARK
GROUP CHIEF EXECUTIVE'S REVIEW 22
"We see plenty of investment opportunities to grow our existing ports network. We plan to invest more than £400m in our UK ports over the next 10 years." BO LERENIUS
ABP'S OPERATIONAL MANAGEMENT 24
"We make sure that managers change positions periodically to experience different aspects of the group's activities. It has an invigorating effect. Four of our team took on new responsibilities in 2004." BO LERENIUS
OPERATING AND FINANCIAL REVIEW 26
"We decided to extend the share repurchase programme begun earlier in the year by a further £75m. Once the current programmes are complete, the group will have returned over £300m to shareholders since the beginning of 2000." RICHARD ADAM

NEW ROLL-ON/ROLL-OFF TERMINAL AT IMMINGHAM OUTER HARBOUR

PROJECT OVERVIEW
A £35m project to develop a new roll-on/roll-off terminal at the Port of Immingham in partnership with DFDS Tor Line. ABP is investing £27.5m in dredging some 40 acres of inter-tidal mud-flats and creating riverside berths in the outer harbour. A further 50 acres of adjacent land will be redeveloped to provide operational space. Project partner DFDS Tor Line is investing in site infrastructure such as buildings, terminal equipment and roll-on/roll-off ramps.

CURRENT STATUS
Construction is under way and the new terminal is expected to become operational in 2006.

BACKGROUND
DFDS Tor Line is a leading supplier of roll-on/roll-off liner shipping services, primarily in the North Sea and Baltic Sea, and transports around 8m tonnes of freight annually. It is part of DFDS, the oldest and largest shipping company in Denmark, which is listed on the Copenhagen Stock Exchange.

Immingham and its sister port Grimsby have been doing business with DFDS since 1885 and the company continues to be a major customer today.

In 1995, ABP built the DFDS Nordic Terminal, a four-berth in-dock roll-on/roll-off facility. DFDS Tor Line's business at Immingham has since almost doubled.

THE ROLL-ON/ROLL-OFF FREIGHT MARKET
Freight transported by roll-on/roll-off vessels can range from driver-accompanied lorries to unaccompanied trailers that are loaded on and off using specialist equipment. Figure 1 sets out an analysis of the roll-on/roll-off traffic handled by the UK's ports during 2003.

Roll-on/roll-off is one of the port industry's fastest-growing sectors. The growth in roll-on/roll-off traffic since 1995 can be seen in figure 2.

* Source: Department for Transport Statistics Report: Maritime Statistics 2003 (latest available data)

FIGURE 1
UK PORTS: 2003 ROLL-ON/ROLL-OFF TRAFFIC*

■ ROAD GOODS VEHICLES 33%
■ UNACCOMPANIED TRAILERS 26%
■ IMPORT/EXPORT VEHICLES 36%
■ OTHER 5%

FIGURE 2
UK PORTS GROWTH IN ROLL-ON/ROLL-OFF TRAFFIC SINCE 1996 ('000 UNITS)*

FIGURE 3
FIVE-YEAR GROWTH IN ROLL-ON/ROLL-OFF TRAFFIC AT GRIMSBY & IMMINGHAM (UNITS)

— The UK's increasing requirement to import finished goods

— The centralisation and rationalisation of production by motor manufacturers

As the market has grown and competition between operators has intensified, the importance of service factors such as high reliability and frequency of sailings has increased. Consequently, there is heavy demand for dedicated port terminals that can be customised to an operator's requirements. There is also a trend towards the use of larger vessels on roll-on/roll-off routes for the economies of scale that they offer.

As the UK's largest ports group, ABP is a major player in the roll-on/roll-off market. The group had a market share of over 23 per cent in 2003. Although passenger services also operate from our Ports of Fleetwood, Hull, Plymouth, Swansea and Troon, freight services are the focus of our roll-on/roll-off activities. This new terminal brings total investment in roll-on/roll-off facilities at our ports since 1999 to over £60m.

Immingham, together with its sister port of Grimsby, is a major centre for roll-on/roll-off traffic. It too has seen significant growth of around 30 per cent since 2000, with over 60 scheduled weekly departures for unit load services.

Notwithstanding the introduction of services through the Channel Tunnel in 1995, roll-on/roll-off volumes handled by the UK ports in 2003 were almost 38 per cent above the 1996 level; volume growth of 45 per cent is forecast between 2000 and 2010.

Factors driving this growth include:

— The growing status of roll-on/roll-off within Europe as the transport method of choice for finished goods, due to the flexibility of the system which allows for rapid loading and quick turnarounds.

CUSTOMER DEMAND
Immingham's location makes it an ideal port of call for roll-on/roll-off services operating on North Sea routes. Located on the Humber Estuary, it enjoys excellent distribution links. It is near to both the main shipping lanes and the UK's industrial heartland; 40m UK consumers can be reached by road within four hours.

DFDS Tor Line already operates the highly successful DFDS Nordic Terminal at Immingham and is looking to expand its business further. It is currently investing in six new vessels for its North Sea services, of which three are already in operation on the Immingham - Gothenburg service.

ABP is developing Immingham Outer Harbour, which is outside the enclosed dock system, in partnership with DFDS Tor Line to create river berths capable of accommodating vessels of up to 225 metres long, 35 metres wide and

with a draught of up to 10 metres at all stages of tide. The new berths will create extra capacity to accommodate the new vessels as they come on stream and will also optimise their handling. In addition, the outer harbour location will provide a high degree of weather protection. These attributes will enable DFDS Tor Line to respond to the demands of its customers by increasing the frequency of its service.

VIABILITY
Given its strategic location and the proven success of DFDS Nordic Terminal, Immingham was the natural choice for DFDS Tor Line as it looked to expand its operations on the east coast of the UK, especially as its UK headquarters are already there.

ABP was able to use its proven relationship with the company to design a bespoke solution. A 25-year agreement that incorporates an annual facility fee and a guaranteed minimum volume

arrangement ensures that the project meets the group's investment criteria.

Negotiations for projects of this scale do not take place overnight, which is why ABP took the initiative and applied for planning permission for the development in advance. To achieve this, we established a pioneering agreement with leading conservation bodies. They agreed to support our planning application in return for a commitment by ABP to provide alternative wildlife habitats to compensate for the group's port developments on the Humber Estuary.

CONCLUSION
Investing in long-term contracts with quality customers is at the heart of ABP's growth strategy. This project typifies our approach. By working closely with DFDS Tor Line, we have been able to expand the Port of Immingham in a low-risk way while accommodating the needs of a valued customer.

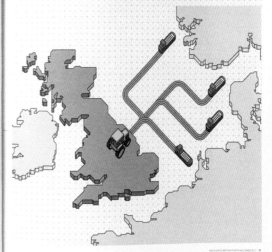

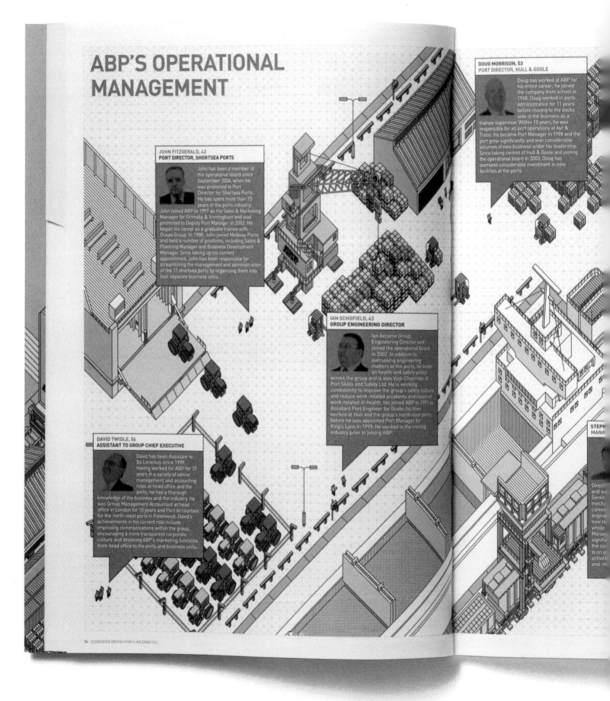

ABP'S OPERATIONAL MANAGEMENT

JOHN FITZGERALD, 42
PORT DIRECTOR, SHORTSEA PORTS

John has been a member of the operational board since September 2004, when he was promoted to Port Director for Shortsea Ports. He has spent more than 15 years in the ports industry. John joined ABP in 1997 as the Sales & Marketing Manager for Grimsby & Immingham and was promoted to Deputy Port Manager in 2002. He began his career as a graduate trainee with Ocean Group. In 1988, John joined Medway Ports and held a number of positions, including Sales & Planning Manager and Business Development Manager. Since taking up his current appointment, John has been responsible for streamlining the management and administration of the 11 shortsea ports by organising them into four separate business units.

DOUG MORRISON, 53
PORT DIRECTOR, HULL & GOOLE

Doug has worked at ABP for his entire career; he joined the company from school in 1968. Doug worked in ports administration for 11 years before moving to the docks side of the business as a trainee supervisor. Within 10 years, he was responsible for all port operations at Ayr & Troon. He became Port Manager in 1998 and the port grew significantly and won considerable volumes of new business under his leadership. Since taking control of Hull & Goole and joining the operational board in 2003, Doug has overseen considerable investment in new facilities at the ports.

IAN SCHOFIELD, 43
GROUP ENGINEERING DIRECTOR

Ian became Group Engineering Director and joined the operational board in 2002. In addition to overseeing engineering matters at the ports, he leads on health and safety policy across the group and is also Vice-Chairman of Port Skills and Safety Ltd. He is working consistently to improve the group's safety culture and reduce work-related accidents and cases of work-related ill-health. Ian joined ABP in 1991 as Assistant Port Engineer for Goole; he then worked at Hull and the group's north-east ports, before he was appointed Port Manager for King's Lynn in 1999. He worked in the mining industry prior to joining ABP.

DAVID TWIDLE, 56
ASSISTANT TO GROUP CHIEF EXECUTIVE

David has been Assistant to Bo Lerenius since 1999. Having worked for ABP for 37 years in a variety of senior management and accounting roles at head office and the ports, he has a thorough knowledge of the business and the industry. He was Group Management Accountant at head office in London for 10 years and Port Accountant for the north-west ports in Fleetwood. David's achievements in his current role include improving communications within the group, encouraging a more transparent corporate culture and devolving ABP's marketing functions from head office to the ports and business units.

STEPH...
MANA...

Direct... and wa... Servic... mech... caree... engine... now r... whole... Manag... signifi... the co... is on e... activiti... and -h...

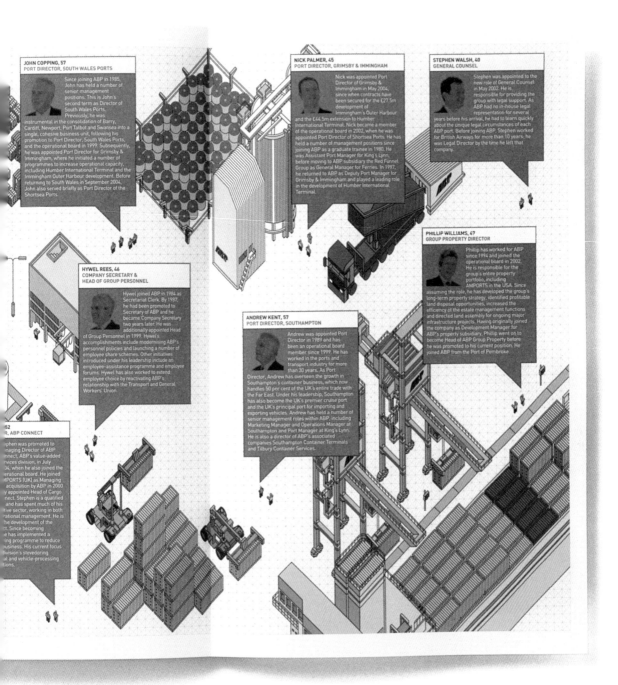

JOHN COPPING, 57
PORT DIRECTOR, SOUTH WALES PORTS

Since joining ABP in 1985, John has held a number of senior management positions. This is John's second term as Director of South Wales Ports. Previously, he was instrumental in the consolidation of Barry, Cardiff, Newport, Port Talbot and Swansea into a single, cohesive business unit, following his promotion to Port Director, South Wales Ports, and the operational board in 1999. Subsequently, he was appointed Port Director for Grimsby & Immingham, where he initiated a number of programmes to increase operational capacity, including Humber International Terminal and the Immingham Outer Harbour development. Before returning to South Wales in September 2004, John also served briefly as Port Director of the Shortsea Ports.

NICK PALMER, 45
PORT DIRECTOR, GRIMSBY & IMMINGHAM

Nick was appointed Port Director of Grimsby & Immingham in May 2004, since when contracts have been secured for the £27.5m development of Immingham's Outer Harbour and the £44.5m extension to Humber International Terminal. Nick became a member of the operational board in 2002, when he was appointed Port Director of Shortsea Ports. He has held a number of management positions since joining ABP as a graduate trainee in 1980. He was Assistant Port Manager for King's Lynn, before moving to ABP subsidiary the Red Funnel Group as General Manager for Ferries. In 1997, he returned to ABP as Deputy Port Manager for Grimsby & Immingham and played a leading role in the development of Humber International Terminal.

STEPHEN WALSH, 40
GENERAL COUNSEL

Stephen was appointed to the new role of General Counsel in May 2002. He is responsible for providing the group with legal support. As ABP had no in-house legal representation for several years before his arrival, he had to learn quickly about the unique legal circumstances of each ABP port. Before joining ABP, Stephen worked for British Airways for more than 10 years; he was Legal Director by the time he left that company.

HYWEL REES, 46
COMPANY SECRETARY &
HEAD OF GROUP PERSONNEL

Hywel joined ABP in 1984 as Secretariat Clerk. By 1987, he had been promoted to Secretary of ABP and he became Company Secretary two years later. He was additionally appointed Head of Group Personnel in 1999. Hywel's accomplishments include modernising ABP's personnel policies and launching a number of employee share schemes. Other initiatives introduced under his leadership include an employee-assistance programme and employee forums. Hywel has also worked to extend employee choice by reactivating ABP's relationship with the Transport and General Workers' Union.

PHILLIP WILLIAMS, 47
GROUP PROPERTY DIRECTOR

Phillip has worked for ABP since 1994 and joined the operational board in 2002. He is responsible for the group's entire property portfolio, including AMPORTS in the USA. Since assuming the role, he has developed the group's long-term property strategy, identified profitable land disposal opportunities, increased the efficiency of the estate management functions and directed land assembly for ongoing major infrastructure projects. Having originally joined the company as Development Manager for ABP's property subsidiary, Phillip went on to become Head of ABP Group Property before he was promoted to his current position. He joined ABP from the Port of Pembroke.

ANDREW KENT, 57
PORT DIRECTOR, SOUTHAMPTON

Andrew was appointed Port Director in 1989 and has been an operational board member since 1999. He has worked in the ports and transport industry for more than 30 years. As Port Director, Andrew has overseen the growth in Southampton's container business, which now handles 50 per cent of the UK's entire trade with the Far East. Under his leadership, Southampton has also become the UK's premier cruise port and the UK's principal port for importing and exporting vehicles. Andrew has held a number of senior management roles within ABP, including Marketing Manager and Operations Manager at Southampton and Port Manager at King's Lynn. He is also a director of ABP's associated companies Southampton Container Terminals and Tilbury Container Services.

[...]EPHEN [...]62
[...]R, ABP CONNECT

[...]phen was promoted to [...]aging Director of ABP [...]nnect, ABP's value-added [...]vices division, in July [...]4, when he also joined the [...]erational board. He joined [...]PORTS (UK) as Managing [...] acquisition by ABP in 2000 [...]y appointed Head of Cargo [...]nect. Stephen is a qualified [...] and has spent much of his [...]ive sector, working in both [...]rational management. He is [...]he development of the [...]ct. Since becoming [...] he has implemented a [...]ng programme to reduce [...] business. His current focus [...]vision's stevedoring [...]al and vehicle-processing [...]tions.

ABP Annual Report 2005

Client Associated British Ports *Design* Jodie Wightman *Year* 2005

A striking solution was arrived at, driven by a distinctive illustration led visual language, and supported by a typographic style and layout that achieve optimum clarity and a contemporary tone. Illustrator Lucinda Rogers was commissioned to develop an animated series of sketches, which have been applied to the front and back cover and dividing pages. The images reflect the scale and complexity of a port and thus, ABP's business.

Chairman's statement

I am pleased to report that the group achieved a satisfactory operating performance and made significant progress on its major Humber projects during 2005

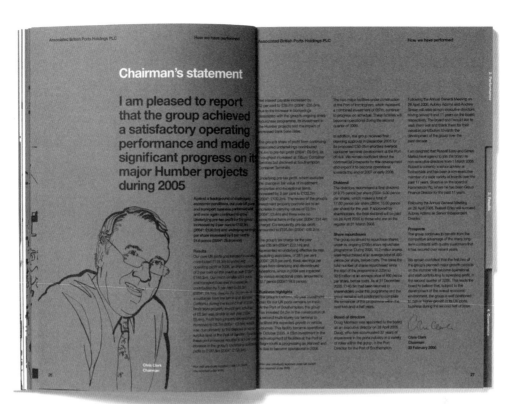

Chris Clark
Chairman

26

27

Chris Clark
Chairman
22 February 2006

Our long-term agreement supporting ABP's investment in Humber International Terminal, Phase 2, is a valuable part of our fuel supply strategy

Peter Emery, Production Director, Drax Group plc

Humber International Terminal: generating revenue from coal

Facts and figures

- **£58.5m** is the cost of the terminal, being built by around
- **150** people at any one time over the
- **24** months it is taking to build, for
- **5** quality customers, so that approximately
- **180** coal-laden vessels can call at Immingham each year, to be loaded on some
- **130** trains every week, to bring in up to
- **9.5** million tonnes of coal per annum, which is enough coal to generate over
- **7%** of the UK's electricity needs.

Immingham coal volumes
(million tonnes)

2001	2002	2003	2004	2005

16

17

How we have performed

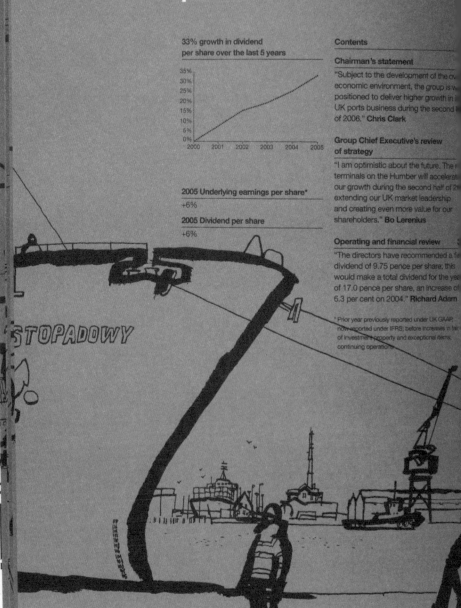

33% growth in dividend
per share over the last 5 years

35%
30%
25%
20%
15%
10%
5%
0%
2000   2001   2002   2003   2004   2005

2005 Underlying earnings per share*

+6%

2005 Dividend per share

+6%

* Prior year previously reported under UK GAAP,
now reported under IFRS; before increases in fair
of investment property and exceptional items;
continuing operations.

Contents

Chairman's statement

"Subject to the development of the ov
economic environment, the group is w
positioned to deliver higher growth in
UK ports business during the second
of 2006." **Chris Clark**

Group Chief Executive's review
of strategy

"I am optimistic about the future. The
terminals on the Humber will accelerat
our growth during the second half of 2
extending our UK market leadership
and creating even more value for our
shareholders." **Bo Lerenius**

Operating and financial review

"The directors have recommended a fi
dividend of 9.75 pence per share; this
would make a total dividend for the yea
of 17.0 pence per share, an increase o
6.3 per cent on 2004." **Richard Adam**

2

2. Performance

3. Results

4. Governance

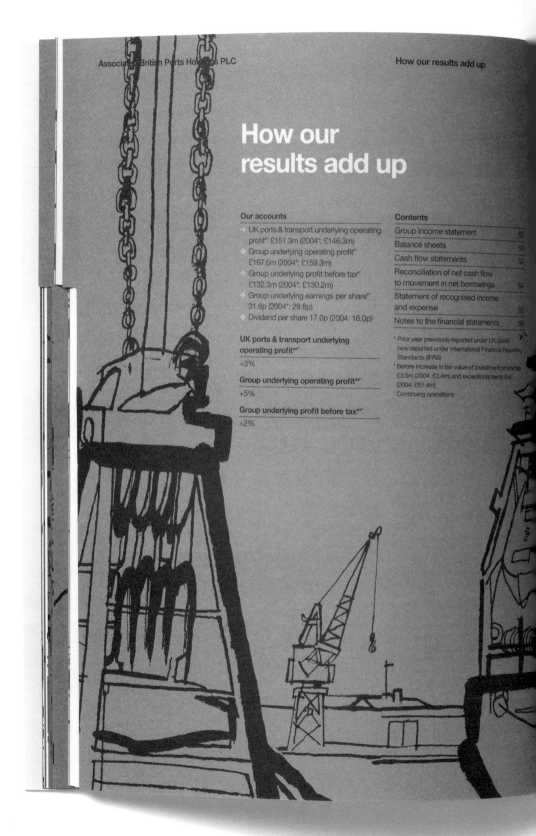

How our results add up

Our accounts

- → UK ports & transport underlying operating profit*' £151.3m (2004*: £146.3m)
- → Group underlying operating profit' £167.6m (2004*: £159.3m)
- → Group underlying profit before tax' £132.3m (2004*: £130.2m)
- → Group underlying earnings per share*' 31.6p (2004*: 29.8p)
- → Dividend per share 17.0p (2004: 16.0p)

UK ports & transport underlying operating profit**'

+3%

Group underlying operating profit*'

+5%

Group underlying profit before tax**'

+2%

Contents

* Prior year previously reported under UK GAAP, now reported under International Financial Reporting Standards (IFRS)

' Before increase in fair value of investment properties £3.5m (2004: £3.4m) and exceptional items £nil (2004: £51.4m)

'' Continuing operations

3

Monsters Ink

Client NB:Studio *Design* Jodie Wightman *Year* 2006

Monsters ink is a self-initiated project created as a giveaway for an NB:Studio Halloween party. The book also acts as a promotional piece for copy writer Vivienne Hamilton and illustrator James Graham. Monsters stir our hearts with an uncommon intensity. They lend a vital edge to our daily lives -a vague malevolence in the office, a creeping uneasiness on our walk home and a disquieting sense of danger at bedtime-. In the interest of 'feeling the fear and doing it anyway', we brought together an indispensable guide to all that's ghastly, misshapen, ghoulish and generally hideous.

After researching mythical monsters throughout different cultures, we commissioned James Graham to illustrate a selected few in his eccentric and eclectic hand drawn style. Text and image was lovingly screen printed in white onto black paper to give a really contrasting and dark feel to the book.

346

A malevolent, shape-shifting monster
whose origins are probably Arabic.
A **Ghoul's** favourite habitat is
a burial ground or barren land
where it likes to feast on corpses
supplemented with the flesh of young
children it might lure into its path.
It can assume the guise of many
animals (hyenas are common) and
has even been spotted riding on
dogs and hares. Not to be confused
with other types of 'undead' namely
vampires and zombies.

A monstrous race of super-strong
huge beings as tall as mountains
with shaggy hair and dragon scales
on their feet. From Scandinavia
to Eastern Europe all **Giants** are
typified by a remarkable stupidity
with a penchant for tossing boulders
and cannibalism. Although fierce,
if encountered their intellectual
incompetence offers intended
victims a good chance of survival
by outwitting them.

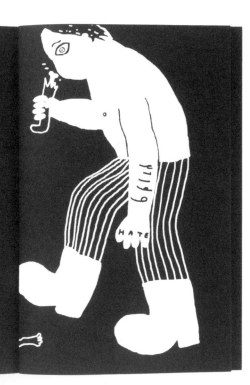

Originally very beautiful women transformed into hideously ugly monsters, **Gorgons** are identified by the crown of writhing live snakes on their heads. Noted in many classical Greek texts as Queens of the Underworld, their additional features include a round flat face, lolling tongue and sometimes the tusks of a boar. The most famous example of this fearsome creature is undoubtedly Medusa, who, like her sisters, could turn onlookers into stone.

Tate Membership

Client Tate *Design* Sarah Fullerton *Art Direction* Alan Dye, Ben Stott, Nick Finney *Year* 2006

A membership pack that provides 'added value' to being a member.

We set out to create a desirable, must have, product. By creating a distinct style, solely for membership, we generated an exclusive feel extending across a range of collateral. We wanted to avoid a corporate look, so shuned the existing Tate colour palette in favour of photography of real people interacting with art in any of the four galleries. Working with photographer Matt Stuart we softened the images to make them 'Tate'.

The result was a product which communicates that Tate values its members, creating valued loyalty in return.

350

Welcome to a whole year of unlimited
free visits to outstanding exhibitions
at all four Tate galleries.

This pack contains:

— your membership card showing
  your current membership type,
  any additional benefits you have
  requested and your personal
  membership number

— a Members handbook to help
  you make the most of your
  membership

— the current Tate guide to what's
  on which will be sent to you
  every other month

Handbook
Tate Members

TATE

Please bring this card with you
whenever you plan to visit Tate.

TATE

Credits

p 9 — Jeff Koons
         *Three Ball Total Equilibrium Tank
         (Two Dr J Silver Series, Spalding
         NBA Tip-Off)* 1985
         © Jeff Koons
p 12 — (image 1) David Nash
         Pyramid, Sphere, Cube —
         part of the *David Nash* exhibition
         at Tate St Ives 2004
         © The artist
      — (image 2) Sir Thomas Brock
         Eve 1900
      — (image 3) Robert Bevan
         Horse Sale at the Barbican 1912
p 16 — John Singer Sargent
         *Essie, Ruby and Ferdinand, Children
         of Asher Wertheimer* 1902
p 19 — (image 1) Kara Walker
         *Grub for Sharks: A Concession
         to the Negro Populace* 2004
         © The artist
         Courtesy of Brent Sikkema NYC
      — (image 2) Friedrich Kunath
         Going to Quauhnahuac 2003
         and *No I don't really want to die,
         I only want to die in your eyes* 2004
         © The artist, Courtesy BQ, Cologne
p 20 — (image 1) Alberto Giacometti
         Collection of works in situ
         © ADAGP, Paris and DACS,
         London 2005
      — (image 2) John Currin
         Honeymoon Nude 1998
         © The artist, c/o Tate
p 23 — Patrick Heron
         Window for St Ives 1992
         © Tate, 2005
p 24 — Barbara Hepworth
         Sphere with Inner Form 1963
         © Bowness, Hepworth Estate, 2005

Please note that as Tate's exhibitions and
displays change regularly, the works of
art illustrated in this handbook may no longer
be on display at the time of your visit.

Tate Members registered charity no. 313021.

Design by NB Studio
Photography © Matt Stuart

354

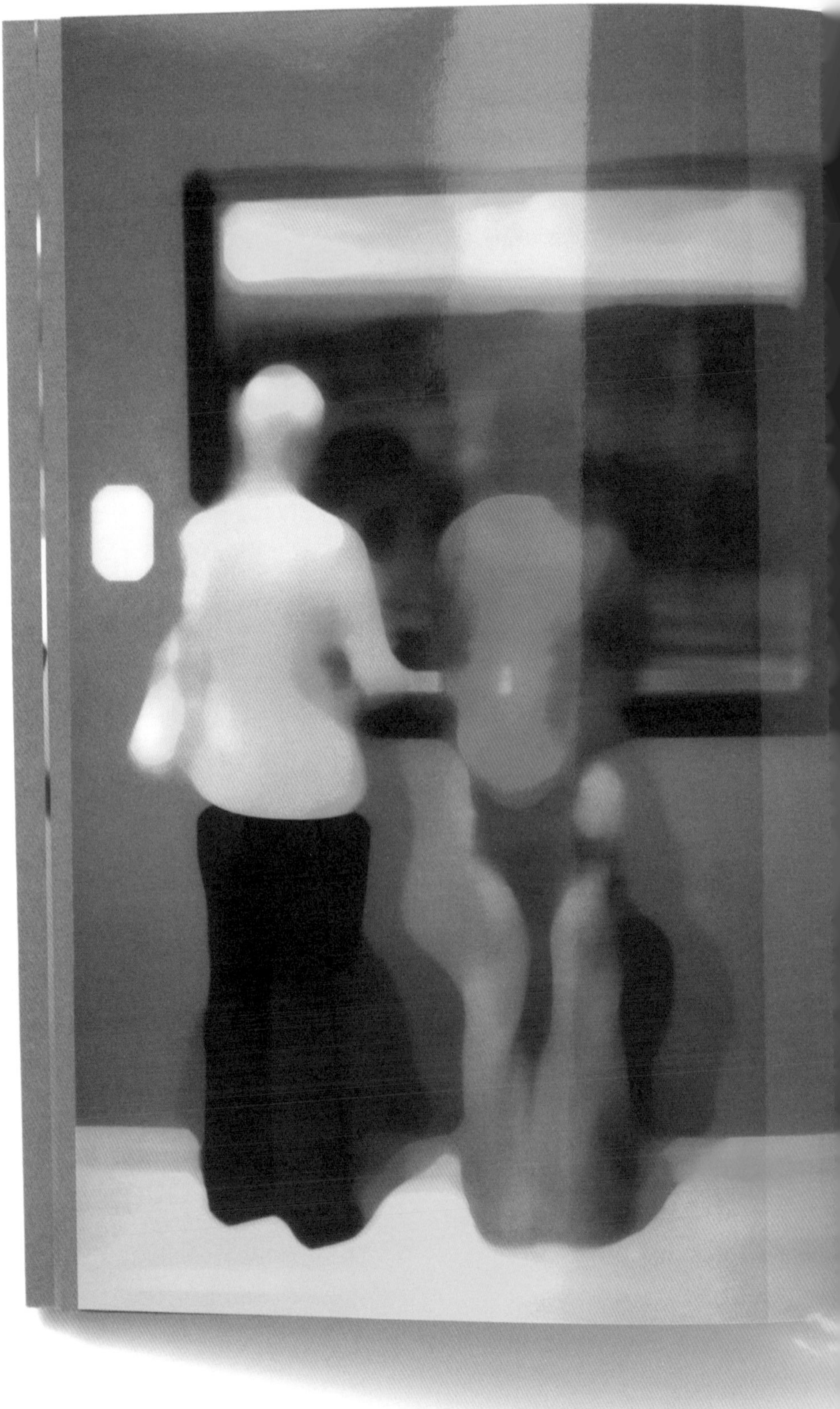

Membership benefits
Special access to exhibitions

As a Member you enjoy unlimited free access to around fifteen special exhibitions across all four Tate galleries throughout the year, giving you the flexibility to visit and revisit favourite works of art and discover less familiar artists at no extra cost. In St Ives you can also visit the Barbara Hepworth Museum and Garden free of charge. Members may bring up to six family children aged sixteen or under with them to exhibitions and Members Rooms.

One of the other great benefits of membership is not needing to queue for tickets. As a general rule, Members do not need to obtain a ticket for exhibitions — simply show your membership card at the entrance and present it for scanning. The exception is very popular exhibitions when, to ensure maximum viewing comfort and safety, timed tickets are issued to all visitors and there may also be a short wait to enter the galleries. When timed tickets are required, you should arrange your tickets ahead of your visit to ensure availability of your preferred time — this service is included in your membership package at no additional cost. Book tickets online at tate.org.uk/members or call Membership Services on 020 7887 8752. We will write to let you know when it is advisable to book in advance.

We also recommend you book ahead if you plan to visit at the weekend or at the beginning or end of any exhibition, as these too tend to be busy times.

The Portrait Now
Client The National Portrait Gallery *Design* Daniel Lock, Eng Su *Art Directors* Alan Dye, Ben Stott, Nick Finney *Year* 2006
The Portrait Now presents over ninety of the best contemporary portraits from across the world, including the most recent work of internationally acclaimed artists. Images of the work was backed up by tight typography and rigorous layout.

his project to include other cities in Western Europe, the United States, and Asia. In these photographs, buildings and cars become as evocative as human faces. Accustomed to hurrying through the city with an almost unseeing eye, we are encouraged, in the artist's words 'to give pause, to move to investigative viewing'. Struth also makes portraits of friends and acquaintances, usually in intimate gatherings, as if contrasting the public environment of architecture with the private space of the family. These photographs are explorations of social dynamics, showing how people within a tightly-knit group arrange themselves in front of the camera.

Sam Taylor-Wood
Ed Harris, from the series 'Crying Men', 2002
C-print mounted on aluminium
862 x 1117mm
(33 15/16 x 43 15/16")
© Sam Taylor-Wood, courtesy Jay Jopling/White Cube (London)

Sam Taylor-Wood graduated from Goldsmiths College in 1990. Her work in photography and film is distinguished by an ironic and subversive use of the media, which centres on the creation of enigmatic situations replete with a latent but explosive energy. In films like *Noli Me Tangere* (1998), and photographs such as *Wrecked* (1996) she explores the boundaries between the sacred and profane, fusing religious imagery informed by the Renaissance and baroque periods with the secular, urban and contemporary landscape which she inhabits. Since her solo show at White Cube in 1995, Taylor-Wood has had numerous shows including Fundico La Caixa, Barcelona, Hirshhorn Museum, Washington DC, and Matthew Marks Gallery in New York. In 1997 she received the Illy Café Prize for the Most Promising New Artist at the Venice Biennale and was nominated for the Turner Prize in 1998. The Hayward Gallery hosted a major survey of Taylor-Woods's work in 2002.

Juergen Teller
Yves Saint Laurent, 2000
C-print
254 x 304.8mm
(10 x 12")
© Juergen Teller

Juergen Teller was born in 1964 in Erlangen, Germany and after a short spell working as an apprentice bow maker, he began his career as a photographer. He studied at the Bayerische Staatslehranstalt für Photographie in Munich between 1984 and 1986, and then moved to London in September 1986. His ad campaigns have included work for Marc Jacobs, Helmut Lang, Yves Saint Laurent and Calvin Klein. He has photographed amongst others, Charlotte Rampling, Pele, Barbara Cartland, Kate Moss, William Eggleston, Kurt Cobain, Bjork, Elton John, O.J. Simpson and Arnold Schwarzenegger. Recent exhibitions of his work include: *Louis XV*, Contemporary Fine Arts, Berlin, 2005; *Fashioning Fiction*, MoMA, New York, 2004; *Ich bin vierzig*, Kunsthalle Wien, 2004, and an exhibition at The Cartier Foundation, Paris, 2006.

Mario Testino
The Prince of Wales with sons Prince William and Prince Harry, 2004
© Mario Testino

Mario Testino was born in Lima, Peru. He studied Economics, Law and International Relations before moving to London to begin his formal training in photography. Mario travels extensively shooting for American, British, French and Italian *Vogue*, *L'Uomo Vogue* and *Vanity Fair*. He has worked with many high-profile celebrities including the British royals, and has contributed to the images of leading fashion houses. *Mario Testino: Portraits* opened at the National Portrait Gallery in London, February 2002 and the exhibition has travelled around the world stopping in Milan, Amsterdam, Edinburgh and Tokyo. As well as many other international solo exhibitions, Testino has been involved with several book projects. Recently, a collaboration with Marie Stopes International, Interact Worldwide and the United Nations Population Fund (UNFPA) called *Women to Women: Positively Speaking* was launched to raise awareness of women living with HIV/AIDS.

Andrew Tift
Alexander and Eun Ju, 2004
Acrylic on canvas
1127 x 973mm (44 3/8 x 38 1/4")
© Andrew Tift

Andrew Tift graduated with a first-class honours degree and a Master of Arts degree from the University of Central England. In 1995 he had a portrait-based solo exhibition at the National Portrait Gallery in London following a visit to Japan, which was sponsored by BP. He has exhibited in the BP Portrait Award at the National Portrait Gallery nine times and has been short listed for the prize on three different occasions. His painting of the Rt Hon. Tony Benn for the Palace of Westminster collection won third prize at the 1999 BP Portrait Award. Tift has won many other awards including The Japan Festival Award, The European Painting Award at the Frissiras Museum in Athens and the Emerson Group Award at the Manchester Academy of Fine Arts. In 1998 he was commissioned to paint the portraits of Neil and Glenys Kinnock for the collection at the National Portrait Gallery, London, which was unveiled in 2002.

Wolfgang Tillmans
Peter Saville, 2002
C-print
610 x 508mm (24 x 20")
© Wolfgang Tillmans

Wolfgang Tillmans was born in Remscheid, Germany in 1968 and studied at Bournemouth & Poole College of Art and Design. He is widely regarded as one of the most influential artists of his generation. His work, whilst appearing to capture the immediacy of the moment and character of the subject, also examines the dynamics of photographic representation. From the outset he ignored the traditional separation of art exhibited in a gallery from images and ideas conveyed through other forms of publication, giving equal weight to both. His expansive floor to ceiling installations feature images of subcultures and political movements, as well as portraits, landscapes, still-lifes and abstract imagery varying in

scale from postcard to wall-sized prints. His work has been shown at the Museum of Modern Art, New York in 1996 and at Tate Britain, London, in a major retrospective in 2003. He was awarded the Turner Prize in 2000.

Daphne Todd
Me in a magnifying mirror, 2001
Oil on panel
412.8 x 406.4mm (16 1/4 x 16")
© Daphne Todd, by kind permission of Messums Gallery

Daphne Todd studied at the Slade School of Fine Art, as both an undergraduate and postgraduate (1964–71), under the direction of Sir William Coldstream. While she was there she was awarded the Tonks Drawing Prize; the intercollegiate David Murray Award for landscape painting and the British Institute Award for figurative painting. She taught part time at the Byam Shaw and at the Heatherley School of Art in the 1970s, and then spent two years in Spain painting landscapes. She returned to become Director of Studies of Heatherleys (1980–86). She exhibited widely in group shows during the period including the Royal Academy's *Summer Exhibition*, but ceased to submit after objecting publicly to their *Sensation* exhibition. Major prizes include first prize for the Hunting National Art Prize in 1984, and the Ondaatje Prize for Portraiture and the Gold Medal of the Royal Society of Portrait Painters in 2001.

Francisco Toledo
Self-Portrait XXXVIII, 2000
Mixed colour intaglio
280 x 220mm (11 1/4 x 8 3/4")
© Francisco Toledo

Francisco Toledo was born in Oaxaca, Mexico in 1940. He studied at the Escuela de Bellas Artes de Oaxaca and the Centro Superior de Artes Aplicadas del Instituto Nacional de Bellas Artes, Mexico, where he studied graphic arts. In 1960 he moved to Paris from where he travelled throughout Europe. In 1965 he returned to Mexico and started to promote and protect the arts and crafts in his native state of Oaxaca; he designed tapestries with the craftsmen of Teotitlan del Valle and in 1988 he created the Instituto de Artes Graficas de Oaxaca. Toledo's outstanding creativity has been expressed in pottery, sculpture, weaving, graphic arts and painting. He has had exhibitions in Argentina, Brazil, Colombia, Ecuador, Spain, Belgium and the USA. Toledo is a patron of the arts and crafts of Oaxaca.

Luc Tuymans
Portrait, 2000
Oil on canvas
670 x 390mm (26 3/8 x 15 3/8")
Courtesy Zeno X Gallery, Antwerp

Tuymans was born in Mortsel, Belgium in 1958. He has been recognized in Europe for creating a powerful body of work that reaffirms the importance of painting in a climate that continually questions the legitimacy of the medium. Tuymans feels that painting must continually confront the power and fragmentation of the media. The human condition on the heels of two World Wars and the current proliferation of media images of global bloodshed and disaster have pushed humankind to the point of numbness. For Tuymans this imaging trend represents 'absolute horror and absolute indifference at the same time; it is a perversity that creates itself entirely in images. In my view, the perversity of these images is the right idea to start from'. Solo exhibitions include: The Renaissance Society, Chicago, 1995; Kunstmuseum St Gallen, 2003; Helsinki Kunsthalle, Finland, 2003; Pinakothek der Moderne, München, 2004; Museo Tamayo, Mexico City, 2004; K21 Düsseldorf and Tate Modern, London, 2004. He lives and works in Antwerp.

Bettina von Zwehl
#5 from the series 'Alina', 2004
C-print
598 x 464mm (23 1/2 x 18 1/4")
© Bettina von Zwehl

Bettina von Zwehl was born in Munich, Germany in 1971 and studied in London, firstly at the London College of Printing (BA Photography) 1997, and then at the Royal College of Art, London (MA Fine Art Photography) 1999. Solo exhibitions include *An Anatomy of Control* 2000, Lombard-Freid Fine Arts, New York, 2000; Victoria Miro Gallery, The Project Space, London, 2002; and The Photographers' Gallery, London, 2004. A monograph of von Zwehl's work will be published by Steidl and Photoworks in 2006.

Gillian Wearing
Self-Portrait at Three years old, 2004
Digital C-print
1820 x 1220mm (71 3/4 x 48 1/2")
Courtesy Maureen Paley, London

London-based artist Gillian Wearing is known for her clever and acutely poignant photography and video work, exploring the complexity of human relationships. Gillian Wearing was born in Birmingham, England, in 1963. Winner of the prestigious Turner Prize in 1997. Wearing has participated in major exhibitions showcasing young British art, such as *Brilliant! New Art from London*, the Walker Art Center, Minneapolis, 1995, and *Sensation*, the Royal Academy, London, 1997. Wearing was honoured with a mid-career retrospective at the Serpentine Gallery, London, in 2000.

Antony Williams
Robert, Anne, and Henry Tann, 2004
Egg tempera
1168.4 x 1708.15mm
(46 x 67 1/4")
© Antony Williams, courtesy Petley Fine Art, London

Antony Williams is a member of the Royal Society of Portrait Painters, and his solo exhibitions include: Alternate Gallery, London, 1997; Sala Parés, Barcelona, 1999; Messum Gallery, London, 2000; Galería Leandro Navarro, Madrid, 2001; Petley Fine Art, Monaco, 2003; Petley Fine Art, London, 2004. He has won the Ondaatje Award, 1995, the Carroll Foundation Award, 1991 and 1995, and the Discerning Eye Award for Still Life, 1998.

assume vivid astro focus
y.o., 2002

Decal, CD
Variable dimensions (maximum size unlimited) Edition of 3, AP

The one man 'collective', assume vivid astro focus, works in a variety of mediums and draws from a plethora of inspiration. This portrait of Yoko Ono is intended to be installed on the floor and can be printed to any size. avaf gleefully appropriates art, music, images, and motifs from any resource he finds stimulating, including such disparate influences as psychedelia, glam, pop, and kitsch. In this case, the final montage portrait looks as equally drawn from Brazilian carnival costumes as it does from an acid trip, or even hippie renditions of Tibetan devotional imagery.

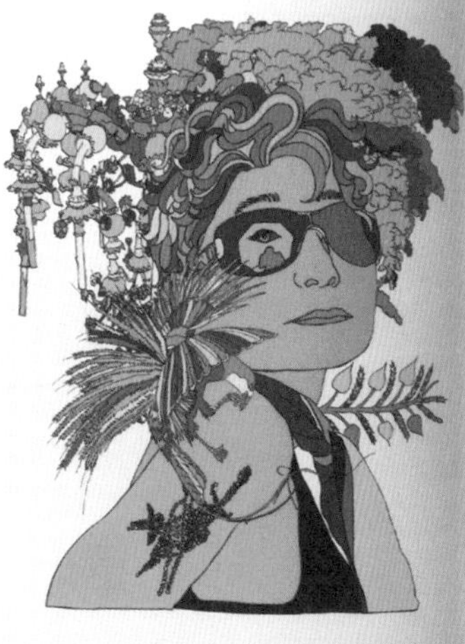

Gary Hume
Green Nicola, 2003

Gloss paint on aluminium
1800 x 1390mm
(70 7/8 x 54 3/4")

In this portrait, Gary Hume depicts fellow British artist Nicola Tyson. The portrait typifies his love of bright colours and adeptness in creating simple compositions. The shiny aluminium surface is bold and the process is simple, but the portrait is imbued with Hume's painterly touch. Hume's style draws inspiration from the worlds of fashion, poster design, and painting, gaining complexity from the tensions that exist between each. While the portrait might also reference certain aspects of advertising, or billboard displays, the reference is more critique than homage.

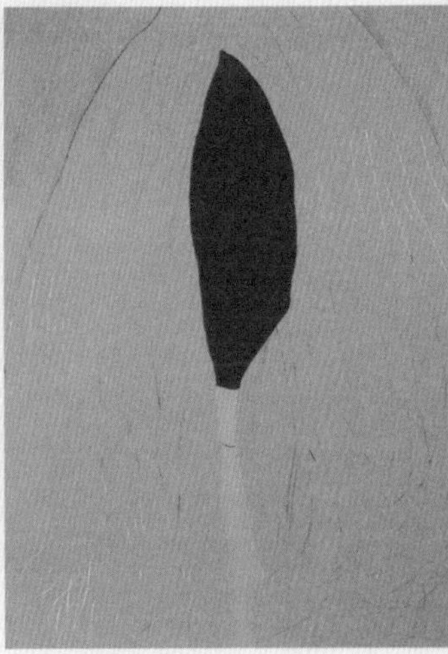

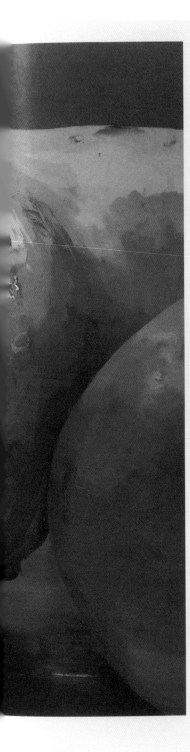

Jenny Saville
Reverse, 2002–3

Oil on canvas
2133 x 2439mm (84 x 96")

Reverse demonstrates Saville's skill at using her own body as a prop. The painting is part of a sequence of self-portraits, all of which came out of the artist's exposure to plastic surgery in New York City. During this time, Saville witnessed the manipulation of the human body, and subsequently sought to incorporate a similar quality in her work. In *Reverse*, 'The flesh becomes like a material,' Saville says, which allows her work to retain its characteristically raw, emotive style. 'I do hope I play out the contradictions that I feel, all the anxieties and dilemmas,' Saville comments. 'I see it as empowering that I manage to use my body to make something positive, whether I like it or not.' It is with both this positive attitude and her dedication to a truthful portrayal of the human condition that Saville approaches her work.

'Faces are the most
interesting things we see;
other people fascinate me,
and the most interesting
aspect of other people –
the point where we go
inside them – is the face.
It tells all.'

David Hockney
Peter Goulds Standing, 2005

Oil on canvas
1212.9 x 908.1mm (47 x 35")

David Hockney has been engaged with portraiture throughout his career. His self-portraits and portraits of his family and friends represent a visual diary of his life. Hockney's creative development and concerns about representation can also be traced through his portrait work. This portrait of his Los Angeles dealer, Peter Goulds, is one of a series of full-length standing figures produced entirely from life in 2005. These paintings are the culmination of many of Hockney's preoccupations with the painted portrait over the past fifty years. They follow on from a series of complex double portraits in watercolour also produced from life in 2002 and 2003.

Nick Bell Design
5.06 Tea Building
56 Shoreditch High Street
London E1 6JJ
+44 (0)20 7033 2991
www.nickbelldesign.co.uk

AJOS

Che Guevara: Revolutionay & Icon

Client V&A Publications *Designed by* Nick Bell Design *Creative director* Nick Bell *Designer* Sven Herzog *Year* 2006

A book not about Che Guevara but a particular photograph of him. The photograph by Alberto Korda, taken on 5 March 1960, is thought to be the most reproduced image in the history of photography. It has become an icon, symbolising anti-establishment thought and action. This book tells the extraordinary story of the image, bringing together photography, posters, film, fine art, clothing and artefacts from all over the world.

364

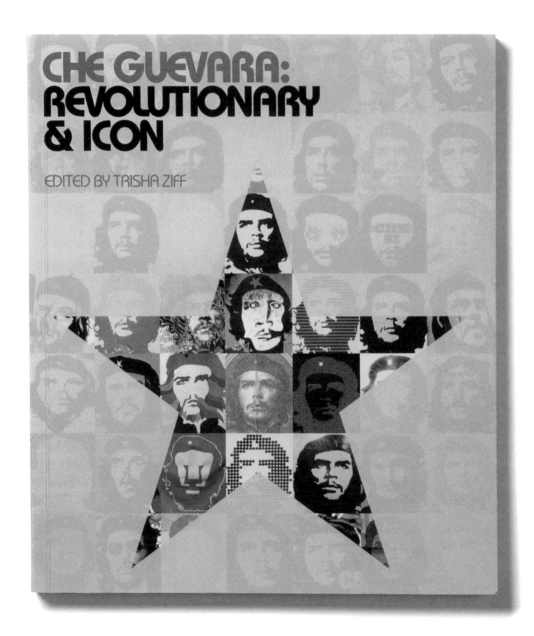

*Popular fast food ads featuring
a talking Chihuahua have offended
some members of Miami's Cuban
exile community who think the
latest commercial glorifies leftist
revolutionary Ernesto "Che"
Guevara.*

*The most recent in a series of
ads starring the dog with big ears
and bulging eyes has him posing
as a beret-wearing revolutionary
who appears before a crowd in a
public square and says "Viva
Gorditas," sending onlookers into
a cheering frenzy.*

*Some members of Miami's
800,000-strong Cuban exile
community interpreted the ad as a
parody of the stage play and movie
"Evita" and saw the Chihuahua
as Guevara. Taco Bell vice
president Peter Stack said the ads
were meant to portray revolution
"generically" and did not seek
to glorify any revolutionary figure.
In tests on Hispanic audiences, he
said, the response was "over-
whelmingly positive."*

*"The advertising is about our
revolutionary taco," Stack said.
"It's about Gordita-ism and not
any other kind of 'ism' out there."
Excerpt from MIAMI (Reuters)
1998. Copyright 1999 Reuters
Limited. All rights reserved.*

Come Alive! The spirited Art of Sister Corita
Client Four Corners Book *Designed by* Nick Bell Design *Creative director* Nick Bell *Designer* Helene Samson *Year* 2004
Admired by Charles and Ray Eames, Buckminster Fuller and Saul Bass, Sister Corita Kent (1918-1986) was one of the most innovative and unusual pop artists of the 1960s, battling the political and religious establishments and encouraging the creativity of thousands of people – all while living and practicing as a Catholic nun in California.

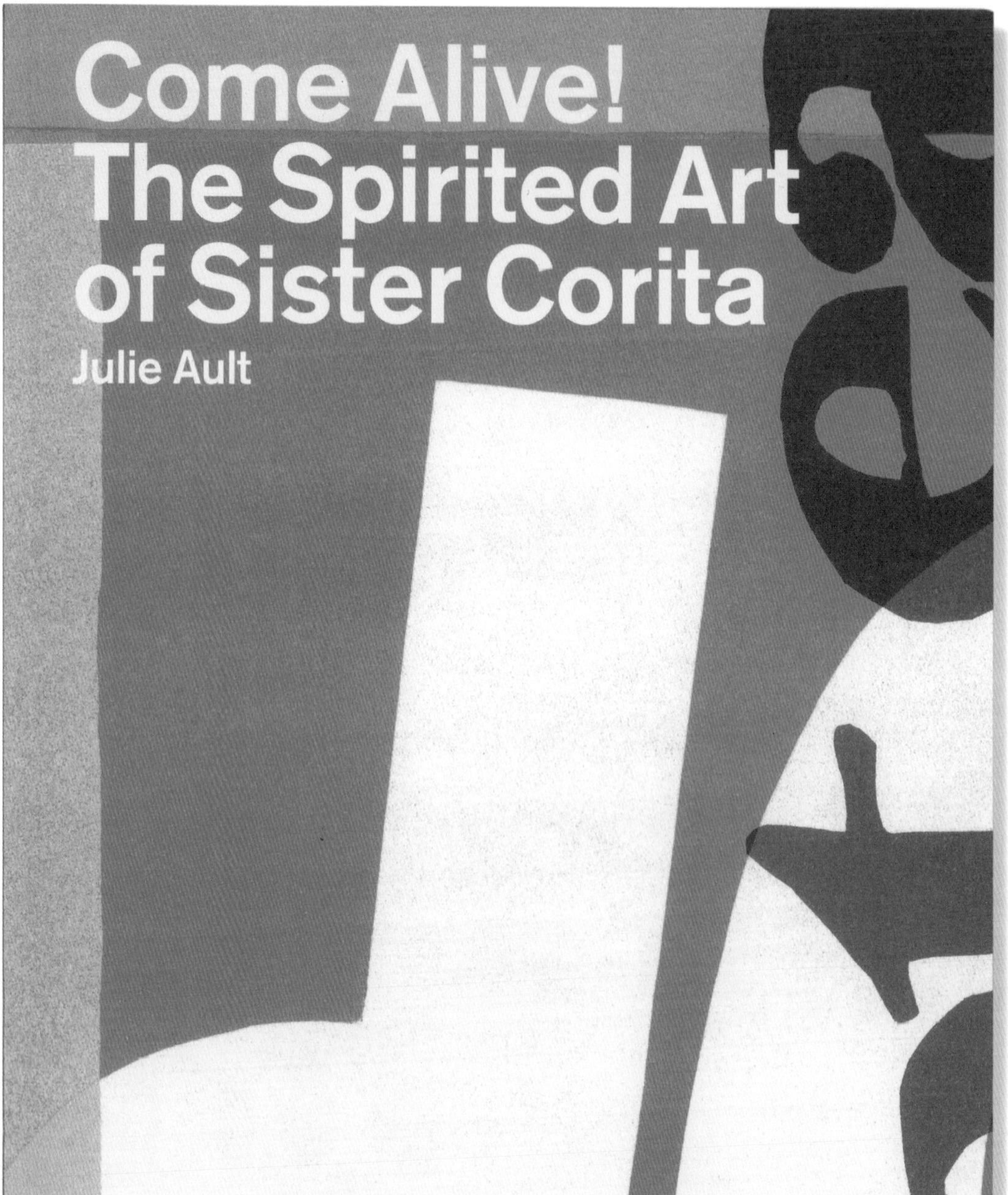

Eye 54 cover
Client Quantum Business Media *Designed by* Nick Bell Design *Creative director* Nick Bell *Designer* Jayne Robinson, Kate Mansell *Year* 2004
The cover shows a collage by Nick Bell using a few manipulated photographs from typeface designer Tobias Frere-Jones' collection.

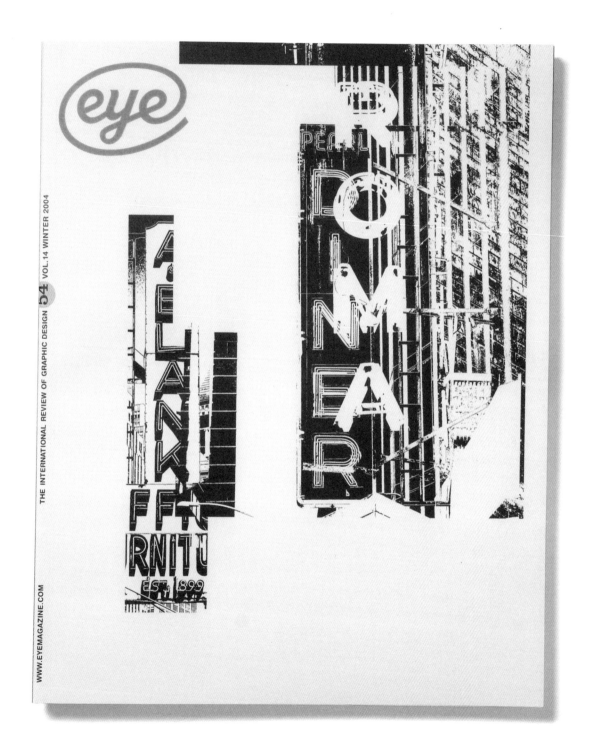

Client Universities UK *Design Director* Nick Bell *Design* Helene Samson, Sven Herzog, Paul Tisdell *Year* 2006
This is not a book for public sale but operates as a lobbying tool for those wanting to maintain and increase funding for research at UK universities. It's intention is to celebrate the discoveries and developments made in UK universities over the last 50 years.

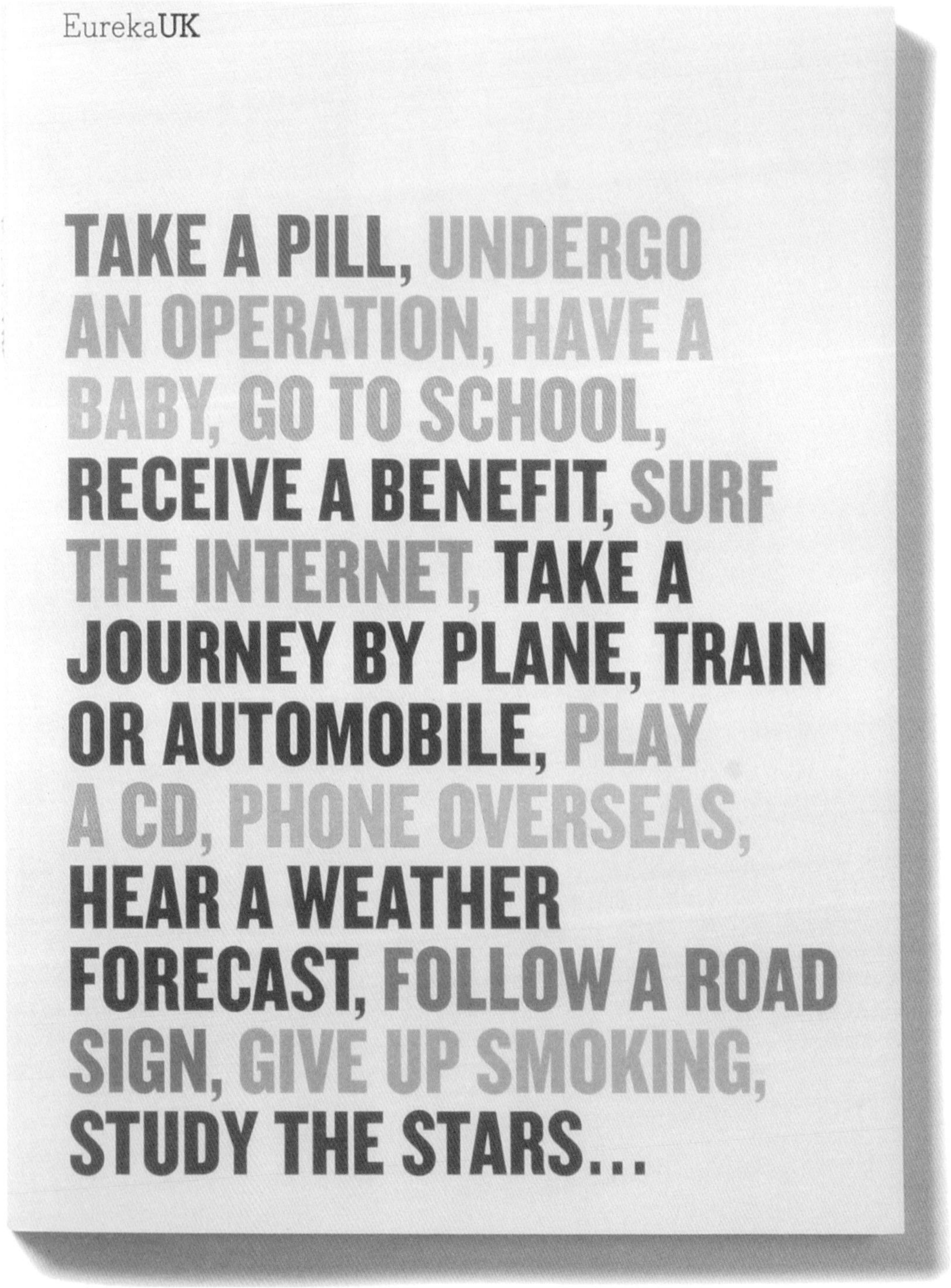

368

EurekaUK

TAKE A PILL, UNDERGO AN OPERATION, HAVE A BABY, GO TO SCHOOL, RECEIVE A BENEFIT, SURF THE INTERNET, TAKE A JOURNEY BY PLANE, TRAIN OR AUTOMOBILE, PLAY A CD, PHONE OVERSEAS, HEAR A WEATHER FORECAST, FOLLOW A ROAD SIGN, GIVE UP SMOKING, STUDY THE STARS…

LOOKING BACK IN TIME

370

THINGS ARE HEATING UP

In the 1950s, meteorologists assumed that the Earth's climate was more or less stable, and few people had then heard of 'global warming'. The pioneering climatologist Hubert Lamb was instrumental in establishing the study of climate change as a serious research subject.

Academic researchers at the Unit have created computer models to simulate the effects of increased carbon dioxide on the planet. Others have used tree rings, ice cores and coral to put together a comprehensive picture of climate patterns over the past millennia.

Without research, the UK wouldn't be able to plan for extreme weather

As well as establishing the character of climate change, Lamb was also known for his research into how major weather events impacted on people in the past.

Lamb's legacy is the Climatic Research Unit he founded in the School of Environmental Sciences at the University of East Anglia, which is a world centre for research on climate variability and the role of human-induced changes, such as the greenhouse effect.

Many of the researchers are working to get a better understanding of the flooding that has had such a devastating effect on UK regions such as Cornwall, especially over the past decade. Without such research, the UK and other countries would not be able to plan for the extreme weather events that are becoming increasingly common.

372

LASTING EFFECTS

The instant catastrophic impact of flooding was brutally
exposed by the tsunami disaster in late 2004, one of the
world's worst natural disasters. But researchers at
Middlesex University have shown that this is really just
the start of the problems: people suffer from stress,
sleeping problems and depression long after the flood-
waters have receded.

We have under-estimated the long term psychological impact of floods

The research has helped to raise awareness of these impacts in Government circles, increasing the emphasis on the 'social' consequences of flooding and helping to boost budgets for flood defence in the UK by hundreds of millions of pounds.

Surveys of recent flood victims in England by the University's Flood Hazard Research Centre have found that we have up to now under-estimated the long term physical and psychological impact that flooding can cause.

The effects on individuals, households, and communities can last for years, with for example loss of possessions and the perceived security of the home causing lasting psychological damage, such as high anxiety and stress levels.

The lessons on how to assist different communities in dealing with flood emergencies and their aftermath are likely also to have continued value: flooding, locally and worldwide, is expected to increase over the next 50 to 100 years due to the effects of global warming.

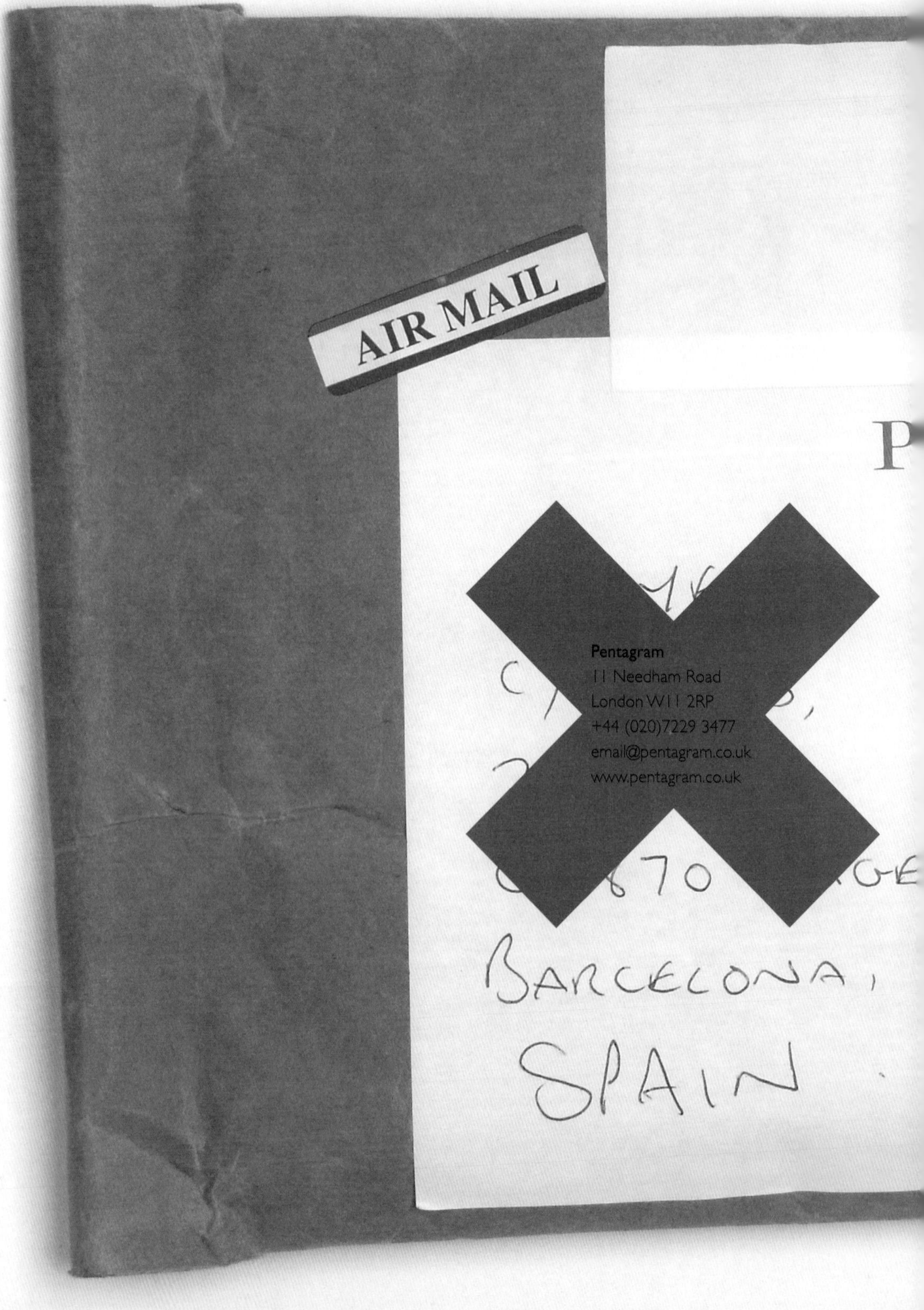

AIR MAIL

P

Pentagram
11 Needham Road
London W11 2RP
+44 (020)7229 3477
email@pentagram.co.uk
www.pentagram.co.uk

870

BARCELONA,

SPAIN

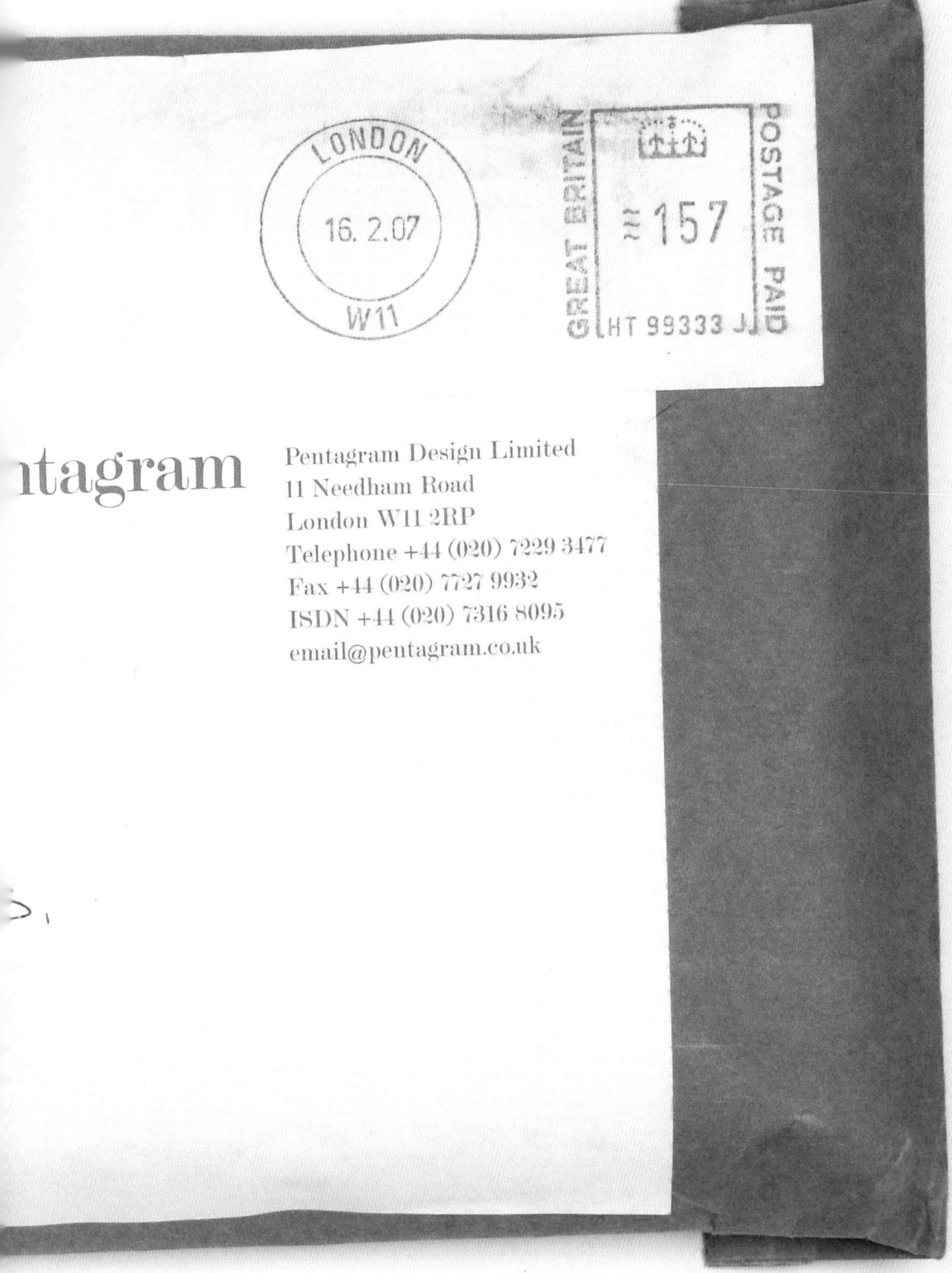

LONDON
16. 2.07
W11
GREAT BRITAIN
157
HT 99333 J
POSTAGE PAID
ntagram
Pentagram Design Limited
11 Needham Road
London W11 2RP
Telephone +44 (020) 7229 3477
Fax +44 (020) 7727 9932
ISDN +44 (020) 7316 8095
email@pentagram.co.uk

the TESS

more than a job

The Times Educational Supplement
Scotland. Friday November 17, 2006
No 2085 £1.30
www.tes.co.uk/scotland

Across the UK: discover our new 64-page glossy magazine

Packing up: what happens when you break up a secondary
School closure 12-13

Packing in: how one head got 600 parents through the doors
Primary 14

Experiential learning at Lumphanan Primary as the Countryside Classroom on Wheels rolled into town. Full story, page15. Photograph: Simon Price

An inspector didn't call

Scottish schools should be inspected within a seven-year cycle, following a 2002 ruling. But dozens have remained uninspected since the 1980s. Henry Hepburn reports

TES SCOTLAND can reveal that more than 300 Scottish schools have not been inspected in the past decade, and some have not seen an inspector report for nearly a quarter of a century.

Using records from the Scottish Parent Teacher Council, HM Inspectorate of Education and local authorities, *TESS* compiled a master list showing schools whose last full inspection report was published in December 1995, or earlier — a total that came to

almost 300, including 32 whose last inspection report was in the 1980s. For three schools — in East Dunbartonshire, Highland and West Lothian — the last recorded full report dates back to January 1983.

The news has been described as "appalling" by the Scottish Parent Teacher Council, but HMIE insists that plans for fresh inspections of every school in Scotland are on schedule.

Judith Gillespie, SPTC develop-

ment manager, said: "I know that in that time certain schools have been inspected more than once — and not even problem schools. This is not acceptable. No school should be left as long as some have been — it's appalling."

She said that HMIE inspections were important in detecting problems at an early stage. "Some schools can actually slide without anyone picking it up — HMIE does play a very important role.

"HMIE's own target is that schools will be inspected in the lifetime of each pupil. Schools have to ensure that they are keeping up to benchmarks, but who is keeping an eye on HMIE?"

Caroline Vass, president of the Scottish School Board Association,

praised HMIE for stepping up its rate of inspections in recent years, but added: "As a parent, I would be a bit concerned if a school had not been inspected in more than 20 years. The school may be self-evaluating and the local authority will also have done things, but it's HMIE that has a national perspective."

HM Inspectorate of Education started its Generational Cycle programme in 2002, where it told parents to expect reports within seven-year cycles for primary schools and six for secondary schools, meaning every school should have been inspected by 2009.

A spokesman said: "HMIE
Continued on page 4

TES JOBS

The Times Educational Supplement
Friday 24 November, 2006
Full jobs index: page 3

www.tes.co.uk

Brent Teacher Recruitment Service

For a Brent N.Q.T. information pack for Secondary or Primary teaching please contact Maxine Kildare.

tel: 020 8937 3233

email: teacher.recruitment@brent.gov.uk

or write to:
Maxine Kildare,
Teacher Recruitment Unit,
Chesterfield House, 9 Park Lane,
Wembley, Middlesex HA9 7RW.

website: www.brent.gov.uk/teachers

---

more than a job

Further Education Focus
The Times Educational Supplement
Friday November 24, 2006

www.tes.co.uk/fefocus

AoC training arm leaves £1m debts

Inquiry launched as scale of losses after closure is revealed at national conference

By Ian Nash

---

more than a job

The Times Educational Supplement

the TES

www.tes.co.uk

David Oyelowo: Broadway-bound, thanks to his best teacher
Magazine, page 12

Ditch the gym: you too can keep fit in the classroom
Magazine, page 32

Thousands take pay cut

... but some senior staff reap benefits of new responsibility payments

By Jonathan Milne

Cooking up a storm: the hotel chef's kicking Jamie out of the canteen
Magazine, page 8

---

the TES *magazine*

GASTRO GRUB
sets the school bells ringing

WORK THAT BODY
use your classroom as a gym

24.11.06

ALL THE WORLD'S A STAGE
Thanks to my best teacher
David Oyelowo remembers

the

TESS

more than a job

The Times Educational Supplement
Scotland. Friday November 24, 2006
No 2086 £1.30
www.tes.co.uk/scotland

**Across the UK: discover
our new 64-page
glossy magazine**

See hear: children
learn what it's like to be
deaf and blind
Primary 15

**Glasgow girls: the
Drumchapel pupils who
fought dawn raids**
Asylum-seekers 12-13

Samira I. Rudig Sotomayor took the top award for academic excellence at the SQA's annual awards (page II). Photograph: Ashley Coombes/Epic Scotland

Key reforms under threat

Staff development initiatives face a major setback as councils are hit by budget cuts

By Neil Munro

THE SCOTTISH Executive's major drive to invest in teachers' skills is facing a growing crisis because of the pressures piling on council spending.

Headteachers' leaders in primary and secondary schools are reporting slashed budgets for continuing professional development, despite specific executive funding which is now £13.5 million a year and has totalled £60.5 million since 2002.

This will re-ignite the debate about government cash for key initiatives in schools passing through education authorities and appearing to go astray.

John Stodter, general secretary of the Association of Directors of Education in Scotland, acknowledged that general financial constraints were forcing councils to cut spending where it did not directly affect front-line services.

Authorities which had large staff development budgets would reduce their contribution if there was money from the executive to take its place, he said. "You've always got to make difficult choices."

One authority has enraged its heads by insisting that staff members who wish to attend any in-service course in another part of Scotland must have approval from a senior manager in the education department.

Another straw in the wind, according to CPD co-ordinators, is that some candidates planning to take the Scottish Qualification for Headship have been told their employer cannot afford the fees.

Charles McAteer, president of the Headteachers' Association of Scotland, said it was clear council budgets were under strain and that continuing professional development was one of the casualties.

Bill Milligan, professional advice convener for the Association of Headteachers and Deputes in Scotland, said it was the view of many of his members in primary schools that spending on CPD was now inadequate.

One secondary head, who did not wish to be named, said it would be impossible to deliver many of the executive's key reforms without investing in the skills of teachers. His CPD budget had been £32,000 last year and was £18,000 now. "It's a soft tar-

get," he said. "But it's a short-sighted saving and will not pay dividends in terms of delivering what the executive expects."

Margaret Alcorn, national CPD co-ordinator, confirmed that reports from her colleagues round the country pointed to the fact that "money allocated to CPD is not being spent on CPD".

The pressures on continuing professional development could not have come at a worse time as the executive prepares to launch its "teachers for excellence" initiative, which is an implicit acknowledgement that support for staff development is an essential component of its curriculum reforms.

CPD: latest developments,
pages 8, 14, 16, 22

The Glasgow Girls who are fighting sweeps on school mates by immigration officers. (From left) Jennifer McCann, Agnesa Murselaj, Emma Clifford, Roza Salih, Amal Azzudin, Emlina Smith and Toni Lee   Henderson. Photographs: Chris James/Epic Scotland

Snatched from their beds in secret

The pupils of Drumchapel High have coped for years with friends disappearing overnight. Jean McLeish reports on the campaign of the Glasgow Girls to win greater rights for the children of asylum-seekers

GENTIAN IS A LOVELY BOY WHO, WHEN HE RETURNED TO SCHOOL AFTER THREE WEEKS IN A DETENTION CENTRE, STOPPED SMILING – SIMPLE AS THAT

How Roza fled Saddam

6   *Subjects*   The Times Educational Supplement
Friday November 24, 2006
www.tes.co.uk

music

Pots and pans concerto

Want to encourage youngsters to take up classical music? Launch a "groove search". This, at least, is the ambition of the Philharmonia orchestra based on London's South Bank. Its teen-friendly initiative aims to combat the reservations many young people feel towards high culture.

The orchestra is challenging members of the public to send in a 30-second "groove" – anything from a guitar riff to a rhythm bashed out on pots and pans with suggestions on how it might be adapted for a 45-piece orchestra.

The book will then be performed by the Philharmonia, lead by its new conductor, Finnish maestro Esa-Pekka Salonen.

This project really is open to everyone, regardless of age or musical ability," said a spokesman.

A visit to the Philharmonia's newly launched Myspace site proves they are in earnest. Their virtual "friends" include Jamie Cullum and jazz crooner Corinne Bailey Rae.

● adè.bloom@tes.co.uk

phse

Online parent practice

Forget Tamagotchis – the "virtual baby" is the new way to introduce children to the wonders, or otherwise, of child-rearing.

The new application, developed by BBC Jam, the corporation's online learning service, invites pupils to adopt an online tot. They must then learn to bottle-feed, change nappies and work tantrums in a bid to increase their baby's happiness score.

The child comes with its own sandpit, beach ball and wall charts. Players can select from a range of babies on a menu.

It is part of Child Developments, a learning zone that features video clips of growing children and excerpts from the popular Lord Robert Winston-lead series *Child of our Time*.

The pages will be launched in January.
● jam.bbc.co.uk

enterprise

Turning business ideas into action

By Irena Barker

They said it could not be assessed, but secondary pupils are now being given the chance to earn qualifications in enterprise. The Qualifications and Curriculum Authority has finally given the go-ahead for two GCSE-level awards in "developing enterprise capabilities", which encourage creative and innovative thinking.

The awards are broader than existing business and entrepreneurship qualifications, with pupils developing ideas and putting them into action.

Pupils will be assessed on the basis of a project, which could be anything from setting up a charity to a real company. Some pupils are already working towards the enterprise-only qualifications, but up to 500 are expected to have signed up by January. The qualifications were initiated by the Academy of Enterprise, established to promote enterprise learning.

Alastair Falk, the academy's director, said: "Pupils taking the qualifications will devise, develop and evaluate their own project in any area of the curriculum. It is about encouraging pupils to be enterprising and innovative."

He said that the purely enterprise-based qualifications was a breakthrough, because there had previously been concerns from the Government over how it could be assessed.

The original concept of the certificate was developed over four years by William Percy, director of business and enterprise at the Elibow Hall school in Dudley. More than 200 pupils in Year 10 at the school have started working towards the qualifications this year.

Mr Percy is also working on a PhD on how the subject can raise pupils' aspirations. He said: "It is a great way to engage the disengaged and raise aspirations and self-esteem. The qualifications have only just gone live but there is a lot of interest. It is a student-centred course which has the flexibility to mould to local needs."

The Level 2 award and certificate are both awarded by Northern Council for Further Education, which is working to introduce an A-level equivalent qualification in enterprise by September 2007.

Last week, the Government announced a £110million package to boost social enterprise in schools and the wider community.
● irena.barker@tes.co.uk

geography

In praise of field trips

At last, a boost for the much maligned geography field trip. Alan Johnson, Education Secretary, will outline the Government's commitments to different education when he launches a Manifesto for Learning Outside the Classroom on Tuesday.

The Institute for Outdoor Learning, one of the organisations, is campaigning to reduce the bureaucracy associated with excursions.

The institute believes trips are crucial for budding team skills and confidence. It wants greater numbers to take part and is lobbying the Government to get school trip programmes monitored by Ofsted.

"We believe the manifesto has the potential to significantly improve outcomes for children and young people," said Steve Lenartowicz, chairman of the group.
● news@olt@tes.co.uk

history

Top-notch teachers

A new chartered history teacher category is likely to be introduced recognising outstanding contributions to teaching within a school and across the history community.

The Historical Association is in talks about introducing the status after it obtained a Royal Charter from the Privy Council last month.

Detailed rules have yet to be finalised, but teachers are likely to be able to apply for the status once they have had five years in the profession. They would also need to be Historical Association members. The badge would not come with any additional salary, but could be used, for example, as evidence for threshold applications.

Heather Scott, chairwoman of the association's secondary committee, said: "This would be something for top-notch history teachers. We hope every teacher wants to aim for it."
● network.man@tes.co.uk

maths

Low marks, big ideas

Finding that students in countries with the lowest international maths scores are the most self-assured about their abilities have shown that instilling pupil confidence should not be the top priority for maths teachers, experts say.

Boosting self-esteem is no substitute for rigorous instruction, according to researchers at the Brookings Institution. US think-tank. They found that pupils in the highest-performing nations show the greatest insecurity.

The researchers compared pupil achievement at 13 with their own appraisal of their abilities, using data from the 2003 Trends in International Mathematics and Science Study.

It revealed that confidence was highest in low-performing Jordan, Egypt and Ghana; it was lowest in high-flying Japan, Korea and Hong Kong. The study has sparked much soul searching in America which, despite being the world's wealthiest nation, came in ninth out of 46 in pupil achievement, while ranking among the world leaders in pupil confidence. The findings call into question America's infatuation with the happiness factor in education, the report said.

Professor William Schmidt, of Michigan State University, said the difference between confidence and achievement reflected variability in national curricula. He said: "The maths you are being asked to learn has a lot to with your perception of whether you're competent.

"Most 13-year-olds in the US are still doing foundational arithmetic, but in more demanding countries, kids are really being challenged."

Professor Schmidt said the study undermined the importance of international benchmarking. "The world is a global economy, no country can afford to only look internally," he said.
● news@olt@tes.co.uk

For lots of brilliant classroom ideas, see *TES* magazine. And visit our resources and review bank at www.tes.co.uk

ict

Special tips and tricks

Children with special needs will soon be able to benefit from a new remote assessment service, to help them make best use of ICT.

AbilityNet's Barrier Free Assessment will mean youngsters can have their computers adjusted to their needs without receiving a face-to-face visit from a specialist. The system uses a combination of broadband video streaming, websites and the telephone to help an expert decide remotely what changes to make.

Equipment such as alternative keyboards and speech-recognition software can then be borrowed from the charity. Changes can also be made to Windows. Children with visual impairments, dyslexia, learning difficulties and physical disabilities could all benefit from the service.
● For more information, call AbilityNet's hotline on 0800 269545 or go to abilitynet.org.uk

english

Reading only for exams

We are spurning the life out of our most important subjects by forcing constant literacy tests on pupils, according to a polemical pamphlet published by the English Association. It will be released in December to mark the association's centenary. The pamphlet argues that British pupils, despite performing well, are among the least interested in reading in the world.

"Back in 1922 George Sampson complained that the fledging subject of English was widely seen as something that could be examined, tested, marked," said Geoff Martin, an association fellow. "That obsession with testing remains deadening characteristic of English today. It has led to a narrowing of the curriculum and an apparent loss of confidence by teachers in how to teach the subject in a way that the ignites youngsters' enthusiasm."

The association contends that in an era of global competition and an internet economy, a passion for English is needed now more than ever. "It is not just another of those whinge-fests," said Mr Martin. "It's a plea to scrap exam-centred and reignite the core of creativity."

● One hundred years of English teaching: the problems that won't go away, can be obtained from the English Association on 026 232 9982; email engassoc@cix.co.uk

A paean to prose and poetry, page 27

inside your TES

Creationism tag dogs Vardy's hard work
Will creationist teaching accusations threaten future of academies? Page 8

Japan fights to stem suicide spate
Exam pressure and bullying are being blamed for the rise in suicide rates in Japanese schools.
Page 10

Research
Power to the pen
Children's drawings can provide an insight into their emotional world, if you know what to look for. Page 30

Pupils on par for a career in golf
Head hopes that help from a professional coach will attract more to his Mill Hill school.
Page 5

Snatched in secret
Glasgow Girls battle to obtain greater rights for the children of asylum seekers
Page 22

Comment
Supernanny soap
Libby Purves on the Constantine Street parenting saga.
Page 25

FE Focus
Whoops!
AoC business arm leaves a £1million debt. Page 3

Jobs
Top vacancies are advertised in our full colour section

Online
Everything for the teacher on our website, www.tes.co.uk

A Week in Education

By Warwick Mansel

ANTI-BULLYING week opened with a statistic that won headlines, and no doubt much needed attention, for the campaign every day, 20,000 pupils are so scared about intimidation from their classmates that they play truant.

The Beatbullying charity, which released the figures, said one in three 11 to 17 year olds have skipped school at least once after being victimised.

The revelations were backed with calls for action on several fronts. Sir Al Aynsley-Green, the Children's Commissioner, said that some heads responded to parental concerns by merely denying the problem. He wanted parents to be given the right to complain to independent panels, while councils should appoint anti-bullying advisers.

Meanwhile, Alan Johnson, Education Secretary, announced plans to increase the number of pupils acting as "bully mentors" and Sara Cox formed an advert.

Another form of bullying was going on elsewhere in London's Evening Standard attempted to beat up Baroness Perry, the former chief inspector, over Tory plans to scrap school catchment areas.

The peer said that the move would give children in poor areas the chance to attend better schools elsewhere. But would this not mean that some middle class children would lose out on entry to their good local school, she was asked? "That certainly might be something in the early stages we just have to live with," she replied.

Oakwood technology college, Rotherham, was also subjected to a bashing after it was revealed that it planned to replace a traditional Christmas dinner with a Muslim halal chicken alternative.

The school backed down after complaints from parents and Denis MacShane, the local MP.

Traditional turkey will now be offered alongside halal chicken and a vegetarian option. Finally, several papers reported that Eton College is among schools considering abandoning A levels in favour of the Cambridge Pre U, as revealed in the TES in September. A slow news week, perhaps? You read it here first.

they said...
Targets to focus on less able pupils
('Financial Times' and others)

we say...
Alan Johnson, the Education Secretary, is to consult on a new statistical measure to be used in league tables and target setting.

Although details are scarce, the indication will seek to assess the progress pupils make between one key stage and the next, as measured, presumably, by test and exam performance.

Mr Johnson said that the current central league table rankings, which focus on pupils' "raw" results, are "too narrow". This is a hint that they give schools incentives to concentrate on middle ability pupils at the expense of others. Many will take that as a welcome admission. But it seems that the "raw" rankings will continue alongside the new measures in the league tables.

The plans won a few national headlines for Mr Johnson. However, teachers will now be entitled to question whether the is yet another stick with which to beat them.

Radio DJ Sara Cox is fronting an anti-bullying advert. Photograph: Getty

---

Big Brother's exam database

Employers and academics can check individual records to combat qualifications fraud

Madeleine Brettingham

The days of embellishing your CV will soon be over, for both pupils and teachers. A new database could in the future allow potential employers or universities to call up an individual's exam results and other qualifications, including bars taken at age seven.

The Learner Achievement Record system, set up that year by the Qualifications and Curriculum Authority to manage vocational qualifications, will be extended to include GCSEs and A levels within 12 months, and could eventually display every thing from a student's primary bar scores to their degree results, researchers said.

Log in, and a user's birthdate turns up and red screen, which resembles an online banking screen, lists your completed qualifications, from college courses to on the job training in subjects like IT.

With a few clicks of the mouse, the information can be sent to a third party such as a potential employer or a school admissions officer, which allows unprecedented access to individual academic records.

The database is likely to become a standard source of verification for employers and educators alike, combating academic fraud. The

Invasion of privacy?

A new children's database which will contain details of everything from a child's vaccinations to whether they are eating enough vegetables will "shelter" family privacy, according to academics.

The Children's Index, which was planned in response to the death of eight-year-old Victoria Climbie in 2000, who was tortured to death by her aunt, had been intended to act as an early warning system for abused children.

National Union of Teachers supports the setting up of the database, but described proposals to include primary test scores as "over the top". It said that teachers should not be responsible for its accuracy and maintenance.

The programme is being tested on thousands of learners at UK training centres, and will be rolled out across England, Wales and Northern Ireland by 2010.

The Learning and Skills Council said it fully supported the venture, which was "designed to fit within a more flexible and responsive qualification system," according to Janet Ryland, qualifications director. It will allow teachers to help pupils plan for the future by selecting appropriate

courses, and has the ability to put an end to skills shortages, according to Alan Saunders, project manager.

He said: "In advance of big construction projects we would be able to see if there are enough workers in training. If not, the government could provide incentives schemes, or students could retrain. It is a powerful tool to help us identify learner trends."

Concerns similar to those dogging the government's £12.4billion NHS database – which doctors are currently boycotting over

could be rolled out to GCSEs and A levels in future, potentially revolutionising the way these qualifications are managed.

The software forms part of QCA plans to shake up vocational training by allowing "packets" of learning completed at work and in evening courses to count towards formal qualifications.

Under the new Qualifications and Credit Framework, small chunks of training will earn "credits", which will add up to form a certificate such as a GCSE or diploma. While the system is aimed at vocational training, it

fears of hacking – have inevitably resurfaced. Greg Watson, the chief executive of the OCR exam board, has warned schools and colleges not to get "embroiled" in the QCA initiative. He said: "Such large-scale developments are neither necessary, nor desirable."

Employers will be able to access results of tests taken as young as seven. Photograph: Shannon Fagan

Exams supremo resigns - suddenly

By Jonathan Milne

The man in charge of the Government's 14-19 and post-primary resources to deliver test and exam targets has resigned suddenly as the government seized back control.

Mark Patison was appointed chief executive of the national strategies in March last year when the private company Capita won the five-year contract.

Mr Patison had been briefing officials in the Department for Education and Skills twice a week, but the relationship is thought to have become fraught.

When Capita took over, the Government beefed up the gives so that they became the main mechanism for ministers to achieve targets for test and exam results. One source said the DfES was portraying Mr Patison as the sacrificial lamb required by the Government to atone for disappointing key stage 2 results.

The Government came under fire this year for "burying" the key stage 2 results by publishing them at the same time as the more positive GCSE results. They showed primary schools had missed the Government's target in national English and maths tests.

On Tuesday, Ian Harrison, Capita's managing director of the strategies, went on several other team appointed acting in the

over on an interim basis as Mr Patison moved on to "new challenges". He wrote: "The DfES has indicated that it is keen to take a more direct role in the strategic leadership of the national strategies with Capita."

A Capita spokeswoman said the DfES played no role in Mr Patison's departure.

Mr Patison came to the role with impeccable New Labour credentials. He had been at Bradford council where he turned around the authority's failing pioneered education service. Before that he had been director of education at Blackburn with Darwen council, where he also worked closely with prime minister Tony Blair.

The weekly for the entertainme

www.thestage.co.uk

STAGE

£1.20

Thursday May 18, 2006

Kevin Spacey

"I'm here trying to
build something that
is bigger than me"

Continental
collision

How the UK can
rule Eurovision
once again

Cream of
the crop

Celebrating
25 years of
Cats

The showman must go on

Derren Brown has used psychology to make his subjects steal, believe they are raising the dead and even to help himself dodge death. He tells **Alistair Smith** why he plans to take a more serious direction as well as make his mark onstage. Pictures by **Sahba Saberian**

There are many ways one might attempt to categorise Derren Brown – magician, mentalist, illusionist, psychic even – but I think it is fair to say 'normal bloke' would probably not make it far up many people's lists.

And yet, and I'm sure this will disappoint some, shorn of his showman's eccentricities – no costume, no patter, no clasped hands – and sat opposite me pushing some equally unclassifiable pub food around a plate and sipping on an orange juice, he of the demonic goatee and all-knowing gaze seems just that. Distinctly normal.

Down to earth, one might say. He is also polite to the point of obsession (he insists on holding doors open and paying for drinks), remarkably decent (he makes a point of introducing himself to all the backstage staff working his gig the evening I meet him) and above all, affable. Honestly, I am not a stooge.

Whatever you want to call him, as Brown explains, his style is rooted in magic. "As I say at the beginning of everything I do, it's magic, suggestion, psychology, etc. So it's rooted in magic but it just has a different take on things. Some methods are shared with conjuring and lots are more peculiar to what I do.

"I would much rather that people saw it as a particular type of magic or a different way of looking at magic, rather than thinking, 'He has this set of skills – he's a psychic, he's a hypnotist'."

While at university in Bristol studying law and German, Brown did indeed begin his career as a hypnotist, having been impressed by a performance by a certain Martin Taylor. He soon moved away from the sector, though, becoming disillusioned with having to get people to take their clothes off and behave stupidly to entertain audiences.

Instead, he tried his hand at close-up magic, performing his new show in the very restaurants and bars where he had previously taken his hypnotism. Next, he began to combine the two disciplines and introduced a psychological theme to some of his tricks, shifting into a field broadly known as mentalism.

It was then he was approached by Objective, a television company looking for a showman to front a new TV magic show, in an attempt to build on the success of hit US magician David Blaine and his new style of street magic.

"Objective, I found out later," explains Brown, "had been looking for someone for a couple of years to do this kind of thing and there aren't that many people who do mentalism.

> "It was really lovely to get an [Olivier Award]. It ended up being far more exciting than a TV award. There was the genuine feeling of being a complete fraud in a room of proper theatre people"

"So that was that and I got a phone call, they came and saw a lecture I was giving to some magicians and they signed me up. That was in 1999 and the first TV show came out in 2000."

His team, including fellow mentalist and actor Andy Nyman and producer Andrew O'Connor, were still unsure of exactly what form the show was going to take. At one point the idea of having Davina McCall front the show was mooted but not followed up on. Eventually, in December of 2000, the first Mind Control special came out and Brown was introduced to the UK viewing public.

"Some things in that first special reflected the sort of material I was already doing – a bit like a comic using his jokes up on his first show. But it was very different doing it on TV and I had to learn a lot in terms of pacing and efficient writing. I think I was probably quite a self-indulgent performer.

"The biggest difference is when you work on your own, you are your own director and editor and everything. It's only when you start working with other people that tell you what they really think and tell you what is good and bad, that you realise how many bad habits you have as a performer."

He has now produced three series of Trick of the Mind, in addition to his original Mind Control shows and a number of specials including a controversial Russian Roulette performance, a faked seance and his latest, The Heist, in which he used a sales seminar to influence a group of business people to steal £100,000 in an armed robbery.

Each series takes about eight months to devise, with Brown and his collaborator Nyman thinking up new tricks and scenarios. However, according to Brown, they spend most of their time "farting and laughing".

"I'm genuinely surprised we get anything done," he continues. "We really challenge and bully each other as well, which I think is the real value of having someone like that you are comfortable with.

"It is up to me to come up with the stuff, though, at the end of the day. I have to be the driving force behind it and, if Andy isn't around, there are other people I bring in and use. Having those other voices is really important. I think with most modern magicians it all gets farmed out to people to come up with the ideas and I don't like that. I like to be behind it."

Brown's persona has always been integral to his work and it has developed over the seven years since he was first taken on by Objective.

"I think the key to it is that it has to be a theatrically tweaked version of yourself – a heightened version of yourself," he explains. "I'm sure I've changed a lot as a person since I started, so probably that has been why that shifted on the show as well.

"In the early specials it was about trying to get known, really trying to make a claim and it wasn't soft, it was very hard. It was very, 'this is real'. Now I think it's important, especially ☞ **30**

LISTINGS

Listings contact

To have your show included in *The Stage* listings, please email a full press release – including cast list, production credits, press night and press contact – to listings@thestage.co.uk at least three weeks before first night

Harriet Walter in Antony and Cleopatra at the Swan, Stratford-upon-Avon

ABERYSTWYTH
Arts Centre (01970 623232)
Dara O'Briain (May 4)

BAGNOR
Watermill (01635 46044)
Market Theatre Johannesburg – The Island (from May 5); Twenty Thousand Leagues Under the Sea (to May 6)

BARNSTAPLE
Queen's (01271 324242)
The Magical Dance of Ireland (May 6); Theatre Alibi – The Crowstarver (to May 5)

BASINGSTOKE
Anvil (01256 844244)
Amics Forever (May 10)
Haymarket (01256 465566)
The Opera Group – The Nose (May 5); Wuthering Heights (from May 8)

BATH
The Egg – Theatre Royal
The Ignatius Trail (May 5)
Rondo (01225 463362)
Sardine Circus – Clown Atlas (to May 6)
Theatre Royal
(01225 448 844)
Exuberous Obsession (from May 8);
The Safari Party (to May 6)
Theatre Royal, Ustinov Studio
(01225 448844)
Out of Inc – Night-Light (to May 5)

BEDFORD
Corn Exchange (01234 269519)
What a Feeling – The Rock's Pop Musicals in Concert (May 10)

BELFAST
Circus School (028 90 760403)
Man To Man (May 4); Re-cline (May 5)
Catalyst Arts
Annie Gilpin – Drowned (May 5)
Lyric (028 9038 1081)
Return to the Forbidden Planet (to May 6)
Old Museum Arts Centre
(028 9023 3332)
Noel Faulkner – Shake, Rattle and Roll (to May 4); Singin' I'm No a Billy, He's a Tim (May 5-6)
Sugar Room@The Potthouse
One Flew Over the Cuckoo's Nest
(to May 4)
Waterfront Hall (028 9033 4455)
Dara O'Briain (May 5)

BILLINGHAM
Forum (01642 552663)
I Can't Stop Loving You – The Genius of Ray Charles (from May 8); Red Hot Chartbusters (May 4)

BIRMINGHAM
Alexandra (0121 643 1231)
Christmas National Opera – Rigoletto (May 7); The Rocky Horror Show
Hippodrome (0121 622 7486)
Birmingham Royal Ballet – Apollo/ Pulcinella/The Firebird (to May 6); Birmingham Royal Ballet – La Fille Mal Garde (from May 10)

BLACKPOOL
Grand (01253 290190)
The Rat Pack Live from Las Vegas (from May 8)
Pleasure Beach Arena
(01253 341707)
Hot Ice
Pleasure Beach, Horseshoe
(0870 444 5566)
Mystique (from May 5)

BLISLAND
Village Hall (07785 550032)
Miracle Theatre – The Case of the Frightened Lady (May 5)

BOLTON
Octagon (01204 520661)
Blue/Orange

BOURNEMOUTH
BIC (0870 111 3006)
Blood Brothers (to May 6)

BRACKNELL
South Hill Park Arts Centre
(01344 484123)
God's Official (May 4)

BRADFORD
Alhambra (01274 432000)
Trainspotting (from May 8)
St Georges Concert Hall
(01274 752000)
Grumpy Old Women (May 5)

MAC (0121 4403838)
Hospofloi – The Imposter (to May 5);
Pandora's Box (from May 8); Rumpelstiltskin (May 7)
Repertory (0121 236 4455)
Present Laughter (from May 8); Trainspotting (to May 6)
Repertory, Door Studio
Katherine DeSouza (from May 6)

BRADFORD-ON-AVON
Wiltshire Music Centre
(01225 860 110)
Henri Oguike Dance Company (May 5)

BRENTWOOD
Brentwood Centre
(01277 262616)
Solid Silver 60s Show (May 4)

BRIGHTON
Komedia (01273 647100)
Carl Talk – Barb Jungr; Claire Martin; Mari Wilson (from May 10); The Ignatius Trail (May 7); The Treason Show (to May 6)
Marlborough (01273 647100)
Immaculate (May 6)
Nightingale (01273 702563)
Ten Thousand Several Doors (from May 6)
Pavilion, Dome (01273 709 709)
Beckett Trilogy – Molloy/Malone Dies/ The Unnameable (May 7-8)
Theatre Royal (08700 606 650)
Fimbles Live! (May 5-7); Paradise Lost (from May 9)

BRISTOL
Hippodrome (0870 607 7500)
The Blue B Stard Project (to May 6); Snow White on Ice (from May 10)
Jongleurs (0870 7870707)
Danny Buckler/Dave Williams/Jeff Innocent/Dave Best (to May 6)
Old Vic (0117 987 7877)
The Taming of the Shrew
Old Vic, Studio (0117 987 7877)
Johnathan Pram – Go/Off (to May 5); Out of Inc – Night-Light (May 8); Sketty – Imogen (May 6)
Tobacco Factory
(0117 902 0344)
Five Sides of a Circle (from May 9)

BROMLEY
Churchill (020 8460 6677)
Strangers on a Train (to May 6)

BURNLEY
Mechanics (01282 664400)
Mark Steel (May 4)

BUXTON
Opera House (0845 12 72190)
English Touring Opera – Jenufa (May 5); English Touring Opera – Tosca (May 4, 6)

CAMBRIDGE
Arts (01223 503333)
Losing Louis (from May 8); Present Laughter (to May 6)

CANNOCK
Prince of Wales
(01543 578762)
The Dolly Parton Story (May 5)

CANTERBURY
Gulbenkian (01227 769075)
Alex Horne – When in Rome (May 4); Labyrinth – Mystery of the Monster in the Maze; Will Smith – Misplaced Childhood (May 8)
Marlowe (01227 787787)
Beauty and the Beast
Tonic Bar (01227 784826)
Shappi Khorsandi/Joe Wilkinson/Earl Okin/ Rob Collins (May 10)

CARDIFF
Jongleurs (0870 7870707)
Keith Fields/Karl Spain/Jim Jeffries/Chris Corcoran (May 5-6)
New (02920878889)
Buddy (from May 8); Diversions Dance Company – Struck by Lightning/Chase the Growing Hours with Flying Feet/In Our Own Image (to May 6)

CHELMSFORD
Civic (01245 606505)
Beyond the Barricade (May 4); Newcastle (May 5)
Cramphorn (01245 606 752)
Coward Tones Three – Funned Oak, Still Life, Red Peppers (to May 5)

CHELTENHAM
Everyman (01242 512 515)
Dylan Moran – Like Totally (May 7); English Touring Opera – Jenufa (May 10); English Touring Opera – Tosca (May 9); Simply Ballroom (to May 6)

CHERTSEY
Comedy Club
Barry Castagnola/Dave Dynamite/Jenny Bennett/Tom Wrigglesworth (May 10)

CHESTER
Gateway (01244 340392)
God's Official (May 5); The Vagina Monologues (from May 8)

CHICHESTER
Festival (01243 781312)
Entertaining Angels (from May 5)

CHRISTCHURCH
Regent Centre (01202 479 819)
The Warrior and the Poet (May 7)

CLARE
Town Hall (01787 277 726)
Theatre Royal, Bury St Edmunds – Intimate Exchanges (May 6)

COLCHESTER
Mercury (01206 573948)
The Bay at Nice/Family Voices (to May 6); Return to the Forbidden Planet (from May 9)
Mercury, Studio (01206 577006)
Brass Balls (to May 6)

COVENTRY
Warwick Arts Centre (02476 524524)

After the End (from May 8); Labyrinth – Mystery of the Monster in the Maze; Merton's Imaps Chesno (May 5)
Warwick Arts Centre, Stage
(024 76 52 3734)
Puss in Boots (May 6)

CRAWLEY
Hawth (01293 553626)
Funny Bones (May 6); Mojeeeo –
The Satan Party (from May 8)

CROYDON
Ashcroft (020 8688 9291)
Rentaghost – the Musical (May 6);
Clocktower (020 8253 1030)
Little Fish Big Storm (from May 9);
Soul Sister (May 6)
Fairfield Concert Hall
(020 8688 9291)
Jim Davidson (May 5)
Warehouse (020 8680 4004)
Oddbodies – The House of No Fun

CUMBERNAULD
Cumbernauld Theatre
(01236 732887)
The Wizard of Oz

DARLINGTON
Arts Centre (01803 863073)
Newscastle (from May 3)
Civic (01325 486555)
Beyond Reasonable Doubt (from May 8)

DARTFORD
Orchard (01322 220000)
Girls Night (from May 8); What a Feeling – The Rock'n'Pop Musicals in Conc... (to May 8)

DERBY
Assembly Rooms (01332 255800)
Jo Brand (May 7)
Playhouse (01332 363275)
Into the Woods

DERRY
Millennium Forum (028 71 264455)
Blue Bayou – Roy Orbison the Legend (May 7)

DORKING
Dorking Halls (01306 879200)
Derren Brown – Something Wicked Comes (May 5)

DUNDEE
Repertory (01382 227630)
Monkey (from May 10)

DURHAM
Gala (0191 332 4041)
Swan Man/Seymour Mace/Carol Gritton; Sasha (May 7); Wrestling Wall (to May 6)

EAST KILBRIDE
Arts Centre (0355 261000)
Tape

EASTBOURNE
Congress (01323 412000)
That'll Be the Day (May 7)
Devonshire Park (01323412000)
The Hollow (from May 9)
Royal Hippodrome (01323 412000)
The Great British Variety Show
Winter Garden (01323 412000)
Keith Duwn/Silky/Michael Legge (May 8)

EDINBURGH
Festival (0131 529 6000)
English National Ballet – Swan Lake (to May 6)
Royal Lyceum (0131 248 4848)
Les Liaisons Dangereuses
Stand Comedy Club
(0131 558 7272)
Melting Pot (May 9); Miss Behave (May 9); Gillick/Dave Ingram/Barry McElhinney; MacAulay (May 5-6); Red Raw (Bank Holiday)
Sunday Night Laugh-in (May 7)
The Thursday Show – Nick Wilty/Jim Gillick/Danny McGinlay/Fred Macaulay (May 4); Whose Lunch is it Anyway? (May 7)
Traverse (0131 228 1404)
Gorgeous Avatar (from May 5)

ENNISKILLEN
Ardhowen (028 6632 3233)
I Dreamt I Dwelt in Marble Halls
(May 5-6)

EXETER
Northcott (01392 493493)
English Touring Opera – Pagliacci
(to May 6); The Reduced Shakespeare
Company – Completely Hollywood (Abridged)
(from May 9)
Phoenix (01392 667060)
Majnoon (May 9)

FAREHAM
Ferneham Hall (01329 231942)
Morrow by Night (May 6); Scotty – The Izzy
Wizzy Holiday Show (May 7)

GAINSBOROUGH
Sands (01427 811 118)
Clarke Martin (May 5)

GLASGOW
Citizens (0141 429 0022)
Charlotte's Web; Elizabeth Gordon Quinn
(to May 6)
Eastfield Community Centre
(01416 418319)
The Collection (May 4)
King's (0141 240 11 11)
Stuart Little (to May 6)
Ramshorn (0141 552 3489)
Tosa
Stand Comedy Club
(0870 600 6055)
Dance Monkey Boy Dance (May 8); Greg
Crook/Jesse Long/Craig Hill (May 5-6);
Michael Redmond's Sunday Service –
Greg Crook/Dave Ingram/Michael Redmond
(May 7); Red Raw (May 9); The Thursday
Show – Greg Crook/Jesse Long/Craig Hill
(May 4)
Theatre Royal (0141 332 9000)
Scottish Opera – Don Giovanni
(May 4, 6, 10)
Tron (0141 552 4267)
Bella and the Beautiful Knight
(to May 5); How to Steal a Diamond
(from May 5)

GUILDFORD
Laughing Horse (01483 572410)
Mark Felgate/Paul Kerensa/Juliet Meyers/
Nick Cowan (May 7)
Yvonne Arnaud (01483 440000)
The Best of Friends (to May 6); Wars of the
Roses (from May 9)

HALIFAX
Square Chapel (01422 349422)
A Gran For All Seasons (May 10)
Victoria (01422 351 158)
Birmingham Stage – The Jungle Book
(to May 6); The Chuckle Brothers –
Or What and the Return of the Garlics
(May 7)

HARTLAND
Parish Hall (01805 603201)
Journey to the Centre of the Earth (May 5)

HASTINGS
White Rock (01424 462288)
Chisinau National Opera – Rigoletto (May 5)

HATFIELD
Weston Auditorium (01707 284004)
Union Dance – Sensing Change (May 10)

HAYES
Beck (0208 561 8371)
Derren Brown – Something Wicked This Way
Comes (May 4)

HEREFORD
Courtyard (0870 1122330)
Lady Chatterley's Lover (May 6)

HIGH WYCOMBE
Swan (01494 512000)
Chisinau National Opera – La Boheme
(May 8); Dara O'Briain (May 10); Marrying
the Mistress (to May 6); What a Feeling –
The Rock'n'Pop Musicals in Concert (May 7)

HORNCHURCH
Queen's (01708 443333)
Room at the Top

HORSHAM
Capitol (01403 750 220)
The Magical Dance of Ireland (from May 10);
Wuthering Heights (to May 6)

HOVE
Old Market (01273 736222)
There is a Rabbit in the Moon (from May 10)

HULL
Hull Truck (01482 323638)
Mark Steel (May 7); Men of the World
New (01482 226655)
Anything Goes (from May 9); Old Big 'Ead in
the Spirit of the Man (to May 6)

JERSEY
Opera House (01534 511000)
Dr Bunhead's Recipes for Disaster
(from May 10)

KENDAL
Brewery Arts Centre
(01539 725133)
Labyrinth – Mystery of the Monster in the
Maze; The Tiger Trail (May 7)

KING'S LYNN
Corn Exchange (01553 764 864)
Jo Brand (May 10)

KINGSTON
Laughing Horse
Shelley Cooper/Luke Shaw/Neil Price/
Tom Parry/Aaron Rice/Mark Penney/Aggie
Elsdon/Holly Walsh/Leony Peters (May 6)

LANCASTER
Grand (01524 64695)
Circus Hilarious – The Magical Moorhef Tour
(May 6); I Want That Hair (May 4)
Nuffield (01524 594151)
Heelz on Wheelz (from May 9); Will Smith –
Misplaced Childhood (May 10)
Dukes Theatre – Fairy Tale (May 5-6)

LEAMINGTON SPA
Royal Spa Centre (01926 334418)
Grumpy Old Women (May 10)

LEEDS
City Varieties (0113 243 0808)

LIVERPOOL
Academy of Arts
(07762 385894/0151 709 8735)
Talking Heads (to May 6)
Empire (0151 709 1555)
Chisinau National Opera – La Boheme (to
May 6); Chisinau National Opera – Rigoletto
(May 4); Rentaghost – the Musical (May 7)
Everyman (0151 709 4776)
Paradise Bound
Philharmonic Hall (0151 937 863)
Dara O'Briain (May 6)
Royal Court (0151 709 1808)
Super Vision (to May 6); Will Smith –
Misplaced Childhood (May 10)
Unity (0151 709 4988)
16 (R)evolutions (May 5-6)
Valley Community (0151 488 0364)
Heelz on Wheelz (May 6)

LLANDUDNO
North Wales Theatre (01492 872000)
Dancing in the Streets (May 7)

LONDON
Albany (0207 387 5706)
Signs of a Diva (May 5-6)

Bo Poraj and Stella Gonet in Hilda at the Hampstead Theatre, London

Mark Steel (May 5); Will Smith – Misplaced
Childhood (May 7)
West Yorkshire Playhouse
(0113 213 7700)
Foxes (to May 6); Janus (from May 9)

LEICESTER
De Montfort Hall (0116 233 3111)
16 (R)evolutions (from May 8); Cats
(from May 8); Dancing in the Streets
(May 5)
Guildhall
The Daughter (from May 9)
Haymarket (0870 330 3131)
The Good Woman of Setzuan (to May 6)
Haymarket Studio (0870 330 3131)
Natural Breaks and Rhythms (to May 6)
Peepul Centre (0845 310 3344)
The Emperor's New Machine (to May 6)

LICHFIELD
Garrick (01543 412121)
An Enemy of the People (to May 6)

LINCOLN
Theatre Royal (01522 525555)
Teen Scream

BAC (020 7223 2223)
Alice Bell (from May 10); Slow Thinking –
Working (from May 10); Words Words
Words (from May 9)
Barbican, Pit
Beckett Evolutionary Festival – Krapp's Last
Tape (to May 6); The Mirror for Princes
(from May 10)
Barons Court (020 8932 4747)
The Magic Carvers Sunday Matinee (May 7)
Blue Elephant (020 7701 0100)
Evronvision (to May 6); Flatland (from May 10)
Broadway Studio
Easy to Love – The Story of the Great
American Songwriter
Bush (020 7602 3703)
Crooked
Bush Hall
Sprung (to May 6)
Cambridge (020 7850 8710)
Chicago
Camden Head
Ruth Pickett (May 9)
Canal Cafe (020 7289 6054)
NewsRevue (to May 7); Penny Spubb's Party

with Anna Crilly and Katy Wix (May 8);
The Sunday Delicrumer (May 7)
Charles Dickens Museum
(020 7631 1011)
The Sparkle of Albion (May 10)
Coliseum (020 7632 8300)
La Belle Helene; Madam Butterfly
Comedy (0870 060 6622)
Donkey's Years (from May 9)
Comedy Camp, Bar Code
(0871 223 2794)
Lucy Porter/Nina Benjamin/Paul Sinha/
Paddy Lennox/Simon Happily (May 9)
Criterion (020 7287 2875)
Mack and Mabel
Dominion (0870 607 7400)
We Will Rock You
Donmar Warehouse
(0870 060 5624)
Phaedra
Drill Hall (020 7307 5060)
A Dangerous Age; Dress Suits To Hire
(to May 7); What Tammy Needs to Know
(May 9)

Duchess (020 7494 5075)
Breakfast with Mugabe
Duke of York's (0870 060 6623)
Embers
Elcetera (020 7482 4857)
Night, Mother
Finborough (020 7244 7439)
Loyalties; Our Miss Gibbs (May 7);
Perspective Productions – Lucky Nurse and
Other Short Musical Plays (to May 5)
Fitzroy Tavern (0207 580 3714)
Brian Damage/Krysztal/Anthony Miller/
Jimbo/Heb Barker/Dizzy High/Brian Gittins/
Tom Wright/Vince Mancey/Richard Brophy/
Flemming Jenkin/Katy Bagshaw/Robert
White/Kate Wilkins (May 10)
Fortune (0870 060 6626)
The Woman in Black
Garrick (020 7494 5085)
One Flew Over the Cuckoo's Nest
Gate (020 7229 5387)
In Celebration of Harold Pinter – A Kind of
Alaska/A Slight Ache (to May 6)
Gielgud (020 7494 5085)
The Crucible

Greenwich Playhouse
(020 8858 9256)
Prospero's Will (from May 9)
Greenwich Theatre
(020 858 7755)
Tartuffe (to May 6)
Hackney Empire
(020 8985 2424)
Babel Junction
Hampstead (020 7722 9301)
Hilda (to May 9)
Her Majesty's (020 7494 5400)
The Phantom of the Opera
Hobgoblin (020 7639 5590)
Not About Heroes (from May 9); To WH
(to May 5)
Jermyn Street
(020 7287 2875)
Late Night Magic (May 5-6); Preachersssity
(to May 6)
King's Head (020 7226 1916)
Road to Nirvana
Laughing Horse Wimbledon
Jay Sodagar/Griff Griffiths/Rik Moore/

Jennifer Banks/Ava Alexis/Bill Moody/
Aggie Elsdon/Stella Ratner (May 7)
Laughing Horse Camden Town
Paddy Lennox/Patrick Worthington/David
Longstaff/Ben Inemer/Sajeela Kershi/Neil
Price/James Cann/Tom Parry (May 10)
Laughing Horse Oxford Circus
Peter Tennant/Lewis Bryan/Kat Sommers/
Graeme Harkins/Anthony Miller/Jay Sodagar
(May 8)
Laughing Horse Soho
Aggie Elsdon/Raymond Blake/Nick Cowan/
Nick Evans/Jimbo/Ed O'Meara/Matt Rudge/
Martin Donald/Lee Nelson (May 9)
Laughing Horse Walthamstow
Mike Belgrave/Ian McDonald/Paul Sheff/
James Sherwood/Lianne Rose/Laura Nunn/
Garry Daly/Sion James/Duncan Edwards
(May 4)
Laughing Horse Wimbledon
Jay Sodagar/Rick Kiesewetter/Lewis Bryan/
Chris Brown/Griff Griffiths (May 5)
Lilian Baylis (020 7863 8198)
Lost Musicals – Nymph Errant (May 7)
Little Angel (020 7226 1787)
The Very Thirsty Giraffe (from May 6)
Lyceum (0870 243 9000)
The Lion King
Lyric (020 7494 5040)
Al Murray – The Pub Landlord... and Another
Thing (May 7); Smaller (to May 6)
Lyric Hammersmith (020 8741 2311)
The Gardener (May 9)
Menier Chocolate Factory
(020 7378 1712)
Breakfast with Jenny Wilkinson
Miller of Mansfield (07899885752)
Nick Revell/Patrick Monahan/Del Strain
(May 5)
Millfield Arts Centre
(020 8807 6680)
The Elves Collection (May 5)
National Theatre, Cottesloe
(020 7452 3000)
The Overwhelming (from May 9)
National Theatre, Lyttelton
(020 7452 3000)
The Voysey Inheritance
National Theatre, Olivier
(020 7452 3000)
The Royal Hunt of the Sun
New End (020 7794 0022)
The Dead Fiddler
New Wimbledon (0870 060 6646)
Seven Brides for Seven Brothers (to May 6);
Chisinau National Opera – Rigoletto
(May 10); Derren Brown – Something
Wicked This Way Comes (May 9);
Paul Merton's Impro Chums (May 8)
Novello (0870 950 0935)
Fontinase the Musical
Old Red Lion (020 7837 7816)
Valparaiso
Oval House (020 7582 0080)
Market Theatre Johannesburg – The Island
(to May 6); Some Mothers' Sons
(from May 10)
Palace (020 7434 0909)
Whistle Down the Wind
Palladium (020 7494 5020)
Sinatra at the Palladium; Solid Silver 60s
Show (May 7)
Peacock (0870 737 0337)
Paco Pena – A Compact to the Rhythm
Phoenix (0870 060 6629)
Blood Brothers
Piccadilly (0870 060 0123)
Guys and Dolls
Place – Robin Howard Dance
Theatre (0207 387 0031)
Earthfall – At Swim, Two Boys (from May 10);
Probe Dance Company – Have We Met
Somewhere Before? (May 5-6)
Playhouse (0870 060 6631)
My Name is Rachel Corrie
Polka (020 8543 4888)
Child of the Divide (from May 5); The Three
Billy Goats Gruff (May 6)
Prince Edward (020 7447 5400)
Mary Poppins
Prince of Wales (020 7839 5972)
Mamma Mia!
Queen Elizabeth Hall, Southbank
Centre (0870 3800 400)
CandoCo – The Journey/In Praise of Folly
(May 5-6); Henri Oguike Dance Company
(May 7)
Queen's (08709500930)
Les Miserables
Red Rose Comedy Club
(07963 618333)
Alex Horne – When in Rome (May 6)
Riverside Studios (020 8237 1111)
The Exonerated

REVIEWS

Classical comedy proves real McCoy

The Pocket Orchestra

Trafalgar Studios 2
April 26-May 20
Authors: Graeme Garden, Callum McLeod
Director: Richard Williams
Producers: Ambassador Theatre Group, Screenstage
Cast: Sylvester McCoy, Paul Arden-Griffith, Sebastian Bates, Emma Correlle, Karen Fisher-Pollard,

Ian Harris, Ella Smith
Running time: 2hrs

With the feel of an extended Edinburgh Festival Fringe show there is something endearing about this comical history of classical music, written by former Goodie Graeme Garden and composer Callum McLeod.

Sylvester McCoy, resplendent in his showman's outfit of a tailcoat, flashing badge and equally red trousers, boots and hair, narrates proceedings as if born to the role. There is always something of the burlesque clown to McCoy and he pulls few punches here. If Doctor Who had been a classical music buff, this is probably what he would have been like.

The humour is light but perfectly suits the show and its target audience, with the music a sort of Classic FM medley mix of favourite classical tunes.

The stories of the great composers and how their lives intertwined is told in the guise of a soap opera with the musicians playing the various roles.

They perform well, although a little less amateur dramatics-style gurning while offstage would not go amiss. The music – played as they wander about and without sheet music – is often a little discordant but it somehow suits the knockabout nature of the show.

It is all very Radio 3/*Daily Telegraph*. So much so that the audience should be admitted only if they have either a 4x4 or a labrador.

Jeremy Austin

dear john

I've been out of drama school for about a year and now I'm stuck in that classic performer's catch-22 – can't get work without an agent, can't get an agent to look at me because I don't have work. Can you help me break out of the loop?

It might well be a classic catch-22 but it is the kind of classic that would sit very well on a shelf with Snow White, Sleeping Beauty or Cinderella. In other words, it's probably the number one showbusiness fairy tale and certainly the one this advice column hears most often – we've even had the occasional enquiry as to whether we ourselves are taking on acts at present. Although it's always been in the interests of the industry's big bad wolves and up-front fee merchants to keep the 'no agent equals no work' myth alive and kicking, it's a fairy tale that reputable agents are as keen to debunk as anyone else. I would personally tend to be wary of an agent wanting to represent you if they haven't seen your work and you don't have a track record – one would have to wonder what's in it for them? A serious agent on the other hand will be aiming to put some serious time and expense into marketing you – so it follows that they will need to be sure there is something worthwhile to market. From your point of view you should be looking for someone who can take your career to the next level, not someone to take over base level promotion you could easily do yourself, or at least not until you have had a chance to see what's involved for yourself. Then, when you do employ someone to do it for you, you'll have an idea of what you're actually getting in return for the percentage of your earnings

they'll be getting. So given that the process of getting a good agent takes time, what should you do in the meantime, especially if you're at the early stages of your career?

Sara Dee

As a professional actress who also works in the PR field and is frequently involved in organising and hosting industry events, Sara Dee has experience of artist promotion from both sides of the fence:

"The first thing I advise is to begin with what you can do and stop thinking of what you can't do. You can still go for jobs without having an agent – in fact that's the way most performers build up their showreels and get themselves into places that will get them seen.

"As you build up your work this way, make a point of writing (briefly and politely) to people you would like to represent you, to invite them to come and have a look.

"If you do get a job that requires you to go through an agent, it's a very good opportunity to call your best option and ask them to represent you for this one job – something which is a lot easier to agree to if you've kept them in touch with your progress along the way. This business is 80% PR, office work and networking – possibly more when you first start out – and 20% doing the job you love.

"If you have persistence and perseverance things will happen eventually. When something does happen, it's up to you to contact everyone in the business again and repeat all of the above steps armed with this new piece of experience, information and renewed confidence.

"It's that easy – or that tough. The rest is down to luck and good

timing but the likelihood of bo— tends to increase the more har— work you put in."

John Woolvett

John Woolvett is a character a— who turned professional later — life but has made up for lost tim— with featured roles in shows su— Shock Treatment and The Rev— Game. John offers some furthe— practical steps you can take rig— away:

"If you are absolutely new to— business you will probably hav— build a CV by doing some fring— plays, student films, etc, to sho— your talent. Resources like PC— and Shooting People – and of c— The Stage – are a good source.

If you have a CV and set of— photographs that actually look — you – many don't – then be pro— active and market yourself at e— opportunity by mailing to casti— directors, networking with othe— actors, subscribing to casting ser— vices, to get your name circulat—

Focus on getting work to be s— and to get better at what you do— not on getting an agent. That w— happen also but you need to sho— not just that you believe in you— but also that you are willing to— demonstrate that belief by inves— time and hard work on the less— 'exciting' administrative side of— business so that someone else m— feel it's worth believing in you to— that extent too."

I should point out that while both Sara— John have agents – no doubt as a res— putting into practice what they sugge— here – both are also still actively invol— in doing their own networking and— promotion work. The ideal performer/a— relationship is a partnership where bot— parties do their best in their own area— expertise and as well as doing your bi— stage you'll often make contacts yourse— that your agent may not necessarily co— across. Perhaps the most important po— to stress that while you'll be looking fo— good agent who works hard for their ca— you'll need to bear in mind that this m— they will currently be working hard on— behalf of their existing clients. So whil— fully support John and Sara's 'network— and keeping people informed' advice, y— need to keep your contact with potenti— agents brief and polite. Update when y— have something of real interest to shar— not every other week. Letters are bette— than phonecalls and often better than— emails too – and instant messages are— never a good idea. It's your performan— power not your pester power you're ai— to bring to their attention.

In addition to his own work as a— cartoonist, writer and broadcast— John Byrne is a business coach— and career advisor to the arts an— media industries. He has a regula— slot on the Valley Fontaine show— Saturdays and Sundays, 2-6am— (BBC London radio 94.9FM).— Questions for Dear John and lin— back on answers already publish— are welcome to dearjohn@— thestage.co.uk or via the Dear Jo— section of The Stage website, whe— previous Q&As are collected.

---

showpeople

Jordan Clarke

Stage scholarship winner
Sylvia Young Theatre School

Jordan, age 11, lives in Margaretting, Essex and has already featured in several award-winning movies.

How did you get involved in showbusiness?
It was all a bit of a surprise, really. My mother (Sharon) was asked to pick up a friend's son from drama school. I went with her and the drama teacher suggested I join. He gave us the option of a free trial for a few weeks and I enjoyed it so much I stuck with it.

Are your family very supportive of your work?
I have three older sisters and they are all very supportive. My mother works at home and she is always helping me prepare for auditions. My room has been converted into what the family call JJ's studio and we rehearse in there. My school has also been very good and let me go on auditions regularly.

What auditions have you been on recently?
I have been given a recall for Andrew Lloyd Webber's new production of The Sound of Music which is very exciting but the details are all top secret at the moment. I go on a lot of movie auditions and I really like working on a film set. I have done a few films already including a movie called Too Many Gods, which won awards at the Chicago Film Festival and a film for Unicef called All the Invisible Children.

What was your favorite film you worked on?

I really liked working on Finding Neverland with Johnny Depp and Kate Winslet. I was a body double for one of the children and the director liked my work so much I also had a role as one of the Lost Boys. It was great fun filming at Pinewood and Shepperton.

Are you a fan of Mr Depp's work?
He is probably my favourite actor. I really admire him and the work he does. I am a big fan of Pirates of the Caribbean.

What do you think you would do if you did carry on acting?
I really like acting and thanks to the scholarship at Sylvia Young I am looking forward to working in the industry. I really enjoy maths and English at school and most sports, especially football but I have enjoyed my time on set so much that if I didn't continue as an actor I would probably end up working behind the scenes as a director or something like that.

Paul Vale

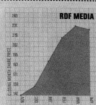

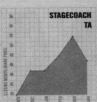
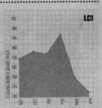

OF buoyed by de Mol

alysts' claims that prices for TV
ies RDF and Shed are inflated
old be disproved with ex-Endemol
s John de Mol showing interest in
DF Meanwhile the performing arts
nchise Stagecoach has had to
stend with a second – greater – six
onthly pre-tax loss for the period to
vember. However, turnover is up
th losses down to new investment
schools. Casino operator LCI can
ok forward to a climb, thanks to
eculation about a mystery bidder.

BIZ 2 BIZ

Hull Truck smashes audience records

Visitors rise by 10,000 in 2005/6

Regional theatre

Hull Truck Theatre has announced
record-breaking audience figures for
the last 12 months.

A total of 70,000 people came
through the doors of the venue
between April 2005 and April 2006,
an increase of 10,000 from the
previous financial year. Meanwhile
total sales have gone up by 18%.

Recent shows A Kick in the
Baubles, Up on Roof and I Want
That Hair, made a major contribution, with the latter almost doubling
predicted ticket sales. In addition
Hull Truck Youth Theatre's performances of Once a Catholic completely
sold out – a first for the group.

Gareth Tudor Price, associate
artistic director, commented: "These
record figures are a tremendous
success for us and we would like to
take this opportunity to thank our
audiences for their continued support
while we look forward to the opening
of our brand new city centre home."

Hull Truck is starting work this

An artist's impression of the new Hull Truck Theatre

season on construction of a new
location in place of its Spring Street
home, before moving to the new
building in Hull. The new site will
include a 440-seat auditorium,
136-seat studio theatre plus rehearsal
and education spaces as well as bar
and business facilities.
• Former manager of West End
venue Trafalgar Studios Jo Ditch has
been appointed as the first general
manager of the new Grove Theatre
in Dunstable.

The 750-seat, £16 million arts and

entertainment centre opens in spring
2007. Owned by South Bedfordshire
District Council, it is operated under
management contract by Leisure
Connection. It will function as a
professional receiving house and
offer drama, music, dance, comedy
and film, in addition to community
arts performances.

In her previous job she was
responsible for the relaunch of the
Trafalgar site, formerly the Whitehall.
Prior to that she was manager of the
Phoenix Theatre in London.

TEA '06 unveils list of sponsors

Theatre technology

One of the biggest events in stage
technology, TEA '06 – the Theatre
Engineering and Architecture
conference – has announced its
full roll call of sponsors.

Some of the biggest international
theatre companies are taking part,
alongside top British names. The
categories include gold, silver and
bronze sponsors, plus a single
platinum sponsor, which this year is
leading automation firm Stage
Technologies.

Delstar and Unusual Rigging are
the show's gold sponsors with British
Harlequin, Gerrets, J&C Joel/
Triple E, Theatre Projects Consul-
tants, White Light, Serapid and
Waagner Biro in the silver section.

In addition, a total of 24 firms
are registered as bronze sponsors,
among them Siemens, SBS-Dresden,
the Theatres Trust, Northern Light
and Sansei Yusoki of Japan.

The TEA conference is a three-day
event starting on Sunday, June 11.
It takes place at 1 Great George
Street, London.

An estimated 40% of the delegates
are expected to be from foreign
companies. The last conference was
held four years ago.

Disney sails into Med market

Cruising

Disney, a relative newcomer to the
cruise industry, is targeting the
Mediterranean in its expansion with
tours of eight European cities,
starting in Barcelona.

The entertainment group, which
boasts Disney-themed entertainment,
began operating voyages in 1998 in
the Caribbean. However, it remains a
minor player in the cruise industry.
Market leader Carnival currently
runs a 79-ship fleet and has plans
to add a further 16 by 2010.

Sheffield now for Stanley

Gaming

Stanley Leisure has added Sheffield
to its portfolio of new casino sites,
just days after securing permission
for a building in Liverpool.

The latest acquisition is the first
time Stanley has established a
presence in Sheffield and the finished
building is scheduled to open at the
start of 2008.

Its accounts have been swelled by
the sale of its string of betting
shops to William Hill for more than
£504 million in 2005. The company

has spent nearly £100 million on
upgrading its existing casinos.
Stanley Leisure achieved pre-tax
profits of £22 million for the half
year to October 31.
• Gambling industry website
www.gamingfloor.com estimates that
the number of casinos in the UK now
tops 140. The figure for the start of
2006 was:

London	24
Rest of England	100
Scotland	12
Wales	4
TOTAL	140

Boost for Manchester TV 'village'

Television

Plans to develop Greater Manchester's reputation as a world-class
television production base have been
boosted by the decision of the North-
west Regional Development Agency
to approve funding of £30 million for
the development of a Media Enterprise Zone in the city.

While the scheme remains subject
to approval from Whitehall and
Brussels, its prospects have been
enhanced by the BBC's proposals to
relocate significant commissioning
and production to the north-west.
The MEZ aims to house a host of
independent production and technical
facilities and complementary services
with the BBC as the 'anchor tenant'.

Corporation management recently
announced its two preferred sites
for the development of the MEZ –
Quays Point at Salford Quays and
Manchester's Central Spine, with
a final decision on the winning site
expected in the summer.

Steven Broomhead, NWDA chief
executive, said: "Developing a vibrant
Media Enterprise Zone in Greater
Manchester as part of the BBC's
proposed relocation to the region is
highlighted in the new Regional
Economic Strategy as a key trans-
formational action and so today
marks an important step forward
for the region."
• RDF Media, which makes Wife
Swap (pictured), has hired an executive from American network ABC to
head its US development arm.

Greg Goldman has been the executive director of alternative series
and specials at the broadcaster and
was in charge of popular series such
as The Bachelor and new Simon
Cowell project American Inventor.
He will oversee all of the production
house's US output.

BY AIR MAIL
par avion
Royal Mail

Plan-B Studio
Studio 12
25 Horsell Road
London N5 1XL
+44 (0) 207 700 1166
www.plan-bstudio.com

Plan-B Studio 16-24 Underwood Street London N1 7JQ tel.+44 (0) 207 253 8732
info@plan-bstudio.com / www.plan-bstudio.com

Please do not bend

23rd Union Fanzine
Client Stiff Records *Design* Steve Price *Year* 2006
23rd Union is a club night hostted by Stiff Records who just happen to manage Boy Kill Boy and The Enemy, amongst a host of previous and current bands and artists. This fanzine was produced for their club night to promote their new signings and celebrate the history of their label and club night.

The Voom Blooms

That's a weird name for a band, why are you called that?
The name came from Thom. He was watching a Japanese film a few years ago, forget what it was called now, but there's one scene where some guy shouts out something in Japanese about 3 or 4 times, and it sounds like he's shouting "VOOM BLOOM! VOOM BLOOM!" ... He's probably not though.

How are you going to change the music world then?
We're gonna go on a journey to find Michael Jackson, ask him how he did it, then give him a swift roundhouse kick to the face the way Chuck Norris told us to.

You've done a bit of touring this year - What do you get on your rider?
Nothing exciting like socks or ravioli. Just the usual really; beers, waters and a selection of sweet and savoury snacks including crisps and chocolate. We specify Nik-Naks and Boosts, but we never get them. Cnats.

Describe The Voom Blooms in no more than 23 words
George Guildford, Thom Mackie, Craig Monk and Brett Young play the tawdry, stylish indie rock sounds of The Voom Blooms – www.wikipedia.org

Which bands have influenced you?
List time? ... Syd Barrett, Pharrell Williams (The Neptunes), Beach Boys, The Libertines, Television, Kanye West, Sigur Ros, Interpol, Joy Division, The Clash, The Cure, Jackson 5, Aphex Twin, DJ Krush, Photek, Nick Drake, Bright Eyes.
More recently on the stereo: Boards of Canada, Larrikin Love, Animal Collective, Matmos, TV on The Radio, Isolee...

What does the future hold for you lot?
You never know what's round the corner. Unless of course its a corner on a street you know well, in which case i suppose you do, like your mate's house or a shop or something like that. We're pretty new round here though. Its a bit rough too. Full of thieves, fools and vultures. We're in love with it though, and when the time's right I think we're gonna get drunk down the park, throw some bricks through a few windows and then do one to a place we can't be found.

boy kill boy
interogated by corporal jones

You've just done a big tour of America. Are the people there really as fat as they look on the TV?
Some are a little larger than life, but others aren't - they do say the telly puts extra pounds on you though. If you ever meet us in person you'll see we're all actually considerably thinner than Kate Moss.

Apart from obviously laughing at the morbidly obese, what was the best bit about your American tour?
It was really cool to get to play to a whole new bunch of people most of which hadn't even heard of us and get such amazing responses. But if you're after something a little less boring it was probably the night we all nearly got our faces kicked in at a bowling alley in a truck stop.

You have 23 words to describe your album 'Civilian' which is out now in all good, and some average, record shops. Go...
Civilian is the debut album by Boy Kill Boy, featuring the singles 'Back Again', 'Suzie', and 'Civil Sin'. Go and buy it now.

Where do you think you played your best set yet?
Probably Frog in London a few weeks ago or Bar M in Ibiza for Ibiza Rocks with Dirty Pretty Things. We're always developing so the recent gigs are generally the best. We've yet to support a puppet show so until then these will probably have to do.

You recently trashed the Manumission villa in Ibiza. At any point during this debauched behaviour did you feel a pang of guilt about what your mother's might say when they found out?
No, they get up to far worse than we do. They're extremely proud of any raucous behaviour by us as it takes the spotlight away from them.

When you do a DJ set as a band, do you argue about who gets to do the DJing or do you just put a mix CD on and pretend?
We actually argue about who gets to put the mix CD on and pretend they are DJ-ing. Seriously though we love DJ-ing and we're going to get out there as much as we can after gigs and stuff to educate the masses with songs from Sesame Street.

The life of a rock and roll band never stops, have you written any new material that we can look forward to you performing soon?
Yes.

"THERE'S NO PLACE FOR HALF HEARTED BANDS – YOU'RE IN IT FOR THE LONG RUN OR YOU'RE NOT IN IT AT ALL. NONE OF US OWN A CRAVAT OR POINTY SHOES – BUT WE'RE STILL HAVING IT. JOBS ARE RUBBISH – YOU'RE THERE FOR 40 YEARS AND THEN NICE ONE, YOU'VE WASTED YOUR LIFE. YOU'RE TRAINED AT SCHOOL TO BE A SAP WORKING FOR THE MAN. WHAT'S THAT ABOUT? IT'S ABOUT MODERN LIFE. IT'S ABOUT WHAT WE ARE AND WHO WE ARE. WE DO IT TO KEEP OUT OF TROUBLE."

- THE ENEMY

The Grand Union Alumni
Just some of the artists we have worked with over the years

Amen

Killing Joke

Pleasure

Raging Speedhorn

Scanners

Viking Skull

23

1. Humans have 23 pairs of chromosomes.
2. Jamie Hewlett Uses the number 23 a great deal and also references the Church of the subgenius and the illuminatus trilogy in his illustrations and writing for Tank Girl and Gorillaz.
3. W, the 23rd letter of the Latin alphabet has 2 points down, 3 points up.
4. Purple 23 is the location where Kramer sets the air conditioner in the parking garage episode of Seinfeld.
5. 23rdian is a person who constantly witnesses the number 23 in high concentration.
6. The 23rd moon of Jupiter is called Carme.
7. The earth's axis is tilted at a 23.4 degree angle
8. In William Shakespeare's Julius Caesar, Caesar was stabbed a total of 23 times.
9. The Twenty Threes is a secret society at Wake Forest University.
10. In The Big Lebowski, the Dude and his friends always use Lane 23 at the bowling alley.
11. Late author William Burroughs was so gripped by numeric coincidences surrounding. 23, he kept a scrapbook of his findings. It is said he was alerted to the number's power when a Captain Clark told him he had run a ferry from Spain to Morocco with no problem for 23 years. Hours later it sank, killing the skipper.
12. Band Psychic TV were obsessed with 23. They released 23 live albums, each on the 23rd day of 23 months running.
13. William Shakespeare was born and died on April 23. His first folio of plays came in 1623. Wife Anne died in 1623.
14. Car giant Nissan is touched by a numerical coincidence. In Japanese, "ni" is 2, and "san" is 3. So Nissan would be 23.
15. The sound system Spiral Tribe referred to the number 23 extensively. They held parties on the twenty third day of the month; their flyers, posters and artwork featured 23 imagery; their record label was called Network 23; and some music was released under the moniker SP23. Oddly enough, twenty-three members of the group were also arrested immediately after their Castlemorton party event.
16. On average, every 23rd wave crashing to shore is twice as large as normal.
17. In the disaster movie Airport, the bomber has seat 23.
18. It takes 23 seconds for blood to circulate through the body.
19. IN THE Beatles film Yellow Submarine, The Butterfly Stomper, who destroys all things of beauty, wears a shirt with the number 23. So does David Beckham.
20. ROCK star Kurt Cobain was born in 1967 and died in 1994. Both years bizarrely add up to 23 if counted as individual digits: 1+9+6+7=23. 1+9+9+4.
21. On a normal modern Latin alphabet "QWERTY" keyboard, the 23rd letter W is right below and between 2 and 3.
22. It is believed that Adam and Eve had 23 daughters.
23. Actor River Phoenix, was born on August 23, 1970. He died at the age of 23, on Halloween 1993.

Tim Ten Yen

The sinister cat is most often seen keeping an eye on the proceedings of everybody's favourite singing salaryman TIM TEN YEN, at his live shows. Under his beady gaze, he ensures the crowd rocks, rolls, sways and grooves to the sweet, sweet sound of Tim's voice. But who the fuck is he?

Sinister Cat. I've seen you at Tim Ten Yen's gigs. What do you actually do?
You takin' the rise? You WANT some DO YA??? Look, I run things. I'm in charge. Tim is my puppet. He does what I say. I write the songs. I choreograph the dance moves (well, the less shit ones). I basically do it all. Now fback off before I paw your throat out.

Describe Tim Ten Yen in no more than 23 words.
The bastard love-child of David Byrne, Graham Coxon, Nik Kershaw, Prince, David Lee Roth and all them other 80's gayers...recorded live at Top Of The Pops on a Sony Walkman.
OK, that's 32, but that's what you're getting

Why wouldn't you let us interview Tim?
He's busy changing my litter tray. (The sinister cat shouts 'Master Tim, get the piss out of my tray sharpish or I'll claw ya...fucking skivvy...').
Err, sorry, what were we talking about?

Did you frame Roger Rabbit?
Look, these rumours have been hanging over me for a long, long time now. It's getting boring. I know I was quoted on NME.com at the time as saying he was getting above his station, and I was going to claw his teeth off, but fuck it, I'm a cat, I can't talk and I'm bored – leave me alone

Tim Ten Yen releases 'When The Song Applies To You' on 7" vinyl on Monday 28th August
http://www.myspace.com/timtenyen

23RD UNION

words by Josh Jones
design by Steve Price (www.plan-bstudio.com)

23rd Union Fanzine
Client Mercury Records *Design* Steve Price *Year* 2006
Josh Jones, been the music savvy kind of guy, was approached to design a fanzine for boy Kill Boy.
He came and asked me to design it. The result was a 26pp fanzine festival of black and white beauty, all of it designed during one day.

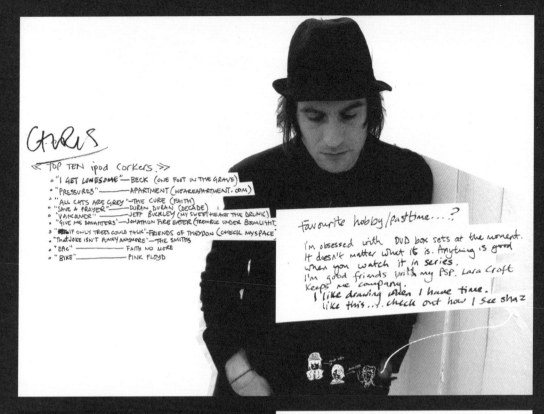

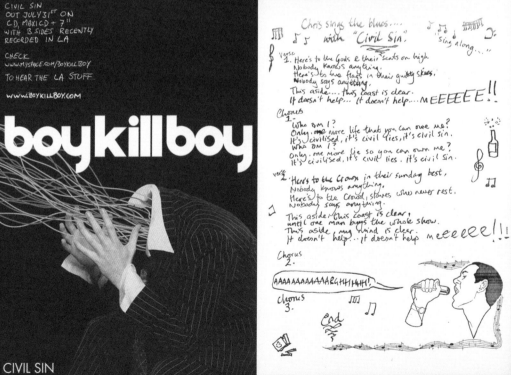

400

Some lovely memories

Playing Reading 05
Playing the Royal Albert Hall
The evening of the night we signed our record deal
Playing with and meeting Graham Coxon
Not unwell, actually actually everyone
The view from the top of the hill in San Francisco
The first time we heard our song on the radio
Living in the middle of the forest at sawmills
Seeing Dave Rangware backstage at T in the Park
Watching Chris fall off a boat
Meeting some of you lot at signings and babores

Pete's current iPod top 10

1) Queens Of The Stone Age: No One Knows
2) Jim Noir: My Patch
3) Johnny Cash: Folsom Prison Blues
4) Kanye West: Addiction
5) John Lennon: Mother
6) The Meters: Darling Darling Darling
7) Michael Jackson: Billie Jean
8) The Strokes: Reptilia
9) Blur: Trimm Trabb
10) G-Love and Special Sauce: Gimme Some Lov

Favourite hobbies/pastine?! Gdf.

TOP 10 IPOD TRACKS...>>>

Graham Coxon >>> Hero, I think we scared him.
Simon Williams >>> Gave us our first break releasing the original
Suzie on his label Fierce Panda.
Hard-Fi >>> Top guys. Took us out on our first tour last year.
Robbie Knox >>> Works on Soccer AM and introduced us to the show.
Spread a nasty rumour about me in my home town, but I forgive him.

1. Caught By The Fuzz >>> Supergrass
2. Pump It Up >>> Elvis Costello
3. One Armed Scissor >>> At The Drive In
4. The Rat >>> The Walkmen
5. Freakin' Out >>> Graham Coxon
6. Been Caught Stealing >>> Janes Addiction
7. When The Song Applies To You >>> Tim Ten Yen
8. If You Want Me To Stay >>> Phoenix
9. Run Run Run >>> Sly & The Family Stone
10. Groove Is In The Heart >>> Deelite

10 QUESTIONS FOR KEV BY PETE...>>>

1. Where do you live?
London
2. Where were you born?
London
3. What's the name of your local boozer?
Sambucca
4. What is your proudest moment?
Signing our record deal
5. What is your most disgraceful moment?
No comment
6. Have you ever had an altercation with a nightclub bouncer?
Yes, more than once.
7. What is your favourite Book, Film and Album?
Book: Any colouring in book
Film: Dog Day Afternoon
Album: I Should Coco by Supergrass
8. Do you prefer Blondes or Brunettes?
Brunettes, but blondes are good too.
9. Flowers or Chocolate?
Flowers
10. Favourite Boy Kill Boy track?
Exit

CHRIS OFFERS GREAT HAT ADVICE...

"Hats are special. You can never get bored of hats. Abuse them I'd say. Here are some helpful tips..."

"Visors are great for this time of year. And what with the 80's trends, you'll look very dishy on the beach."

"Never be afraid to get dandy with your head. Accessorise with a cravate perhaps."

"Always have a fold-away hat handy for that all important down-time."

"From time to time you may be in unsafe environments, like in a girls about mosh pit. Come prepared. Again, perhaps accessorise with a cravate or moustache."

"Never be afraid to modify."

"You know, sometimes it's effective to just keep it simple. An honest chapeau can often woo the hearts of many."

"Thanks for your time folks. In the next edition, we will be exploring Shower Caps, Berets, bonnets, Top hats and crowns."

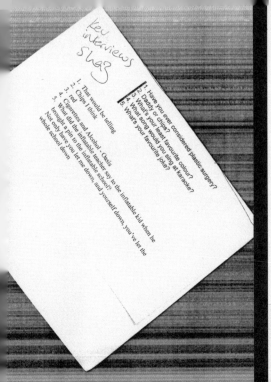

Kev
interviews
SHAZ

1. Have you ever considered plastic surgery?
2. Dandy or chips?
3. What's your least favourite colour?
4. What song would you sing at karaoke?
5. What's your favourite joke?

1. That would be telling
2. Chips I think
3. Red
4. Cigarettes and Alcohol - Oasis
5. What did the inflatable teacher say to the inflatable kid when he brought a pin to the inflatable school? Not only have you let me down, and yourself down you've let the whole school down

Dandy Tips from Pete

The Neck Scarf/Cravat

Always double up around...
reef knot (remember from sco...
are my preferred patterns.

Shoes

Smooth and dainty with...
leather generally looks mor...
Leather soles are a must. B...
kept minimal. Less is more...

Posture

Your posture should be...
but not too much. Back str...
Shoulders and toes, shoulde...

Smoking

No plastic lighters pl...
roll-ups.

How to hold your money at a...

Fold a £20 note length...
to make it rigid. Now hol...
your 1st and 2nd finger with...
your elbow on the bar. Sho...
get your drinks.

More tips next time

Pete Hammond

Boy Kill Boy's Five-Step Guide to Grooming

1. Wake up. Never wash off yesterday's eyeliner – it must build up all week for that all-important Sunday night at the Goth bar. Brush teeth. There's no room for furry teeth in Hollywood or Essex.

2. When the timing is suitable, apply afternoon garments. Perhaps a simple pair of skinnies and an old t-shirt (which makes no statement). Trainers may be appropriate, but only if they are over two years old.

3. Hair must always be groomed well – especially for our fans in the press who love to talk about it all the time. See Kev's hair dos and don'ts if unsure how to do this.

4. Evening arrives and a change of clothes is essential. Cravats, braces (for your socks as well), cummerbunds, and maybe a good hat should, at some level apply. See Chris guide to hats if unsure how to do this.

5. Wearing a brand new layer of eyeliner and threads clinging to your moist body, one is now ready to enjoy the evening's proceedings. Never remove the cravat, and make sure one is home for two hours beauty sleep to be ready for the next day's events.

① Muse - Knights of Cydonia
② Foo Fighters - In your honour
③ Ride - Cool your boots
④ Pulp - Don't you want me anymore?
⑤ Jeff Buckley - Lover, you should have come over
⑥ Razorlight - In the morning
⑦ 22-20s - Such a fool
⑧ Graham Coxon - Do what you are told
⑨ Taylor Hawkins and the coattail riders - Running in place
⑩ The Who - Pictures of Lily

Favorite Recreational Pastimes

Being in a band

Sitting in front of the tv with some mint choc chip ice cream and watching a movie

SHAZ interviews

- What size shoe are you U
- When was the last time you
- What's your favourite thing
- What will you do on your ne
- Have you ever fallen asleep
- If you had to live in one plac it be - Near month
- Who's your favourite cartoo
- How many kids do you want
- What was the last thing you
- Have you ever had any swim
- What's your favourite chat u
- Would you beat me in a race
- How about an arm wrestle
- What are you doing tomorrow
- Would you kiss Kev for a fi
- If you had to swap instrume would it be Chris - C
- If Lilly Allen asked you to m
- Do you have a foot fetish
- What would you ask the que
- Will you cook dinner for me

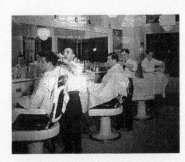

Kev's Hair Do's and Don'ts

1. Visit your hairdresser
2. Indulge in some mild form of banter or small talk, possibly about the weather or where you're gong on holiday this year
3. Tell him / her you want to look 'salon beautiful'
4. DO: Brush from left to right / Wash your hair regularly / Feel free to correct it during the day
5. DON'T: Use hair straighteners / Use a hairbrush

SHAZ
by Kev

Climate Report
Client Cooperative Bank/ Friends of the Earth *Design* Steve Price *Year* 2006
The objective was making the whole report feel and look very easy - easy to read, and easy to understand. The primary focus was on the 'roadmap'
designed to look like just that on the opening spread the roadmap illustrates the path to combating climate change.

402

THE FUTURE STARTS HERE:
THE ROUTE TO A
LOW-CARBON ECONOMY

Illustration 1: Cutting carbon dioxide steadily, starting now, enables a smooth transition. Delay and we have to take much more drastic action.

Government Total	Aviation (Int.)	Shipping (Int.)	Actual Total (2004)
150 MtC	9 MtC	5 MtC	164 MtC

Table 1: The Government's assessment of carbon emissions fall well below the real figure.

MtC = Million Tonnes Carbon

6 WHY WE NEED TO ACT NOW

THE BUDGET
The key findings of *Living Within a Carbon Budget* are that:

• The UK must emit no more than 4.6 Giga-tonnes of carbon between 2000 and 2050 if it is to deliver its fair share of emission cuts to achieve a concentration of 450 parts per million carbon dioxide in the atmosphere. This is our "carbon budget". (Whether the UK aims to deliver its fair share is a political and moral question that this report does not attempt to address.) A carbon budget of 4.6 Giga-tonnes is equivalent to roughly 28 years' worth of current emissions. That is to say, if the UK continues to emit carbon dioxide at its current level, then in 2028 the entire carbon budget will have been used and the UK will need to stop emitting carbon dioxide completely (illustration 1) – a technical impossibility.

• Carbon dioxide emissions have not fallen in the UK since 1990, despite claims to the contrary by the Government which has ignored emissions from international aviation and shipping (Table 1).[2] Emissions have actually increased in recent years.

• Immediate government action to reduce energy consumption and drive innovation is needed and possible. A comprehensive programme of action must be implemented within the next four years (ie by 2010). If action is delayed much beyond this then the scale of cuts will have to be much greater.

• As long as action is taken now it will be possible to live within this carbon budget and have a healthy, growing economy and enjoy lifestyles not radically different from today. The longer we leave it, the more radical the changes will need to be.

The research made a number of assumptions: the amount of biomass energy is constrained by sustainability limits (because land is also needed for food production and biodiversity protection); the structure of the economy remains broadly the same and continues to grow; and nuclear power is undesirable (because of intractable waste problems and security concerns).

The Tyndall Centre was not asked to consider economic aspects of climate change, but to concentrate on the science and technologies. Others have looked at economic impacts. The Group of 8 richest nations (G8) stated in 2005 that:

Improvements to energy efficiency have benefits for economic growth and the environment, as well as co-benefits such as reducing greenhouse gas emissions, preventing pollution, alleviating poverty, improving security of energy supply, competitiveness and improving health and employment.[5]

The 14 chief executives of some of the biggest businesses in the UK told Tony Blair on 6 June 2006:

Bold leadership on domestic climate change policy has the potential to deliver significant economic benefits to the UK. These include improvements in economic performance through increasing energy efficiency; improved growth as a result of technological innovation; greater energy security; and access to significant global export markets for low carbon technologies [...] However, the UK will only access these potential economic benefits if domestic policies provide strong incentives for technological development.[6]

Other social, personal and economic benefits from a low-carbon economy will include cleaner air and fewer road accidents, and better health as more people choose to cycle and walk. It will mean spending less money on flood defences and less on cleaning up after floods, and it will mean less expenditure helping poorer countries deal with floods, hurricanes and land loss.

GOOD FOR PEOPLE
The way we live daily life does not need to be radically different in a low-carbon economy. We will have warm houses – in fact with the right policies more people will have warmer homes. We will have jobs, leisure, and mobility. What will change radically is how energy efficient our lives are, and where we get our energy from.

GOOD FOR THE ENVIRONMENT, GOOD FOR THE ECONOMY 7

	Oil	Coal	Gas	Nuclear	Biofuel	Renew	Total
2004	81.6	39.4	89.4	19.6	14.7	1.5	246.0
2030	57.5	42.2	53.9	2.0	21.0	16.6	194.2
2050	31.7	34.1	24.8	0	15.3	17.2	118.1

Table 2: Total energy supply 2004–2050, Million Tonnes of Oil Equivalent

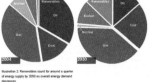

Illustration 2: Renewables count for around a quarter of energy supply by 2050 as overall energy demand decreases.

40 ENERGY – A BIG ISSUE

"The research suggests that in 2030 total energy use could be reduced by 20 per cent and fossil fuel use by over a third."

How the UK satisfies its energy needs in the future has rightly provoked keen political debate.

THE FIRST COMPREHENSIVE STUDY
Had the Government's own 2006 Energy Review been more comprehensive it might have provided clarity on how the UK could provide for its future energy needs - including transport which is a fast-growing source of emissions. It could also have taken on board latest scientific understanding that carbon dioxide concentrations need to be kept below 450 parts per million and not the 550 parts per million previously thought. The Review failed on both counts. Living Within a Carbon Budget is more comprehensive, looks over a longer period and is scientifically up to date.

REDUCE DEMAND FIRST
Cutting energy demand is critical to meeting carbon dioxide targets as well as switching dependency away from imported fossil fuels. Today the UK gets around 90 per cent of its energy from fossil fuels (oil, coal and gas). Since 1990 oil consumption has increased by almost a third and gas use has almost doubled, while coal use has almost halved. Total energy use has increased by over 10 per cent.

The research suggests that in 2030 total energy use could be reduced by 20 per cent and fossil fuel use by over a third. Using cleaner fuels and capturing carbon dioxide from power plants and storing it could result in carbon dioxide emissions being reduced by 70 per cent. By 2030 renewable power and bio-fuels could provide a quarter of all energy needs.

Looking further, by 2050 energy use could be reduced by half and fossil fuel use by 70 per cent. Emissions of carbon dioxide could be reduced by 90 per cent. Bio-fuels and renewable energy could provide 40 per cent of renewable energy.

Key findings on energy from
Living Within a Carbon Budget
include:

· Innovation is critical.
· Government intervention is needed to drive innovation.
· Greater levels of innovation or more aggressive Government action could achieve even greater cuts in emissions and further reductions in fossil fuel use.
· There is a need for a strong focus on reducing energy.
· With greater support renewables can play a very significant role in meeting energy needs.
· Hydrogen, produced by renewables and fossil fuels incorporating carbon capture and storage, will be an important energy carrier in the future.
· It is possible to satisfy energy needs and live within this carbon budget without recourse to nuclear power.

44

Look Book SS'07- Red Dot Clothing

Client Red Dot Clothing *Design* Steve Price *Year* 2007

Together with Red Dot and copywriter Josh Jones we developed the concept that the Look Book should be designed in the style of a glossy ga magazine. It should be an interview with the son and grandson of William Samuel DeBon - the ficticious character that the SS07 collection is ba upon. Creating an elaborate, and intrinsic story to accompany the photoshoot was a lot of fun as was designing it in this style.

Peregrine stands in the rose garden on the spot where his father's decapitated body was discovered by the family poodle, Sasha. Peregrine wears a Sky Blue Safari Jacket by Red Dot.

Father and Son relax in the Cinema, seated in 2 of the 3 chairs given to William Samuel De Bon by Adolf Hitler during World War 2.
Peregrine wears Blue Strap Waisted Chino Pants, a Navy Blue De Bon Air T Shirt and a Blue Ike Jacket while Sebastian wears Grey Strap Waisted Chino Pants, an Ecru Goggles T Shirt and an Ecru Ike Jacket, all by Red Dot.

Left: Sebastian looks out across the rolling fields of the De Bon family estate, its boundaries stretching farther than the eye can see. He wears Ecru Cable Print Track Pants and a Cloudy Sky Hoodie with matching T Shirt, all by Red Dot.
Above: Sebastian sits in his favourite spot where William Samuel De Bon first taught him to smoke as a child. He wears Stone Girly Paisley Print Safari Shorts, a Black Girly Paisley Print Polo Shirt and Stone Girly Paisley Print Safari Jacket, all by Red Dot.
Below: A discarded Yellow Sunglasses T Shirt on the back of a Dining Room chair. T Shirt by Red Dot.

of his companies when I turned 18, but his sudden death put paid to that."

After the death of William Samuel, what has happened to his many companies? I see some of them have already been sold.

Peregrine: "It's all about money, I needed some more, so I sold some stuff, I think that father would have approved. I saw a number of opportunities and decided to strike while the iron was hot. Experience told me that opportunities of this kind do not come along more than once in a life time so I acted swiftly."

Sebastian: "Your experience? Have you read the financial pages recently? Or not? Speed & Co. Crane Suppliers' profit forecasts are triple what they were when you sold the company 6 weeks ago. And

"THERE IS SOMETHING VAGUELY REWARDING ABOUT WORKING ALTHOUGH I WOULDN'T RECOMMEND IT AS A FULL TIME OCCUPATION"

PEREGINE AND SEBASTIAN

IN AN *Oi!* EXCLUSIVE PEREGRINE AND SEBASTIAN DE BON HAVE OPENED THE DOORS TO THEIR FAMILY ESTATE IN HAMPSHIRE

Above: Father and Son enjoying a late morning stroll in the 300 acre grounds of the De Bon family estate. Peregrine wears a Cloudy Sky Polo Shirt and Sebastian a Cloudy Sky Hoodie with matching T shirt underneath, all by Red Dot."

1

Above: Father and Son stand staring on the stairs. Sebastian wears Ecru Cable Print Track Pants, a Blue Marle Wayward Seamen Yacht T Shirt and a Navy Blue WanchorS Hoodie while Peregrine wears Ecru Artists Pants, an Ecru WanchorS Polo Shirt and a Pink Cable Print Fleece Tank Top, all by Red Dot

Above: Peregrine on the stairs leading to his father's private apartments which are rumoured to by haunted by the ghost of William Samuel De Bon's Grandfather, Sparky De Bon Fire. Peregrine wears an Ecru Wanchor5 Polo Shirt and a Pink Cable Print Fleece Tank Top, both by Red Dot.

Above: Sebastian on the stairs leading to the back passage where he can often be found. Sebastian wears Ecru Cable Print Track Pants, a Blue Marle Wayward Seamen Yacht Club T Shirt and a Navy Blue Wanchors hoodie, all by Red Dot.

The Enemy Fanzine
Client Warner Records *Design* Steve Price *Year* 2006
Having designed fanzines for Boy Kill Boy, and 23rd Union, Mercury Records enlisted myself and Josh Jones (editor of all three fanzines) to write and design a fanzine for the Sheffield born 'soon-to-be-bigger-than-god' band, The Enemy.
So well received was our effort that the record label have decided to reprint 30,000 of them.

410

ANDY

BASS GUITAR / BACKING VOCALS IN
THE ENEMY.
Don't worry 'bout it, fuckin kickin arse
yeah!

Right I've come straight out of
sunny Coventry, made it through
school and spent months and months
fuckin round in stock rooms and on the
booze and birds. Still ain't bored of them
so ladies don't be shy yeah...
Now I'm ready to forgll my ambition and
show people what we're really about. Signed
the deal and gonna have as much fun
as poss coz thats what liges about
aint it ..... Laters

THE ENEMY

At what point are you going to start wearing really, really skinny jeans?
HOWS ABOUT NEVER!? STUPID QUESTION, NEXT. ANYWAY THEY LOOK LIKE LEGGINGS, YOU GOTTA LET THE OLD MAN BREATH AIN'T YA. LOOK AT PELE, HE SUFFERED FROM THE 80'S TIGHT JEANS REVOLUTION. LOOK AT THE OLD BOY NOW. HE CANT GET IT UP FOR SHIT, SMACKED OFF HIS TITS ON VIAGRA TO GET A LOB ON. MAYBE WE SHOULD USE HIM TO RAISE AWARENESS?

Tell me who you are
WE ARE THE FUTURE

How are you going to change the music world then?
WE'RE JUST GONNA WAKE EVERYONE UP. TOO MANY DORMANT AREAS. ALL THIS FASHIONISTA BULLSHIT. TOO MUCH 'STYLE' AND NOT ENOUGH SUBSTANCE. STRIPPED DOWN, NO NONSENSE, BALLS OUT ROCK AND ROLL IS WHAT ITS ABOUT. IT AINT ROCKET SCIENCE. WE'RE GONNA TALK ABOUT WHATS REALLY HAPPENING, WHY ARE BANDS AFRAID TO WRITE CHORUSES THESE DAYS. EVERYTHINGS JUST SO FOOKING BORING AND BLAND. NOBODY IS SAYING FOOK ALL!

Is heroin cool?
ABOUT AS COOL AS A KICK IN THE BOLLOCKS. SEEN IT DESTROY HOMES AND NEIGHBOURHOODS WHERE WE'RE FROM. ANYONE PROMOTES IT ROUND ME AND I'LL LAUNCH EM!

You're from Coventry. Is it any good there?
YOU TAKING THE PISS? ITS HELL ON EARTH. BUT WE WOULDN'T CHANGE IT FOR THE WORLD.

What would you say to the head of Peugeot if you met him?
FIRSTLY, I'D ASK HIM WHY HE HASN'T GOT THE BOLLOCKS TO SIT DOWN INFRONT OF ALL THE PEUGOT WORKERS TO LISTEN AND TAKE ON BOARD WHAT THEY HAVE TO SAY. TO ANSWER THE QUESTIONS THEY NEED TO ASK ABOUT THEIR FUTURE WHEN IT MATTERED. SECONDLY I'D LOVE TO FOOKIN LAUNCH HIM..... OOOOOUCE!!! SIMPLY BECAUSE HE SOLD FAMILIES, GENERATIONS, LOYALTY AND THE CITY OF COVENTRY DOWN THE RIVER JUST TO BECOME COST EFFECTIVE AND FOOKING GREEDY! FILLING HIS AND HIS COMPANIES POCKETS AT THE EXPENSE OF THOUSANDS OF FAMILIES. SHIT COMPENSATION PAYOFFS AND HARDLY ANY WARNING, IN AINT ON! THEN I'D TAKE HIM FOR A BEER DOWN FOLLY LANE SOCIAL AND LET ALL HIS EX WORKERS SHOE THE HEAD OFF HIM. MOONWALK ALL OVER HIS FACE. WHAT A CUNT!

TOM

SINGER + GUITAR — THE ENEMY,

WHAT HAVE I GOT TO SAY
FOR MYSELF?

YES HEADS, LETS TALK ABOUT
THE FACT THAT THE WORLD
IS LIVIN IN A SHIT 9-5
ROUTINE AND NO ONE'S
QUESTIONIN IT, WHATS ALL
THAT ABOUT? WAKE UP
YEH? LETS CHANGE IT,
HAVE A LAFF INSTEAD,
TELL YOUR BOSS TO
FUCK OFF AND DO
SOMETHING THAT YOU WANNA
DO, IN A BITCH

THE ENEMY

If you happen to be young, intelligent and restless, Coventry is a surprisingly inspiring place to be today- if only for all the wrong reasons. What was a once proud, vibrant town that was known around the world for its motoring exports (Jaguar, Peugeot) has succumbed to economic progress and is fast becoming an identikit British city of chain stores, franchised nightlife and abundant apathy. After spending the first 18 years of life watching the soul get ripped out of their hometown, the three members of The Enemy are determined to connect their own frustrations up with that of an entire country.

Already mutual friends beforehand, The Enemy became genuine music allies in February of 2006. Andy Hopkins brought along his bass and boyish good looks, Liam Watts added a fearsome drumming prowess that blows away tub-thumpers twice his age and the young Mark E. Smith look-a-like Tom Clarke provided all the swagger and sneer that anyone could possibly expect from someone who has to sing and play guitar at the same time. Initially, the main motivation for the band was simply boredom in its many forms. "There's nothing to do," states Tom bluntly. "Although I did most of my growing up in Birmingham, it's still very similar to Coventry when it comes to being bored. You're either down the pub or you're not so starting a band represented doing something a bit different to everyone else we know." What started out as an exercise in keeping yourselves occupied soon developed into something more serious as the band realized that a) what they were doing was really, really good and b) they preferred it more to their day jobs by a distance of several light years.

Just eight months (eight months!) later, The Enemy are releasing their sinister yet pulverizing first single '40 Days, 40 Nights' on the newly rejuvenated punk label Stiff records that once brought the world of the seminal early work of The Damned and Elvis Costello. Proof that they are already making a racket loud enough and impressive enough to awaken a sleeping giant. With the songs continuing to come thick and fast and the lofty comparisons to such luminaries as Oasis and Kasabian adding an element of early vindication, sticking with it seems like the only sensible option because as Tom continues, the alternative is a painfully stifling one.

"It's either this or get some shit 9-5 job, work your arse off for a relatively small amount of money and not have any real aims or ambitions… just like everyone else.
If you look at most people that you know, they work in jobs that they either dislike or hate and their only goals are to get a decent girl and settle down in an average house. Everyone just seems to think 'that's life' but it doesn't have to be at all."
Having seen various members of their families live and work to this unsatisfying blueprint (until the grave in the case of Tom's grandfather who worked at the recently closed Browns Lane Jaguar factory), The Enemy intend to reiterate that being working class doesn't have to be merely another incarnation of adult slavery. "Why should you just accept that life is just work and work and work until you die? If you actually stop to question your regular routine, you'd be pissed off. All you're doing is making someone else a lot of money. I'm not trying to be Billy Bragg or even to be political necessarily, we just want people to wake up."

The time to rise, has been engaged.

words: Hardeep Phull

LIAM

Dirty, sweaty Drumming bastard ~~for~~ the enemy. Loving every minute.

Born in geodic coventry. Did school n that. A lot of lazy days, ~~xxxxx xxxxx~~ and now im here. In a Signed band, going ~~round the~~ country doin what im good at, ~~Drumming n ase off.~~ Meeting a lot of cool people some not so cool people. But loving it all the same. Cant complain

I aint looking too far into the future right now. Just enjoying each day as it comes. Dont even know what day of the week it is to be honest. Its all good tho. LAAATERS!

Roundel
7 Rosehart Mews
Westbourne Grove
London W11 3TY
+44 (0)20 7221 1951
info@roundel.com

Please do not bend

AX

Royal Mail

POSTAGE   PAID   UK
14/03/07   £6.69   W8
133006   4-2077673-1

ROUNDEL ®

airsure ®   PRIORITY MAIL

DELIVERY CONFIRMATION   AIRSURE Exprès ®

LY 3222 5097 5GB   No sig req

LY 3222 5097 5GB   No sig req

LY 3222 5097 5GB

Scan   No Signature

Ikono In Line Off Line

Client Zanders / M-real *Design* Paul Ingle, John Bateson *Year* 2003

The book is split into four main sections showcasing a surface from the Ikono paper range. These divisions are filled with a wealth of figurative and graphic imagery that are used to employ a multitude of print techniques and finishes that demonstrate the benefits of the Ikono range.

420

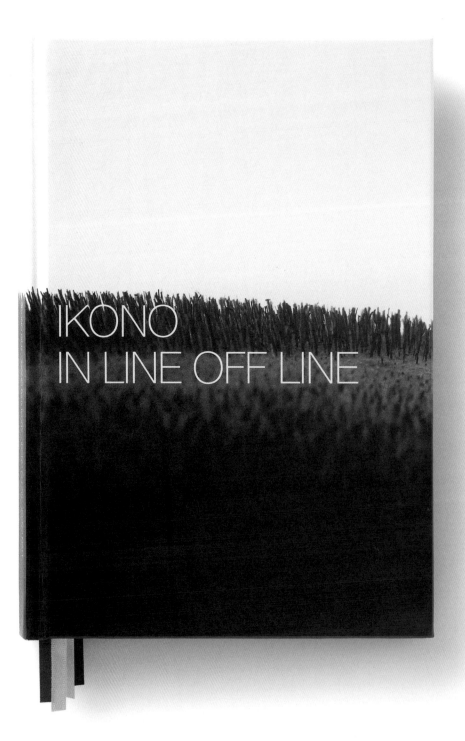

422

426

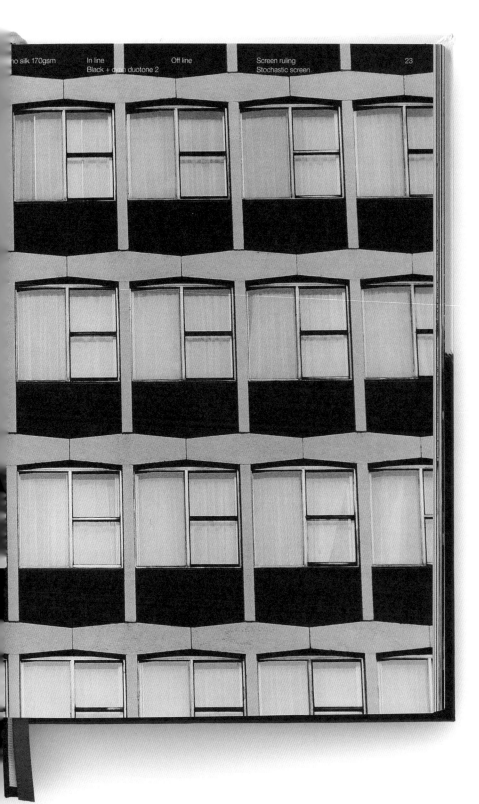

Nut Free
Client Zanders/ M-real *Design* Mike Denny, Adam Browne *Year* 2006
We created a series of tongue-in-cheek benefits promoting the environmental and design advantages of the new product and service.
Working closely with an illustrator we refined ideas and developed a series of images to be used throughout the campaign.

Fat free

The new Zeta recycled range,
50% of pulp comes from managed, sustainable forests

Unleaded

The new Zeta recycled range,
manufactured with 50% post consumer waste

All day confidence

The new Zeta bespoke watermark system,
added company prestige, enhanced corporate image

Durable finishes

The new Zeta recycled range,
available in 3 finishes; Hammer, Linen and Wove

BY AIR MAIL
par avion

Sampsonmay
4 Tanner Street
London SE1 3LD
+44 (0)20 7403 4099
studio@sampsonmay.com
www.sampsonmay.com

bend

SampsonMay

Sampson May
Client Self-promotional *Design* Ricky Sampson *Year* 2007
Self-promotional book about the studio.

SampsonMay
ShowMe

Our design agency is shaped by SE1.
The stimulating shelves of Tate Modern's
bookshop. The tastes of Borough Market.
The sayings of The Bard on open-air
boards. The fancy footwear on cobbled

SampsonMay
SmallMighty

Working on design projects for huge
FTSE 100 companies, we pay attention to
the smallest detail. Finding design solutions
for smaller clients, we come up with big,
powerful ideas. On all projects, we offer

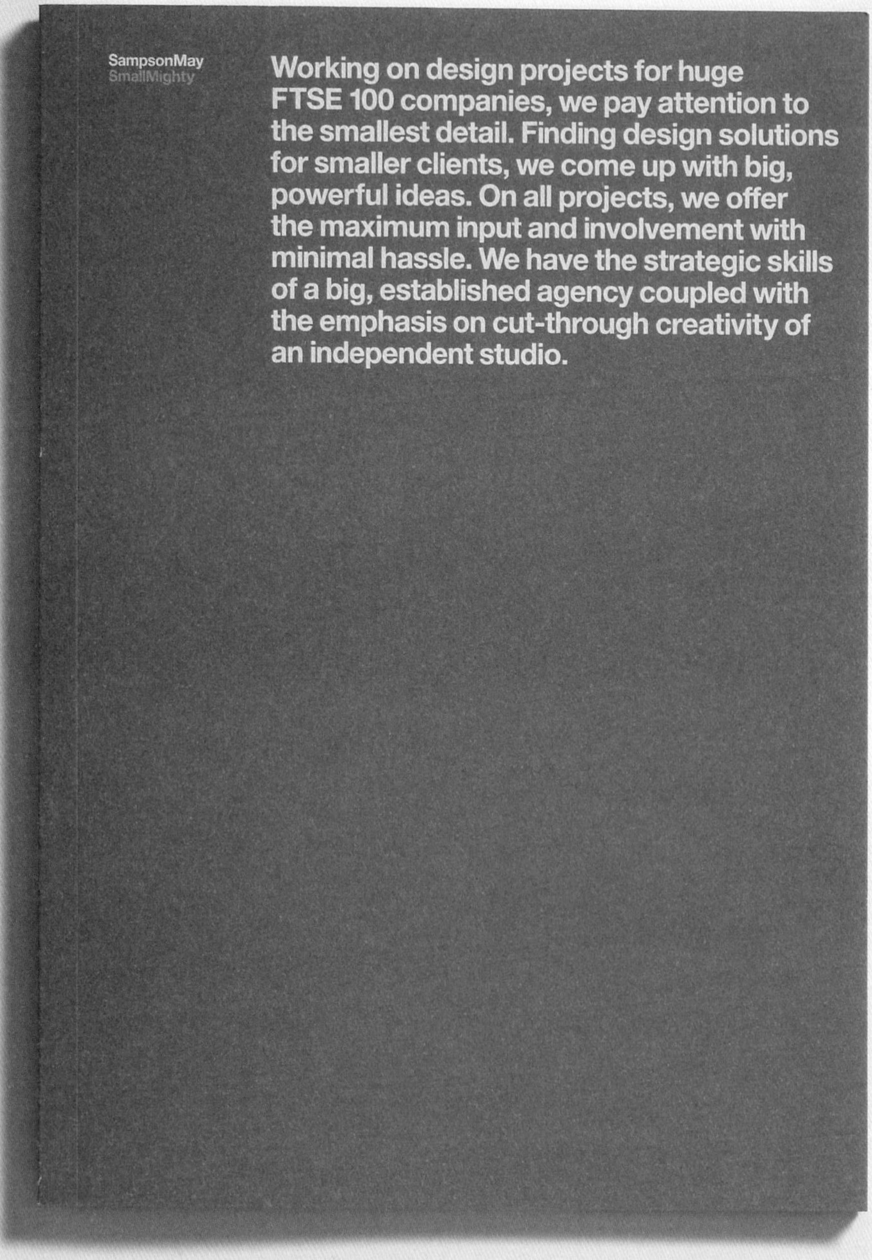

SampsonMay
SmallMighty

Working on design projects for huge FTSE 100 companies, we pay attention to the smallest detail. Finding design solutions for smaller clients, we come up with big, powerful ideas. On all projects, we offer the maximum input and involvement with minimal hassle. We have the strategic skills of a big, established agency coupled with the emphasis on cut-through creativity of an independent studio.

SampsonMay
SmallMighty

Sucden (UK) Limited
Corporate Advertising

SampsonMay
SmallMighty

You can skip this page. The best way to learn about our thinking is to look at our work. We believe that it speaks for itself, without the need for preamble, explanation or rationale. We'll simply say that all the work in this brochure is the result of our belief that creative solutions should be communication-led, not design-led.

To this end, we work closely with our clients to understand their business goals and communication issues. We make sure that the intricacies of our clients' products or service are clear to us. Throughout the process, we take a disciplined approach to design, channelling our creativity in the agreed strategic direction.

During the implementation stage we make sure that our ideas are executed in the most efficient way, targeted towards a precisely defined audience. Then, when the project's completed, we carry out a detailed debrief with our client to see what lessons we can learn.

This is our thinking

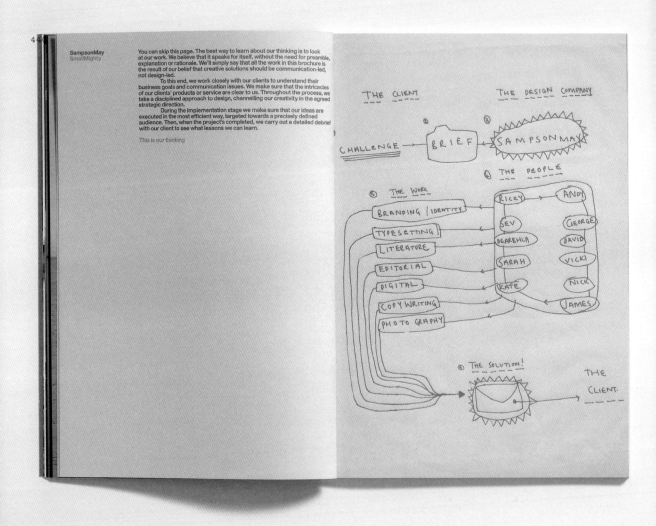

SampsonMay
SmallMighty

Ri2k – John Richmond
Advertising and Branding
Autumn/Winter

444

SPAIN

Barcelona,

08870 SITGES,

08870

Saturday
Biscuit Building 3rd Floor 10
Redchurch Street
London E2
+44 (0)20 7749 4500
www.saturday-london.com

1
25
43
87
46
48

LONDON
19.02.07
E2

GREAT BRITAIN

PB 253279

0102

POSTAGE PAID

GQStyle

LUXE
Feel the quality

TERRY'S HOMBRES

By TERRY RICHARDSON

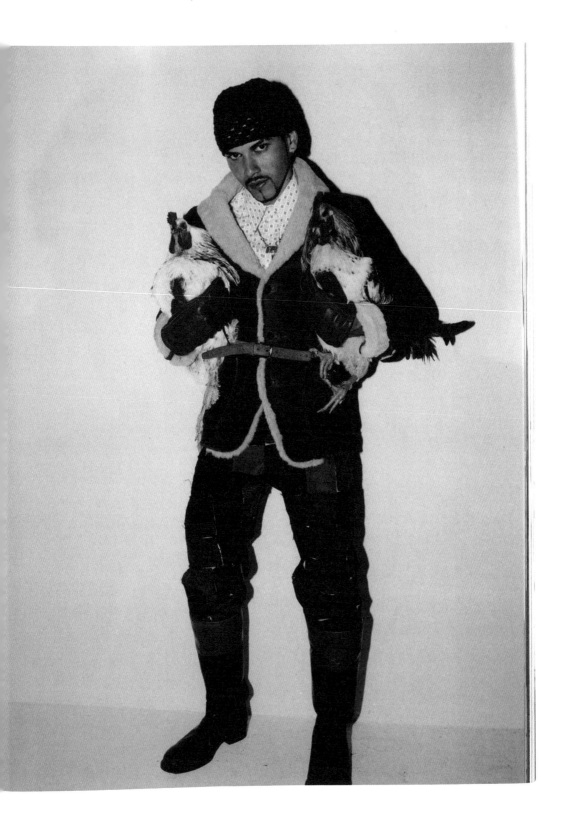

Captain Chris Johnston
AT SHAIBAH LOGISTICAL BASE, IRAQ
PHOTOGRAPHED BY SUSAN SCHULMAN

the sunbathers

'In war films soldiers always seem to have plenty of downtime, so I was surprised when I realised how little time there is to relax,' says Captain Chris Johnston of the Duke of Wellington's Regiment. That's him sitting on the foldaway chair, but he insists that this photograph in Iraq illustrates a rare opportunity to soak up some sun before heading home to the UK.

'Sometimes you'll be out for 20 hours, driving and visiting villages. It doesn't leave much time for relaxing, particularly as there are always weapons and vehicles to clean when we're not on active patrol. He doesn't have a distinct working week. 'You just grab any downtime whenever you can.'

Because the threat level is so high, the troops don't leave the base to socialise in local bars or restaurants – as has happened in previous conflicts. Although some bases are quite sophisticated, with a Subway or Pizza Hut, and have rooms showing Sky Sports, others are rudimentary places, not much bigger than a couple of football pitches, where there's nothing to do but listen to the British Forces Broadcasting Service.

Johnston joined the army four years ago after a successful stint as a professional rugby player for both London Scottish and Leeds Tykes, and, unsurprisingly, he still plays a lot of sport. 'Watching football is very popular, and we play volleyball, football and touch rugby, as it's vital to keep the guys fit.' When he's asked if the officers always pick the sides, he says, 'When we're at

rest, there's no real distinction between the officers and the lads. Some of them are only 18 years old, and I'm amazed at their professionalism. I think back to what I was doing at university when I was their age, and it's very different.'

Is blogging as popular among the British troops as it seems to be with the Americans? 'There is internet access,' he says. 'But I've not heard of anyone writing a blog. From what I can tell, they spend most of their time checking "Hot or Not" to see how girls are reacting to their photos.'

At some point during a tour, every soldier has two weeks to rest and relax back in the UK. Although most of the lads cram in as much partying as they can, when he's back home, Chris sees the time to chill out. 'Until you go home, you don't realise how on edge you are. On my first day back, I walked down Oxford Street with my girlfriend, but I spent the whole time scanning for booby-traps. After an hour I'd had enough. When I'm at home I need to wind down, so I go out for the odd meal with my girlfriend, see friends and family, and maybe go to the theatre.'

Does the modern-day army have its equivalents of Dame Vera Lynn and Bob Hope, visiting the troops to boost morale? 'Sort of,' Johnston says. 'We've had John Barnes over doing tricks and talking to the guys. Jakki Degg and Leilani have also been here, posing for photos with the troops. I wasn't there, but by all accounts they went down well.' *David Amand*

AUTOPIA
by Phil Poynter

MEN WILL DISCOVER FOR
THEMSELVES THE BENEFITS OF CARING
FOR THE SKIN ON THEIR BODIES

Rosignano Solvay Sea 2 (1998)
PHOTOGRAPHED BY MASSIMO VITALI

Work's out

Leisure once meant picnics
and cricket. But modern
man – atomised, infantilised,
credit-crazy – has a lifestyle
to consider. So, are we
enjoying ourselves?
by Michael Bracewell

Back in the 1930s a young man called Peter Fleming – who happened to be the brother of Ian Fleming, the creator of James Bond – set off by train from London on a journalistic mission to Manchuria. He would later begin his account of this journey by describing the English suburbs and countryside as he saw them from the window of the boat train.

It was the start of a fine weekend. 'England was looking her best,' he wrote. From his few details, we get a good idea of leisured ease in the 1930s. He saw people setting off with picnic hampers and tennis rackets strapped to the back of their cars; a man fishing beside a quiet river; cricketers assembling on a village green; golfers striding from clubhouse to fairway; people walking their dogs or pottering in the garden. Simple pleasures – camaraderie?

Fleming became so wistful at the sight of these cosy, comforting, leisured pursuits that he very nearly gave up the whole idea of spending two and a half weeks on a succession of trains and mules in order to reach a hailowpy province of deepest China. Why bother with adventure, when it's so much nicer at home? In all these tennis rackets and golfers and picnic hampers was the very essence – the lifeblood, so to speak – of order, routine and familiarity, as welcoming, friendly and reassuring as a favourite pair of old brown shoes.

Since Peter looked out from the boat train, a great deal, of course, has changed in British society. If you were looking for common denominators of that change, you'd probably hit such concepts as 'acceleration' and 'fragmentation'. Everything moves faster these days, and there's a far less distinct sense of order. For better or worse, old ideas of work, leisure and class have been rearranged, and we now inhabit a consumer menu-environment in which most things are available most of the time. It is a modern paradox, therefore, that when people get home from work, they tend to get bored a lot more easily. After all, one toffee-nut mochaccino tastes much the same as another.

In the midst of all of this confusion, how – if at all – have men's attitudes towards their leisure time changed? In the first place, social evolution has dismantled the old divisions and hierarchies that used to frame our every move. If you look at the short documentary films made by the British Film Institute's Experimental Films Fund during the 1950s, you see a world in which class, above all, is the defining social structure – but one gradually >

Images curated by Jimo Toyin Salako

452

"A CLOAK CONVEYS A SENSE OF MYSTERY, HISTORY AND PROTECTION"

ALEXANDRE PLOKHOV, CLOAK

New York, Wednesday 9 February. Menswear in New York is a battered beast, with few shows dotted through the womenswear-dominated schedule. So it's a thrill to attend the menswear-only show by Cloak, which menaces the safe Manhattan catwalks with a welcome defiance.

We are big fans of Alexandre Plokhov, the man behind Cloak. There's a nascent quality about his collections that makes them very appealing. Even though he's now acting on a global stage – his recent Best New Menswear Designer win at this year's CDFA awards ensured that – his clothes (and there's more to him than just cloaks) still seem personal, and carry a great deal of conviction.

There is little advice you can give with a cloak – either you've got the balls to wear one, or you haven't. If you go ahead, make sure the trousers that peek out below are in a background colour. The shape of the cloak will do the shouting for you, making a statement that doesn't need to be fought against.

PHOTOGRAPHED BY TOMO BREJC

FROM LEFT: ROBIE WEARS CLOAK, LOUIS VUITTON. CARDIGAN, £190, SILAS. SHIRT, £24.99, RIVER ISLAND. JEANS, £40, TOPMAN. LEATHER TIE, £12, URBAN RENEWAL AT URBAN OUTFITTERS. JAMES WEARS CROPPED CAPE, £250; TROUSERS, £180; AND SHIRT, £180, ALL DERYCK WALKER. CHELSEA BOOTS, £135, HUDSON. BAG, £3950, FENDI. UMBRELLA, £145, BURBERRY LONDON. MARCH WEARS CAPE, £1300, DIOR HOMME BY HEDI SLIMANE. SHIRT, £205; CARDIGAN, £505, BOTH DSQUARED2. JEANS, £210, PRADA. OLIVER WEARS CAPE-COAT, FROM £850; SHIRT, FROM £170, BOTH CLOAK. JEANS, £250, PRADA. BAG, £695, MULBERRY. SEE DATA FOR DETAILS.

Scott King
+44 207 359 2316
info@scottking.co.uk
www.scottking.co.uk

AX

Royal Mail

POSTAGE   PAID   UK
19/03/07   £5.41   N5
81004   2-2792522-1

28 BAJOS

STITGES

ONA

Royal Mail® | PRIORITY MAIL

airsure®   AIRSURE Exprès

DELIVERY CONFIRMATION

LY 1819 4527 5GB   No sig req

LY 1819 4527 5GB   No sig req

LY 1819 4527 5GB

Scan   No Signature

SLEAZENATION

A BARRAGE OF BLEEDING EDGE FASHION, ART, MUSIC AND DESIGN WITH THE ODD VINTAGE THATCH

Militant Pop

Do you believe in revolution?

AD ROCK • STEPFORD LIVES • STREETWEAR SPECIAL • PORN TO ROCK
ZOOT WOMAN • NOBLE AND SILVER • CRAFT WORK • DANIEL JOHNSTON

SLEAZENATION

AN ABUNDANCE OF SUBLIME FASHION, ART, MUSIC AND DESIGN WITH A PEEK AT BLONDIE'S FLUFFER

Some people should be shot
Our photographers take on Britain

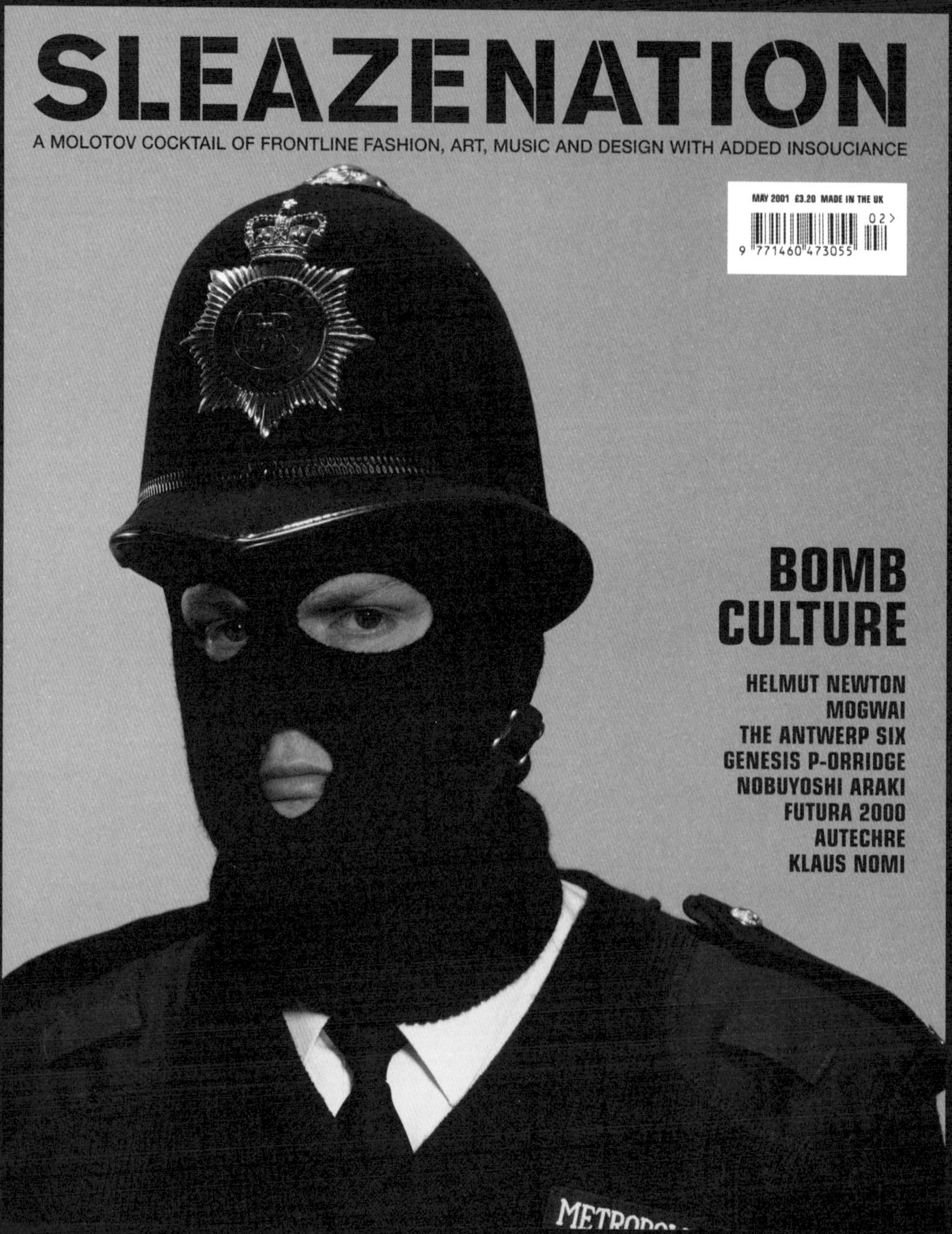

458

SLEAZENATION

A MOLOTOV COCKTAIL OF FRONTLINE FASHION, ART, MUSIC AND DESIGN WITH ADDED INSOUCIANCE

MAY 2001 £3.20 MADE IN THE UK

9 771460 473055

02>

BOMB
CULTURE

HELMUT NEWTON
MOGWAI
THE ANTWERP SIX
GENESIS P-ORRIDGE
NOBUYOSHI ARAKI
FUTURA 2000
AUTECHRE
KLAUS NOMI

METROPOL

SLEAZENATION

AN IDEAL FOR LIVING THROUGH HONEST FASHION, ART, MUSIC AND DESIGN

I'M WITH STUPID

JARVIS COCKER & BARRY 7 • ARAKI FASHION EXCLUSIVE • BIBA • THE HIVES
DJ BIRD • KILLED BY DEATH • CHARLIE LUXTON • RAPING STEVEN SPIELBERG

NOV 2001 £3.20 MADE IN THE UK

9 771460 473055   02 >

460

Chair throwing England fan wears replica Accrington Stanley
Football Club shirt, shorts by Next

Wet England fan wears T-shirt by Daily Star and jeans by Pepe

Mike Egerton/Empics

Missile throwing England fan wears shirt Hackett ● Bleeding England fan wears shirt by Aquascutum

464

epidemic

a
fashion
story

Story Scott King
Courtesy of Magnani, London

Scuffling England fans left to right: Replica England shirt by
Umbro, jacket by Harrington, jeans by Lee ● Replica England
shirt by Umbro, jeans by Chipie ● Shirt by Ted Baker and jeans
by Duffer of St. George ●Victimised fan wears jacket by
Chevignon, jumper by John Smedley

SEA Design
70 St John Street
London
EC1M 4DT

Telephone
020 7566 3100
Facsimile
020 7566 3101

Email
info@seadesign.co.uk
Website
www.seadesign.co.uk

Sea Design
70 St John Street
London EC1M 4DT
020 7566 3100
info@seadesign.co.uk
www.seadesign.co.uk

EA

S

Surface Seduction
Client GF Smith *Design* SEA *Year* 2006
Phoenix Motion is a smooth white uncoated paper by GF Smith.
The brief was to produce promotional material that showcases the quality of the paper.

115/135
150/170
250GSM

XENON/
XANTUR

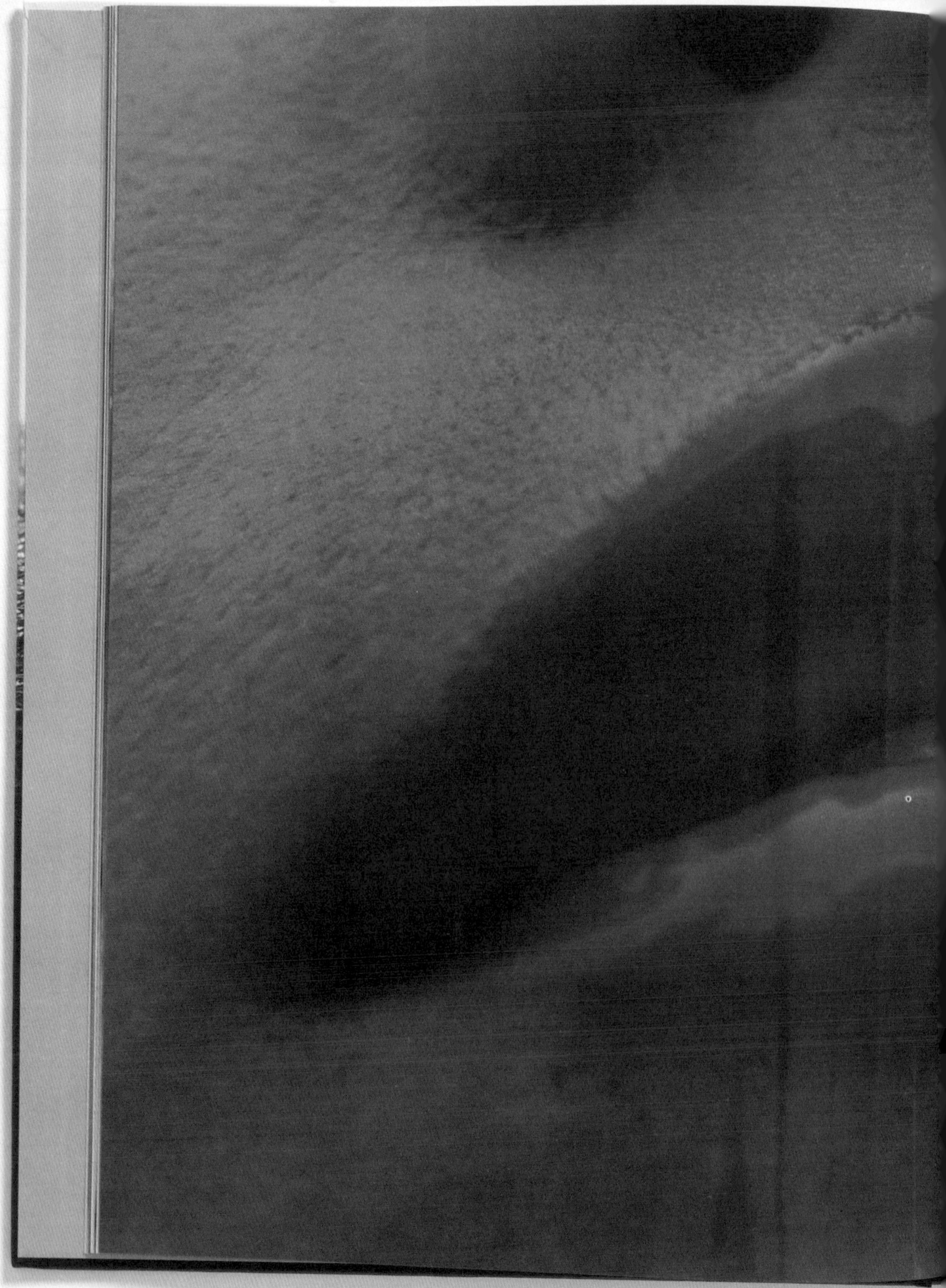

Grafik Magazine
Client Grafik *Design* SEA *Year* 2006-2007
Grafik magazine wanted to update its look and increase sales by appealing to a wider audience.

fiKjg
grfiK
read
my
grafiKj
filthy
salt lips

Special Report
Editorial Design
Profile
A Practice For
Everyday Life

November 2006 £8

474

Showcase
February

02

01

03 **04**

Noki
Noki
Nokia
/Tverskaya

PRINT
IS DEAD

MATCH DA

FOOTBALL PROGRAMME

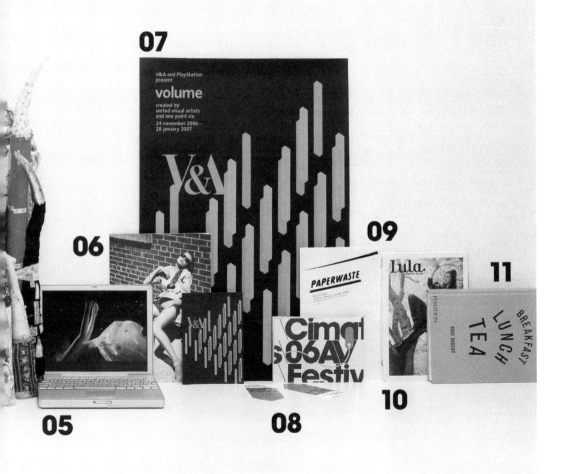

TEDDY BOYS
AND GIRLS

HEY HO
LET'S GO

01
Booklet

02
Hey Ho Let's Go
Installation

03
Hey Ho T-shirt

04
Hell A Toys badges

05, 06
Posters

01

02

03

04

05

06

Letterform
Bridge Type 'E'
René Knip

Amsterdam has over six hundred bridges and canal locks; all are numbered and some of them even have their own name. Around 1930, it was decided to design identical nameplates for these bridges, consisting of a series of cast-steel capital letters 70 mm in height.

We do not know for certain who was responsible for the design, but it was probably Anton Kurvers (1889–1940). He worked for the Amsterdam Public Works Department, which commissioned the project. In addition to being an architect, Anton Kurvers was also a painter and graphic designer; among other things, he designed book covers and posters.

The style of the letters and the architecture of the bridges is typical of the Amsterdam School tradition: geometric, decorative, original and unorthodox. The letters are well known as architects' letterforms: letters without typographical refinement.

A striking feature of the 'E' is the raised middle bar. A raised or lowered middle bar is characteristic of the style of that period. The tapering is a typical stylistic change that has its origins in the architectural rather than the calligraphic tradition.

Atelier René Knip has been interested in the world of architectural and environmental typography for about ten years now. Because letters of this type do not have to compose large bodies of text, they are frequently more spontaneous and whimsical in form. They are able to escape the iron laws of legibility.

A-R-K is currently working on an architectural type collection of its own, which will appear in 2007.

www.atelierreneknip.nl

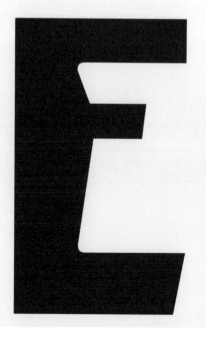

Photo graphy

The best photographers of 2006

01 Kim Hiorthøy
Melanie Bonajo. She's been photographing smoke a lot in 2006. There's one of just a cloud on the floor which I know of and which is fantastic.

02 Kerr Noble
Alice Hawkins. Particularly her Texas shoot for Pop Magazine. Beautiful and weird.

03 Michael C. Place, Build
Rred Delicion, NYC (http://rr9000d.com). He has such a great eye for composition, the colour in his shots are great—and he's a lovely guy.

04 Daniel Eatock
The Groot Wassink and Ruben Lundgren. Two Dutch guys, very nice, they made the book Wassinklundgren. Is Still Searching (www.wassinklundgren.com).

05 Ben Parker, MadeThought
Richard Learoyd. Experimenting with a brand new way of taking photographs for the last two years. Richard has pioneered a technique that captures the most beautiful and sublime images. Most of his works are either portraits or still lifes, and they paradoxically shift between looking like oil paintings and hyper-real renders. They are ethereal, emotive and amazingly detailed—qualities that so much modern photography seems to omit. They not only redefine Richard's approach to photography but define a new way to experience it.

06 Matt Pyke, Universal Everything
Erwan Frotin (www.bigactive.com). King of the sculptural photography still life fusion.

07 Experimental Jetset
Dutch duo Neils Schumm and Anuschka Blommers. Do check out their recent anthology (Anita and 124 Other Portraits, published by Valiz and designed by Joo van Bennekom). Another favourite photographer is Johannes Schwartz.

08 Jon Forss, Non-Format
Zoren Gold & Minori, aka Zoren Gold and Minori Murakami. They're amazing photographers but they're also incredible illustrators and they combine the two skills in ways that I've never seen before. Their work has a simple graphic quality that appeals to my Pop Art sensibilities but these are often elements of fine detail and craftsmanship that constantly shift their work in surprising directions. I look forward to getting their book and I can't wait to see what they come up with next.

09 Jonathan Ellery, Browns
Juergen Teller has an ability to straddle the worlds of art and commerce effortlessly. He works on large, lucrative accounts for the likes of Marc Jacobs while still contributing to public collections such as the V&A, Fondation Cartier and L'Art Contemporain, Paris.

10 Elisabeth Arkhipoff
Tim Walker. Stern has just published a 'Photografie on his work.

01
Cloud by
Melanie Bonajo

02
Lauren wearing Ghost from the Texas shoot for Pop by Alice Hawkins

03
Anna Ruth Sophie still by Red Delicion

Paper Collection 2

Grafik Paper Collection 2—Eco-Papers

Everyone's talking about reducing their carbon footprint, and as a designer there's really no excuse not to steer your clients towards paper with excellent eco-credentials. Luckily the paper manufacturers have anticipated the growing interest in 'green' papers and have been busily manufacturing some top-quality stocks that will not only make your work look great, but will be good for the environment too.

See for yourself with the second instalment of Grafik's Paper Collection, which contains the following swatches of eco-friendly paper.

Arjowiggins

With growing numbers of companies pushing a greener corporate social responsibility agenda, designers are looking to highlight environmental credentials in fully satisfying clients' briefs. All Arjowiggins Fine Papers products are environmentally friendly, but for those customers looking for an even higher commitment to the environment recycled and Forest Stewardship Council (FSC)-certified products with a high-quality finish are available.

Conqueror Recycled—FSC-certified
Manufactured using a minimum of 70 per cent FSC-certified Mixed Source Virgin Pulp and 25 per cent Post-Consumer Recycled Fibres, the range is available in three of Conqueror's most popular finishes: Texture Laid, Smooth/Satin Wove and Smooth/Satin CX2) in watermarked and unwatermarked options. Comprising of 100g, 160g, 300g and 370g grades as well as DL envelopes, these papers are perfect for all business and corporate identity literature. The stock is fully guaranteed across all major print processes, including offset litho and desktop laser and inkjet print and offers superior bulk and stiffness.

Inuit
A new brand of premium-offset papers and boards, Inuit is certified under the FSC credit material system using 100 per cent FSC mixed-source pulp. Clean, fresh and white sheets offer a modern alternative for eco-conscious clients, Inuit comes in three shades across the white spectrum: Brilliant White, High White and Oyster, available in two finishes: Ultra Smooth and Tactile and nine weight options from lighter paper weights (80gsm) through to heavier boards. With a matching collection of envelopes also available, the range is ideal for reports and accounts as well as a range of high-volume business and commercial applications, including invitations, business cards and direct mail.

And as the annual reports season approaches, London design company Bloat has created an engaging yet simple mailer to showcase Inuit's four key benefits: economical, environmental, excellent print performance and wide range, demonstrating how it is particularly suited for this application.

Samples can be obtained by visiting www.arjowigginsfinepapers.co.uk

Fenner Paper

Colorset
Following the recent trend for high-quality recycled products, German the papermaker August Koehler together with UK-based merchant Fenner Paper have jointly developed a new collection of recycled text and cover papers called Colorset. The range combines twenty-six colours from neutral hues to bright, vivid shades including black and is manufactured using 100 per cent post-industrial waste, for which it has been awarded the Blue Angel environmental mark.

Colorset can be used for a wide variety of uses, from covers to cards, folders and text. Angus Hyland of Pentagram used a selection of different Colorset colours for a run of limited-edition silkscreened posters promoting a lecture at the University of Plymouth. Colorset was chosen, not only because of the colour range but it also because the entire range is available in a B1 sheet size.

Colorset is an economical alternative to other premium-priced coloured ranges. Fenner Paper is the exclusive distributor for the new Colorset range and holds UK stock of all shades in 120gsm and 270gsm in B1. New swatches are now available.

For further information about this new range contact samples@fennerpaper.co.uk

Tullis Russell

Advocate
Scottish papermaker Tullis Russell, in collaboration with exclusive UK distributor PaperCo, recently made some radical changes to its Advocate range. A brand new look with an enhanced and broadened range addresses new and changing market demands for uncoated papers.

Significantly, the changes included the introduction of the first Tullis Russell brand made with FSC-certified pulps and also offers the whitest shade yet manufactured at the Markinch mill. Developed originally for PaperCo as a business paper range in the late Nineties, the new Advocate family now also embraces distinctive cover and text qualities and has been extended in terms of finishes, shades and sizes to broaden its design and printing capabilities.

"With new Advocate, Tullis Russell has provided exactly what the market has been telling us it wants—a top-quality, uncoated all-rounder with the varying visual and tactile strengths to suit corporate communication applications across the board," says PaperCo marketing director Bob Ide. "It gives us a renewed opportunity to address the growing demand for our market, 'touchy-feely' cover and text stocks and ensures we can continue to offer the optimum in prestige business papers.

"In addition to the dramatically improved white shade, Xtreme White, other innovations include a pleasingly tactile and bulky matt finish, Advocate Rough, a smoother wove finish, Advocate Smooth, and an improved traditional laid paper, Advocate Laid. A super-translucent, called Advocate Ghost, completes the range. All are manufactured with 100 per cent elemental chlorine-free pulp from sustainable forests and are available in a comprehensive range of popular sizes with matching envelopes for business and direct mail uses."

For further information please contact the PaperCo marketing department on +44 (0) 1733 441560, mail info@paperco.co.uk or visit www.paperco.co.uk

Glossary

Blue Angel
A German eco-label for recycled paper.

Chlorine
A bleaching agent used in the woodpulp production process to create whiter, stronger paper.

Chain-of-Custody
The step-by-step verification process through which products are traced from their origin to the final end product. For paper this means the forest to the finished product.

FSC (Forest Stewardship Council)
An international, non-governmental organisation, which promotes responsible and sustainable forest management. The FSC system of forest certification and product labelling allows papermakers to identify woodpulp that comes from well-managed forests. Its chain-of-custody sources woodpulp from the forest to the final user. FSC is the only eco-label endorsed by WWF, Friends of the Earth, Greenpeace and the Woodland Trust.

Post-Consumer Waste
Waste collected after the consumer has used and disposed of it. Recovered printed materials that can be de-inked to form a recycled pulp.

Pre-Consumer Waste
Also known as best white waste, typically these are unprinted offcuts, scraps, trimmings, overruns etc from printers and converters that are then formed into a recycled pulp.

Processed Chlorine-Free
Recycled paper in which the recycled fibre content is unbleached or bleached without chlorine or chlorine derivatives. Any virgin material portion of the paper must be TCF.

Recycled Paper
A broad term that needs to be clearly defined. Recycled paper could mean anything from a 100 per cent post-consumer waste to paper made from paper machine offcuts. There is no one clear definition of a recycled paper, so it's best to specify the fibre content.

Recyclable
All paper is theoretically recyclable, but systems must be in place to ensure that this happens before this term can be applied.

Recycled Fibre
Fibre obtained from recovered paper.

A full version of this glossary can be downloaded at www.ourtelinepapers.com

478

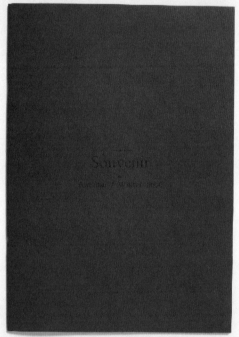

Pete Hughes and Simon See
Souvenir

Lots of T-shirts come our way at Grafik mansions but we're quite particular about them. By far the best (and the only ones that prompted us to dig deep and actually make a purchase) were Pete Hughes and Simon See's Souvenir range. The very seductive Souvenir look-book lured us in with its excellent photography (by Ben Weller) and its informative article about the history of the T-shirt. What really got us, though, was the concept behind the range—each has a story of its own based on a memory recounted by the designers.

Thus, Hughes and See play with the very notion of what T-shirts are as message-carriers and garments we purchase and wear in commemoration of an experience. Currently, plans are afoot for a new autumn/winter 2007 range and, while the details are top secret, we can reveal that it will involve collaborations with designers across the world. The industrious pair are looking for sponsorship or agency representation to launch the new line internationally. Potential patrons should form an orderly queue and contact pete@souvenirstudio.co.uk.

www.souvenirstudio.co.uk

Cla-se
Pedro García

and provide one of the year's most interesting fashion identity projects. Barcelona-based studio Cla-se has worked with shoemaker Pedro García for over fifteen years and the graphic collateral Cla-se produced for its spring/summer 2006 campaign is clearly the work of a studio and client beautifully in tune with each other. The photography sets the shoes in a series of interesting locations that emphasise the artistic qualities of the products.

Shoes and art: it's the seductive combination that couldn't fail to capture our imaginations

Thus we find elegant footwear fraternising with literary classics and Cubist prints at a Belgian antiques shop, or posing sublimely among an installation of Anish Kapoor sculptures. Cla-se collated these visuals to create extravagant A0 promotional posters that also act as unconventionally formatted look-books. We'd be most happy to frame them on our walls—if only we had the space.

www.cla-se.com

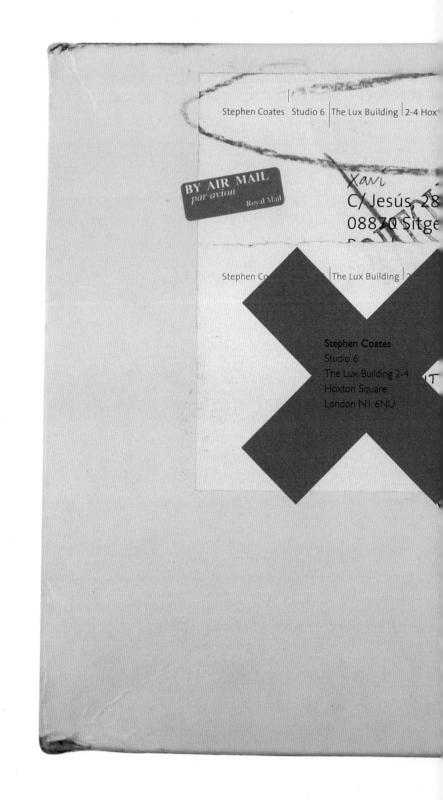

20

e Lor   20 7684 6525

A

Royal Mail
POSTAGE   PAID   UK
14/01/08   £3.98   EC1V
28003   7-3067538-1

QS

re | London N1 6NU | t: 020 7684 6535 | f: 020 7684 6525

AJOS

reat Britain
ecommandé
edfor **R**
ernational

DELIVERED FOR REASON HAND

RETURN TO SENDER

RI 9842 8810 7GB
PRIORITY HANDLING & REGISTERED DELIVERY

482

THEDRAWBRIDGE

Failure

Issue Four/Spring 2007
£2.50/€4.00

There's a quiet passion beyond triumph and defeat. Cradle it, curse it, steal it if you can

Rub the dice and scare yourself

By DBC Pierre

I've had a long look at failure. The thing is like an old die carton, at once rudimentary and infuriating, one you can turn over in your hands and examine, but can't quite grasp the mechanics of. It clinks and clunks, whirrs when you pick it up off the floor, but doesn't go anywhere when you put it back down.

I haven't been around forever, but I've turned that bastard over in my hands a few times. And here's the point: it's the very idea of a mechanism that makes stuff fail. A business, a marriage, a life – in constructing them with mechanisms and balances in mind, we wire the failure ourselves. We're so fucking clever, full of buzzwords and concepts and snippets from the smaller column in the press; we go no farther than tacking together towers of what's expected.

As if defining the thing intellectually helps us deny the real source of triumph and defeat: energy.

There's an aristocracy of energy in the world, made up of people who have failed, and might fail again, but who realize that breasts, winds, and gales of energy are at the heart of all fortune. You'll know these people when you come upon them. No zealots or enthusiasts are among them, neither pragmatists nor fatal hearts. Still passion quietly ripples everything they say and do. They feel the breeze each morning and walk in its stream all day.

Backgammon is the way to meet and confirm that energy. Play backgammon, play it drunk, play it high, play it sober, deploy the dice in every mood and before and after good and bad and best sex. Play without dice cups, refuse to play with anyone who insists on using a cup to throw the dice. Dice are an organ from beyond the body, hold them in your hands, rub them, rattle them. That's where energy will sing.

Steal energy if you have to. Tell your opponents they will lose, chances are their power will default to you. Just play, use the doubling cube, play for money, frighten yourself. At the height of a solid game you'll find that the numbers you call are the numbers you get, once, twice, thrice. And in that game you'll ace the source of all endeavour sparking unambiguously, guaranteed, you'll feel the heat of its shine.

Energy. Neither triumph nor defeat. Arriving without a notion of itself. Just raw fortune.

Raise a drink to it, court it.
Call it motherfucker, call it sweetheart. Say hi from me.

"He either fears his fate too much,
Or his deserts are small,
That puts it not unto the touch,
To win or lose it all."
Marquess of Montrose, 1612–1650

DBC Pierre is the author of Vernon God Little and Ludmila's Broken English (both Faber & Faber).

It is a dubious exercise to ask "What if…?"

Regrettable regret

By Perry Anderson

No emotion is more regularly brigaded by hypocrisy. "To my regret, I am unable to attend…" "Regretfully, we cannot extend…" Such formulae are the daily coin of social insincerity or commercial threat. Even innocent of this counterfeit ring, regret has a poor reputation. Popular wisdom takes a dim view of it – what other adjective is so regularly attached to it as vain? Homely images of spilt milk, over which no sensible child will cry, are an early lesson in the futility of the feeling. A successful life, by definition, is one in which it plays no part. The defiant chanteuse, belting out *Je ne regrette rien*, sings of a moral heroism we applaud as warmly as the vibrato.

One sub-class of regret alone attracts approval. Remorse is ethical. Redeemed by repentance, regret is raised to a virtue. Otherwise it remains, in general estimation, a vice. Why so? It is the counter-factual among emotions. What haunts regret is the reflection: "if only…" But as the most accredited historians explain, counter-factuals are a dubious exercise, for questions as pointless as "What would have happened if…?" In life, imagining alternative outcomes can only be demoralising. In youth, we may on occasion regret what we have just done. When older, regret for what we have not done – the opportunities missed, possibilities rejected – is commonly more acute. Neither can alter the record, only our comfort with ourselves. Yet the dysfunctional sensation is not banished so easily. Regrets are born of a vision no one escapes: the vertigo of choice with the irreversibility of time. Its offspring are often unhappy. Should we be more lenient with them?

Perry Anderson teaches history at University of California, Los Angeles.

The night wasn't silent and the dogs were out

Jesus Christ, please tell him to shut up

By Gerry Adams

Sam Beckett had the business about failure not about right. Fail? Fail again. Fail better. I paraphrase the learned scribe. I don't believe in failure. Even though Anglo-Irish history is chock full of glorious failures. It depends how you come at these things. Some of my more melancholic friends would have you believe that every silver lining has a cloud. Me? I'm with Beckett. I'll give you an example.

It was Christmas Eve in Long Kesh. Long Kesh was a British prison camp outside Belfast. It was 1974. We were to be blessed with a midnight mass. It would be celebrated in the half hut which was the only bit of our cage which was not used as living accommodation. There were four large Nissen huts in each cage. There were occupied by a motley mix of male internees who ranged from teenagers to old-age pensioners. There were about one hundred and twenty of us in each cage. We spent our sleeping hours piled on top of each other to decrepit bunk beds. The rest of the time we did our time. Most of us were from the north, city folk and country men in equal measure, with a handful of blow-ins from the south. Duby and culchies, again in equal measure.

At its height there were about twenty-two cages in Long Kesh. The conditions were awful. Especially during the winter. Particularly on Christmas Eve. But this Christmas Eve was going to be different. That is for me and three trusty compañeros. This Christmas Eve we were going to vamoose, skedaddle, get outta the place. This Christmas Eve we were going to escape.

The plan was simple. We had a trapdoor cut in a blind spot in the cage fence, not visible to the tall watchtowers which glared down at us. Our cage had four such towers with their heavily armed Brit soldiers and Colditz searchlights and sirens. Once out of the cage we were to crawl our way towards the perimeter fence, cutting our way through acres of barbed razor wire. We had procured bolt and wire cutters for that purpose. We had also smuggled in camouflaged clothes and sewed a change of clothing into this heavy fatigue gear. The plan once we got beyond Long Kesh was to change into the civilian clothes and make our way

> "Hi Brit. What rank are you? Is that dog taking you a walk? What, you're only a private? My mate is twenty-three and he's a general."

to civilization. In case of emergency we each had a twenty pound note, some change for phone calls, a Mars Bar and an Ordnance Survey map.

So far everything was going hunky dory. We were outside the cage, the four of us belly-flat on the ground inching our way along the gap between our cage and the one next to it. We didn't expect to make much progress until midnight mass was over so I was content to listen to the sound of the cage choir rehearsing "Oíche Ciúin" ("Silent Night") and other seasonal offerings. The sounds of slightly melodious male voices drifted out from the half hut to where we lay.

Then a slight mist came down. Extra sentries were put on the walkway alongside us and into the cages. We timed the sound of their footsteps approaching us and lay soundless and motionless till they passed. Then we edged forward another wee bit. Midnight mass came and went. We heard our comrades being locked up. To our relief our absence was unbeknownst. Long Kesh went to sleep. Christmas Day arrived. The mist stayed. So did the extra sentries. We could hear the snatches of their conversation as they passed on their weary beat.

Then all hell broke out. Sirens wailed. Searchlights lanced the darkness. There was the sound of running feet, shouted commands. Dogs barked excitedly.

We were caught. A gang of Brits and prison warders converged on the area we were crawling through. One of our group stood up in a vain attempt to distract attention from the rest of us.

"He no fse," he shouted. "Happy Christmas everyone."

It didn't work. One by one we were pried from the barbed wire. I was beaten about the face. My spectacles scarred a bloody track across my cheek. We were frogmarched, batons raining down on us, towards the punishment blocks.

I was glad to get into the cell. By now I was naked. Our clothes were stripped from us, our belongings, including the Mars Bars, confiscated. Alone in my cell I pulled the rough jail blanket around me and lay in the foetus position on the plank bed.

"Ach well. *Sin é* (That's it)," I thought to myself.

"You alright?"

It was one of my captured compatriots. I shouted in response and each of us yelled back and forth to each other. I pulled myself up to the cell window and peered through the bars. Right outside there was a line of Brit soldiers with ferocious war dogs. They, the Brits not the dogs, screamed abuse at me.

"Get down ya Irish bastard."

Then to my horror one of my friends yelled back in defiance.

"Fuck up ya bollox. My name is Gerry Adams and if you come in here I'll knock yer neck in."

"Jesus," I whispered as I slid back on to the bed.

The verbal abuse continued.

"Hi Brit. What rank are you? Is that dog taking you a walk? What are you, you're only a private? My mate is twenty-three and he's already a general."

I stayed quiet. Well nearly quiet. Between clenched teeth I hissed at my friend next door.

"Shut up you imbecile. Give me a break. Jesus, Mary and Joseph tell him to shut up."

By now the Brits and their dogs were in the corridor. The dogs were off their leashes. They ran excitedly up and down barking madly as their masters drummed our cell doors with their batons.

Then all went quiet. My cell door slowly opened.

A young British soldier stood looking in at me. I stood up fists clenched eying him.

"Here you are."

He flung a packet of cigarettes at me.

"You want a light, Paddy?"

I looked at him in disbelief. He pushed a lit match towards me.

"Happy Christmas," he grinned.

I sucked on the cigarette.

"My name's not Paddy."

"I know, Paddy. Happy Christmas."

I grinned back at him.

"Happy Christmas," I said.

Gerry Adams is President of Sinn Féin and the abstentionist Westminster MP for Belfast West.

The red tenda of Bologna
'I should begin with how I loved him, in what manner, to what degree, with what kind of incomprehension…'
Exclusive short story by John Berger, page 5

By David Shrigley

GO DOWN THE HOLE

STAY DOWN THE HOLE

Borders blur, barriers fall and utopias crumble – all for the better

Remains of past identities

By Massimo Genghini

In most simple and straightforward terms, "home" may stand either for your own home, your native land or a general sense of belonging. Yet each of these three concepts exists not only in its proper but also in a degenerate form – rather like the types of Greek government, which as monarchy, aristocracy and democracy, the government of one, of an élite or the people, immediately evoke their corrupt counterparts, tyranny, oligarchy and demagogy.

Your native land may therefore be a sum of traditions, customs, history and language that generates a sense of belonging which isn't static, but continuously evolves in order to meet other related realities, and contributes to a reciprocal and general enrichment. But it may also, and this is unfortunately the form history has proven to be more prevalent, constitute a "convention ad excludendum", an appropriation vis-à-vis your neighbour, an expression of the Roman concept "imperium" rather than the Greek idea of "koinè", which embraces transmission of thought, culture and beauty. Such an understanding of native land triggers imbecilic, arrogant notions like "My country, right or wrong", employed to justify the worst of colonialist violence. A flag is always an ambiguous, highly ambivalent symbol; the flag of the invader is never of the same colour as the one of those fighting the invasion!

If we observe – objectively – today's global migration phenomenon, and in particular its causes, effects and possible developments, the concept of a "native land" crumbles quickly: borders are permeable, the idea of citizenship a cracked container, and the legal system can only lag behind the phenomenon, trying to adapt to the status quo. Ethnic and religious phenomena have a unifying capacity by far more pervasive than the traditional idea of belonging to a fatherland.

A change of similar dimension has also reached "the home" – or whatever we call our own living space. Its walls are as permeable as national borders; television and internet alone, in influencing mass behaviour, have swept away all barriers. Not only do we observe in our offspring words, gestures, mannerisms and attitudes that are perfectly strange to us, we even ignore where they come from. The effects aren't solely negative, in some cases they break taboos and open new perspectives. But in others, they simply produce vulgarity, brutishness, a loss of harmony, and allow a dive into shallowness and (mass-induced) individualism that is a more relapse mode of conformism.

No less heartbreaking is the falling apart of a shared sense of belonging: Who are we? What do we feel we belong to? Be it religion, a philosophical system, a political group, the larger cultural categories (Westerners, supporters of democracy, pacifists, environmentalists, etc.), we perceive that the great utopias have run aground and lost their power of attraction and therefore propulsion. They appear to us as dried-out and shrivelled; their remains leave us doubtful, uncertain and in some cases horrified. On too many occasions have their symbolic flags been waved in order to commit atrocities and deceit; the heralds of great ideas have turned out to be traitors who pursued the opposite of what was publicly declared.

Well, if we feel a great sense of liberation, now that we see what we do and what we decide to be, and if "we do not belong", so much the better! The only possible common denominator still always be the respect of man - the idea which made Einstein reply to a customs officer asking for his ethnicity: "Human!" ∞

Massimo Genghini is the former president of Italy's Supreme Court. Now retired, he tours Europe pursuing his passion for opera.

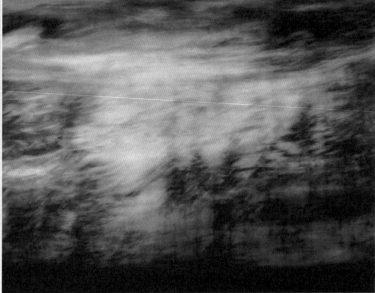

The Clearing

The Israeli photographer Ori Gersht took a train trip through the forests of Galicia in the Ukraine. Here, near Rzow, his father-in-law Gideon Engler, had hidden from Nazi persecution for two-and-a-half years.

Mirroring the train journey of the imprisoned Jewish population to Auschwitz, Gersht made a series of photographs aimed at capturing the landscape's "memory" of the atrocities it witnessed 60 years ago. Gersht's subtle approach defies a pure documentation of Gideon Engler's particular hiding place. It portrays the longevity of memory.

The series not only shows a stylistic kinship to the German Romantic movement, especially the paintings of Casper David Friedrich, such as *Morning Fog in the Mountains* finished in 1808, Friedrich himself had mythologised the very same forests – an idealisation which was later hijacked by Nazi nationalists.

Gersht's series is slanted towards poetic obscuration, but the depth and clarity of understanding found in the individual photographs, as well as their bleached and dark-ened exposure, testify to a thoughtful and resonant record of the history held within these forests. M S-A

Above: Galicia, 2005, from the series entitled 'Liquidation', published in the book The Clearing

---

Out after curfew, a boy gets shot at. His quiet logic defies the pain. "Places have to be separated – it's what kilometres are for!"

The two banks of a river

By John Berger

He was thirteen, perhaps fourteen. He already had a man's voice but not the pace of a man's voice. He was in pain and determined not to show it. K and two other kids had knocked on my front door and woken me up. Who's there? trouble and bloodshed people often come to consult me, because they know I work to the pharmacy. And I assume this role, for, contrary to what some might think, it makes my life easier. Raf was wounded in the leg and couldn't put his right foot on the ground. They had carried him hobbling, his two arms round their shoulders. His name's Raf, they told me.

In the times we're living through, spontaneous courage begins young. What comes with age is endurance – the cruel gift of years.

They shot at him from one of their jeeps; he was out after curfew. He managed to crawl under an abandoned truck and then hide in a ruin. I told the kids I would examine him alone in the pharmacy. That way if the lights there attracted attention – it was past midnight – they wouldn't be implicated.

We fetched a stretcher from the shop. Laid Raf on it, carried him back along the broken road and then shifted the stretcher on to the sickbed that's permanently in the pharmacy's back room. He'd apparently lost a fair amount of blood.

I told K he could come back in an hour or so if he wanted, and if, by any chance, he found the pharmacy without lights and bolted, it would mean I had taken Raf urgently to the hospital.

The three of them stared at me as if I'd become immensely large. Probably won't be necessary, I said reassuringly, I'll do our best to avoid it, but we have to imagine every-

thing, don't we? If we're here, you knock three times on the door.

When we were alone, Raf smiled at me. Strange smile for someone so young – as if we had both, the two of us, qualified for something, and the smile was its proud acknowledgement.

They shot five rounds and I think three missed, he said.

Where's your mother?

In the village.

What are you doing here?

Working.

You work late!

You're working late too, he replied, and he screwed up his eyes. I wasn't sure whether in pain or as a sign of conspiracy. Perhaps both.

I eased off his jeans, swabbed his leg and cut with scissors the tourniquet at the top of his thigh. There was no sudden surge of blood so the artery, thank God, was untouched. He was watching me, curious, but not about his immediate condition: You know what I'm dreaming about? he asked.

I tested his reactions by scratching the sole of his dusty bloodstained foot and his leg twitched as it should. Its nerves were functioning. I washed his feet.

You know what I'm dreaming about? he repeated.

No, tell me. I'm going to examine your wound now, if it hurts too much, you whisper to me.

I'm dreaming, he said, of lying on the deck of a motor-launch and you're driving it, and we are far from the coast and the boat's thumping the waves. Thump. Thump.

There were two sounds which were adjacent. One was long and not very deep and the other was ugly and small and profound. My guess was that the bullet, which caused the first, had entered at a tangent, because shot from above, and had re-emerged where the wound ended above the knee.

Where's our boat going? I ask him as I pick up with my left hand the little clip instrument for holding open the lip of a wound. The bank of a wound as the French say, like a river bank.

In my right hand I have a canula and with

its tip I tap very gently along the length of the gash, waiting to hear a metallic click, or to touch suddenly the hardness of metal. You're more likely to register an embedded bullet like this than to see it with your eye.

So where are we going? I'm on my back on the deck and you're steering, he asked. To where?

There was no bullet. I let the lip fall back.

Now for the ugly one.

You know something about the dreams of men, all of you men? I ask him.

Tell me, he says gruffly.

You love dreaming of conflict...

I was probing and I thought I heard the click of metal. I tapped twice more. A bullet. And women what do they...? Abruptly he clenched his teeth.

We're going to do something to stop it hurting, Raf.

Don't go.

You think I'd leave you on the deck? Wait thirty seconds.

I stepped across to the analgesics where I found the diamorphine I was looking for.

I'm going to give an injection into your shoulder.

I did so (5 mg), and we both waited.

So what do women dream of? he eventually asked.

Of places no longer being separated, I tell him.

Places have to be separated, it's what kilometres are for!

The quiet logic of his reply reminded me of the forceps a proteinish bullet like a ration tooth. He didn't so much in a flinch. Neat I dripped butadine into the wound until it overflowed like a volcano does. He clenched his right fist, nothing more.

Picking up, with a pair of tweezers, the lemon Unt bullet, I showed it to him. Don't look now, I whisper, shut your eyes. With my eyes shut I get scared, I see their Ua's to pointing straight at me.

Then look at my face not my hands.

So you have dimples! he said, you still have dimples.

From the bottom of the wound I extracted with the forceps a proteinish bullet like a ration tooth. He didn't so much in flinch. Next I dripped butadine into the wound until it overflowed like a volcano does. He clenched his right fist, nothing more.

Tying the knots made me remember my grandmother's fingers and the way they moved when she was embroidering. They were defter than mine.

I fix two dressings, I place a pillow under his head. And I rock the stretcher in imitation of a boat riding the swell of the waves.

It was 3.30 am. We were alone, we were waiting, it was quiet. ∞

John Berger's latest book, Here is Where We Meet, was published by Bloomsbury in 2005.

Happy families Christoph Niemann

484

2

Issue Four
Spring 2007

To subscribe to *The Drawbridge*
visit the website at
www.thedrawbridge.org.uk

How going straight can ruin your legacy

Death, lies and old newspapers

By Rebecca Gowers

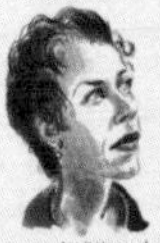

In the 1840s, government stamp duty kept the minimum price on an English newspaper at four pence, a sum way beyond any ordinary labourer. In recompense for this tax, supposedly, newspapers could be sent through the post for nothing: the postal system also belonged to the government. By this means, information would wend slowly from the cities into the countryside. It was illegal to perforate or otherwise mark a newspaper so as to send the recipient a coded message, effectively a free letter. It was also illegal to publish any sort of newspaper without paying stamp duty on it.

Edward Lloyd's fabulously successful idea was to print one-penny newspapers that circumvented the law by virtue of the fact that not a single story in them was true. He was already familiar with the tastes of the impoverished reader, being a premier publisher of pamphlet-form "penny bloods" – serial novels of erotic gore, highwaymen and horror. He was also busy poaching customers for the serial parts of Dickens's novels, bringing out instant improvements on each new installment under titles like *Oliver Twiss* and *David Copperful*. Weak copyright protection allowed for this form of piracy, but a pseudo-newspaper was, legally, a different proposition. The importance of defining "news" here can be deduced from Lloyd's having only narrowly avoided prosecution when, on January 8, 1843, one of his editors carelessly included the genuine report of a lion loose in London that had escaped from somebody's zoo.

Within a few years, Lloyd was amongst the richest newspapermen in the land. Demand for his product was so high that he had to plant his own forests to generate enough

He was familiar with the tastes of the impoverished reader, a publisher of serial novels of erotic gore, highwaymen and horror.

paper. But here's the question. If one were compelled by the authorities to fill a penny newspaper with anything but news, avoiding in particular all metropolitan topicality; if one wished to make a fortune out of fantastic, faked stories, bent information and suitable lies, what would be the plan for charming ill-heeled Londoners of the 1840s into giving up their beer money? – beer, not water, being the cheapest liquid it was safe at the time to drink.

It is important to note that you decidedly didn't want to print anything quite so plausible that it provoked the investigative arm of the law. There was also in this period the offence of "circulating false news", designed in part to prevent the weary hawker from trying to shift a heap of the day's unsold papers by yelling out, say, that the Duke of Wellington had just been struck down dead. You definitely didn't want to be fingered as an exploitative pseudo-alarmist: that, too, was a crime.

Lloyd came up with several answers to these constraints. Principally he told tales from long ago, dressed up to look like news. On July 12, 1840, for example, he had the headline: A COOK BOILED TO DEATH IN SMITHFIELD. Self-evidently, this is brilliant. And the first four words of the article? "In the year 1530..." Or what about this for a front-page account of a shocking murder? "A more detestable instance of deliberate ferocity than the following has rarely disgraced humanity: On the 25th April, 1759..." So what if the story was eighty-one years out of date and never happened anyway?

Lloyd could get away with items on recent assaults only if they were presented as having taken place in foreign lands, such as the havoc wrought by a bride-eating Philippine alligator. And if he couldn't resist the English? It seems he was permitted to tell stories of the English so long as they were at sea.

One might protest that the English being at sea could hardly have been thought to constitute news, let alone fake news. The English at sea? This isn't news, by any stretch of anybody's imagination. And while we're on the subject, why does the phrase "at sea" imply incapacity and limitation? Surely for the English being at sea ought to mean being exhilaratingly in conversation with the waves and the stars, the stars and the waves, the fish, the wind, the salt, the spray. Did we or didn't we rule the waves once upon a time? No? Can we really have crept out onto our great oak ships and stood around, embarrassed, as little gusty breezes sank the Spanish Armada?

Oh well. It is worth noting that if you are drawn to old newspapers, especially ones that were required by law to be pure invention, then the daily papers of your own age start to seem utterly ridiculous, not to mention the narrative of your own life.

So did Lloyd learn the lessons of the bride-eating alligator? Absolutely not. No, he decided to go straight. It had been his habit to use the editorial columns in his fake papers to rail against slavery, capital punishment and the utter tedium of bona fide news stories, and yet in 1876, he used his vast wealth to buy himself a legitimate title, the *Daily Chronicle*, successfully turning it into an ever more respected Liberal organ. At the same time, he seems to have deployed agents to trawl through bookshops looking for his earlier works in order to purchase and destroy them.

A century and more later, this canny attempt to revamp his reputation is as nought. After decades of mergers – including one with the *Daily News*, a paper first edited by Dickens back when Lloyd was pirating his novels – the *Daily Chronicle* at last sank from view. Nowadays it stands as merely a dim detail in the prehistory of a right-wing tabloid, the *Daily Mail*. By contrast, precious issues of Lloyd's false newspapers are preserved in the country's most august libraries, while surviving copies of his penny bloods – known for their extreme rarity – are worth thousands.

Worse, what has proved to be Edward Lloyd's most potent cultural legacy springs from an example of his very lowest output. The work in question, tumbled together in 1846 by the hack writer Thomas Peckett Prest, was, typically of Lloyd's penny titles, a souped-up rehash of popular, ghoulish whispers. Furthermore, and also typically, it was tempting to semi-believe. Yet much though it followed a general pattern, *The String of Pearls: A Romance* struck a particular chord. The publisher is all but forgotten, the author a mere footnote, but its central character, Sweeney Todd, "the Demon Barber of Fleet Street", skulks in the backs of our minds to this day.

Rebecca Gowers is the author of The Swamp of Death: A True Tale of Victorian Lies and Murder *(Hamish Hamilton/Penguin). Her first novel,* When to Walk, *is published by Canongate.*

By Bela Borsodi, art directed by Stefan Sagmeister

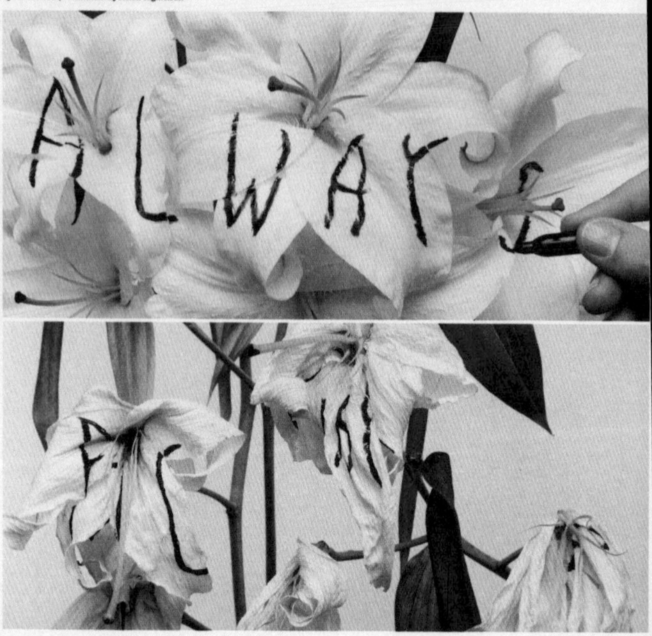

Moral condoms

By Vincenzo Ruggiero

If looking to Goethe, *The Sorrows of Young Werther* might come to mind as a classic depiction of failure. The story of the love-struck suicide, for all its literary worth, famously engendered a Europe-wide wave of copycat self-harm. Yet Goethe's subsequent novel, *Wilhelm Meister's Apprenticeship*, suggests a subtler approach to the topic. One evening, Wilhelm Meister meets Philina, who flirts with him and then, rather invitingly, walks off towards her hotel. Wilhelm follows her but is hampered by a number of unexpected encounters: an acquaintance to whom he has promised a loan, someone who greets him with affection and, once in the hotel, the receptionist looking at him suspiciously. Even in Philina's room, he has to negotiate his decision to follow the woman with Mignon, a friend who is present yet whom he completely ignores, sensing that his desire is becoming frustrated by a series of insignificant obstacles.

According to literary critic Franco Moretti, the bitterness of Wilhelm's disappointment is mixed with a curiously vehement feeling of possibility. Failure, such a reading proposes, is a transitory affair. It liberates, it reawakens the quotidian (which is always precarious), and at the same time it is unpredictable as to the potential further achievements it promises.

Don Quixote is a prime example for such failure. He is comical, unrealistic and he expresses a surreal form of resistance manifested in his refusal to see where he fails and his permanent attempt to unveil the new possibilities his failures anticipate. Further there are the two street robbers, Rinconete and Cortadillo, towering creations in Cervantes' *Exemplary Novels*. They fail to adapt to organized crime, its hierarchy, moralistic values and asphyctic rules, and prefer to pursue their career as independent thieves, roaming unknown towns in search of opportunities.

English literature, too, is replete with failures – namely heroes and heroines who try to express their individuality and nonetheless respect their particular societal conventions. They simply affirm their distance from them. Their existence is punctuated by transgression, but their conduct is a celebration of the system allowing it – a hymn to the principles according to which singularity must not challenge the uniformity of the challenged. In sum, individuals are allowed to be different, maverick and proud, as long as they appreciate that they are "insider deviants", "included losers". They must respect the winners and refrain from perturbing the rules allowing them to be such.

Many nineteenth-century English novels remind us of the functionalist sociological analysis which posits that a certain degree of transgression and crime is desirable because it reinforces the righteousness and solidarity among the law-abiding community. These novels provide the body to a literature clad with gloves and "moral condoms", one which dissects the ills of society while offering no possibility for change. Failure, in this case, brings no opportunity. For failure to convey a feeling of possibility one has to look elsewhere. Perhaps one should be proud of Virginia Woolf, who wore no gloves. For her, the society in which she lived and which led to the massacres of war deserved no polite criticism, maverick transgression or "condomised" condemnations. It needed outright rejection. Hers was a form of failure bearing the marks of possibilities.

Vincenzo Ruggiero is Professor of Sociology at the University of Middlesex in London and at the University of Pisa in Italy. His latest books are Crime in Literature *(Verso, 2003) and* Understanding Political Violence *(Open University Press, 2006).*

One man's struggle to beat the boredom of Civil Service after the RAF. And another's arguable success

Shooting at shadows on a bottle a day

By Gerald Mars

After demob it was back to the Civil Service in London, to an office job on the sixth floor of an office block, St George's Court in New Oxford Street. But being tied to a Civil Service desk after the RAF was mountingly unsatisfactory – to me and the service. Any job, anywhere, I thought, must be better than "working under well-defined instructions", as the description for clerical officers put it. So, desperate for travel and adventure and buoyed by youthful immortality, I searched for a position abroad.

Previous attempts to see the world had been notably unsuccessful. During National Service the RAF had even turned down my request to serve in Korea. Perhaps because my cynical world-weary Flight Sergeant had filled in the all-purpose form "Application for a Medical Examination" and under "Symptoms" written "Volunteer For Overseas Service". Later I accepted an Internal Ministry job in Cairo and was ready to go just when it was cancelled. Being a Jew and with the Arab-Israeli conflict at one of its peaks, they belatedly thought to save themselves another possible "remains returned home" incident.

And then suddenly a job turned up in Kenya – with prospects of adventure, life in the sun and a chance to experience the Empire, all on full pay. This was the fifties however, and Kenya was in the news. Mau Mau terrorists as we called them, or Freedom Fighters as they did, were running a bloody campaign to rid themselves of the British, though not as bloody as the British were waging to rid themselves of the Mau Mau. But the advertisement for "Administrative Assistants" made no mention of the troubles. They were, it seemed, trawling for clericals. The pay was fabulous, "everything was found" and all you needed was a school certificate, to be over 21 and fit. Here I was, well qualified on all counts, except possibly the fit bit. Two of us applied from the same South Kensington hostel. My co-applicant, a six-foot-four blond giant, was also 21. Though not the most reflective of men, he was an excellent rugby player. And he, like me, was eager to experience the world while it was still there. He so obviously was an embryonic colonist. Was I?

Mr Breeze, my section's Higher Executive Officer, called me in. He was about five feet four with a white toothbrush moustache, a peppery well-intentioned paternalist.

"I hear you've applied for a post in Kenya? Then let me give you a piece of advice. Before you go into that interview, you're to repeat to yourself twelve times: 'I'm Proud To Be British; I'm Proud to be British; I'm Proud To Be British.' Got that?"

"Yes Sir."

"Good. And Good Luck."

Armed with this tip from the top, I determined to make this application succeed. I would obviously need to be prepared. To be sure, they'd want awareness of the troubles and for me to offer the appropriate 1950s imperialist views. I could do that. "Native peoples throughout the Empire are increasingly aiming for independence. It should be given them – but only when they prove capable of taking on its responsibilities." With the "Proud To Be British" jingle, that meant two nonsenses. I could live with two.

The morning of the interview was wet and dismal and so were the Kenyan Protectorate's offices. The walls, dominated by dark panelling, were embellished with even darker oil paintings, all of solemn Victorian Empire-builders. The décor emanated established verities with a musty whiff of White Man's Burden. I was ushered to an anteroom and then almost immediately called to interview. Facing me was a panel of four burden-carriers, all lean, interrogative, middle-aged men with mahogany faces.

"Mr Mars. Do sit down."

I sat.

"Tell us. What do you know of the present position in Kenya?"

The tone was superior, interrogatory, crystal. My prepared specialism! With measured deliberation, seemingly thinking it out as I went, I moved in: "Native peoples throughout the Empire are aiming for self-government… (pause for careful thought)… I think it should be given them… (good so far, now a longer pause here, before the conventional *fait accompli* about responsibility)…

"You surely don't mean…? You can't possibly…?" The fool took it for a full stop. He couldn't be restrained. His colleagues on the bench waded in and bayed their support.

Their few remaining questions were more pointed and my answers not carefully restrained – though they didn't appear very interested in answers. Luckily the process did not last for long.

There is a law about interviews that needs wider provenance. You can swan through interviews with a degree of truth. But outright lies must be thoroughly rehearsed.

My co-applicant was of course successful. He wrote me a letter that took some time to arrive. The boat trip to Mombasa had been fabulous, straight out of Somerset Maugham. The morning after arrival he'd reported to his briefing address and was immediately taught how to fire a Smith & Wesson. Then a crash course in how to drive a Land Rover. After lunch it was map reading. Finally, in the late afternoon, he had to drive to "his territory" some two hundred miles away. Here he would be the only white man. Before he left he was sworn in as a magistrate and warned he had sentencing powers of up to twelve years – but could only recommend, not order, the death penalty. He was settling in well. He liked the responsibility; not many jobs gave such opportunities to a 21-year-old with just a school certificate. But after some weeks he found he was drinking a bit. A bottle of whisky a day. And, he wrote, he was shooting at shadows.

I couldn't possibly be glad I had failed in the first place, but this wasn't a clerical post in the sun; it was just another case of organizational deceit.

Gerald Mars is Honorary Professor of Anthropology at University College London and Visiting Professor at London Metropolitan University.

By Toby Morison

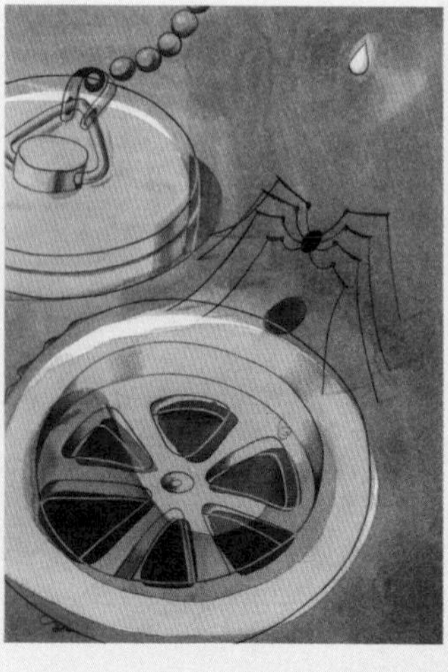

ssue Four
pring 2007

To subscribe to *The Drawbridge* visit the website at www.thedrawbridge.org.uk

3

On treasuring the loser in his will not to will

Crush me, Muse

By Lisabeth During

Modernism prefers the losers. There are exceptions, one-man galaxies like Picasso, seemingly unable to fail at anything he tried. The sun kept shining, the pictures kept coming, as did the love and the money. Picasso is the artist who defies the myth of the sacrificial artist. His success, as John Berger points out, was his disaster. Frustration is supposed to be the price of integrity in modernist mythology, which is a Jansenist heresy infatuated with the pleasures of self-doubt. "*Le moi est haïssable*," said Pascal. It can be fun to attack the self. Freud thought the artist had the privilege of a prolonged childhood, his egoism unconstrained by the negations that make the rest of us civilized. But modernism, beginning its long history of psychoanalytic misreadings, argued that anxiety is good for you. Being comfortable with the world creates only the desire to repeat its forms, and produces the happy, timeless art of naturalism. Abstraction, the art of spirit, needs a quarrel with the world, an awareness of inadequacy.

When defeat becomes a virtue, we begin to value those whose lives involve compromise and incongruity. Picasso on the beach is one thing; Stevens writing in his breaks from the insurance office, Kafka filling in his forms are closer to our ideals of avant-garde purity. Certainly the ambivalence towards commercial success counts. Baudelaire knew the moment had come; midway through the nineteenth century: finally the artist has nothing but himself to sell in the market. Our greatest modernist, Henry James, wanted nothing better. James's disastrous siege of the stage was not an experiment but a compulsion. It soaked up years of his life, while this shy, misanthropic man surrounded himself with a glut of exhibitionists, venal entrepreneurs, callous and inept impresarios, showmen and women aware of just how far this innocent could let them lead him. Everything here was poison to his sensibility. Yet that was precisely the attraction. Public performance for James, as for his Bostonian heroine Olive Chancellor, offered an unmixed opportunity for catastrophe. The very excesses and tawdriness of the commercial theatre were what made it irresistible. It was war, one he speaks of to his brother as "waging ferociously", mocking himself for trying to be "heroic" in what soon looked like a "ghastly and disgraceful farce", where the victory and the spoils would not outweigh the "humiliations and vulgarities and disgusts, all the dishonour and chronic insult incurred".

The crash came. We could remember the master only in Lamb House or a London dining room, admired and lionized. But the image of James at the St James's Theatre for the première of *Guy Domville* is the one that matters: the catcalls from the gallery, the author too frightened to sit in the audience, but quiet and briefly composed on stage after the curtain fell in the face of what meant the end of his fantasy, failure in large letters. After the death of ambition, James turned to ghost stories. Living on, or belatedness, distinguishes the modernist writer. Sometimes the very idea of survival is intolerable.

When it comes to the cloying death of a culture, the Austrian writers Thomas Bernhard and Elfriede Jelinek are unsparing. Art is no redemption. The discriminations of intellect only clarify the disgrace which that intellect made possible.

In Bernhard's novels corruption settles like a miasma; nothing is too base to avoid further infection – the language, the money, the food, the emotions. Perhaps by the strenuous cultivation of failure the artist can make a kind of bargain with form, can leave behind something halfway decent. He can become a Glenn Gould; he can "play himself into the impasse" from which he will die (the carefully tended lung disease is an afterthought, Bernhard's invention). He can crush his own virtuosity. But better if it disappears entirely, which takes a lot of art. Extinction is hard. Bernhard's writing deals coldly with the heroics of modernist asceticism, as with the cheap pathos of late European memory. Gould's fellow students crave renunciation, envy the fidelity to negation they can never fully possess. The genius is better at failure just as he is better at everything else, and his failure makes the rest of us look little, makes our success look stupid. This is something Adorno understood, and credited to the aesthetics of the latecomer. Art is still art when it tries to take itself back; the modern Doctor Faustus devotes his time to the de-creation of music, but the music doesn't go away. Vestiges of achievement always threaten to betray the artist's best efforts. The attendant spirit of modern Austrian literature is Schopenhauer's will not to will at all, and this is a demanding muse.

Lisabeth During teaches philosophy and aesthetics at Pratt Institute in Brooklyn, and is interested in heroic as well as everyday asceticism.

The last movement of Beethoven's Ninth, anthem of the European Union, literally deconstructs itself

An ode too Turkish for Europe

By Slavoj Žižek

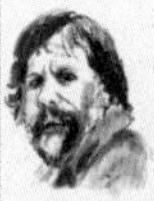

The anthem of the European Union, heard at numerous political, cultural and sportive public events, is the "Ode to Joy" melody from the last movement of Beethoven's Ninth symphony, a true "empty signifier" that can stand for anything. In France, it was elevated by Romain Rolland into a humanist ode to the brotherhood of all people (the Marseillaise of humanity). In 1938, it was performed as the highpoint of the Reichsmusiktage and later for Hitler's birthday. In the China of the Cultural Revolution, in an atmosphere of rejecting European classics, it was redeemed as a piece of progressive class struggle, while in today's Japan, it achieved cult status, being woven into the very social fabric with its alleged message of "joy through suffering". Until the 1970s, i.e. at a time when both West and East German Olympic teams had to perform together as one, the anthem played for the German gold medal was the Joy song, and, simultaneously, the Rhodesian white supremacist regime of Ian Smith, which proclaimed independence in the late 1960s in order to maintain apartheid, also proclaimed the same song its national anthem. Even Abimael Guzman, the (now imprisoned) leader of the *Sendero Luminoso*, when asked what music he loves, mentioned the fourth movement of Beethoven's Ninth. So we can easily imagine a fictional performance at which all the sworn enemies, from Hitler to Stalin, from Bush to Kim Jong Il, for a moment forget their adversities and participate in the same magic moment of ecstatic brotherhood.

However, before we dismiss the fourth movement as a piece "destroyed through social usage", let us note some peculiarities of its structure. In the middle of the movement, after we hear the main melody (the Joy theme) in three orchestral and three vocal variations, at this first climax, something unexpected happens. It has bothered critics for the last 183 years since its first performance: at bar 331, the tone changes totally, and, instead of the solemn hymnic progression, the same Joy theme is repeated in the *marcia Turca* (Turkish march) style borrowed from the military music for wind and percussion instruments that eighteenth-century European armies adopted from the Turkish Janissaries. The mode is here that of a carnivalesque popular parade, a mocking spectacle (some critics even compare the "absurd grunts" of the bassoons and bass drum that accompany the beginning of the *marcia Turca* to farts), and after this point, everything goes wrong. The simple solemn dignity of the first part of the movement is never recovered.

The mode is here that of a carnivalesque popular parade, a mocking spectacle, and after this point, everything goes wrong.

After this "Turkish" part and in a clear counter-movement to it, in a kind of retreat into the innermost religiosity, the choral-like music (also dismissed as a "Gregorian fossil") tries to render the ethereal image of millions of people who kneel down embraced, contemplating in awe the distant sky and searching for the loving paternal God who must dwell above the canopy of stars ("*ueberm Sternezelt muss ein lieber Vater wohnen*"). However, the music as it were gets stuck when the word "*muss*", first rendered by the basses, is repeated by the tenors and altos, and finally by the sopranos, as if this repeated conjuring presented a desperate attempt to convince us (and itself) of what it knows is not true. It turns the line "a loving father must dwell" into a desperate act of beseeching, and thus attests to the fact that there is nothing beyond the canopy of stars, no loving father to protect us and to guarantee our brotherhood.

After this, a return to a more celebratory mood is attempted in the guise of a double fugue which cannot but sound false in its excessively artificial brilliance – a fake synthesis if there ever was one, a desperate attempt to cover up the void of the absent God revealed in the previous section. But the final cadenza is the strangest of them all, sounding not at all like Beethoven but more like a puffed up version of the finale of Mozart's "Abduction from Seraglio", combining the "Turkish" elements with the fast rococo spectacle. (And let us not forget the lesson of this Mozart opera: the figure of the oriental despot is presented there as a true enlightened master.) The finale is thus a weird mixture of Orientalism and regression into late eighteeenth-century classicism, a double retreat from the historical present, a silent admission of the purely phantasmatic character of the Joy of all-encompassing brotherhood.

We can easily imagine Hitler and Stalin, Bush and Kim Jong Il, participating in the same magic moment of ecstatic brotherhood.

If there ever was a music that literally deconstructs itself, this is it: the contrast between the highly ordered linear progression of the first part of the movement and the precipitous, heterogeneous and inconsistent character of the second part could not be stronger. No wonder that as early as 1826, two years after the first performance, a reviewer described the finale as "a festival of hatred towards all that can be called human joy. With gigantic strength the perilous hoard emerges, tearing hearts asunder and darkening the divine spark of gods with noisy, monstrous mocking…" Of course, these lines are not meant as a criticism of Beethoven, quite to the contrary; in an Adornian mode, one should discern in this failure of the fourth movement Beethoven's artistic integrity: the truthful indexation of the failure of the very Enlightenment project of universal brotherhood.

Beethoven's Ninth is thus full of what Nicholas Cook called "unconsummated symbols": elements which are in excess of the global meaning of the work (or of the movement in which they occur), i.e. do not fit this meaning nor make clear what additional meaning they should carry. Cook lists the "funeral march" at bar 513 of the first movement, the abrupt ending of the second movement, the military tones in the third movement, the so-called "horror fanfares", the Turkish march and many other moments in the fourth movement. All these elements, according to Maynard Solomon, "vibrate with an implied significance that overflows the musical scenario".

It is not simply that their meaning should be uncovered through an attentive interpretation. The very relation between texture and meaning is inverted here: if the predominant musical scenario seems to set into music a clear pre-established meaning (the celebration of joy, the universal brotherhood), here the meaning is not given in advance, but seems to float in some kind of virtual indeterminacy. It is as if we know that there *is* (or rather *has to be*) some meaning, without ever being able to establish *what* this meaning is.

What, then, is the solution? The only radical solution is to shift the entire perspective and to render problematic the very first part of the fourth movement: things do not really go wrong only at bar 331 with the entrance of the *marcia Turca*, they go wrong from the very beginning. One should accept that there is something of an insipid fake in the "Ode to Joy", that the chaos entering after bar 331 is a kind of "return of the repressed", a symptom of what was wrong from the start. What if we domesticated too much the "Ode to Joy", what if we got all too used to it as a symbol of joyful brotherhood? What if we should confront it anew, reject it in what is false in it?

And does the same not hold for Europe today? Though inviting millions, from the highest to the lowest (the worm) to embrace, the second strophe ominously ends in: "But he who cannot rejoice, let him steal weeping away from our circle ("*Und wer's nie gekonnt, der stehle weinend sich aus dem Bund*").

The irony of Beethoven's "Ode to Joy" as the European anthem is, of course, that the main cause of today's crisis of the Union is precisely Turkey. Opposition to Turkish membership can be grounded in rightist-populist terms (the Turkish threat to our culture, the Turkish cheap immigrant labour) or in liberal multiculturalist terms (Turkey should not be allowed in because, in its treatment of the Kurds, it doesn't display enough respect for human rights). So, should Turkey be allowed in or should it be left to steal itself weeping out of the union? Can Europe survive the Turkish march? And, as in the finale of Beethoven's Ninth, what if the true problem is not Turkey, but the basic melody itself, the song of European unity as it is played to us from Brussels' post-political technocratic élite? What we need is a totally new main melody, a new definition of Europe itself. The problem of Turkey, the perplexity of the European Union with regard to what to do with it, is not about Turkey as such, but the confusion about what Europe itself is.

Slavoj Žižek is a professor at the European Graduate School, International Director of Birkbeck College and a senior researcher at the University of Ljubljana. Most recently, he introduced and presented Robespierre: Virtue and Terror *and* Mao: On practice and contradiction *(both Verso Revolutions series, January 2007).*

Mother's right

By Dubravka Ugrešić

You should always sauté chopped onion for a long time. Good health is what matters most. It is tough to get rid of wine stains. Liars are the worst people. Lettuce is good for you. Old age is a terrible tragedy. Beans are best in salad. Cleanliness is next to godliness. Stand up straight when you walk. Always throw the first water out when you cook kale.

I took note of this authoritarian voice of hers. I am sure she has been saying sentences like that her whole life, it's just that amid the sea of other sentences, I hadn't spotted them. But now, everything has gotten smaller. Her heart has shrunk. Her veins have shrunk. Her footsteps are smaller. Her repertoire of words has narrowed. Life has narrowed.

She has reduced her movement to a daily visit to the nearby open market. She takes this little walk by relying on a shopping cart on wheels. (*I always buy meat at this butcher's. As far as lettuce is concerned, I only buy the tenderest kind.*) She uttered her stereotypes with special importance. Stereotypes give her a feeling that everything is fine, that the world is precisely where it should be, and that she has things under control, that she has power, because, here she is, deciding, here she is, buying something, because, here she is, knowing which kind of lettuce is best. Her mind still works, her legs still work, she can walk, though only with the help of a shopping cart, but she is walking, and she is a human being like any other and she still has her work to see to.

She wields her stereotypes as if with an invisible stamp of approval, which she smacks everywhere, eager to leave her mark. The desire grows stronger with her awareness that death is growing stronger too. (*When I die, this porcelain coffee service will be yours. When we bought it, it was the most expensive service around. It cost us a whole month's pay!*) She has intended the service for me. In her opinion it was the most valuable thing in the house. She had something different in mind for my brother and his family. She explained this to me not long ago on the phone.

"You know, I have decided to have them over for dinner even more often from now on. The children love everything I cook for them. They say to me: Grandma, you are the best cook in the world! It is exhausting, but the way I see it, I'll cook for them even if I have to on my hands and knees. That way they will have something to remember me by."

"There will be plenty of things for them to remember you by," I said cautiously.

She didn't answer. Instead she remarked:

"You sound a bit congested. Do you have cold? Have some tea with lemon. Tea with lemon is the best way to combat a cold."

I hung up the phone and sighed with relief. All was right with the world. My eighty-year-old mother was doing fine. Her message – what she'd said about the tea with lemon – foamed, buzzed and shimmered into the air like the lively colours of a divine sparkler.

Dubravka Ugrešić's most recent books are Ministry of Pain *and* Thank You for Not Reading. *Her new essay collection* Nobody's Home *will be published in August 2007 by Telegram/Saqi.*

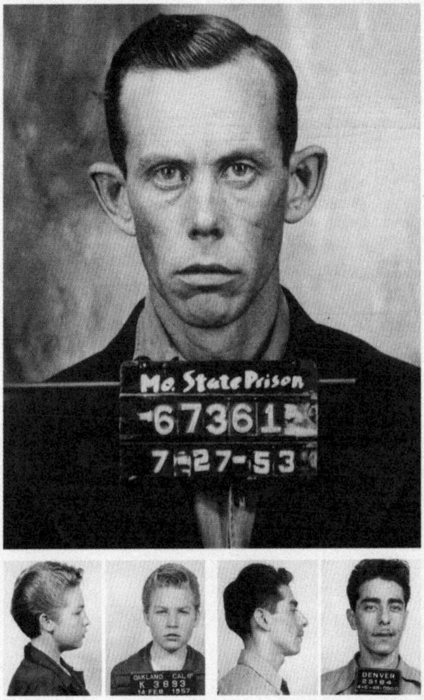
Mo. State Prison
6736
7-27-53

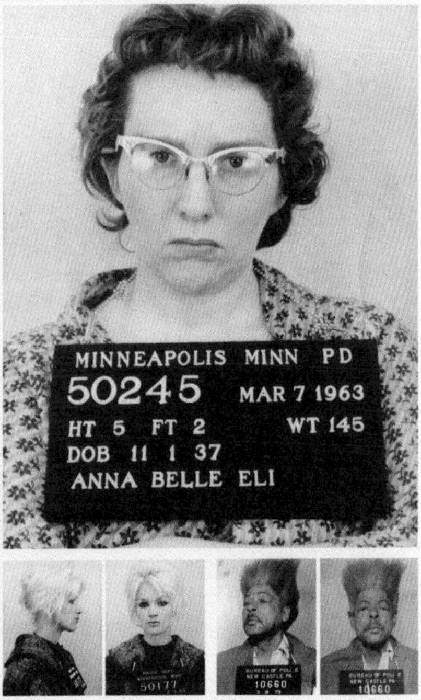
MINNEAPOLIS MINN PD
50245 MAR 7 1963
HT 5 FT 2 WT 145
DOB 11 1 37
ANNA BELLE ELI

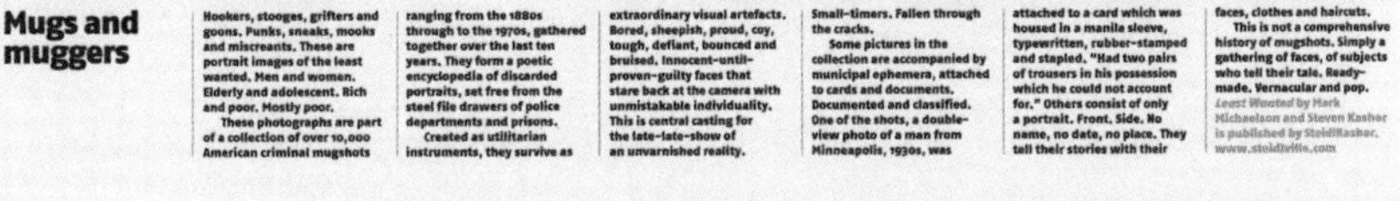
OAKLAND CALIF
K 3893
14 FEB 1957
DENVER
50177
BUREAU OF POLICE
NEW CASTLE PA
10660

Mugs and muggers

Hookers, stooges, grifters and goons. Punks, sneaks, mooks and miscreants. These are portrait images of the least wanted. Men and women. Elderly and adolescent. Rich and poor. Mostly poor.

These photographs are part of a collection of over 10,000 American criminal mugshots ranging from the 1880s through to the 1970s, gathered together over the last ten years. They form a poetic encyclopedia of discarded portraits, set free from the steel file drawers of police departments and prisons.

Created as utilitarian instruments, they survive as extraordinary visual artefacts. Bored, sheepish, proud, coy, tough, defiant, bounced and bruised. Innocent-until-proven-guilty faces that stare back at the camera with unmistakable individuality. This is central casting for the late-late-show of an unvarnished reality. Small-timers. Fallen through the cracks.

Some pictures in the collection are accompanied by municipal ephemera, attached to cards and documents. Documented and classified. One of the shots, a double-view photo of a man from Minneapolis, 1930s, was attached to a card which was housed in a manila sleeve, typewritten, rubber-stamped and stapled. "Had two pairs of trousers in his possession which he could not account for." Others consist of only a portrait. Front. Side. No name, no date, no place. They tell their stories with their faces, clothes and haircuts.

This is not a comprehensive history of mugshots. Simply a gathering of faces, of subjects who tell their tale. Ready-made. Vernacular and pop.

Least Wanted by Mark Michaelson and Steven Kasher is published by SteidlKasher. www.steidlville.com

By Paul Davis

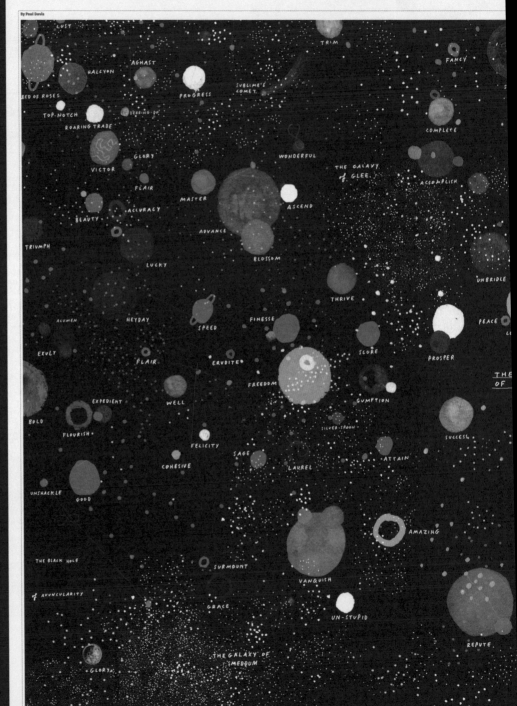

Issue Four
Spring 2007

To subscribe to *The Drawbridge*
visit the website at
www.thedrawbridge.org.uk

7

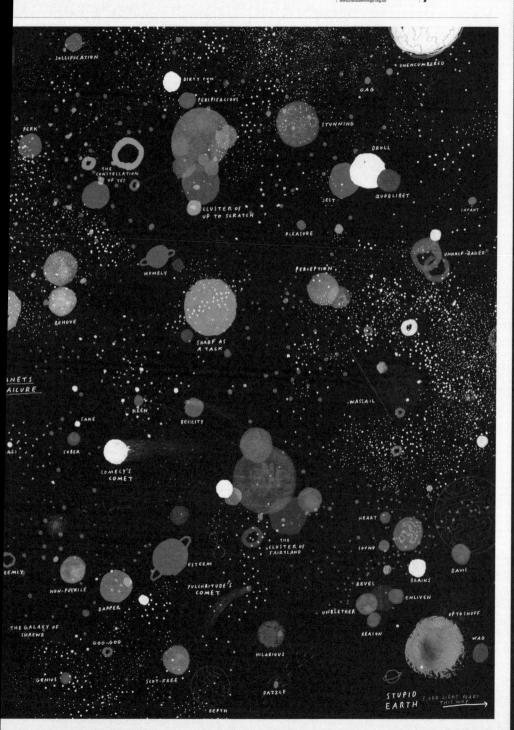

Issue Three
Autumn 2006

By Toby Morison

Appeasing the locals in rural France

Entente most cordiale

By Alice Waugh

An Englishwoman's home is her castle, so they say, and mine have stood up to various attacks. From the neighbour who jumped my parents' fence one day, brandishing a chainsaw, to cut down an inoffensive birch tree that had been upsetting his dog – itself a vicious Alsatian trained to draw blood first and ask questions later – to the strange glazed-eyed ladies who appeared at my door a week after I had set up house in a small Japanese fishing village to teach me about Jehovah, I have usually been able to repel intruders. Even the SWP types who used to let themselves into my room at university and wait patiently for me with a pile of *Morning Stars* were eventually got rid of with protestations of eternal Catholicism – and the Catholics with vows of undying Socialism.

Not so with the French. There is a marauding ex-plumber in the village where I now live who is engaged in a one-man struggle against the English invasion, with reckless disregard for personal safety. Rather than adopting the traditional method of retreating to the forest and firing the occasional salvo, he has embarked on a campaign of aggressive friendship. He starts his rounds of the village at about quarter to twelve each day, when he sets out from home to the nearest foreign house. A loud cry of "*Salut!*" is the only warning his victims get before he walks into the kitchen, pours himself a Ricard and settles into his favourite chair to pontificate. He prefers to drink two Ricards before moving to the next stop on his itinerary, where the process is repeated. At one o'clock he goes home for lunch and, presumably, to sleep it off before starting his evening round at five-thirty.

Claude has two important weapons: the ability to expound on any subject for unlimited amounts of time and his vocabulary, a conglomeration of 70s Paris and timeless Languedoc that leaves the uninitiated lost and reeling. He is also unhindered by any fear of repeating himself and has never heard of political correctness. Recent monologues include "The Importance of Sport to the Soul", "How to Grow Parsley" and "Why Le Pen Will Always Have My Heart". He is abetted by the growing sense of shame amongst the foreign community, desperately middle-class and eager to fit in with the village but secretly aware that they would far rather play bridge and drink G&T with their compatriots. This makes it impossible to turn away the locals, even someone like Claude who turns up every day, twice a day. Most of his regulars buy Ricard only for him.

My position is slightly worse; he has a key to my castle. Others may lock the door and cower under the covers when they hear his battle cry, but the last time I did that he came straight up into my bedroom and demanded to know why I wasn't at home. My feeble response that "*Je suis très fatiguée*" was treated with the contempt it deserved. When I left my key in the lock to stop him using his own, he stood in the courtyard and yelled for ten minutes before he eventually got bored and went away. The next time we met, he informed me that he needed to be able to get into the main house at all times, regardless of whether he was welcome. He has even come down to my garden to look for me.

Anywhere else, I would think he was a stalker. In this little village, though, he is clearly the vanguard of a people fed up with occupation. The chattering classes are undaunted by the bills for extensive renovation, nor do they feel anything other than amusement when confronted by French rudeness. So the locals have taken the fight in a different direction. A sign on the road outside announces that you are about to enter "*Un des Plus Beaux Villages de France*". The annual village sports now include the running of the pigs, where two village teams chase their respective pigs round the ramparts with large buckets of water, used to spur on the animals but also to splatter any second-homers who have turned out to luxuriate in the "rustic" nature of the festivities. They are trying to out-twee us; they will never succeed. Claude continues his solitary mission to infuriate us into leaving; I will offer him my west wing and stack it with Ricard – it wouldn't be too cruel, rather traditional, in fact.

Alice Waugh is currently stationed in the south of France.

A life played out in the prairies of Country Club, Rutherford and Harbour Park

The parking lots of home

By Craig Taylor

I think of parking lots when I think of home. I think of the parking lots of Nanaimo, BC, Canada. Parking lots that sit about as far West on the North American continent as you can put them before you get ocean and ocean and then the parking lots of Japan begin. These lots come with their own memories. My life has played itself out in them. The Woodgrove Mall lot is where I pushed friends around in shopping carts in the middle of the night. We drove them hard. After a day's work those carts must have been terrified to see us approach in denim jackets, in acid-wash jeans. Maybe we were hard on the shopping carts, but that's what surplus teen energy gets you in the middle of the night, slightly drunk on stolen rosé, as the grey light comes over the movie marquee that announces the films that are playing in this mall. It was 1989, a good year to be thirteen, and the movies hinted at possible outcomes of our new lives: *Parenthood. Twins. Glory. Dead Calm. The Abyss.*

One of these friends went on to become an architect; the other a cross-dresser.

We smashed stuff in the parking lot. We ran from tired police cruisers and lazy sirens. We got back to the parental houses before anyone was up, inserting the key with care to ensure the lock wasn't scratched awake.

Country Club Mall had the parking lot closest to our record shop, the best record shop, where the snobbery was most potent. After each trip, I tapped the CD cases on the roof of the car while waiting for the driver. Some days we stood in the parking lot with our purchases and watched the new Wal-Mart, the first in the city, being birthed. It aged too, just like us. Wal-Marts grey. The greeters got older and the blue lettering lost its lustre. Finally, Wal-Mart left home, moved north to be with a newer mall. Country Club was left with a crater and a lot of empty space in the parking lot.

There was always space in these parking lots for the boys with trucks to leave tyre-mark slashes; space to wander while feeling that strange, encompassing sensation that came from smoking someone's parents' stash of weed. The parking lot in Rutherford Mall was at the top of a large hill. At the bottom of the ravine lay the mangled remains of more shopping carts. Each year the Canadian winter rusted them. Each year we pushed more down, like sending buffalo off a jump. Our prairies: there was space to watch our girls lean up against Volkswagens and begin their love affairs with cigarettes. We huddled around them, eating McNuggets and watching those slow billows of smoke coming from their mouths. There was space in those parking lots for searing, fucking searing, love. And there was space for that walk you had to take to that far side of the parking lot with that girl to have that talk. The parking lot changed when I walked back alone after being dumped for the first time. That night I actually fell asleep in the parking lot. I wandered off and lay down on the white lines while AC/DC played out of someone's car door. There was always a movie marquee in sight, but the films of 1991 didn't look as optimistic. *Slacker, Dying Young, Life Stinks and Love Hurts.*

The last of my parking lots is attached to Harbour Park Mall, though the name has since changed. This parking lot is furthest from my childhood home. When I go back now to my town the West Coast drizzle is still there and the Wendy's still serves from its 99 cent menu. I sit in a car. I don't lay on the pavement. I watch obese people enter the Great Canadian Casino and wait for the ferry that takes me to a small island where my family has moved to and where there are no malls or parking lots. The ferry comes once an hour and so I wait as best I can. Droplets turn to rivulets on the windshield and the shopping trolleys roll all around me. These days, I don't need to destroy them, send them down hills, bash them against concrete. We eye each other in the parking lot and I let them peacefully roll on their way.

Craig Taylor produces a zine called One Million Tiny Plays About London.

By Jeff Fisher

Escaping the humid valleys of Northern Italy for the calm of Mexico City

Ritalin for loners

By Carlo Pizzati

I was on my way to catch a flight to Mexico City when I first felt the need to draw a diagram of my life. The train was racketing away from Valdagno, my hometown in the humid valleys of Northern Italy near Venice. At the time a correspondent for *La Repubblica*, Italy's national left-leaning daily, I had been covering the Latin American beat for three years and was heading out for one last, particularly dangerous assignment. And it struck me there and then, on the train to the airport, that exactly half of my life was over and the other half was about to begin.

If I have any choice in the matter, I remember thinking, that second half will be lived as far away from Valdagno as possible. My hometown is shrouded in fogs, falls away into dark valleys and seems allergic to Italy's reputation as a sunlit, cheerful place. Winter closes like a lid over the town, which sits near the foothills of the Dolomites and has been fittingly described by visiting friends as "Transylvanian". But I doubt Dracula ever entertained himself with the nation's highest rate of lap dancers per capita. Nor is it likely that he expiated his sanguinary conscience by consulting the massive population of nuns and priests (and alcoholics) who live nearby. Perfectly two-faced, aggressively pious by day and wanton by night, Valdagno is just like many a small northern Italian town, only darker – much, much darker.

Another thing the town is, particularly when you're sixteen years old, is a good place to flee. Which I did, for Pensacola, Florida, where I was an exchange student at first, and then, having fallen in love with my host family, a default American boy for the following eleven years.

So I start drawing this diagram, on the train, to explain to myself how it came to be that, at this particular moment in life, I am about to board a plane to put myself in harm's way three thousand miles away.

At the centre of the paper I see a small, dimensionless dot. It is the "I" around which memory, solitude, family, friends, job, vocation and Her rotate with the oiled ease of so many satellites.

But solitude should not be a satellite so much as a colour, I decide, and make solitude the colour of the yellow pad on which I write, the same yellow as the streetlamps shining through the windows of the moving night train as it flies past sleeping villages.

Memory is the thickness of the sheet.

Women are the smell of the paper, friends the wrinkles.

My job is the handwriting.

The things of this world are the sound of the crumpled paper.

Family is the shape of the paper.

The vocation is the pen.

Strangers are the empty space around the notepad.

And the "I" is not the hub at the centre at all, as it turns out, but rather something spread around the entirety of the paper on which the diagram sits. It is the power of the page you're reading to make sense.

"*Passaporte!*" screams the man with the moustache. The plexiglass between us reflects me back as a gaunt, jet-lagged ghost overlapping the officer's face. The trip was exhausting, but my exhaustion wasn't only physical.

Look in his eyes without challenging him, don't be flip, adjust a calibrated smile, I repeat to myself.

I know that in my bordeaux passport there are too many stamps – twenty Mexican, a dozen Argentinian, eight Chilean, four Peruvian, two Ecuadorian, several Brazilian, a couple each from Uruguay, Bolivia, Panama, Cuba, Jamaica, Venezuela, Kenya, Morocco, Hong Kong, the Philippines and Tahiti as well. And I know that there'll be a small hitch while the officer digests this fact.

Sure enough, he's giving the standard response. Equally intrigued and bewildered, his stern young face is lit with the faint hope that he's "got one"; that he's nailed a smuggler or contraband-artist of some kind. His hope is that he can stop me. And he's right, I should be stopped. Someone should stop me from this insane travelling.

Why do I do it, still? It wasn't merely the job; I'm no longer a correspondent. It's some larger form of restlessness. It's related, perhaps, to my own hybrid status as Americo-Italian, a border dweller, an interstice-seeker, a happy inhabitant of ontological cracks. I've always felt at home in the alienation of fast-food restaurants, and in those impersonal vast barns of commerce that are Latin American shopping malls. Alto Las Condes in Santiago, Palacio de Hierro in Mexico City, Jockey Plaza in Lima are zones of the world where the pitch and hum of the impersonal finally reach a frequency that allows me to rest.

Doctors prescribe the stimulant Ritalin to hyperactive children, and on the same principle, I prescribe myself the loneliest places in the world as a cure for my loneliness, and it works.

Carlo Pizzati is currently in a small hut in the Tolfa Mountains, an hour north of Rome, possibly thinking of going elsewhere.

An island too small and a goat too many

Peace comes dropping slow

By Rowena Macdonald

"I will arise and go now, and go to Innisfree,
And a small cabin build there, of clay and wattles made:
Nine bean-rows will I have there, and a hive for the honey-bee,
And live alone in the bee-loud glade.

And I shall have some peace there, for peace comes dropping slow…"

This was Yeats' dream. Sometimes it is my dream too. It was fed to me by my parents. They met in 1972 picking tomatoes on a nursery on the Isle of Wight. "I spied her through the tomato vines," my father always says. I like to think their fingers touched as they reached for the same fruit.

My mother's first memory of my father is in the hut where they took their tea breaks; he rolled a cigarette and offered it to her. She declined because she didn't smoke, but the other pickers, Stollfuss, the German prisoner of war, and Kath, the Island woman he had married, chuckled knowingly.

Not long after, my father came into the hut, the sleeves of his shirt torn on broken greenhouse glass, his hair long, his face thin and bearded "like a picture of Our Lord". He ripped off the sleeves in front of them all and said, "And He rent His garments." My mother knew then she had to marry him.

He was living in a caravan on the nursery. His ragged clothes were all mildewed on one side where they had touched the condensation on the caravan wall. She was living in Newport with her sister, her widowed mother and her grandmother; three generations of women in a crumbling Victorian villa decked with geraniums and a veranda. He moved in as a lodger but he and my mother were not allowed to carry on together; they had to get married first, because even though it was 1972, in rural backwaters that was the way it was back then.

After they were married, they went on honeymoon to Scotland in an Austin A60 van with my father's lobster pots tied to the roof. He dreamed of living off the land in splendid isolation on a croft in the Highlands; he had read my mother's copy of *Walden* by Thoreau. But the van broke down, their wedding night was spent arguing in a lay-by near Swindon, my father slapped my mother – the only time he ever hit her – and my mother was sick on the verge in shock. When they got to Scotland, the croft had no toilet and no electricity, the locals were even more morose than Islanders, they poured condensed milk in their tea for a treat, and the nearest piece of civilization – a corner shop which sold plastic bread – was two hours' walk across flint and bracken.

"The final straw," my mother said, "came when your father got up in the middle of the night to pee into an empty baked bean tin instead of going outside. He put the tin down and accidentally kicked it over."

Back on the Island they wandered the blackberry lanes between the fields farmed by my mother's uncle. They found a derelict farm called "Sullens" in a valley shaded by old holm oaks.

"You don't want to live there," said Uncle Albert drawing out every vowel as if he had all the time in the world, "I got a much nicer place for you."

And so it was that they came to live for three pounds fifty a week in Rose Cottage on a lane marked Loverstone, Rill and Cridmore. My first home.

I remember feeding the goats with dandelion clocks and in turn I was fed with their milk. Three goats we had – two nannies, Katie and Bella, and a castrated billy called Harwood, one of triplets, named after a very fat priest at my father's school. All three met unhappy ends. Katie was hit by a VW Beetle on the lane, Bella died of anaphylactic shock after my father inadvertently pegged her stake into a wasps' nest, and Harwood fell into a ditch and was strangled by his own tethering rope. Bella's kids, sired by a goat called Socrates from a neighbouring farm, were butchered but it was hard to eat them, particularly Plato, who was very sweet natured.

The van broke down and their wedding night was spent arguing in a lay-by near Swindon

The bees they kept at the bottom of the garden went too after they turned angry and swarmed against my father. He didn't realize he was allergic to stings, spent a week in bed, his face swollen like a football, fighting a fever of 102 degrees.

There were two bedrooms in Rose Cottage. Mine overlooked the front garden. My earliest memory, apart from the goats and the bees, is standing in my cot in my room, sweaty fingers clenched around the rails, and looking down on my mother through the window, her red hair shining in the sun, as she walked down the garden path with my father towards the fields, blazing yellow under a vast blue sky. My mother was walking away from me into the world beyond. I screamed and screamed.

Thirty years later, I wake up in my father's orchard overlooking the green sweep of the Malvern Hills. I am lying between the young apple trees, the feathered maidens, my face cushioned by a plastic bag that I had intended to fill with wild cherries. I had lain down to watch the branches against the sky, the sun glinting off the tonic water cans that stop the rain rotting into the tree stakes, and to listen to the flurries of rabbits and birds in the hedgerows. A tractor in the next field wakes me and I see my mother, her hair now grey, disappearing below the curve of the land. "Where are you going?" I call in panic.

"I'm going to build a hut here, a small cabin," says my father, as we sit under the big oak in his orchard and he feeds small sticks into the volcano kettle, waiting for the water to boil for tea. "A small cabin with a bed. So I can come and sleep out here when it all gets too much with your mother."

The builders across the way hammer from dawn till dusk, the neighbour's pit bull barks its throat sore, sirens reel in the distance, drunks on the street argue over cans of Special Brew, and I sometimes dream of the time when I too will have a cabin of my own.

Rowena Macdonald was born on the Isle of Wight in 1974 and now lives in London. She is currently completing a novel about the eroticization of illness, Tending the Sick.

Interiors

To subscribe to *The Drawbridge*
visit the website at
www.thedrawbridge.org.uk

9

When country, street and city rhythms fail

Raga Puriya

By Geoff Dyer

Not just in Varanasi, on the banks of the Ganges, but in Camden, too, over the dank canal, the sun sets for the last time. It will be back but, as of yesterday, the world it returns to each day has changed. Not that – in London at least – it's anywhere to be seen. The sunniest July "since records began" has been followed by a monsoon August. It's raining hard now, hard enough to drown out – almost – the wail of the police siren.

I was in the Café Konstam near Kings Cross waiting for my eggs (over-poached, as it happened) when I read of the death of Bismillah Khan. It's a cycle ride away, Konstam, but there's nowhere nearer home than I like as much. To be precise I'd just sent back my cappuccino on the grounds that it was milky as a latte. I turned the page and there was his picture and a lengthy obituary. When the guy – they don't really have waiters – brought back my cappuccino he must have been able to see the brink of tears in my eyes. Bismillah Khan had passed away. He'd lived and died – aged 90 – in Varanasi (Benares).

Written in his native Buenos Aires, Borges's poem "Benares" is a tour of an "imagined city" which the writer has "never seen". He pictures this city vividly, hears "the voice of a muezzin" calling from a high tower. This strikes a slightly odd note since Varanasi is the epicentre not of Islam but of Hinduism. The confusion is all to Borges's purpose, however, for even while he conjures these "doubtful images" he acknowledges that there is also a real city whose "precise topography" is very different to the one he has imagined. But this city, too, has the quality of a hallucination, is "peopled like a dream".

Bismillah Khan was given a full state funeral in the dream-city. What a day that must have been, in a city where an average day is... where there's no such thing as an average day. In India flags were flown at half-mast and a day of national mourning was declared – but it was a day of mourning the world over.

I saw him play once, in London, but couldn't remember exactly. The internet revealed that he had played here in November 1993. I consulted my diary for that year and saw that that was it: 22 November. But quite a week for Indian music: Ram Narayan (16th), Subramaniam (17th), Trilok Gurtu (18th). The concert, I discovered now, had been recorded (by the Navras label) and within twenty minutes I had downloaded it. That's the music you can hear now, in the background. The swaying shehnai, slinky, funky, spiky; the teental gallop of the tabla. Puriya (to be played after sunset).

I remember him on stage at the QEH: a sprightly little guy with a white beard; ancient-looking even then, thirteen years ago. He gave a speech at the end of the concert. I couldn't understand a word – wasn't even sure what language he was speaking – but everyone who could was cracking up.

I also spent part of today looking, unsuccessfully, for a tape made by my friend Charlie (now antiquair). A *jugalbandi* (duet) of Bismillah and the sitar maestro, Vilayat Khan. I have a CD of them playing Raga Yeman on another occasion (a Gramophone Company of India CD with no information about where and when it was recorded) but it's not nearly as good. It must be here somewhere, in one cupboard or another but, for now, it's unfindable. Home: a place where things are never lost and, as often as not, never found. In the 1980s, Charlie, another friend, Chris, and I used to get stoned and listen to music together. The number of things I heard for the first time, back then, at a Crownstace Court (my place in Brixton) and 133 Notting Hill Gate (Charlie's)! One of the tasks, as you get older, is to try to maintain a flow of things you are experiencing for the first time. The more time you spend at home the more difficult this becomes. Hence the need for travel, which constantly expands the area of the world in which you feel at home – thereby generating the need for further travel.

In February, to cut a long story extremely short, I went to Varanasi for the first time. What a waste of a life never to have gone there, never to have seen for yourself that such a place exists. There's how you imagine it and there's how it is – and the latter is so much stranger than the former could ever be. People said then that Bismillah was very ill. I remember thinking how odd it must be, to be a Muslim in a place where Hindus have all the fun. But by all accounts he liked it well enough. It was where he felt at home.

As for me, here... Well, it's where I live, it's where my stereo and CDs are to be found (except for the ones I can't find) and it's reasonably handy for several international airports. But it's not home in the sense of the place where everything converges, a place one has no desire to leave. It's not Varanasi, it's not Benares. Varanasi, home to Muslims, Sikhs, Hindus, holy men, saints, hucksters, backpackers, ethnomusicologists – and, for as long as I was there, me! For now, though, I'm listening to Raga Puriya in a house I like, in a street I hate, in a city I don't much care for, in a country I've given up on. Not that it matters. There's a certain amount of wisdom in the title of another album of homely duets, by Charlie Haden (bass) and Hampton Hawes (piano): *As Long As There's Music*.

In the twilight, in London and Varanasi, the shehnai sways and dances; the shehnai holds sway still. ▲

Geoff Dyer's latest books include Yoga For People Who Can't Be Bothered To Do It *and* The Ongoing Moment *(both Abacus).*

By Elisabeth Scheder Bieschin

Not quite downing it and wanting more

In praise of wine and nature

By David Blunkett

To have no shape, no form, no existence other than outside your skin, is extraordinary. To have a nose, body and substance is to live.

And so it is with wine. From vine to wine, the grape exists only to be transmogrified: spawn from its skin, translating sunshine into warmth within, bottled like a prisoner, contained and held – a sentence extended by desirability, drinkability, the ability to age – and breathing again only once the cork is removed. Pulled from the bottle, it emerges with the sound that nothing else can replicate; breathing, decanted, swirling at last when poured.

And in breathing has two noses, one providing secrets of hay, of fruit, of sun, of days gone by, the other, snuffing, longing, wanting to sip but waiting. The swirling, taking in the bouquet, waiting to taste, is part of the joy – to pause, only for a short while, but enough

to say "gratification deferred" and then for indulgence to take its part.

And then the body and the blood combined, the edge of just decay turning instead to bursting tastes of life renewed, the first taste lingering, changing on your palate the bliss of Burgundy, the rejoicing of Rioja, the brilliance of Brunello. Give me not the common Claret, import from ancient Aquitaine, but instead the robust body, the lasting pleasure, of the taste of heaven – not of earthly things.

But too much indulgence and the senses deaden, lay heavy, awakened in the night with reprimand; the head in morning's light, half asleep and still awakening, fails to come alive at your command. The second bottle was the culprit from the night before, the tempted hand that pulled the cork, the

remembered pouring, the joy of forbidden fruit taken to excess.

For if pleasure be just one degree below excess, then leave a glass, just one, for another day. Wash your glass, and put away the bottle, knowing that clear heads, lifted hearts and memories sharp enough to bring renewed desire are far, far better still than paracetamols refrained.

So, as night follows day, red and white lay together, one to be cooled for sharpness on the palate, one to be opened to breathe the air and take the oxygen of day to bring the comfort of the night. ▲

David Blunkett is the former Home Secretary. The Blunkett Tapes, *his self-portrait and reflections on the political events of the past nine years, is published by Bloomsbury.*

"In brief, those who do not drink are either imbeciles or hypocrites, who often boast their sobriety while concealing some unspeakable vice. A man who drinks only water has a secret to hide." *Vincenzo Ruggiero,* Crime in Literature: Sociology of Deviance and Fiction.

The temples of phantom runners in DayGlo leotards

Urban strategy 2: The leisure society

By James Harkin

Five years ago this autumn, at an industry forecasting conference in Leiden, we in the strategic development community first woke up to something odd about the way the modern commuter makes his or her way through the metropolis. Using data sent to global satellite positioning systems from the mobile phones nestling our pockets, the consultant delivering the afternoon presentation remarked upon clouds of human activity secreted around areas of the city centre in the early mornings and after work. It was only with the help of enormous complimentary late mini-bar miniatures that a few of us diehard delegates cracked it: home-work-home-pub had been irrevocably interrupted. Indeed, home, for the childless, had been cut out almost completely but for sleep; the pub become a rare, delayed treat. Early morning and early evening, we worked out, they were hiding out in the gym, the swimming pools and leisure complexes. The leisure society had arrived – and we in Leiden congratulated ourselves on being among the first to realize its implications.

Strictly speaking, of course, we were not the first to the intellectual punch. Ever since the 19th century, futurologists and political economists had airily predicted that we would soon be liberated from the workplace into lives of almost unlimited leisure. At the end of that century, the brilliant economist Theodor Veblen noted the emergence of a new "leisure class", a caste of well-heeled dandies who kept their distance from the means of production and were obsessed with showing off symbols of social status. But how could one have known then that sooner or later all of us would – after a cursory week's free trial – morph into paid-up members of a very different leisure society? Who could have predicted that history would have the last laugh – that the siren promise of unlimited leisure would become the jailer of a leisure proletariat who, at the end of the working day, would march like zombies into a "second shift" in the leisure prison of their choice?

Very few, that's who. But what of it? If people want to spend their "leisure time" hidden away in underground carbuncles, the ploughers and post-modernists will shrug their shoulders and say, surely it would be churlish to second-guess them? But one of the agonies of modern life is that there are choices to make, and the tragic plight of the leisured classes is to miss out on the culture that one of the world's capitals can offer. Those hours between seven and nine in the morning, and seven and ten in the evening, are crucial for spiritual and intellectual development. Study after study of longitudinal and ethnographic research from the Western countries points out associations between energetic ritual muscle-use in gyms over many years and incipient mental retardation. Other peer-reviewed research in the Canadian Journal of Child Psychology has identified an association between pampering in spas and malignant narcissism, a condition sometimes brought on by an inappropriate relationship with a sibling as a youth and which can flare up into cross-dressing, ritual homicide, or – and here I refer strategists to *The Silence of the Lambs* – both.

The toxic effects of our "leisure society" are there and obvious for anyone who wants to look beyond better "pecs" and "buns" and examine the evidence. Until now, we have

been distracted by the intellectual schoolboys who pretend that all of our ills are somehow caused by our exposure to the "consumer society". But the society of mass consumption is neither new nor controversial; it has been with us for the last half-century and – barring the wobbly taste of the masses – has done no one any harm. No, the real harm stems from the conspicuous anti-consumption of the leisured middle classes. Rather than existing on the treadmill of a consumer society, they are left to huff and puff on running machines, galumphing at a brisk pace towards MTV screens at which they are destined never to arrive.

What is to be done? The first rule for aspiring strategists is that you are always more useful on the inside. Granted, only a fool – or someone whose complimentary membership comes via their work – would ever hand over money for a health club membership. Most of us, however, survive quite merrily on a conveyor belt of free trials in different leisure establishments, or by walking in and sweet-talking bored receptionists. Every second Friday, to take an example, myself and a small group of strategists – the majority of us freelance, all of us trial members of some years' standing – meet in the jacuzzi of a certain West End gym to discuss strategy and thrash out ideas. Any paying members still in the tub when we arrive are soon shooed away by the younger turks, who blow them kisses or snigger menacingly in their direction.

Like the Manchester factories immortalized by Friedrich Engels, our underground leisure prisons survive because of their invisibility to the naked eye. It would do no harm to name and shame them: Holmes Place (aka Homos' Place), LA Fitness (colloquially dubbed LA Shitness) and Virgin Active (which speaks for itself). Make no mistake, we mute fraternity of urban strategists are plotting at a health club near you, and one day soon we are going to storm the bastilles of the leisure society on your behalf. The humble smoker has already been banished to the margins of urban space. But so much more in need of a short, sharp shock are the shallow-pool swimmers, the machine weightlifters and the phantom runners.

Which one of you would really complain if a number of strategically-placed blast bombs accompanied by brisk telephone warnings were to force the leisure classes onto the pavements of our 21st-century city, to send them scampering blinking into the sunlight, naked and dripping from skimpy togs, slinky swimsuits and DayGlo leotards? A secret army of urban strategists could mingle with the leisure proletariat to counsel the afflicted. It's OK, they could say, holding the liberated leisure masses to their breast, wet and flipping like caught fish; it's OK to cry because everything is going to be all right from now on. Lose bomb all you want, I tell my boys, but don't forget to steal a towel on your way out. ▲

James Harkin is a freelance consultant working on urban strategy.

By Nigel Shafran

By Paul Davis

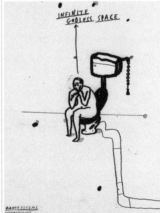

INFINITE GODLESS SPACE

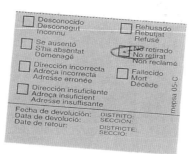

SENDER:
STUDIO8 DESIGN
1 SANS WALK
LONDON
EC1R 0LT
UK

astique Magazine

lient Plastique ***Design*** Matt Willey ***Year*** 2007

esign and art direction of a new women's magazine.

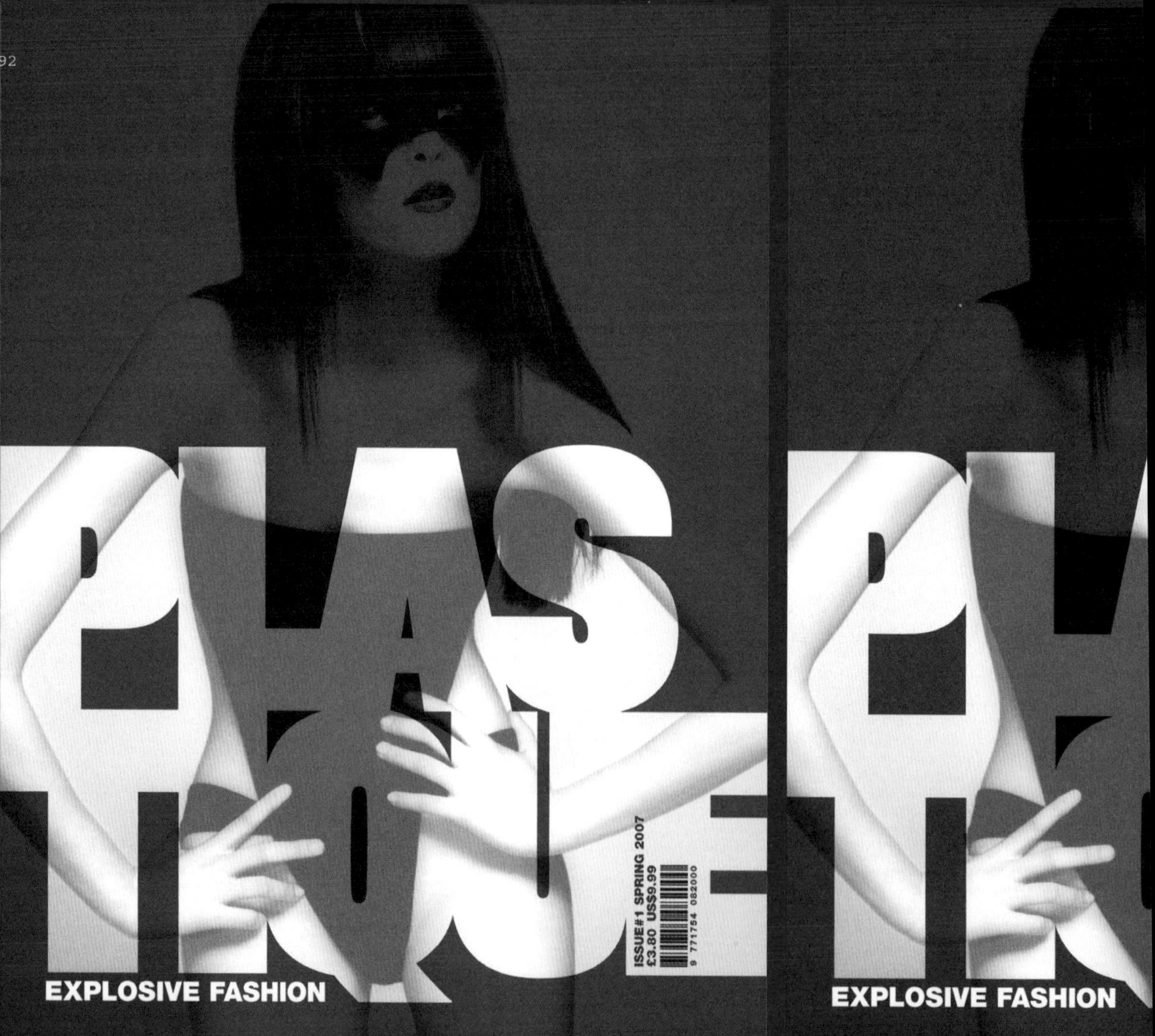
EXPLOSIVE FASHION
ISSUE#1 SPRING 2007
£3.80 US$9.99
9 771754 082000
EXPLOSIVE FASHION

EXPLOSIVE FASHION

ISSUE#1 SPRING 2007
£3.80 US$9.99

9 771754 082000

CONTENTS PAGE TWO

CONTENTS PAGE TWO

CONTENTS PAGE TWO

CONTENTS PAGE TWO

EDITOR IN CHIEF / FASHION DIRECTOR
Brylie Quinn Fowler
brylie@plastiquemagazine.com

ASSISTANT TO THE EDITOR IN CHIEF
Jeanie Annan-Lewin
jeanie@plastiquemagazine.com

BOOKINGS EDITOR
Mai Diallo
mai@plastiquemagazine.com

BEAUTY EDITOR
Emma Miles
emma@plastiquemagazine.com

WATCH & JEWELLERY EDITOR
Toby McLellan
toby@plastiquemagazine.com

DESIGN & ART DIRECTION
Matt Willey / Studio8 Design

PUBLISHER
Benjamin Shrimpton
ben@plastiquemagazine.com

COMMUNICATIONS DIRECTOR
Fabio Ciquera
fabio@plastiquemagazine.com

GROUP SALES DIRECTOR
Houtan Odabai
houtan@plastiquemagazine.com

SALES AGENT – ITALY
Raffaella Giannattasio
Advertising Manager
EDITO S.r.l
Via Conservatorio 22,
20122 Milano, Italy.
PH +39 02 7729 7505
FX +39 02 7772 9259
r.giannatasio@editost.eu

SALES AGENT – FRANCE
PUBLICITAS S.A
Marion Badoller-Reick
26 Victor Hugo F-75116,
Paris, France
PH + 33 1 45 00 66 08
FX +33 1 45 00 94 81

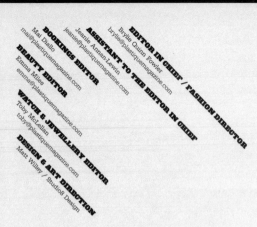

496

PLASTIQUE 2007

MASTHEAD

DAISY DOES...
Daisy Lowe
daisy@plastiquemagazine.com

FEATURES
Ellen Grace Jones / Grace Timothy / Simon Price /
Bee Blundell White / Kelly Carmichael / Peter Davis / Alex Slavycz

CONTRIBUTING PHOTOGRAPHERS
Jeffrey Graetsch / Laurence Ellis / Ram Shergill / David Dunan /
Shawn Mortensen / Katin Berndl / Jason Lloyd Evans / Pieter Henket /
James Ryang / Phillip Volkers

CONTRIBUTING FASHION EDITORS
Anne-Sophie Thomas / Raquel Garcia / Cynthia Lawrence-John

INTERNS
Lucy Kebbell / Ayesha Boone / Dean Hau / Danielle Korma

COVER
Photograph: Jeffrey Graetsch
Model: Andi Muise at MARILYN NY
(see page 73 for full credits)
Grenade: Brayan Marrero

PLASTIQUE
93 Shepperton Road, Pop Floor
London, N1 3DF UK
PH +44 (0)20 7288 1828

CONTRIBUTORS

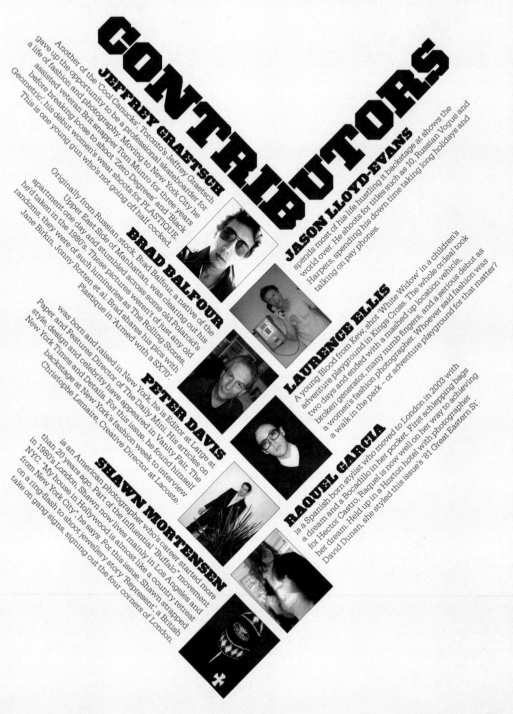

JEFFREY GRAETSCH

Another of the 'Cool Canucks', Toronto's Jeffrey Graetsch gave up the opportunity to be a professional skateboarder for a life of fashion and photography. Moving to New York City he assisted veteran Brit snapper Tom Munro for three years before breaking loose to shoot 'Zero Degrees and Black Geometric', his debut women's wear shoots for PLASTIQUE. This is one young gun who's not going off half cocked.

BRAD BALFOUR

Originally from Russian stock, Brad Balfour, a native of the Upper East Side of Manhattan, was clearing out his apartment one day and stumbled across some old Polaroids he'd taken in the 1980's. These pictures weren't of just any old randoms, they were of such luminaries as The Rolling Stones, Jane Birkin, Jonny Rotten et al. Brad shares his pics with Plastique in 'Armed with a SX70'.

PETER DAVIS

was born and raised in New York, he is Editor at Large at paper and Features Director of The Daily Mini. His articles on style, design and celebrity have appeared in Vanity Fair, The New York Times and Details. For this issue, he found himself backstage at New York's fashion week to interview Christophe Lemaire, Creative Director at Lacoste.

SHAWN MORTENSEN

is an American photographer who's career started more than 20 years ago. Part of the influential 'Buffalo" movement in 1980's London, Shawn now lives almost like a country retreat from New York City 'My house in Hollywood is almost like a country retreat in NYC.' he says. For this issue, Shawn strapped on a ring-flash to shoot jewellery story 'Represent,' a British take on gang signs, signing out the four corners of London.

JASON LLOYD-EVANS

spends most of his life hustling it backstage at shows the world over. He shoots for titles such as 10, Russian Vogue and Harpers, spending his down time taking long holidays and talking on pay phones.

LAURENCE ELLIS

A young Blood from Kew shot 'White Widow' in a children's adventure playground in Kings Cross. 'The whole ordeal took two days and ended with a mashed up location vehicle, broken generator, many numb fingers, and a serious debut as a women's fashion photographer. Whoever said fashion was a walk in the park – or adventure playground for that matter?

RAQUEL GARCIA

is a Spanish born stylist who moved to London in 2003 with a dream and a Bocadillo in her pocket. First schlepping bags for Hector Castro, Raquel is now well on her way to achieving her dream. Held up in a Hoxton hotel with photographer David Dunan, she styled this issue's '81 Great Eastern St.'

GIL CARVALHO

"Never under estimate the power of the stiletto," says Gil Carvalho. Given that he's followed the career route of Mr. Ford, who also gave up architecture for fashion design, Carvalho's ethos is on a par with his vigorous, towering platforms. Covered in vivid python and crocodile skins, with metallic leathers, they epitomise empowerment.

His architectural background is not entirely wasted however: like skyscrapers for the feet, Carvalho has produced a concept collection of soaring, polished steel stilettos – hand-laced elastic string, or satin cord that's woven to mould the foot – unmistakably requiring his construction precision and skill.

For something closer to the ground, Carvalho produces flat-of-foot sandals with slashed leather fronts. Alternatively why not try his made-to-order black rubber and leather thigh-highs? ∎

Todd Lynn is that kid at school that nobody noticed until parents' evening, where his mum and dad were unnecessarily cool and his report card gleamed, despite him being quietly rebellious. With a bespoke-tailor CV reading like a rock 'n' roll-call of the last 40 years in music, it was no surprise his former mentor, Roland Mouret, looked on admiringly in the front row. Lynn's collection was rife with androgynous tailoring and fluid lines that effortlessly sexed up waistcoats, tuxedo jackets, and cropped trousers, which were swapped between the girls and the boys ∎

TODD LYNN

ALEXANDER WANG

Thank goodness he left his San Francisco frat boy beginnings at the door when joining Marc Jacobs as an intern. It no doubt ensured that despite being only 23, his own collection is one of hot sophistication and understatement. Sticking with the cashmere roots planted in his very first 2004 collection with some tasty cardigans and sweaters, Wang also channelled his NYC street cred via sporty playsuits and sexy micro shorts. Think Debbie Harry circa 1977 ∎

Words Simon Price

She latex hot pants so spray-on tight they make Kylies gold numbers look like granny knickers. He: blinding white suit that wouldn't be out of place at a Jackie Treehorn pool party.

This is how Dragonette step out onstage. "Dressing up", explains singer Martina Sorbara "is fun. But it also makes you act differently, and enhances what you do. We would never go onstage in our street clothes. Everything has to look intentional."

Sorbara first met guitarist – and husband – Dan Kurtz at a festival during what he calls "that Nickelback moment" which had gripped their homeland. She was a practitioner of what she neatly terms "simponica" (read whiney acoustic singer-songwriter strumming) he was in an experimental breakbeat trio. "And then," he matter-of-factly recalls, "we screwed".

And screwing around, figuratively speaking, is how Dragonette began. At first, they amused themselves by writing "beyond reasonable" pastiches of 80's pop-rock (invariably sounding like "a bubblegum pop girl singing over a Pat Benatar record"). "The exercise of writing fluffy pop songs," says Martina, "is something I don't think anybody does in Canada. We were trying to make music that wasn't introspective or indie or overly emotional. Songs that weren't full of anguish or angst or social commentary."

Their modus operandi was to rewind to the 80's, and chart a path forward to an alternate, parallel present where grunge never happened, and pop groups aren't ashamed about looking like a pop group. Or sounding like one. Dragonette, who give out mixtapes to their fans at gigs and via MySpace containing names like Prince, Hall & Oates, Talk Talk and INXS, are upfront about their source material. "You can't not be influenced by the 80's if you're a pop band." Sorbara admits "Although for the first 15 years of my music-listening life I was into alternative folk and jazz, so I came to 80's after the fact..."

CANADIAN EXPORT

DRAGONETTE BRINGS PLASTIQUE INTO THEIR WORLD OF ELECTRO-POP ORGIES

Despite landing support gigs with Duran Duran, Scissor Sisters and New Order, they soon realised they needed to flee their hometown of Toronto (where "You couldn't bounce high enough on the trampoline to see over the trees"), and quit North America entirely. Heading for Europe, where they felt their style would be tapped up, they homed in on London ("an exciting place, where everyone's ultra-aware of music"), signed with Mercury, and set about honing their all-killer, no-filler repertoire of sassy, synth-based songs about illicit liaisons and boyfriend theft.

In the meantime, the duo have become in-demand songwriters, collaborating with Martina's first pop heroine Cyndi Lauper. "Seeing her in our crappy 10ft by 10ft basement studio was surreal. There were tears streaming down my face. I muttered 'I think you're god!' under my breath, but I don't know if she heard me." Along the way, Martina became a pop star almost by accident when she was chosen as the voice and face of Basement Jaxx's comeback hit, Take Me Back To Your House (that was her in the video, cossack-dancing in front of a tank driven by Stalin).

Now, it's Dragonette's turn to bust out of the shadows. Oh, the name? "It's a fire-breathing dragon, but it's a chick!" Martina explains. "A dragon in stilettos..."

(Their debut single "I Get Around" is out now. You'll know them when you see them)

CHRISTOPHE LEMAIRE
GIVES PLASTIQUE A LOOK
INTO LIFE AT THE HELM
OF ONE OF TODAYS MOST
WORN SPORTSWEAR
BRANDS – LACOSTE

CRÈME DE LEMAIRE

Words **Peter Davis**
Portrait **Pieter Henket**

OSMAN YOUSEFZADA

Unsubtle pinstripes, pink Ralph Lauren polo shirts – collars popped: the standard City-boy get-up. Somewhat surprisingly then is former banker, Osman Yousefzada's understated collection. Undoubtedly Afghanistan's best export (but let's not get political here). The British raised and CSM educated Yousefzada is in his first season showing Off-Schedule in London. Austere blacks and creams mixed with peachy-nudes and jolts of cobalt blue and red feed through softly tailored dresses and separates. Edwardian style feather ruffles, in varying sizes lent the collection a demure, romantic soupçon. A banker with taste; Who'd've thought? ∎

KIM JONES

It was only a matter of time. With a unisex name comes a unisex shoe. Now girls can finally drop their feet into a pair of Kim Jones' kicks. The high-top and hoodie homeboy responsible for bringing his luxe-chav chic to sportswear mega brand, Umbro, has now made shoes in his Umbro by Kim Jones range available as small as a teeny UK size 3.

Another feature of Jones' spring/summer '07 footwear collection is the 'Runner Lo' sneaker. Sewn completely inside out, like a football boot, the sneaker gives the impression of sleek seamlessness.

Perhaps leading the trend for sports label/designer collaborations, after three years working with the footie giant, Jones has made his trademark refined-casual aesthetic available to a broader, yet no less stylishly discerning audience.

With the current collection of footwear featuring baby blues and powder pinks it's likely all the girls will be elbowing out all the boys in order to grab a pair. ∎
www.umbrobykimjones.com

"I suddenly wanted to dress differently, to wear clothes designed by Hedi Slimane." It may well have been Dior Homme that prompted Lagerfeld's dramatic weight loss, but fortunately now, he can now fit into his own forthcoming range, K Karl Lagerfeld, as well.

Hitting stores this coming autumn, Lagerfeld's new collection for men and women will feature his inevitable 'long 'n' lean' silhouette. The denim line utilizes exclusive fabric treatments; unwashed, waxed, cleaned-up, all coming in neutral blacks, whites and greys. A monochrome palette extends further into a full range of sweaters, trousers, knitted dresses and refined cashmere knitwear – even outer garments. Everything still retaining that trademark sculpted, skinny aesthetic.

For those in the know, a subtle 'K' logo cheekily pops up on buttons, zip and rivet detailing, thus hinting at whose name is on the label. Oh, and don't forget the obligatory skinny tie. Should Hedi be watching his back... ∎

LAGERFELD RANGE

WHITE WIDOW
PHOTOGRAPHY LAURENCE ELLIS

502

DUALITY

STATEMENT LASHES ARE BACK. HERE ARE SOME OF THE BEST NEW MASCARAS FOR ACHIEVING THAT FIERCE-LASH LOOK

Photography **Karin Berndl**
Words **Emma Miles & Grace Timothy**

Plastique/Spring 07/**079**

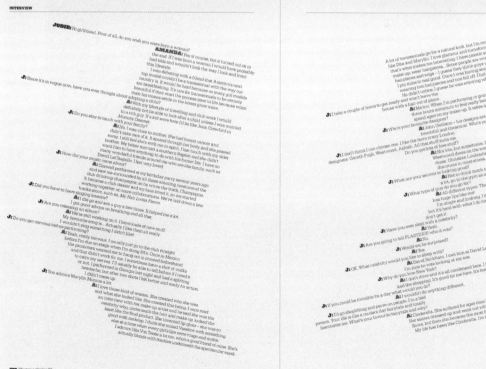

JODIE: Hi girlfriend. First of all, do you wish you were born a woman?

AMANDA: Yes of course, but it turned out ok in the end. If I was born a woman I would have probably had kids and wouldn't look the way I look and lived this lifestyle.

I was debating with a friend that America's next top model couldn't be a transsexual with the way our country is. It would be hard because so many girl models are breathtaking. It's rare for transsexuals to be entirely beautiful if they start the process later in life because when male hormones settle in the bones grow more.

With my lifestyle of travelling and club work I would definitely not be able to look after a child unless I was married to a rich guy. If a kid were here I'd be like Joan Crawford in Mommy Dearest.

J: Do you stay in touch with your family?

A: No. I was close to mother. She had breast cancer and didn't take care of it. It spread through her body and she passed away. I still feel she's with me in spirit. I lost touch with my older brother. My father married a southern Baptist and she didn't want him to have anything to do with his former life. I have so many wonderful friends around me who are like family, such as David LaChapelle. I feel very loved.

J: How did your music come about?

A: Carswell performed at my birthday party several years ago and saw me surrounded by all these amazing creatures at the club drinking champagne, so he wrote the track, Champagne. It became a club classic and my fans loved it, so we started working together on more collaborations. We've laid down a few tracks since, such as, My Hair Looks Fierce.

J: Did you have to have singing lessons?

A: I did go and see a guy a few times. It helped me a lot. I got good advice on breathing and all that.

J: Are you releasing an album?

A: No. I'm still working on it. I have loads of new stuff. My favourite song is... Actually I like them all really. I wouldn't sing something I didn't like!

J: Do you get nervous before performing?

A: Yeah, really nervous. I usually just go to the club straight before I'm done on stage when I'm doing PAs. Once in Mexico the promoters wanted me to have out in crowded beforehand and that didn't work for me. I sometimes have a shot of vodka to calm my nerves. I'll usually be able to tell before if I need it or not. I performed in Georgia last night and had a splitting headache, but after two shots I felt better and ready for action.

J: You admire Marilyn Monroe a lot.

A: I love those kind of women. She created who she was and what she looked like. She created this being. I once read an interview with her make-up artist and he said she was the celebrity who, underneath the hair and make-up looked the least like the final product. She invented lip-gloss - she was so good with makeup. I think she mixed Vaseline with something else at a time when every girl's lips were rouge and matte. I admire Dita Von Teese a lot too, who's a good friend of mine. She's actually blonde with freckles underneath the spectacular mask.

A lot of transsexuals go for a natural look, but I'm much more like Dita and Marylin. I love glamour and transformation and that's what makes me interesting. I have plastic surgery, love make-up, wear hairpieces... Some people are worried about hairpieces and wigs - I guess they think guys will pull them off. I pin mine in real good. Once I was having sex with a guy while wearing hairpieces and one fell off. I hid it under the pillow. He didn't notice, I guess he was enjoying what he was doing.

J: I take a couple of hours to get ready and won't leave the house with a hair out of place.

A: Me too. When I'm performing or going to a party I take three hours minimum to feel really beautiful. I shower, exfoliate, speed ages on my make-up. It takes a lot of work to look like this.

J: Who's your favourite designer?

A: John Galliano - his designs are so over the top and beautiful and theatrical. Who's yours?

J: I don't think I can choose one. I like the more cutting designers: Gareth Pugh, Westwood, Ashish. All that stuff suits me.

A: Nice lots, but sometimes, I have a made-to-measure Westwood dress on the way. Marc [Jacobs] gave me a Vuitton dress. Christian Louboutin gave me the shoes in Paris. I got discounts in most stores.

J: Do you get lots of free stuff?

J: What are your secrets to looking so good?

A: Not to drink much or to do drugs. Rest and exercise a lot, go to the gym as often as possible.

J: What type of guy do you go for?

A: All different types. The latest guy I've been dating has huge lips like me! I'm in the mood for a boyfriend I'm single and looking. I'm in the mood for a boyfriend but it's hard with what I do for a living, so many guys just don't get it.

J: Have you ever slept with a celebrity?

A: Yeah.

J: Are you going to tell PLASTIQUE who it was?

A: No.

J: Would we be surprised?

A: Yes.

J: OK. What celebrity would you like to sleep with?

A: David Beckham. I met him at David LaChapelle's house. I'm sure he was looking at my ass.

J: Why do you love New York?

A: I don't drive and it's all condensed here. I love the partying and the shopping. It's good for me here. It's home.

J: If you could be invisible for a day what would you do?

A: I wouldn't do anything different. I'm a rad.

J: I'd go shoplifting and perve on people. I'm a bad person. Your life is like a modern day fairytale and totally fascinates me. What's your favourite fairytale and why?

A: Cinderella. She suffered for ages then became a princess. Her sisters dressed up and went out while she was left to scrub floors, but then she became the most beautiful of them all. My life has been like Cinderella. I'm happy now.

B1

GREAT
EASTERN
STREET

**PHOTOGRAPHY
DAVID DUNAN**

ZERO
DEGREES

PHOTOGRAPHY JEFFREY GRAETSCH

KILLAH KOLOR

**PHOTOGRAPHY
JOHN LINDQUIST**

At This Rate
Client Rainforest Action Network *Design* Matt Willey *Year* 2006
A booklet produced to raise awareness of the destruction of the Amazon rainforest for the US-based charity Rainforst Action Network (RAN).

506

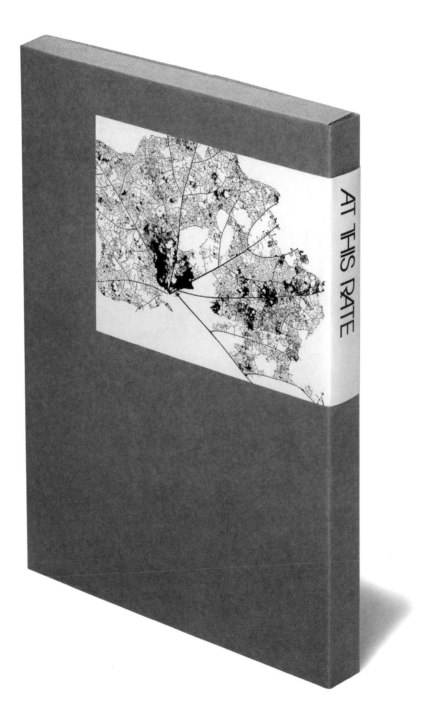

Every day we lose an area larger than all five boroughs of New York City

Our forests, water, and the air we breathe are the lifeblood of our planet. Tragically, more than an acre and a half of tropical rainforests are destroyed every second of every day. Despite the relatively small land area rainforests cover, they are home to over half the world's plant and animal species. In an era of global warming and climate crisis, rainforests play a critical role as carbon regulators and climate stabilizers. Furthermore, forests are home to some fifty million indigenous people and the means by which the planet stabilizes rainfall, protects against desertification and buffers against floods, droughts and erosion. If current rates of destruction continue, half our remaining rainforests will be gone by 2025 and by 2060 there will be no remaining rainforests. If our rainforests are further destroyed, we will lose not only one of the world's greatest treasures, but also our last best chance for the planet's survival.

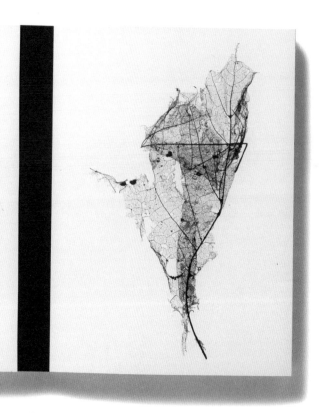

Every year we lose an area three times the size of Sri Lanka

Every second we lose an area the size of a football pitch
Every minute we lose an area 20 times the size of the Sydney Opera House
Every hour we lose an area the size of Central London
Every day we lose an area larger than all five boroughs of New York City
Every week we lose an area 21 times the size of Paris
Every month we lose an area 102 times the size of Barcelona

Extractive industries pose the most severe threat to the earth's remaining intact ecosystems. Timber, oil and mining companies are currently operating in critically endangered areas, clear cutting vast swaths of forest, eradicating critical habitats, poisoning natural ecosystems and displacing indigenous populations.

The current ecological crisis necessitates that logging companies, homebuilders, automakers and multinational banks address the social and environmental impacts of their operations and establish governing policies that ensure the survival of the planet's remaining ecosystems. Establishing an economy based on industries that protect remaining ecosystems is critical to halting the environmental destruction and establishing sustainable forest communities across the globe.

Rainforest Action Network (RAN) works to protect the Earth's rainforests and support the rights of their inhabitants through education, grassroots organising, and non violent direct action. For 20 years RAN has developed dynamic, hard hitting campaigns that work to bring corporate and governmental policies into alignment with popular support for rainforest conservation. RAN works in alliance with environmental and human rights groups around the world, including indigenous forest communities and non governmental organizations in rainforest countries. As a result, RAN has helped convince dozens of corporations – including Home Depot, Citigroup, Boise Cascade, and Goldman Sachs – to adopt progressive environmental policies that set new best practices in their industries. These market transformations have protected millions of acres of forests in Canada, Indonesia, Brazil, Chile and beyond.

But much more needs to be done. For our society to truly break its oil addiction, protect endangered forests, and promote human rights and sustainable finance, everyone must get involved. Please join us. Visit www.RAN.org today.

Design and art direction by Studio8 Design
www.studio8design.co.uk
Photography by Luke Bestell
www.pixieseed.com
Print and reproduction by Granite Colour
www.granitecolour.com

Mixed Sources
This publication is printed on Tesprint Unique FSC, which is produced using a Chlorine Free (ECF) bleaching process. A minimum of 50% of the pulp used is from FSC certified forests.
www.fennerpaper.co.uk

The Forest Stewardship Council (FSC) is an international network which promotes responsible management of the world's forests. Forest certification is combined with a system of product labelling that allows consumers to readily identify timber based products from certified forests. The FSC "tick" logo is increasingly recognised and especially promoted as timber products from furniture and DIY retailers. The FSC is endorsed by Greenpeace, WWF and many other environmental NGO's.
www.fsc.org

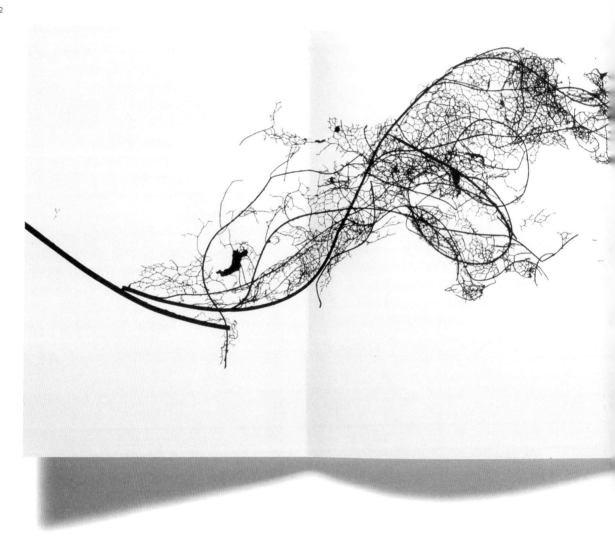

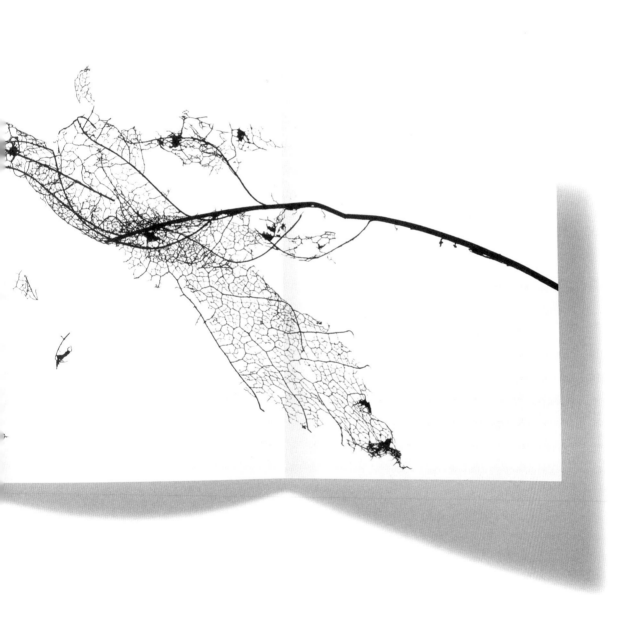

Graphic Magazine

Client BIS Publishing *Design* Matt Willey, Zoë Bather, Matt Curtis *Year* 2006

A wide-ranging, in-depth survey of contemporary visual culture, Graphic examines a particular theme with each new issue. Published twice a year by BIS Publishing, Graphic is sold in over 30 countries around the world.

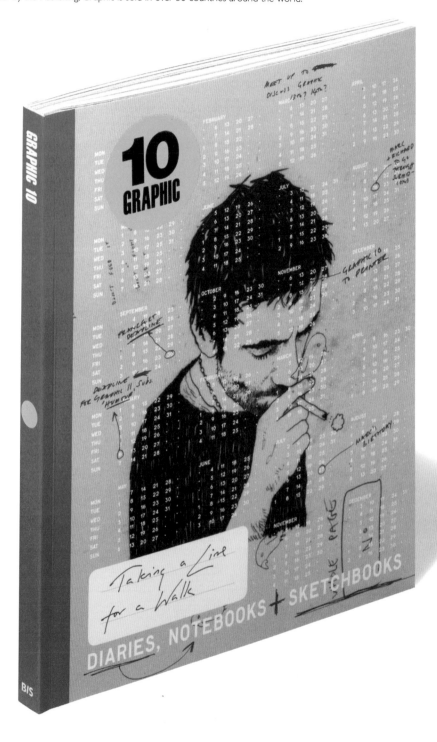

Speak your truth quietly and clearly;
And listen to others, even to the dull and the ignorant;
They too have their story.

TWEED LEDEE TWEED LEDUM

My year of graphic design without ~~clients~~ by **Stefan Sagmeister**

After seven years of running a studio designing CD covers for Lou Reed, David Byrne and the Rolling Stones, I decided not to take on any ~~client~~ projects for a full year. On the surface, the year before had been the most successful to date, our designs had won gold medals from Warsaw to New York, from London to Moscow and the booming economy had filled our coffers. Underneath the surface, however, I was having less and less fun in the office. Work was getting mediocre and repetitive.

I thought I really needed space to experiment and dream up bigger pictures. I wanted some room to re-evaluate what we were doing, decide what I wanted to say, indulge in work-intensive design obsessions for which there was not enough time during regular working times.

During a workshop in Cranbrook I got envious of the students being able to just spend their whole waking hours experimenting. Then Ed Fella came to my studio in New York and showed off all his wonderful sketchbooks with free typographic experiments. That did it: I settled on a starting date of June 2000.

I wanted many people to know about my plan so I could not chicken out of it when June came around. I told our ~~clients~~ about it. They took it rather well, nobody was pissed-off, everybody seemed supportive. I had lunch with veteran designers Ivan Chermayeff and Tom Geismar from Chermayeff and Geismar, where Tom told me that they had been planning a similar move for the past 50 years.

My friend Chee Pearlman suggested I should keep a diary. Here it is:

156–165: MARTHA RICH

PUSHING AN

IDEA

AROUND

Marc Valli talks to **Lee Williams** about how he turned his sketchbooks into the animation film *Tarot*

I have known Lee Williams for some time. When I worked at the (now closed) bookshop Zwemmer, Lee was also a bookseller at the (now also closed) Dillon's Art bookshop on Long Acre. By the time my business partner and I were ready to start our own bookshop (Magma, still open), Lee had moved on and was working for art publisher Booth-Clibborn Editions. He then in turn helped set up the UK office of leading graphic-design publishers Die Gestalten Verlag, or dgv, as they are more widely known.

At Magma, Lee was always a familiar and popular figure. He would come down regularly to our Covent Garden shop to check how we were doing. He would slip in quietly and wander around checking the books until we had noticed him and then burst out laughing. Then you would certainly notice him. Lee has the loudest laugh in the town. But despite his regular visits and his spontaneous and garrulous nature, you could not help feeling that there was something unquestionably shifty about his behaviour. He had the inconspicuous ways of someone who's hiding something.

YRES

'I am for the art of fat truck-tyres and black eyes.'
In addition to the recitation of a creed of such artistic beliefs, Claes Oldenburg's *Store Days* (1967) provides an inventory of his Lower East Side store's products – its plaster Statues of Liberty and Injun Souvenirs, scripts for the four performances or happenings that occurred in Oldenburg's Ray Gun Theater, drawings and photographs, diagrams and typescripts – concluding with a black-and-white photograph of a bath tub in a bare room, which probably influenced Anselm Kiefer's book *Hoffmann von Fallersleben auf Helgoland* (1980). *Store Days* is an artist's book, a Something Else Press book: it also a typical notebook/sketchbook – documenting, notating a present, projecting a future, where a small-scale 'unique multiple' will become a monumental sculpture, or providing a text for a performance which will mean something different at a future time and in a new context. The book contains within its 148 pages a greater, extendible world.

AND MULL

[body text columns largely illegible]

GLASGOW LONDON PARIS WASHI INBU REVIEW

Duncan McLaren is an author and arts writer. He has recently contributed to Infallible. To Seurat at the Beal George Elliot, published by ARTech Press

www.themodernpostitute.com
www.somewhere.org.uk Nina Pope
Karen Guthrie and their BataVille coach trip
www.folkart.org.org
www.blindeed.com Donatov and Brews
www.donadwburgolder.com
www.autobar.co.uk

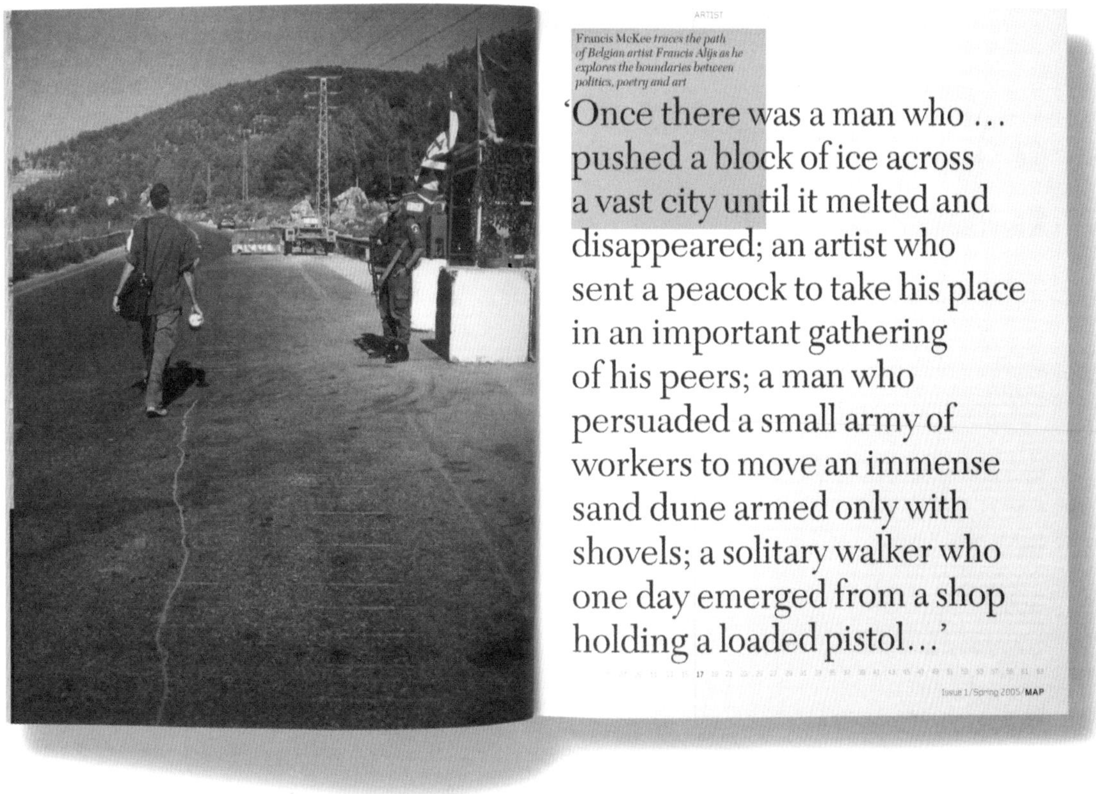

Francis McKee traces the path of Belgian artist Francis Alÿs as he explores the boundaries between politics, poetry and art

'Once there was a man who … pushed a block of ice across a vast city until it melted and disappeared; an artist who sent a peacock to take his place in an important gathering of his peers; a man who persuaded a small army of workers to move an immense sand dune armed only with shovels; a solitary walker who one day emerged from a shop holding a loaded pistol…'

São Paolo suburbia,
near Congonhas airport
Richard Williams, 2004

02 04 06 08 10 12 14 16 18 20 22 24 26 28 30 32 34 36 38 40 42 44 46 48 **50** 52 54 56 58 60 62 64

MAP/Issue 1/Spring 2005

26th Bienal de São Paolo

Brazil has been long established in the European intellectual mind as exotic. What I had not appreciated until this visit was the extent to which Brazilians themselves cultivated their own exoticism. Nor, how in their minds, the exotic was equally a part of the metropolis as the Amazon, of modernity as much as the distant past. One example will suffice: there is a widely-held myth that some middle-class residents of São Paolo are now so terrified of their city that they no longer descend to street level, flitting from one high-rise to another by helicopter. They have, effectively, evolved into a race of aerial beings, as unconnected with ordinary Brazilians as the Tupi-Kawahib. As I left Rio to make my way to the Bienal, my friend's mother – herself a displaced Paolistanos – fixed me with a look of sadness mixed with despair and said, 'May God be with you'. A latter-day Colonel Fawcett, I was going to a lost world and I was not, evidently, coming back.

Arrival in SP naturally dispelled such anthropological fears. As long as you don't look up, or to the horizon, it is just a big modern city, reassuringly busy with work and money. But it is unbelievably vast – 22 million people – and it has a peculiar cityscape all of its own. Its enormity is different from that of Manhattan, where you can always see the edge, or London, whose sprawl is on a human scale and is in any case punctuated by greenery, or even Shanghai, which has the colonial Bund, a sort of Liverpool-on-the-Huangpu. São Paolo, by contrast, seems completely undifferentiated. The entire city, from wherever you stand as far as the horizon, seems to be made of 30-storey point blocks, built in astonishing proximity to one another. The sense of endlessness is greater than in any city I know: it is both terrifying, and in purely aesthetic terms, thrilling.

So to the Bienal, which is found in the strangely picturesque Parque Ibirapuera. In many ways, it matches the city in scale. In terms of visitor numbers, a million in total, it far outstrips any other equivalent biennale, and must be one of the most visited exhibitions in the world. It is enormous: 135 artists from 62 countries. You need a couple of days to do it justice. It was also free in 2004, thanks to the sponsorship of a local bank, and its organisers spoke grandly of the democratisation of art as their principal aim. The scale and ambition of the thing is undeniably impressive, memorialised in its permanent home, Oscar Niemeyer's 1954 Pavilion. The size of the Pompidou, it is both an elegant and exuberant space, the restrained International Style of the exterior containing some spectacular ramps, as if the Illinois Institute of Technology were wrapped around the Guggenheim.

What of the show? It was, to begin with, hard not to be distracted by several things: first, the crowds of schoolchildren, often very young, who made up the majority of the audience on the days I went (I approved of this – it certainly dispelled whatever pretensions to cool the Bienal had); second, the views of the city, which even after several days were still compelling; and third, the incredible noise of many of the exhibits.

On the ground floor, the chief offender was 'Bon Voyage' by Cai Guo-Quiang. This profoundly irritating piece was a 20-foot aeroplane-meets-fish, woven in an open lattice from vines and bristling with thousands of sharp objects recently confiscated from air travellers around the world. In place of the four engines were four electric fans, going full blast, with long streamers attached. This was the source of the racket. What was the point? It made no sense to me: confused in its vision and execution, it offered up every possible

reading and none, so generalised an object as to be meaningless. On the same floor you could find a gigantic climbing frame from which was suspended a spinning VW beetle (Leo Shatzi), an upside-down boat made of mahogany (Simon Starling) and a huge bank of speakers blasting out the sounds of gunfire (Santiago Serra). Upstairs, other things clamoured for attention, not least a circumcision filmed in real time by the Bulgarian artist Nassim, projected on two gigantic screens (the ten-year-old girl sitting next to me asked me, being the only adult around, for an explanation: I was an art historian from Edinburgh, I said, and no, I didn't know what I was doing there either).

But by the second day, these circus-like installations came to seem aberrant. What most artists were portraying was a kind of intuitive anthropology, often casting their own familiar surroundings as other, and recording them through endless lists and photographs. It seemed an oddly appropriate thing to be doing in Brazil, a country which since its origins has been the object of harsh anthropological scrutiny. The Bienal was a good place to think about this systematic, sometimes cruel mode of looking: Juan Britos's photographs of Amazonian Indians clearly fell into this category, as did Edward Burtynsky's images of the Three Gorges Dam in China, and Thomas Struth's pictures of the barriadas on the outskirts of Lima. All were beautiful images, but profoundly disturbing because they aestheticised poverty or displacement for the pleasure of the viewer. In Struth's Lima image, the appearance of Stockbroker Tudor on a slum shack was grimly funny. But it wasn't clear where Struth stood in relation to his subjects, and what he (and I) were laughing at.

It was refreshing by contrast to have the European gaze turned on itself as in Veronika Zapaletalová's gloomy observations of Czech summerhouses, Krysztof Zielinski's grim Wabrezno street scenes, and (most clearly) Noyaya Hartakeyama's snapshots of English suburban houses. Meanwhile the always politically correct Mark Dion sent up the whole business of anthropology, with a faux-naïf reconstruction of Thomas Ende's 19th-century Austrian expedition to Brazil. Dion assembled a seven-man Austro-Brazilian team to retrace Ende's steps, each team member adopting a key role – Dion himself was Ende. The results – a range of documents and drawings, parodying Ende's originals – were displayed as a literally (and metaphorically) wooden museum exhibition.

But all this anthropological reflection had a wearying cumulative effect. We are all other was the clear message, but it was unclear to what extent this differed from a bland multiculturalism of the UN. I was tired. I needed a beer. And it was in the bar over a glass of the always reliable Antártica that I saw unquestionably the best, and possibly smallest, work in the entire Bienal: Miguel Calderón's footballing fantasy. The game between the national sides of Mexico and Brazil was screened on TV monitors over the bar (where else?). It began innocuously enough, but when the underdogs opened the scoring you realised something was amiss. To the accompaniment of a wonderfully convincing commentary, Mexico then opened up a quite preposterous lead. I didn't stay until the end, but when I left, it was 24-nil. Great stuff.

Richard J Williams is an art historian and author of The Anxious City, *published by Routledge, 2004*

São Paolo Bienal 26 Sep – 19 Dec 2004

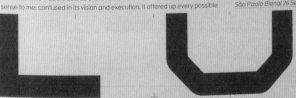

Moira Jeffrey *travels to Monterrey and discovers bright lights at Sodium and Asphalt, a major showing of 12 British artists in Mexico*

I arrive in Monterrey, north Mexico, after dark. To get there I have flown into and out of Mexico City by night. Thirty million people below me and I haven't seen one of them – just an infinite pattern of sodium light. I try to translate that into some kind of human presence: for every streetlight, say, a household. It's like looking at the night sky and trying to imagine each distant star as populous and as complex as planet Earth.

There is no seat belt in my taxi and I try to work up the courage to complain. I don't or can't. I'm weak-willed through lack of sleep. Feeling weirdly untethered I look outside at the view from the highway. A shabby industrial zone gives way to neon signs, billboards, a run of burger bars, car showrooms, low density housing, and a car wash chain that is styled as an African village, complete with a canopy that imitates grass huts.

The taxi driver pulls down a screen above the front passenger's seat: Jennifer Lopez in concert. She is wearing a bright red dress, but I don't recognise the song. He drives me to my hotel, paying more attention to the TV screen than the view through the windscreen. I'm thankful it is late on a Sunday night and the roads seem deserted. I arrive at my hotel, a neat tower at the heart of a downtown grid. They have never heard of me.

The texture of the city, its visual cues, the distinctive way we move through it, the familiarity and the strangeness of the urban fabric, these were the themes of *Sodium and Asphalt. Contemporary British Art in Mexico*. Curated by Ann Gallagher of the British Council and Tobias Ostrander, of the Tamayo Museum, Mexico City, it opened in July 2004 before transferring to MARCO, Monterrey until February 2005.

Sodium and Asphalt could not be described as a survey, nor as a generational show, but it does mark a number of significant developments in British art of the last decade or so. Some of these are age and stage-related, some geographic. Four of the 12 selected artists were Glasgow-based or trained. The youngest artists, Oliver Payne and Nick Relph, are based in New York City. Melanie Smith lives and works in Mexico City.

The exhibition, which grew out of a seminar series on colour and the city at the Tamayo Museum attended by artists David Batchelor and Melanie Smith, also marks a more collaborative structure for exhibition-making at the British Council and coincides with an increased synergy between artists in two countries without any emphatic historical or colonial ties. The last year or two has seen a number of significant shows of Mexican artists in London. In April Mexican collecting gets an airing when a number of works from the Jumex collection will be shown at Glasgow's Tramway as part of Glasgow International, 2005.

What distinguishes *Sodium and Asphalt* from any number of recent themed shows on cities and urbanism

is its particular, although not exclusive, emphasis on formal qualities alongside social realities: on the distinctive visual vocabulary of the urban environment, and its relationship to the history of art, architecture, music and literature.

In the formal spaces of MARCO, a pristine modern concrete building designed by Ricardo Legoretta, the exhibition unfolds as a Baudelairian stroll through a series of different urban environments.

Melanie Smith's installation acts as a kind of transitional zone: a shop front for urban sensations. A series of vibrating striped paintings in acrylic colours of lime green, bright pink – rosa mexicana – and concrete, lean against the gallery wall as though just unpacked. A series of video pieces are shown on televisions sitting on their cardboard boxes. Her paintings form a kind of background hum, a Broadway boogie-woogie, to the more intimate structures of the films. In one of these the camera peers through a fluorescent-lettered window into a downtown aerobics class, the rhythm of pumping bodies, a kind of fleshy parody of the machine age. Above these elements, suspended from the ceiling, is a knot of fluorescent nylon string. An image of the city itself, perhaps, not as a coherent grid but as a tangle.

Nigel Cooke's landscape paintings, with their urban sublime of contemporary ruin and decay, form a kind of exterior wall, albeit one that is characteristically cracked and graffiti-strewn. Jim Lambie's 'Zobop' provides a disco interior, and the film 'Gentlemen' by Payne and Relph, a kind of psychological inner space for the city-dweller.

From David Batchelor's stack of lightboxes to Richard Wright's work 'Untitled (31.3.04)' – a painting of a simulated wooden surface, over which is floated a series of disconnected geometric shapes like ribbons – the language of signage, of simulation and stimulation is a persistent presence.

Kathrin Böhm's installation is part of her ongoing artwork, 'and millions and millions', in which graphic prints are flyposted onto the gallery walls and stacked up on shelves, freely available for visitors to take away.

Mark Titchner and Melanie Smith also contribute billboard projects, posted on commercial plots on the fringes of the city's highway. A set of Richard Wright's delicately modulated posters is slapped up on city walls in an insouciant manner that might make collectors weep (in Mexico City they were flyposted by a crack team specialising in Mexican wrestling posters) and allowed to deteriorate in wind, sun and competition.

Although in many ways some of the artworks selected apparently conform to formal abstraction or minimalism, many emphasise a deliberate disruption of conceptions of purity once associated with it. Mark Titchner's rhythmic billboard-sized piece, 'Y and Y', shown in the gallery, conceals complex coded content derived from industrial punch cards within its geometric patterning.

Opposite
The Magic Hour
David Batchelor, 2004

Quartet: Four Literary Walks Around the V& A

Client V&A Museum/ Playstation PSP *Design* Matt Willey, Zoë Bather *Year* 2006

Containing short stories by Nicolas Royle, Lucy Caldwell, Peter Hobbs and Shiromi Pinto, who were comissioned to write stories for a one-off event at the V&A. Inspired by the museum and its collections, the four stories in 'Quartet' were annotated with directions, mapping the routes described in the writers' narratives and thus enabling readers to follow the stories as they moved through the museum. The routes were also made available as downloads for Sony PlayStation Portable (PSP) consoles.

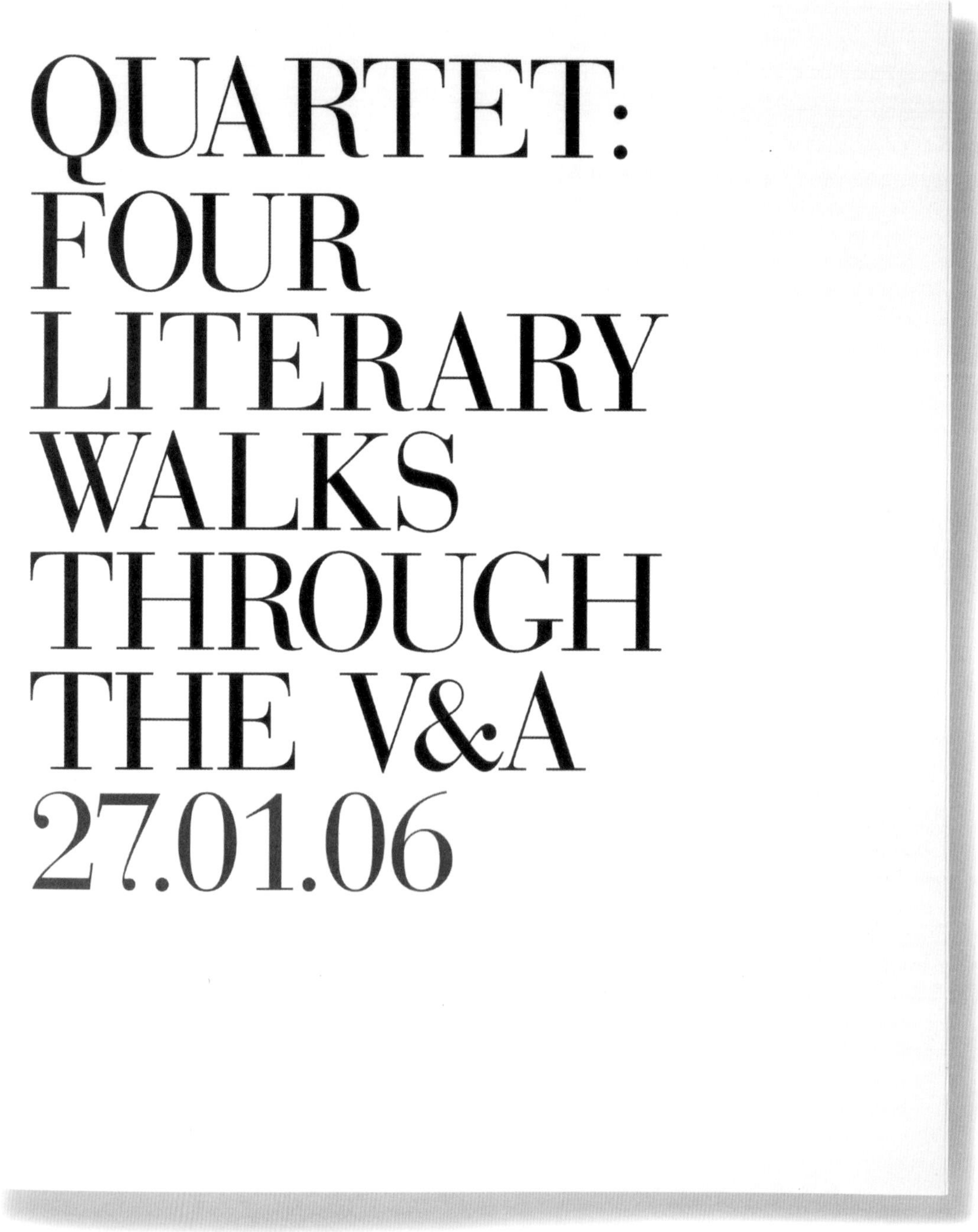

526

QUARTET: FOUR LITERARY WALKS THROUGH THE V&A 27.01.06

NECKLINES THROUGH THE AGES
BY NICHOLAS ROYLE

room within a room. Safe, contained, secure. Sitting inside this 18th century Henrietta Street parlour exquisitely restored and painstakingly reconstructed in the British Galleries of the V&A, Tim should be making notes for his Hitchcock article. In the director's 1972 thriller *Frenzy*, the necktie murderer Robert Rusk lives in a first-floor flat on Henrietta Street. Sitting here in the V&A, in an actual room from that street, would make the film's Henrietta Street scenes come alive, Tim had thought, but all he can think about now is Sarah. The look on her face. The tightly knotted red scarf at her throat.

A young couple sit next to each other on the tube, their legs crossed in opposite directions. They're together, just about, but didn't look it. She's people-watching, hands folded over a book in her lap. Derek Marlowe's 1966 spy novel, *A Dandy in Aspic*, a pink-jacketed film tie-in edition. On the fly leaf she has written her name in pencil, as she does with all her books: Sarah Stone.

Twisted the other way, tense with the effort of keeping his back from resting against Sarah's, Tim flicks through a notebook, rereading his jottings on *Frenzy*, making refinements. He writes with a Fischer Space Pen and when not actually writing he replaces the lid and turns that beautiful brushed steel bullet of a writing implement over and over in his right hand, like a drum majorette twirling her baton. At the front of his much thumbed and closely guarded notebook he has written, in careful block capitals, not only his name, TS Jarvis, but also the address of the flat he shares with Sarah.

At South Kensington, they get off. Walking to the museum, they remain side by side, but without so much as brushing arms. If pedestrian congestion forces them to go in single file, he pauses for the briefest of moments to allow Sarah to go first, and when the pavement widens she slows to let him catch up, but he drags his feet. At the revolving door, he goes first, but waits once he's inside, albeit with a resentful, hangdog look.

'How long are you going to keep this up?' she asks him and when his only reply is to grimace she goes on 'You surely don't think I should have turned it down?'

'You might as well get used to it, because this is beginning to piss me off.'

'Sorry,' he grunts.

'Said with feeling.' She knots the red scarf at her throat, pulls it tight. 'See you later.'

'Where are you going first?' he asks her. The slenderest of silver knots him.

'To look at some Sèvres porcelain. The hero of this book' — she waves the Marlowe novel in his face — 'has a collection of Sèvres porcelain in a vault at the V&A. Chapter one, page two, so it's obviously important. Marlowe lived near here, on Victoria Road, so he probably came here a lot.'

As Tim heads for the stairs, sidestepping the ladders and palettpots of a team of decorators, his falling-out with Sarah occupies his thoughts. They are each researching magazine articles. The trouble is Sarah's has been commissioned by a broadsheet. So she'll get paid a decent whack and her piece will land on a lot of desks. Tim's piece is for a leftfield film magazine, so leftfield it doesn't pay for articles. He should be pleased for her, only he's the one trying to make it as a journalist, while Sarah has no such ambition. She's only writing about Derek Marlowe because a publisher decided to reissue some of his novels and Sarah happens to know someone on the arts desk of the paper. OK, so Sarah is a big fan of Marlowe's. OK, so she's been actively encouraging publishers to get him back into print. OK, so Tim really should be pleased for her. No, he really should be. He knows that. But he's behaved like an idiot, allowing his resentment to ooze slimily out from wherever baser instincts dwell. He said he didn't think Marlowe was that good anyway. (He's so good, why have his books been out of print for twenty-five years? She didn't dignify that with a response.)

Tim looks around the reconstructed parlour with its elegant royal blue walls and wedding cake plaster mouldings. It looks quite different from Robert Rusk's flat in *Frenzy*. It is different. The parlour is from 11 Henrietta Street, while Rusk lives at No 3, and 240 years separate the rooms in time, but both are on the first floor and on the same side of the street only a few doors apart, so the inconsistencies were mere details that didn't get in the way of the particular brand of psychogeography practised by Tim in his speculative articles – speculative in more senses than one – for various non-paying magazines of limited distribution.

Rusk, devilishly played by Barry Foster, commits two of his murders in the flat, its walls covered in green flock wallpaper, the hearth home to a gas fire. Placing one room over the over in his mind, Tim visualises Rusk's bed, where he strangles his victims, in the far corner under the window. A single bed – surprising for such a suave character, a real man about town, but then he never had to worry about sharing it. His guests didn't tend to stay long.

AFTER THE RIVER MAIDEN
BY LUCY CALDWELL

…fore you, My Lord, there is nothing, but I am happy, because I do not know it. After you, there will be nothing too, but then the nothing will be an emptiness.

This is the Imperial Palace in the Forbidden City, and on the throne is the Emperor Kangxi, may he live ten thousand years, and if it were not too presumptuous for a lowly servant girl to mention herself in the same breath, I would say that I am Liu, once the daughter of a river-merchant, and now a hand-maiden in the Hall of Perpetual Light, where dragons carved of jade hang from the heavens, coiled around snakes of lapis lazuli, writhing under the midday sun and the fire of the midnight torches.

The land has been asleep under the blanket of winter, but below the surface, even when you cannot see it, things change, and finally the Eastern winds bring Spring into the palace gardens. The tips of the weeping willows are blue. The grasses grow green, and blossoms appear on the plum and apricot trees. At twilight, the nightingales in their jewelled cages sing their liquid songs. And as the signs of Spring are carried on the eastern winds, the winds that blow from the west bring different news: news of a strange traveller from faraway lands who is bound for the Forbidden City. But although I hear the words, for even from a lonely hand-maiden the Forbidden City holds no secrets, I do not recognize that they are whispering also to me, and my heart remains a sealed chamber.

He stands in the Hall of the Buddhas. He is not like the crafty merchants who come from the lands beyond the Yellow Sea, or the flat-faced traders from the frozen Northeast. He is not like the cruel horsemen who come from beyond the northern deserts, their skin tanned and dried like leather, their short swords dull and merciless. He is not like the cunning doctors from the lands of the Rising Sun, their faces creased and their shoulders stooped under bamboo frames of glittering glass bottles and bitter powders in carved rhinoceros horns. He is tall and slim, pale like a young birch tree, and his eyes are round and clear, the colour of willow rips in Spring. His barbarian clothes are old, and ill-fitting. He is dressed in the spun wool of our peasants, his inner garments sewn with silver metal thread. His outer skirt billows like a robe, but it is not a robe, and his undershirt of colours is not concealed by the top clothes. At his throat like a splash of blood is a scarlet scarf. The other hand-maidens say he does not know it he is man or animal. They say the barbarians speak with strange, thick tongues, that the barbarians are hairy like the beasts that the barbarians do not have our immortal souls. They giggle behind their fans at him. But I do not.

The second time I see him, he is no longer dressed like a barbarian. He is wearing a robe of sky blue silk, embroidered with clouds, and the surging whorls of waves. Red dragons leap in between the crests of the waves, and the yellow sun is in the east. Painted on the inner flap of his robe is Fu, the Symbol of Distinction, and the last of the Emblems of the Ancients. It is a good sign, and it speaks well to those with whom he cannot yet converse: the two characters back-to-back represent the working together of prince and ministers. I see his robes and I see that he will stay longer in the Forbidden City.

He repeats a name. I say his name to myself. His name is Yu, which means Universe.

When I open my hair at night, it falls down my back like the rush of ink from a clumsy calligrapher's pen. But by every bright curl on his head is the carving of a master carpenter. He is crowned with light, in the land where he comes from, men are not born, they are made by hand, by the gods.

In honour of his new name, he drinks tea of jasmine flowers from an ancient jade cup in the Hall of the Four Winds. Sacred incense is burnt in miniature censers of chased silver that come from rare Tang dynasty, more than a thousand years ago. When the tea is drunk, the cup is given to him. It is carved from a single piece of stone, with a shallow bowl carved to fit in the palm of his hand, and three dragons preening on the rim. He bows his head, and his face is grave. The jade cup was made hundreds of years ago. It will endure long after he is gone. He is a barbarian, and so he cannot understand this, but I watch his hands tremble as he holds the cup, and I think that perhaps his heart understands.

THE MECHANICS INSIDE
BY PETER HOBBS

CLOCK
Level 1 / Grand Entrance

ast, before you leave this scene, your eyes upwards. Not
to the rotunda chandelier – eye-catching though it may
be – with its tangle and flash of glass. A little before that,
a little closer to the doors. The collection has already
begun, here with me, suspended between balcony and
arch. And it begins not with *light*, but with *time*.

My history is the museum's history. I have marked time over this
museum for one hundred and forty-nine years. Since the beginning of
this place, almost. My elegant twin faces – no doubt blurred from where
you are standing – were designed by Frank Moody, the same man who
decorated much of the museum. The rest of me – the scrolled gold of my
hands, the mechanics inside – came from Clerkenwell.

I have kept time, and done my time. First relocation, then
relegation into storage (where time passes so slowly, I have
measured it). Fifty two years in the North Court. Sixty years
here. Fifteen long years in storage. And finally, twenty-two
years past, restoration. I have measured them all precisely,
as I have measured your time there beneath me, as I have
done every second of the century before you were born. And
whichever other voices call to you in this place – older, more

beautiful objects, perhaps – remember that few will
be so solid, so functional as I. Not everything is what
it seems to be... well, you are warned. Think on this
now as you stand and watch me for another minute,
two, three. Then, as you all unfailingly do, walk on.

CARTOON: THE MIRACULOUS DRAUGHT OF FISHES
Level 1 / Room 48a

Ignore the dreary old clock; he is quite obsessed with
time. Someone should tell him: a thing of beauty
is a joy *forever*. Take a short cut through the shop
and come see: I am beautiful. My forever began in
fifteen fifteen. A great pope commissioned me made.
Raphael's own hands painted me. Tapestries from
my design adorned the Sistine Chapel.

Look at the drama in me: Three men struggling for fish. Two struggling
for Christ. And the colours... how Christ' reflection is limned pink –
the vermilion enduring long after his robe's fugitive colour has faded.
That mechanical clock, he *means* nothing – I burst with meaning.
Stories of apostles told to legitimate papal succession. Every detail
– the cranes, the swan, the ravens, the eel, the crabs – a code, a symbol,
if you only know how to decipher them.

I tell you – look at my shadow, the tapestry opposite. One hundred
years younger than I, but already impoverished, a pale copy with white
English skin, its weavers terminally unable to replicate my subtle tones.
Attractive, perhaps, but never great. *I* was its blueprint, its precursor.
I was meant to be a patchwork paper mirror, a reverse echo of *its* glory.
Now tell me honestly – is there anyone now who does not think that it is
I who am the original, and it a mere copy, a mere carpet?

HIDE AND SEEK (1)
Level 1 / Room 40

On your right, a world tour: New York, Tokyo, Paris. On your left: a dinner-
suited, headless James Bond, then the invisible woman, corseted. Then
directly in our way a ghostly wedding party. Behind which we hide,
wrapped around blank-eyed mannequins. *Hiding's* all too easy. You
could easily miss us – we fit in so well. A pair of local boys, from down
the road. From your generation, too, very much *in touch*. Fingers (if we
owned them) on the pulse. If that patchwork paper can boast of its age,
we can certainly boast of our youth.

And we're not ashamed to admit that we would
rather not need to be playing this child's game.
We would rather be found than hidden. We
would rather be on bold display, strutting our
stuff. Maybe catch the eye of that cute little
bronze around the corner...

Do we not stand with confidence? With cockiness, perhaps
– but then, compared to how *you're* dressed tonight, we're
unarguably gorgeous. And yet we will nevertheless attest
to a slight twinge of envy as you move past. For as you go,
you leave us imprisoned behind glass; and time, as that
blasted clock so incessantly reminds us, moves on. *Design
classics* we may be, but even classics grow old. There's no
hiding from our future – it's all around us: the fashions of
a previous age, no longer relevant, no longer new.

STATUETTE: WOMAN BATHING
Level 1 / Room 21 / Item Circ. 755-1931

So my young *suit*-ors would like to catch my eye – well my eye
is older than they might imagine. Come see: the renaissance
is only next door...

NB Pulse London
Client Nota Bene *Design* Matt Willey, Zoë Bather, Matt Curtis *Year* 2006
The first in NB Pulse's range of city guides.

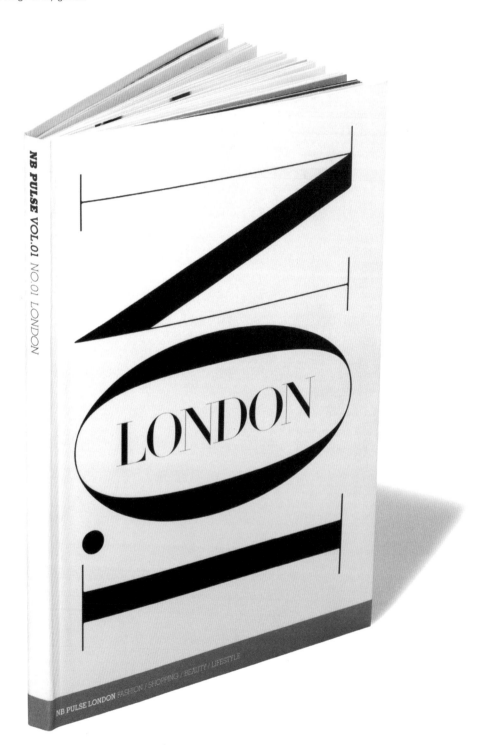

You find no man, at all intellectual, who is willing to leave London. No, Sir, when a man is tired of London, he is tired of life; for there is in London All that life can afford.

NB PULSE VOL.01 NO.01 LONDON

Samuel Johnson English Poet, Critic & Writer (1709 - 1784)

BESPOKEN FOR

AS THE STYLISTIC ZEITGEIST VEERS TOWARDS A DESIRE FOR SOMETHING JUST THAT LITTLE BIT SPECIAL, PULSE ASSESSES THE VARIED, AND SOMETIMES CONVOLUTED, INTERPRETATIONS OF FASHION'S LATEST BUZZWORD. BY EDWINA INGS-CHAMBERS.

STYLE NOMAD #1: MANOLO BLAHNIK

MANOLO

PULSE EIGHT

PULSE PICKS THE TOP EIGHT ULTIMATE FLIGHT KITS YOU CANNOT POSSIBLY TAKE OFF WITHOUT

How ubiquitous the word luxury has become. What then does real luxury mean? For us, the real essence of the word lies in journeying with one's own personal travel kit rather than rely on the substandard offerings provided by most airlines, even in their first class cabins. How often, particularly in take off period, have we sat frozen in icy cold cabins where the crew appear unable to regulate the air temperature. Then it can become insufferably warm. With one's own travel kit you can alleviate some of these discomforts. We list 8 of our favourites, selected for optimum comfort and pure decadence. From the lightweight pack to accompany you on short journeys to the heavier variety, where cashmere blankets and other warmth providing accessories are featured. Think of that long flight back from LA to London, you need never travel uncomfortably again. We also include our favourite combination travel wallet by Smythson in which you can deposit passport, tickets, receipts and other papers. Pack them all away in one place rather than fumbling through handbags and suitcases, and avoid what so often happens — you end up dropping half of them between check in and passport control!

Clockwise from top: Travel bag with matching accessories in retro calf and Malabar canvas by **Rambled**, and the matter case with Malabar canvas accessories **Connolly**, cashmere socks, slippers, spritz and eye mask by **Pure**

Collection in calf and chenille by **Loro Piana**

Storybook rich and luxurious note case by **Hermès**, cashmere pillow and blanket

leather comfort travel bag and leather zipped case by **Bottega Veneta**. Folded cashmere travel blanket in navy and light blue by **Red Envelope**, eye mask by **Pure**

CASE STUDY

FOR HIM

Diverse in terms of style and fashion London throws up something of a conundrum when it comes to knowing what to pack for a trip. The climate is always changeable so your wardrobe needs to be flexible. Whether it's a meeting in the City, an evening at Sadler's Wells, an art lunch in Shoreditch or cocktails at Claridge's, your travelling wardrobe will need to meet any fashion challenge: there should only be one consideration: should together clash. Leaving is important: ensuring your body maintains the right temperature. To keep your silhouette slim, go for the less ostentatious dress. Start with a great suit preferably navy or charcoal grey, too or two in smooth lightweight wool. Subtle pinstripes are stylish but stay clear of the bolder chalk stripe jacket and trousers can be worn

separately, the jacket with jeans and the trousers with knitwear. Buy good quality shirts: two or four, shirtmakers in plain Egyptian cotton that can be worn with or without a tie. Instead in single ply cashmere for early fall and 2 ply for later. Keep it simple and take the sun that fits the body without too much bulk. A multi functional coat is key in layering the look when the weather turns cold. A waterproof outer shell can be worn over suits and knitwear while a detachable quilted inner gilet can be worn casually. Loro Piana does a good example. Don't be afraid to break the suit up for the evening. Mix a luxury cashmere jacket with an open neck shirt and chinos, leather shoes. An elegant watch for example from Cartier will see you effortlessly from day through to evening.

FOR HER

This city of style and epicentre of creativity is on the whole less polished than its fashion city siblings, Paris and New York. Most often the dress code is informal and anything goes from a skinny jean, plain t-shirt by day and elegant for evening, in a simple dress. Madam and Chelsea tend to be glossier affairs, particularly fashion hotspot Brompton Cross where you can experience outfit envy at any time. This contrasts with Notting Hill's bohemian sensibility and East London where the she is decidedly eclectic, urban cool. Leave the big status symbols at home. Arm yourself with a mini umbrella (Fulton design not one the 'super duo') and sunglasses at all times. Practically and fashionably, an oversized bag for the is as essential. A lightweight trench too are fans of Burberry's or for Fall Winter 06 Prada's parka series the same effect. Our Geogr knits (Prada).

Marni, Ralph Lauren and silk and cashmere thermal tees. Hats are useful autumn fillers. When it comes to footwear, flat ballet boots are extremely big in the fashion stakes. Comfortable to walk in and durable enough to withstand any surroundings of conditions. For heels keep pointes for your own unique fabrics like velvet and satin indoors. Eat out as a winter this season. Versatility is key to a metro city wardrobe. Choose pieces with edge that can be mixed to create several outfit permutations.

Pulse Note: Packing is an art form that the most seasoned and stylish traveller will approach with solitary purpose.

Centenary Limited Edition case in gold and tan by Globe-Trotter. For stockist details see page 98.

536

Counter Intelligence 011

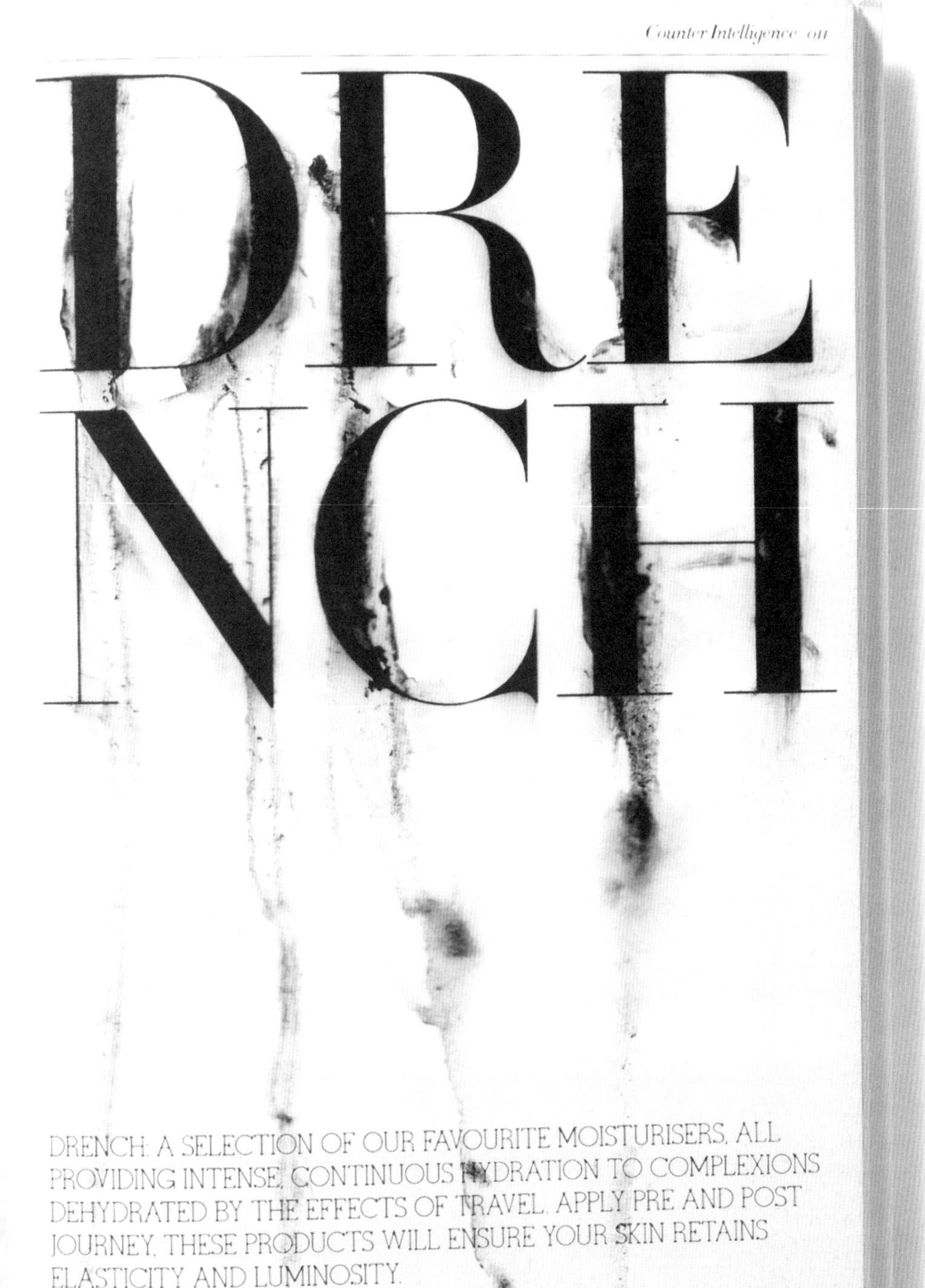

DRE NCH

DRENCH: A SELECTION OF OUR FAVOURITE MOISTURISERS, ALL PROVIDING INTENSE, CONTINUOUS HYDRATION TO COMPLEXIONS DEHYDRATED BY THE EFFECTS OF TRAVEL. APPLY PRE AND POST JOURNEY. THESE PRODUCTS WILL ENSURE YOUR SKIN RETAINS ELASTICITY AND LUMINOSITY.

NBPulse Issue 1 London

Mexico, Martin Parr
Client Chris Boot Publishing *Design* Matt Willey, Nick Bell *Year* 2006
'Mexico' documents the influence of American consumerism on Mexican visual culture.
The book features images by Magnum photographer and collector extraordinaire, Martin Parr.

538

MARTIN PARR MEXICO

Royal Academy of Arts Magazine

Client The Royal Academy of Arts *Design* Matt Willey *Year* 2005-2006

Established 25 years ago, Royal Academy Magazine is the UK's leading arts quarterly and has the largest circulation of any art magazine in Europe. We redesigned the magazine in Autumn 2005 and continue to be responsible for the design and art direction of each new issue.

542

RA
ROYAL ACADEMY OF ARTS MAGAZINE
Nº 90 / SPRING 2006 £4.95

SKY HIGH:
THE SUBLIME LANDSCAPES
of JACOB
VAN
RUISDAEL

DAVID LODGE
ON AMERICANS IN PARIS

JULIA LOVELL ON
THE GREAT WALL OF CHINA

JOHN UPDIKE
ON WINSLOW HOMER

MICHAEL WOOD ON
SHAKESPEARE

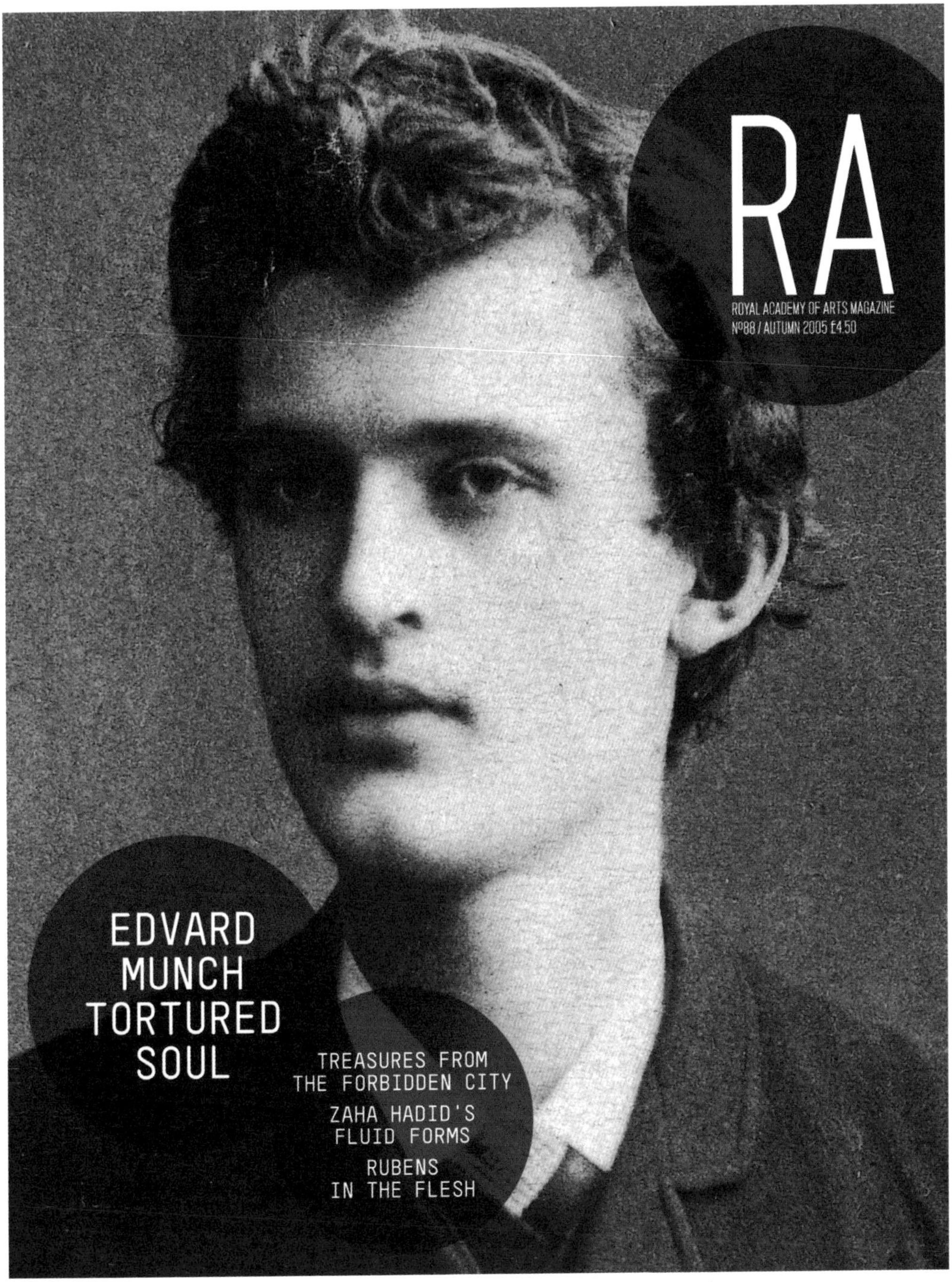

RA

ROYAL ACADEMY OF ARTS MAGAZINE

Nº88 / AUTUMN 2005 £4.50

EDVARD MUNCH TORTURED SOUL

TREASURES FROM
THE FORBIDDEN CITY

ZAHA HADID'S
FLUID FORMS

RUBENS
IN THE FLESH

544

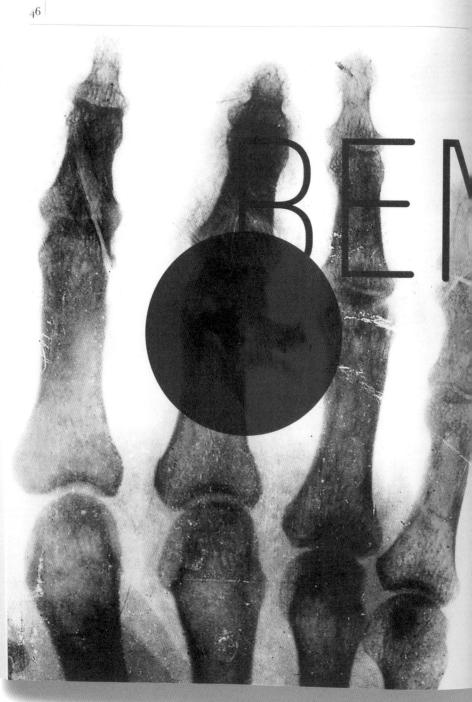

EATH
THE SKIN

Munch's intense relationship with Tulla Larsen came to a bloody climax when a violent struggle left Munch's hand shattered with a bullet. *Sue Prideaux* introduces an extract from her new biography of Munch that tells the dramatic story, and she explains how it inspired some of the artist's most iconic works

Edvard Munch had an enormous number of mistresses, but decided at an early age that he would never marry. Art was his sacred calling. To him, women were mystifying and tempting; they lured men from the path of greatness, spoiling and corrupting them. He would allow them to get within a certain distance, but then always find an excuse to retire, lest the price of intimacy be paid at the expense of his art. He was 35 when he met Tulla Larsen, a generous heiress more than willing to support him financially. A further part of her complicated hold over him was that at their first meeting she insisted upon massaging his head, whereupon he 'saw' the vision of the painting *The Dance of Life* (see page 48). We see her features in the blonde woman standing on either side of the canvas. But Tulla came too close – she announced that they were engaged. This was the signal for Munch to flee. She pursued him through Italy, France and Switzerland, causing him to paint her looking threatening and ugly in *Sphinx*, *Self-portrait with Tulla Larsen* (see page 48) and *A Woman and Two Men in an Interior*, where the third man is Munch's long-dead father who symbolises Munch's own conscience about continuing the affair with a woman he no longer loved. He broke up with Tulla, but two years later she summoned him for a fateful meeting that ended in a shooting incident of some ambiguity. Munch illustrated this in *On the Operating Table* (see page 49) and *The Death of Marat* series (see page 40), where once again we recognise Tulla's features in the murderess Charlotte Corday and Munch's own features in the bloody, dying Marat. The following account of the incident draws heavily on Munch's diaries and letters for its source material; Tulla left no writings to put the case from the other side.

Opposite an X-ray of Munch's left hand taken on 12 September 1902, showing the bullet still lodged in his middle finger

546

CHINESE WHISPERS

Jonathan Fenby anticipates the Royal Academy's landmark exhibition of Chinese art in November and offers a behind-the-scenes look at the unique collaboration with the Palace Museum in Beijing that made it possible

RODIN

He dragged sculpture off its pedestal to create forms that were earthy, erotic and pulsating with life. *Martin Gayford* praises the singular genius of Auguste Rodin, whose passion for the body redefined sculpture

THE CLASS OF 06

In a class of their own **The RA Schools final-year students showcase their art this summer. On the following pages, photographer *Nick Cunard* visits their studios to capture the spirit of the young artists at work. Here *Maurice Cockrill RA*, Keeper of the RA Schools, explains what makes the place so special and praises the outgoing graduates**

When Sir Joshua Reynolds and a score of his contemporaries founded the Royal Academy of Arts in London in 1768, one of their aims was to foster future generations of British artists. The Royal Academy Schools, which lay at the heart of their new institution, was Britain's first art school, and it continues to flourish. Today, with its energetic population of students and teachers, the Schools contribute to making the Royal Academy an academy in the truest sense.

What makes the RA programme unique is its five-year course rather than the standard two-year postgraduate degree, and the photos on the following pages celebrate the progress of the third-year students as they prepare work for their degree show. Dies, the RA Schools Show, has become an annual summer rite. It marks a moment of transition for the students and a chance for the public to glimpse emerging talent.

The three-year course has been in existence continuously since 1768, and allows young artists to realise their creative potential in a way that shorter courses do not permit. Interestingly, when I asked students why the three-year course was so special, they said they recognised its importance in the second year, when perhaps they changed direction or attempted a new idea that didn't work. That extra year gives them the chance to

try and fail and try again. It offers them time and space to reflect and experiment in a way that is crucial to their development as artists.

Our students are largely from the UK, although a good proportion come from overseas, and together they form a critical mass of diverse young artists. A proportion of the artwork they produce involves newer media, such as photography, video, installation or digital print, there co-existing happily with the so-called traditional forms of painting and sculpture. We intend to revitalise the practice of drawing here and also have plans to redevelop and expand studios and other facilities for students, including a new Library, lecture theatre and an exhibition space. Such improvements, as well as running costs and students' fees, are supported entirely from generous private donations because, unlike other similar establishments, the Schools receive no government funding.

Beyond the curriculum, the RA Schools benefit from the wider community of the RA. Many Academicians participate in the Schools, including the Professor of Painting, John Hoyland, and Sandra Blow, Eileen Cooper, Gus Cummins, Ivor Abrahams and Ian McKeever. Architect RAs such as Ian Ritchie come into the Schools to help students make models and complex

structures. Trustees, such as Simon Robertson (now head of Rolls-Royce) give advice on how artists can manage their own businesses, while guest lecturers such as critics Mel Gooding and Tom Lubbock, and dealer Max Wigram, talk to the students about how to survive and thrive in a competitive contemporary art world. Our aim is to prepare students for their future lives as artists. Students also have free access to the RA's exhibition and general education programme.

A school is the sum of its students and these young people represent its buoyant character, its pace, collective energy and direction – striving, variegated, restless but strong and unerring. They are ambitious, but for the work first and foremost, and not for the career, because the latter so one can predict or control. They will create remarkable images and objects in a sense out of the past, but actually from out of this – their hurtling 21st century. I salute them.

RA Schools Show, RA Schools, Royal Academy of Arts (20–29 June), entry is via Jerry Sewall at the back of the RA and accessible via the Dalgan House or the Dalgan Gardens, for the new RA Schools Gallery, see page 84. Platform for Art, an exhibition of work by four RA Schools students. Piccadilly Circus tube station, 6 June–5 Sept, for an e-brochure this summer, see Listings page 89 for more opportunities on the RA Schools, visit www.royalacademy.org.uk

TREASURES

'China: The Three Emperors' overflows with exquisite works of art. But beyond their beauty, these objects are laden with complex symbolism. On the following pages, *RA Magazine* introduces some of the show's most ravishing riches – from enamel to jade, lacquer to paintings – and asks experts to describe their deeper meanings

548

A CULT
ARTIST

Modigliani was the quintessential cult artist. Here cultural commentator *Peter York* looks at what it means to be a cult artist, while on the following pages artist *Adam Dant* maps a 'Modigliography' of cult figures through the ages

wouldn't have worked without the cheek bones. Modigliani, from his photographs, looked a lot like Jim Morrison and was clearly a corduroy abuser. This physical configuration is basic cult artist potential, necessary though not sufficient, but a deal-breaker if it goes, when the artist turns to blob. Which is why it's always better to have croaked it as young as possible, before belly and jowls, before the nose swells from the drink and the eyes hollow from the drugs.

Dying early also means a small sharply etched body of work, as instantly recognisable as Modigliani's nudes from 1917 to 1920, and a constant persona, like Modigliani's again – passionate, ill, 'crazy', the lot. A long and comfortable life doesn't just play hell with the waistline but also with the brand – too much stuff, too many 'periods', the terrible possibility of mainstream recognition, even a long marriage, a mellowing output and a nice suburban house with a garden.

The eighteenth century teen-writer Thomas Chatterton was the first Neurotic Boy Outsider. Chatterton started a respectable two hundred-year plus tradition of conspicuously not belonging. In this sense he's central to the whole idea of individualistic cult artists who appeal intensely to small groups of people, groups who see themselves as Elects. Chatterton was arty and sensitive and topped himself at an early age. Victorians felt he was almost a member of the nineteenth-century Romantic poet posse of ready-made cults, gloriously un-classical. So the pot boiling Victorian oil painting, *The Death of Chatterton* (1856), by Henry Wallis, is the crucial myth-maker (as in 'die young and leave a beautiful corpse').

Cult artists are primarily the province of thoughtful, confused adolescents (meaning, now, anything up to 40). They are role models for imaginative and impressionable people who want to live intensely. As they're sought out and discovered, decade after decade, cult artists blow more minds than mainstream heroes who sell a lot of, say, football kits or CDs.

The key test is whether Johnny Depp could play your man (there are, let's get this on the table clearly, many more male than female cult artists because men are better at epic self destruction than women). And if not Johnny Depp, then Jonny Lee Miller, or someone else thin, young and neurotic. Cult artists need cultists, articulate fans who like to document their terrible lives and their marvellous ambiguities and relate them to their work – who see the life in the work and value it more for that.

Sex is central to cult-artist status. Having a lot of it, ideally as troubled and ambiguous as possible. Tortured or, as middlebrow journalists love to say, dark. Cult artists' sex lives should be as dark and edgy as possible. Ambiguity helps hugely: girl cultists like it and lots of boy cultists can identify with it. The appeal of James Dean – cheek-bones, troubled, died very young – was hugely heightened by his palpable homoeroticism, easy to recognise but impossible to articulate in 1950s America.

Neurotic Boy Outsiders, the key business model in artistic cultdom, all suffered from expressive inarticulacy. There were things they just couldn't say except in their work – that was why they had to write, act or paint. And so the work itself is hugely coded and personal – except to the cultists, who feel they can read it, because it has a message intended for them (and several hundred thousand similarly placed young people).

Mass media, sophisticated PR and the international consolidation of cults meant that Outsiderdom – at its dizzy peak in the 1960s and '70s – became a huge market segment, a vast lonely crowd of youngish people, a Salon des Refusés larger than the mainstream. The twentieth century's biggest cult artist used to be David Bowie. He ticked every box going – thin, handsome, bisexual, nearly dead from drugs, writing awash with ideas, a working method borrowed from William S. Burroughs and every possible fine arts allusion.

But he is un-dead. Bowie's been re-constructed as an entrepreneur who earns millions from selling songs as advertising music tracks to the likes of Microsoft. He's mellow, happily married and he's even had his teeth fixed. He's clearly blown it.

Cult artists are wonderful and terrible. The cult isn't a reflection of quality but a measure of the artist's ability to provoke intense interest and identification long after death. Byron and Rupert Brooke – very different poets – are heaven for biographers and completely on-brand. Ian Curtis and Kurt Cobain had their audiences sussed too – artistic suicide is the link here between doomy Manchester and sunny California. Rimbaud lived as an intense outsider during the Verlaine years and then as good as died when he stopped writing and became another person in another place (North Africa). Meaning he's still there to rediscover.

Now, interestingly, the two-hundred-year tradition of the cult artist has been telescoped by the media. Marketing work on 'the story' – will he, won't he, is he, isn't he? – operates on an instant feedback basis so a life of torment can be a 24-hour webcast. Watch Pete Doherty play it out day by day. Ask yourself about Robbie Williams, who is both a huge, mainstream entertainer and a professional outsider. They haven't exactly staged their own Kurt Cobain farewells yet – but I've met people who thought that was stage-managed anyway.

A2 Magazine

Client Arup *Design* Matt Willey, Zoë Bather *Year* 2006

New magazine for Arup's consulting business. A2 magazine is aimed at introducing Arup Consulting to employees, clients and prospective clients.

CHINA UNVEILS THE
WORLD'S FIRST ECO-CITY

INTERVIEW: *Baroness Ford on regenerating UK communities*
TIME TO START PLANNING: *A new approach to business resilience*
INNOVATIONS: *Exciting new benchmarks in design and technology*

TIME TO START PLANNING

Despite considerable investment in business continuity planning over the last decade, almost 60% of senior managers in the UK are still unsure whether their organisations would survive a major disruption. A recent survey by Arup suggests that organisations, both private and public, need to re-think their resilience strategies. Words: *Matthew Bythell.*

"We know that many organisations have invested in business continuity planning but we believe that many of these systems need upgrading and integrating to ensure that they are more agile and sensitive to different types of threat."

A new approach to corporate resilience:

CASE STUDY: CABINET OFFICE EMERGENCY PLANNING COLLEGE

Making education pay

The UK Government is pushing for all universities to become financially sustainable by 2012. This controversial process is being implemented in universities across the country, but the strategic implications are only just emerging. Words: *Justine Harvey.*

How will university research projects become self-sustainable?

They may have to:

- change some of the types of research they perform
- raise money by charging for the use of research facilities
- share facilities with universities whose costs are lower
- sell parts of their estates that are uneconomic and/or non-beneficial
- bid collaboratively with other universities to get more value into research projects.

CASE STUDY: IMPERIAL COLLEGE LONDON, UK

MAD BRITA

The UK has lost over one million manufacturing jobs in the last five years. In the 1940s, 50% of the nation's work-force were employed in manufacturing. Today that figure is just 15%. Is there a way back for British manufacturing? Words: *Justine Harvey*.

Much has been said about the decline of UK manufacturing and whether there is any serious hope of reversing the trend. According to Tim Hawley, Director at Rossmore Group, part of Arup "The answer is yes and no. Our economy is mature and we have developed higher lifestyle expectations, so we can't compete with emerging economies on direct labour costs, therefore we have to move up the food chain. It's a matter of progression." But Hawley also thinks that manufacturing should not have declined so quickly. "You can't turn back the clock, but I wouldn't like to see UK manufacturing drop any further and I see no reason why it should."

The UK is currently trapped between high value added manufacturing countries like Germany and the USA on one side, and cheap labour countries like China on the other "We need to let go of the middle position and focus on innovation to create and recreate products that respond to the ever-changing marketplace," states Hawley. Research from the London School of Economics suggests that UK productivity is almost 40% lower than in the US and 20% lower than in

E IN
AIN.

Techniques for manufacturing success

- Improve people performance by adopting new techniques, changing culture and best practice, helping people to solve problems out, and improving customer service
- Apply lean manufacturing techniques to take variability out of the process
- Become agile and market responsive: companies need to respond to the consumer
- Reconfigure supply chains: optimise locations to be flexible
- Retain intellectual property close to home to avoid copyright fraud
- See capital investment as an investment in the future
- Embrace the benefits of low-cost economies

France and Germany. "We need to match the Germans in capital investment by using high tech machinery and robots to reduce labour content. In the UK we tend to off shore to China, and yet Germany is the largest exporter of manufactured goods in the world, so there is no reason why we can't do it." Hawley believes that while off-shoring manufacturing suits labour intensive products, it is not always the best solution. "It's not always practical to send manufacturing to China because you have to be market responsive with certain products such as high technology items, and you need to protect intellectual property."

Retaining some production closer to home also reduces supply chain complexity and risk. There are big benefits to sourcing from low-cost economies, but organisations need to become very good at constantly managing and reviewing the cost and opportunities, along with weighing up the risk exposure. "This makes logistics very complicated and very vulnerable, particularly if there are long lead times. You may remember when Sony PlayStation 2 got stuck in transportation on the Suez Canal? It hit market share over a critical Christmas sales period. It is alright if it works, but there are increasing risks from terrorism."

Last year the International Maritime Organization highlighted the vulnerability of the international shipping supply chain to terrorism and the measures being put in place to address security.

Sustainability is also becoming an increasingly important issue with the threat of global warming and environmental disasters making global supply chains a risk. According to Hawley, "Currently most companies move their manufacturing to wherever it is financially viable and often where the environmental legislation is most accommodating, without taking account of the local environmental effects. It seems to be a case of just moving the problems elsewhere so we don't incur the environmental burden at home, but we need to remember that we're still polluting the same atmosphere. There is currently a lack of joined up thinking, but as global warming gets worse and the world becomes more interconnected, there will be more of a ripple effect and we will have to take responsibility on a global scale."

Other improvements can be made to reduce the need to off-shore. As well as capital investment, productivity can also be improved by lean manufacturing models and quality approaches like Six Sigma. Processes need to be tightly

controlled to narrow variation on the production line so you end up with better quality goods. "One example of successful lean manufacturing in the UK is the Nissan car factory in Sunderland," comments Hawley. "It's just a shame that this progress was not home grown, but we should learn from this. We can all do it."

Another productivity weakness relates to management attitudes. "We do suffer from a lot of traditional working practice legacy issues in our mature industries, where there are many restrictive practices, both formalised and cultural attitudes like, 'I can't operate that machine because it's outside my grade,' or, 'Sorry can't do that, I'm on a break.' Labour practices need to be more flexible and focused on problem solving. Employees should be salaried, not waged, team focused, self managing, and able to operate a variety of machines. Why is a company like Toyota able to do it and not Rover? One of the reasons is that Toyota came into the UK and trained people not associated with the car industry, but were assessed for the right aptitude. They knew that culturally the mindset would be different."

While lean is good, companies also have to be agile and responsive to the marketplace. Innovation is the key to future manufacturing success. "We need to design new innovative products or refresh existing products that are responsive to the consumer," says Hawley. "We need to drive product change, be ahead of the competition and keep the market fresh with new ideas. This means we have to effectively educate our young people to ensure that we produce the next generation of ground breaking scientists, engineers and inventors."

Rossmore and Arup have recently been assisting major companies (*see case study, overleaf*) to make some of these changes. "We help companies adopt new processes and thinking. Our history is in manufacturing, operations and business psychology, so we are in a good position to help change the mindset, rather than just processes. It is unlikely UK manufacturing will grow in the coming years because we have lost too much, but if we are clever at what we do and adopt some of these methods, we should be able to stay at our current level and do it well."

E
C
08?0
BARCELON
SPAIN

The Cheese Room
37 Albert Road
Tamworth, Staffordshire
England B79 7JS
www.thecheeseroom.com

42ᴾ

5ᴾ

8, BAJOS

ES

Your shout. Bank Fashion Newsletter

Client Bank Fashion *Design* Lee Murphy *Year* 2006

Newsletter produced for Bank staff across its UK stores.

Focusing on the staff, their lives, events, changing fashions and the development of the business.

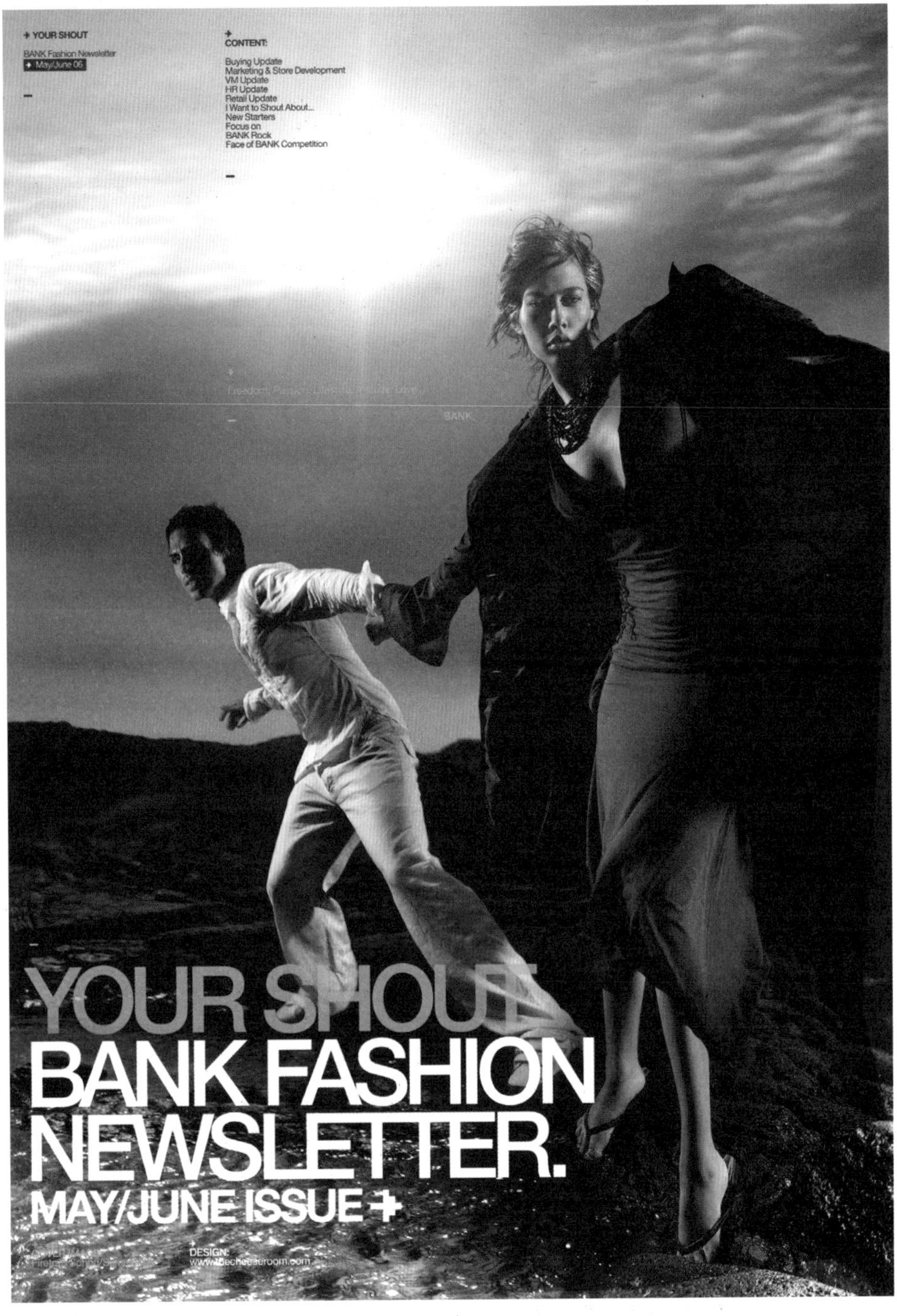

YOUR SHOUT
BANK FASHION
NEWSLETTER.
MAY/JUNE ISSUE +

DESIGN:
www.technetworbom.com

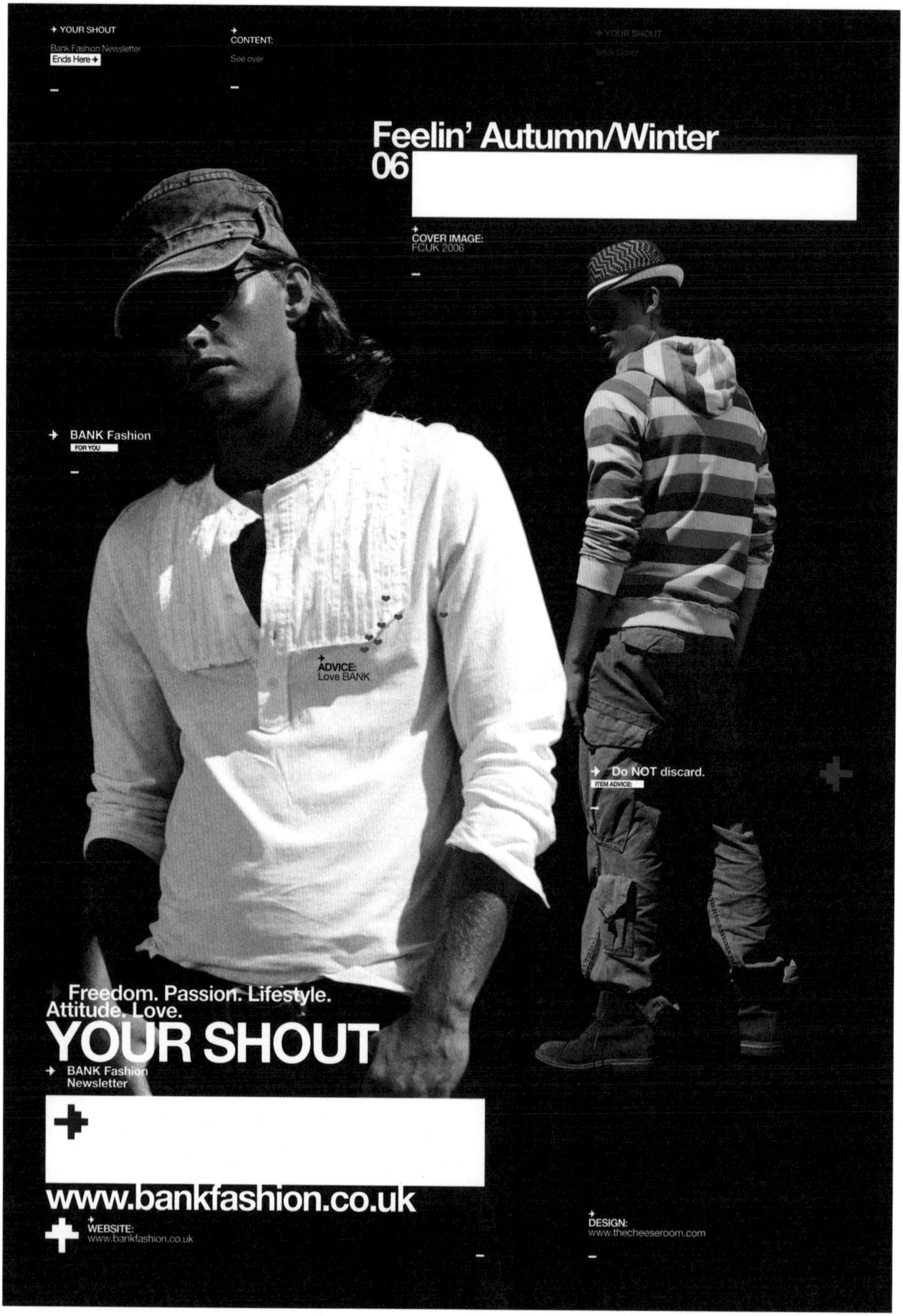

YOUR SHOUT
Bank Fashion Newsletter
Ends Here
CONTENT:
See over
Feelin' Autumn/Winter 06
COVER IMAGE:
FCUK 2006
BANK Fashion
FOR YOU
ADVICE:
Love BANK
Do NOT discard.
ITEM ADVICE:
Freedom. Passion. Lifestyle. Attitude. Love.
YOUR SHOUT
BANK Fashion Newsletter
www.bankfashion.co.uk
WEBSITE:
www.bankfashion.co.uk
DESIGN:
www.thecheeseroom.com

+ YOUR SHOUT

Bank Fashion Newsletter
Ends Here +

–

+ CONTENT:

See over

–

+ YOUR SHOUT

Back Cover

–

+
ADVICE:
Love BANK

+ Freedom. Passion. Lifestyle.
Attitude. Love.
YOUR SHOUT

+ BANK Fashion
Newsletter

www.bankfashion.co.uk

+
WEBSITE:
www.bankfashion.co.uk

+ BANK Fashion
FOR YOU

–

+ Do NOT discard.
ITEM ADVICE

+

Keepin' hot in Winter
06

+ COVER IMAGE:
Fred In Boston 2006

–

+
DESIGN:
www.thecheeseroom.com

–

✚ YOUR SHOUT

BANK Fashion Newsletter
Begin Here ➔

✚
CONTENT:

I Want To Shout About...

–

✚ YOUR SHOUT

Page 12

–

–

IWanttoShoutAbout...

✚ Have you done something to be proud of?

✚ QUOTE ME!
"All the staff did fantastically well over Xmas but a big shout out goes to Robbie Woodhead for working 3 six day weeks when we needed cover and when he was beaten up quite badly and lost a tooth, he was still in work. Deserves an ipod just for that.
Rodney Pierre, Huddersfield

✚ QUOTE ME!
"Vicky Davies is our Supervisor, and has done an excellent job in making sure the store is beating targets when I have been gone. Not only that, but she has also managed to organize several instore moves while running minimal staff instore. Well done Vicky, don't think your hard work has gone unnoticed!"
Mark Broadbent, Leeds

✚ QUOTE ME!
"I would like to thank Jamie Reddoch, Asst. Manager for his hard work and dedication to me and the team. Jamie Worked long hours and worked 6 or 7 days without seeing his daughter".
Andy Martin, Braehead

✚ QUOTE ME!
"I would like to thank my whole team for this help, support and team spirit over the sale/christmas period as without them it wouldn't have happened".
Andrea Bungay, Reading

✚ QUOTE ME!
"I would like to thank Jacky Thrussell for all her hard work since opening. Jacky has been the strongest full-timer. She has given me and the rest of the management team alot of support. Thank you to Jacky the hard work payed off!"
Nikki Coe, Norwich

✚ QUOTE ME!
"I would like you to mention both Laura and Daryl from Milton Keynes as they have done a excellent job over Xmas when the previous manager left in November. I am looking forward to working with them both as they are going to take Milton Keynes store to the top of the Company so everyone watch out!"
Barry Wiltshire, Milton Keynes

✚ QUOTE ME!
"I would like to welcome Nicky Bamber to the company. He has had a fantastic start to his role as IT assistant, and I expect great things from him."
Simon Brassington, It Manager

✚ QUOTE ME!
"I would like to nominate Leanne Ross who is my fantastic Menswear Supervisor. She has done a great job over the Christmas period, putting in 100% effort every day & always working late into the evening, we couldn't have done it without her. Without her we would be lost..."
Nick Workman, Leamington

✚ QUOTE ME!
"A big thank you to my whole team at Redditch for working so hard over Christmas and the sale - Keep it up guys. Also a big welcome to our new supervisor Zoe Jones who's already made a positive impact in store."
Kate Jones, Redditch

✚ QUOTE ME!
I would like to nominate Charlotte Duncker. She only works saturdays but is always showing initiative and never has to be asked twice to do a task. Charlotte approaches all customers with a high level of customer service, and has had several customers praising her service to Tracey and I.".
Beverley Palmer, Macclesfield

✚ QUOTE ME!
"I would like to nominate Laura Sowney for taking on the VM role in store. She is using initiative and working hard to keep the store fresh and exciting.
Colin Bell, Worcester

✚ QUOTE ME!
I would like to give a big shout out to my back of house Supervisor Anthony (T.C.) Cowell for all the hard work and long hours he put in over the Christmas period. The poor lad never saw daylight during the month of December, and never tapped out with sickness once over the three month period. The White Rose crew would also like to give a big shout out to Nigel the van driver!
Lee Robinson, White Rose

✚ QUOTE ME!
My thank you goes to Sarah Waterfall. She is full time sales but does lots more as well. She is always keen to learn new things and so completes paperwork and cashes up as well as being one of our highest sales people. She has been a fantastic help especially when one of management team is on holiday - basically. Thank you!!
Suvi Brent, Wolverhampton

✚ QUOTE ME!
I would like to nominate all of the team, but if I can only choose one, then I would like to select Joan, for her continued devotion, hard work, & conscientiousness - a real team player, always with a smile. Joan also makes very scrummy cakes!
Elaine Walton, Accountant

✚ QUOTE ME!
Adam and I were trying to think of staff that we wanted to thank for their hard work over the Christmas period, but it was hard to single anyone out as everyone contributed to a great Christmas period. We ended up beating target by 10% and won 3 i-Pods out of 24, that's a big contribution for a little Town store, so me and Adam would like to thank all our Bankers for all their help and dedication they showed us in this busy time.
Adam & Dekka, Sutton Coldfield

✦ YOUR SHOUT

BANK Fashion Newsletter
Continue Here ✦

✦ CONTENT:

Retail Update

✦ YOUR SHOUT

Page 13

RetailUpdate

✦ A look into the future...

As you are all aware the last 6 months has been exceptionally difficult. The increase in competition in once BANK only territory, has had an impact on our like for like sales. I use the analogy of £100 per day per store to highlight the impact each store has on our global sales, this at our current size equates to £1.2 million per year.

Over the past year we have seen the rise of Primark and other on trend retailers. According to research the average price of Primark is 48% lower than that of the High Street. As a team we have done all we can to minimise the effect on our business, and as a team you have all done exceptionally well at controlling the payroll spend to offset the fall in sales.

✦ Stay focussed, stay positive, staying ahead
Trying to predict the future

If only we had a crystal ball and could predict the outcome of this season. A few good weeks would restore the confidence across the business. I believe the product is getting better and better. Men's continues to shine and perform well and ladies product is looking stronger than ever.

I know as a sector there are a growing number of retailers who are struggling, recent companies such as Capo, Gadget Shop, Eisenegger, Kaliko going into administration and constant talk in the press of a slow down in retail does not help consumer confidence.

✦ We all need to work together
Working towards Team BANK

This newsletter is the first step in trying to generate better communication across the business and for all those who have contributed at retail I thank you. This is a new season and New Year and as such, its time for a positive start. I know the buyers are working hard on product to ensure we have the best product and we need to work together to ensure we are all doing our part.

We are working hard; especially Steph to develop a lot of support for the retail teams. The introduction of the new selling skills workbook, the new mystery shops will be out soon and the results will be published in the next newsletter. I believe in the direction the company is taking to work towards our "Team BANK" philosophy, and I am very excited about the coming months.

This season I believe will continue to present us with challenges and it is at this point that I ask that we all do our part. At the time of writing this we were just entering our third week of February and three store stand out; with sales above last year these are, Shrewsbury +15%, Telford +4% and Redditch +3% thanks to the teams in these stores.

Thank you for your continued efforts and support.

Craig Roach
Operations Director

+ YOUR SHOUT

BANK Fashion Newsletter
Begin Here →

+
CONTENT:

Mens Update

+ YOUR SHOUT

Page 08

—   —   —

MensBuying...

+ The changing faces of the BANK menswear lineup.

I have now been back with the company for just over a year, and hopefully you are starting to see some changes to the menswear line up in BANK. After listening to our shop managers I have started to faze certain brands out of the business - some gone already like Full Circle – certain brands will be given more space over the next few seasons (Adidas Originals, Duck & Cover and Lacoste) and certain brands have been added to the portfolio, brands I feel may not set the world on fire this season but will definitely plant the seed for seasons to come, these include the much hyped FLY53 and DAC Denim a diffusion line of Duck & Cover.

New for Spring Summer 2006

+ **FLY53** – An exciting brand and one for the future. FLY53 has chosen BANK as its High St partner which is a big compliment as are rivals have been chasing the brand hard, they include Scotts and USC. FLY53 I feel bridges the gap between Bench and Firetrap, it has the feel of Firetrap but with more of a street style edge like Bench. I have already previewed the Autumn Winter 2006 range and believe me it has improved 100% on what you will be receiving for Spring Summer 06.

+ **DAC Denim** – This has been designed as a diffusion range of Duck & Cover, and once again Bank has been chosen as a partner along with House of Fraser to help launch DAC Denim onto the High St, with USC, Scotts, and Republic all chasing hard BANK has once again been established as the most ideal partner to launch new product with, a massive compliment from one of the hottest brands on the High St. DAC Denim has taken influence from both G-Star and Diesel and pitched itself to compete head on with Firetrap Blackseal, but with more focus on tops rather than jeans.

+ **Penguin** – An old favourite returns to the branded market, you couldn't revive the eighties theme without this terrace classic. Penguin has already proved itself to be a success in competitors stores and now we are going to let it shine in BANK for Spring Summer. Admittedly we were not first out of the blocks with this one and will be playing catch up for a couple of seasons with distribution, so to kick off we have only been given Penguin for Bury, Whiterose, Hull, Solihull, Norwich and the long awaited Manchester store. The brand consists mainly of plain and striped polo's in both cotton jersey and cotton pique fabrics. Anybody wishing to see images for Spring Summer 2006 can contact me on my email and I will send you key images of Penguin.

✛ YOUR SHOUT

BANK Fashion Newsletter
Begin Here ➜

✛ CONTENT:

Ladies Update

✛ YOUR SHOUT

LadiesBuying...

✛ What's new?

For Spring Summer 2006 we took a fresh new look at fashion. We have added some new brands, a new colour palette, new things to wear and inspiring ways to wear them!!

The super trend from last season, Boho, has been refreshingly replaced and by flats, skinny jeans, shorts and jackets.

Below is all you need to be new and now...
It's time to update your wardrobe.

✛ **Skinny jeans** - we aren't about to give up the skinny drainpipe jean any time soon, lots of skinny jeans with plenty of choice – Miss Sixty JLot, Replay WV479, Fornarina Nek jean and Firetrap Houston.

✛ **Ballerinas** and **canvas pumps** in Crayola colours look fantastic with jeans and dresses to take you throughout summer – Lacoste Muskateer, BANK.

✛ **Tattoo print** and **rock chic tees** by Amplified/Religion to be worn with skinny jeans and ankle boots – Harlot

✛ Bold and oversized **accessories** – piling on beads and bangles into summer with our newly launched Ribbon accessories line.

✛ **Length** – new longer tees and slouchy long sweatshirts to be worn with thin and chunky belts alike – Henley's, Ribbon,

✛ The relaunch of the **Adidas Gazelles** for a retro / preppy look with boys fit jeans and colourful polo's – Miss Sixty, Duck and Cover

✛ **White is the colour** of the season found on everything clothing, denim, footwear and jewellery.

✛ **Metallics** are still a strong look but with more subtle versions of silvers, pewter and bronze found on footwear and accessories.

✛ **Smart utility** – lots of versions of shorts, cropped combats and belted jackets, stylishly relaxed urban wear ability with cargo styling in earthy neutral colours, raw edges – Bench, Vero Moda, Only

✛ **Value per wear** – save for your favourite branded top, fashion fades style doesn't...

✛ *Finally* tie a **belt** around your waist to reinforce the season's key focal point!!

564

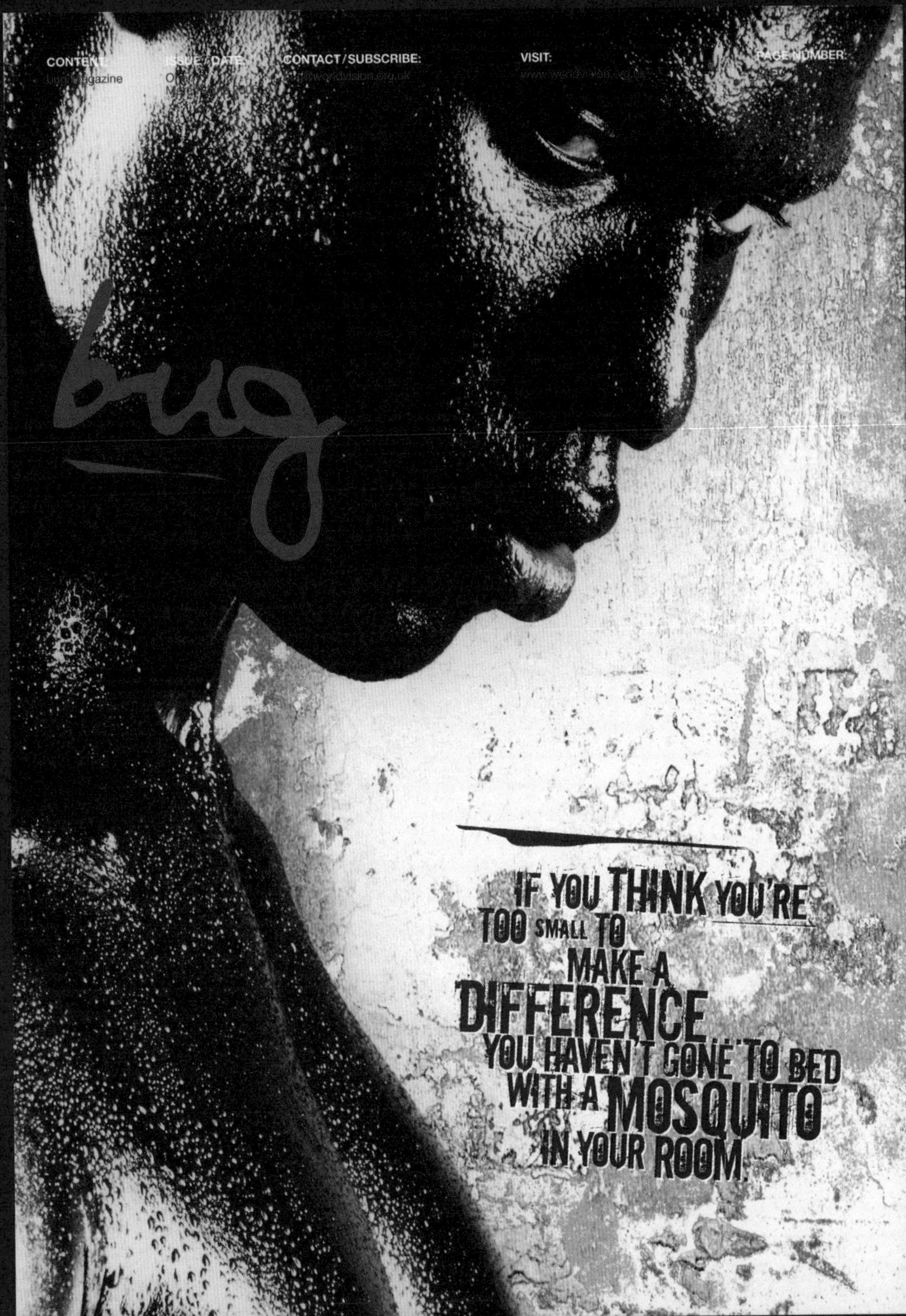
CONTENT:
ISSUE / DATE:
CONTACT / SUBSCRIBE:
VISIT:
PAGE NUMBER:
bug
IF YOU THINK YOU'RE TOO SMALL TO MAKE A DIFFERENCE YOU HAVEN'T GONE TO BED WITH A MOSQUITO IN YOUR ROOM.

CONTENT:
Stop Aids

ISSUE:
Three

CONTACT/SUBSCRIBE:
bug@worldvision.org.uk

VISIT:
www.worldvision.org.uk

PAGE NUMBER:
2420

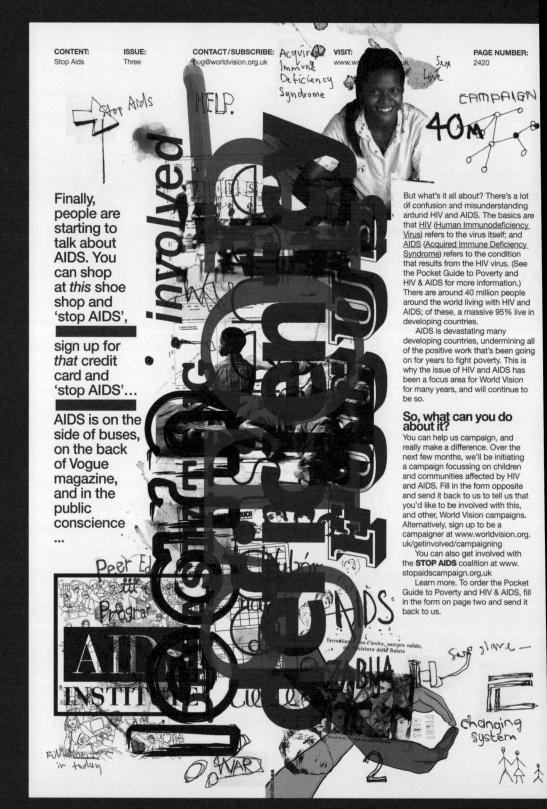

Finally, people are starting to talk about AIDS. You can shop at *this* shoe shop and 'stop AIDS',

sign up for *that* credit card and 'stop AIDS'…

AIDS is on the side of buses, on the back of Vogue magazine, and in the public conscience …

But what's it all about? There's a lot of confusion and misunderstanding around HIV and AIDS. The basics are that HIV (Human Immunodeficiency Virus) refers to the virus itself; and AIDS (Acquired Immune Deficiency Syndrome) refers to the condition that results from the HIV virus. (See the Pocket Guide to Poverty and HIV & AIDS for more information.) There are around 40 million people around the world living with HIV and AIDS; of these, a massive 95% live in developing countries.

AIDS is devastating many developing countries, undermining all of the positive work that's been going on for years to fight poverty. This is why the issue of HIV and AIDS has been a focus area for World Vision for many years, and will continue to be so.

So, what can you do about it?

You can help us campaign, and really make a difference. Over the next few months, we'll be initiating a campaign focussing on children and communities affected by HIV and AIDS. Fill in the form opposite and send it back to us to tell us that you'd like to be involved with this, and other, World Vision campaigns. Alternatively, sign up to be a campaigner at www.worldvision.org.uk/getinvolved/campaigning

You can also get involved with the **STOP AIDS** coalition at www.stopaidscampaign.org.uk

Learn more. To order the Pocket Guide to Poverty and HIV & AIDS, fill in the form on page two and send it back to us.

566

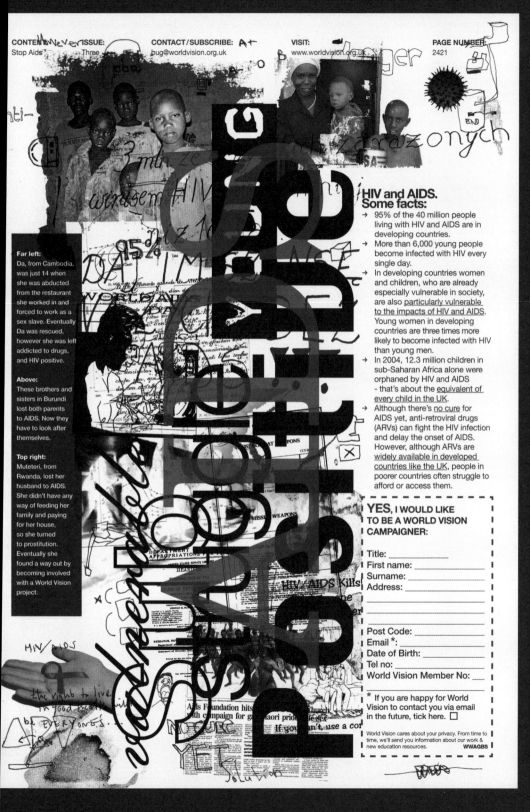

CONTENT THIS ISSUE:
Stop Aids   Three

CONTACT/SUBSCRIBE:
bug@worldvision.org.uk

VISIT:
www.worldvision.org.uk

PAGE NUMBER:
2421

HIV and AIDS.
Some facts:

→ 95% of the 40 million people living with HIV and AIDS are in developing countries.

→ More than 6,000 young people become infected with HIV every single day.

→ In developing countries women and children, who are already especially vulnerable in society, are also particularly vulnerable to the impacts of HIV and AIDS. Young women in developing countries are three times more likely to become infected with HIV than young men.

→ In 2004, 12.3 million children in sub-Saharan Africa alone were orphaned by HIV and AIDS - that's about the equivalent of every child in the UK.

→ Although there's no cure for AIDS yet, anti-retroviral drugs (ARVs) can fight the HIV infection and delay the onset of AIDS. However, although ARVs are widely available in developed countries like the UK, people in poorer countries often struggle to afford or access them.

Far left:
Da, from Cambodia, was just 14 when she was abducted from the restaurant she worked in and forced to work as a sex slave. Eventually Da was rescued, however she was left addicted to drugs, and HIV positive.

Above:
These brothers and sisters in Burundi lost both parents to AIDS. Now they have to look after themselves.

Top right:
Muteteri, from Rwanda, lost her husband to AIDS. She didn't have any way of feeding her family and paying for her house, so she turned to prostitution. Eventually she found a way out by becoming involved with a World Vision project.

YES, I WOULD LIKE TO BE A WORLD VISION CAMPAIGNER:

Title: _____
First name: _____
Surname: _____
Address: _____
_____
_____
_____
Post Code: _____
Email *: _____
Date of Birth: _____
Tel no: _____
World Vision Member No: ___

* If you are happy for World Vision to contact you via email in the future, tick here. ☐

DID YOU KNOW?

2007 is the _200 year anniversary of the end of the slave trade in the UK_. But there is still much more to do. Unfortunately, there are many more stories like those of Nazire and Yen* below. Huge numbers of children and young people are trafficked across borders every year, some into the UK, and forced or manipulated into a life of abuse and exploitation, often as sex workers. Trafficking is an abuse of human rights, and should be wiped out.

This campaign is calling on the UK government to take thr3e small steps that would make a world of difference to children and young people affected by trafficking in 2007:

STEP ONE

That they ratify (confirm, sanction or approve) the Council of Europe's Convention on Action against Trafficking in Human Beings.
Why? Because it will help ensure better standards of protection for victims of trafficking.

STEP TWO

Immediately withdraw its Reservation to the Convention on the Rights of the Child on Immigration and Nationality.
Why? In order to protect all children trafficked into the UK.

STEP THREE

Appoint a national Child Trafficking Rapporteur.
Why? So that there is a specific person responsible for regular reporting on statistics, trends and emerging issues to do with trafficking.

JOIN THE THR3E SMALL STEPS CAMPAIGN

We need you to help us make sure the government takes STEP ONE.

Simply by completing the enclosed post card, you can help us make the government change its policy to protect children trafficked into the UK.

STEP ONE: JOIN US NOW!

We want the UK government to ratify the Council of Europe's Convention against Trafficking in Human Beings without delay.

Here's three small actions you can take straight away to make sure that the UK government takes STEP ONE…

Action 1:

Fill in both parts of the first post card attached.

Action 2:

Post both parts of the first post card (one half goes to World Vision, the other half goes to your MP, visit **www.writetothem.com** to find out the name of your MP).

Action 3:

Give the other two post cards to two people you know - making three people helping to achieve three small steps for children affected by trafficking.

We know from previous campaigns that calling on MPs to make a change does work!

Look out for how to help achieve **STEPS TWO** and **THREE** in the next few issues of bug.

Yen's story

Yen lived alone with her mother in a poor countryside village in Vietnam. When she was just 14 years old, her mother sold Yen to a stranger. She was then trafficked to the UK in a lorry, spending three long months on the road. On arrival Yen was taken to a brothel, where she was shown pornographic videos to groom her for a life of prostitution…

Eventually she managed to escape and, after being on the streets, was taken to a police station. Despite what had been done to her, and her obvious distress, no counselling or specialist support was provided and her asylum claim was refused.

Nazire's story

Nazire was kidnapped at knifepoint one night when she went out to the shops for her mum. She was then trafficked from her home in Armenia to Greece, and forced into prostitution. She was there for seven months until she was rescued. She later testified against her traffickers and there was a trial, but they were found not guilty. Now Nazire has to live in a secret location because her family have received death threats from the traffickers.

* Yen and Nazire are fictional names, but their stories are real.

CONTENT:
Tsunami /
Sri Lanka

ISSUE / DATE:
One /
March-June 2006

CONTACT / SUBSCRIBE:
bug@worldvision.org.uk

VISIT:
www.worldvision.org.uk

PAGE NUMBER:
2416

AFTER THE TSUNAMI, OR HOW TO EAT A SRI LANKAN ELEPHANT

By Jan Butter in Sri Lanka

Aid, both emergency and long-term, is a difficult topic to say the least. There are emotions involved – desperation, empathy, anger, pain, relief and elation – and there are real lives at stake. Aid needs to be focused on real need and it needs to be sustainable. This is eas... As an example Jan Butter, World Vision tsunami Communications Manager in Sri Lanka, talks a bit about the size of the task in Sri Lanka.

"WHY?", people are asking. It's no surprise that donors/the media/the public/survivors sometimes question why more has not been done for Sri Lankan survivors of the tsunami, 'apart from the £300million the British public raised for Tsunami-affected countries, the international community has pledged £1.6 billion just for Sri Lanka. The money's there, how difficult can post-tsunami recovery be?'

The Best Answer To This Question Is Another Question:

How do you eat an elephant? (Stay with me on this one.)

Consider the situation. You arrive in Sri Lanka, an island of 19 million people, nearly 39,000 of whom have been killed in one day by a giant tidal wave. Almost one million people are homeless and many have no way of supporting themselves or their families.

So you get started, providing emergency food, tents, medicines and clean water. But, after a few weeks, it's evident that things need to move on. Schools, roads and hospitals need to be back in working-order, tonnes of debris need to be cleared. There is a need for temporary and permanent housing for thousands of families, fishermen need boats and nets and everybody needs clean, safe water and adequate sanitation.

Quite a challenge – even with millions of pounds at your disposal.

Being a believer in community-based development – rather than flooding a country with 'experts' from other countries, it's best to commission local staff to do the work. This helps local people earn money for their families and regain their independence. However, now more than 300,000 houses are needed. This is a tall order in a country which, in an average year, builds just 5,000 new homes. So, unsurprisingly, there's a shortage of skilled builders in Sri Lanka. There is also, ironically for an island, a shortage of building materials, especially sand.

This isn't the only challenge…

Buffer Zone:

Re-building homes where they used to be, close to the seashore, is not always allowed by the Sri Lankan government, just in case there's another tsunami. Not the best for finding land to build on, and not ideal for fishermen who NEED to be on the seashore to earn a living.

Truth & Lies:

When you do get Government permission to build on land, you find that not everyone who claims to have lost their home in the tsunami actually has. Not that surprising when you consider that Sri Lanka was poor even before the tsunami.

Conflict:

In the south of Sri Lanka where I am, things are marginally easier than in the east and north - here CONFLICT between different groups is regular, dangerous, disruptive and limiting.

Misunderstood:

When you do start a recovery project somewhere, there are those influential political groups who openly and falsely accuse you and your fellow aid agencies of using tsunami-related aid work to "cover up your real work" of converting Buddhists to Christianity. Or colonisation. Or both.

The list of challenges in Sri Lanka goes on, all of them set against an ugly backdrop of political instability.

So then, back to the question of how do you eat an elephant? *Slice by slice.*

How you bring post-tsunami recovery to Sri Lanka with things the way they are right now? *Bit by bit.*

Experts maintain that it will take the island three to five years to recover from the tsunami because of the scale of the disaster. However, there is so much that already has been accomplished since the tsunami. Perhaps, then, the question on everyone's lips should actually be, rather than 'why has more not been done?',

'How has so much been achieved by non-governmental organisations – aid agencies, faith groups, private companies – in just 14 months?'.

How do you eat an elephant? *Bit by bit.*

CONTENT:
Tsunami/
Sri Lanka

ISSUE / DATE:
One /
March-June 2006

CONTACT/SUBSCRIBE:
bug@worldvision.org.uk

VISIT:
www.worldvision.org.uk

PAGE NUMBER:
2417

572

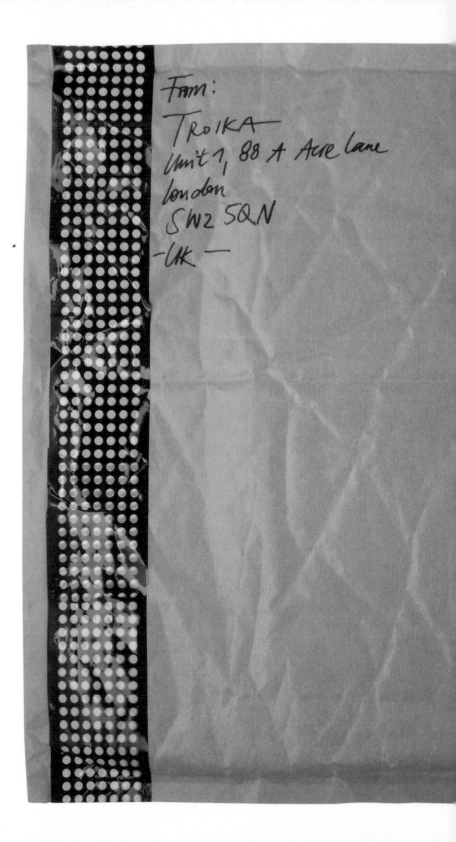

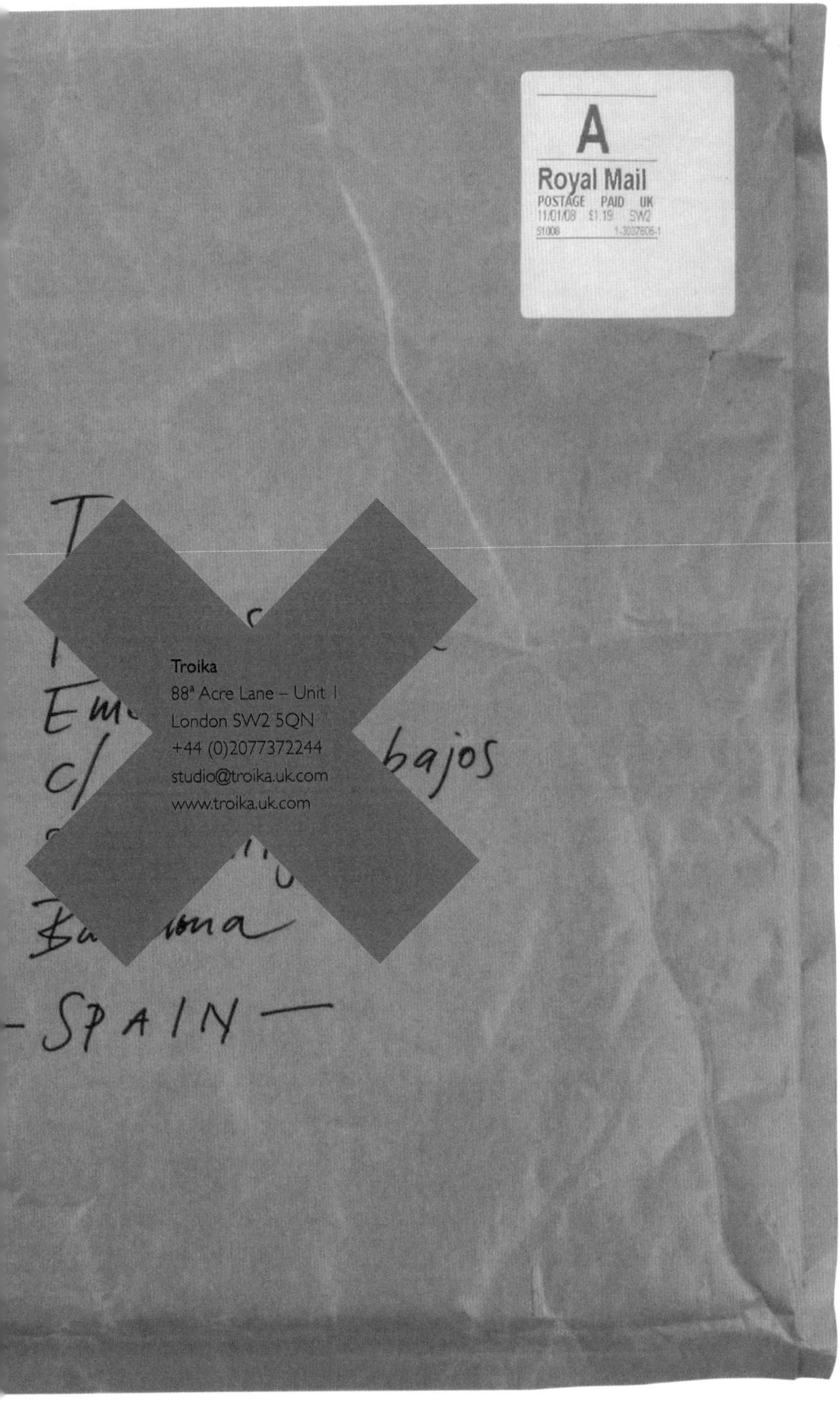

T

Em...
c/
bajos

B...na

— SPAIN —

Troika
88ª Acre Lane – Unit 1
London SW2 5QN
+44 (0)2077372244
studio@troika.uk.com
www.troika.uk.com

Central Saint Martins MA Fine Art Catalogue

Client University of the Arts London *Design* Conny Freyer, Eva Rucki, Sebastien Noel *Year* 2005

We wanted the catalogue to be a useful tool for visitors during the show, while at the same time a catalogue to keep as a reference once the Final Show is over. We chose the size and language of a guide book; the small elongated format makes it easy to hold open in one hand or to carry in your pocket. The page markers and foldout maps refer to colour coded pages with the artworks.

574

01 Taiya N. Kozminsky
02 Daniel Greaney
03 Abigail Howe
04 Alexandros Mangos
05 Gali Timen
06 Theodore Mugkihuly
07 Sarah Hood
08 Sungsu Yu
09 Siu Hong Cheung
10 Adrian Holme
11 Lucille Power
12 Neva Elliott
13 Paul Caton
14 Rebecca Gould
15 Cece Wilden
16 Simon Reuben White
17 Stephen Connolly
18 Taisei Shioda
19 Elena Bajo
20 Johanna E. Laitanen
21 Birgitte Haahr Lund
22 Kleio Gkizeli
23 Toshiyuki Kobayashi
24 Peter Remke
25 Cherie-Marie Veiderveld
26 Mary Anstice
27 Gareth Polmeer
28 Ka Man Yip
29 George Henry Longly
30 Matthew Smith
31 Jane Short
32 Stuart Elliot
33 Samah Hijawi
34 Emily Clay
35 Sue Leavett
36 Arin Sunaryo
37 Andrea Muendelein
38 Boris Kajmak
39 Jeremy Wood
40 Lalie Schewadron
41 Sharon Wyper
42 Jane E Bentley-Taylor
43 Hrvoje Majer
44 Helgi Snaer Sigurdsson
45 Marina Kassianidou
46 R J Hinrichsen
47 Peter Hardy
48 Jennifer Jacobs
49 Vasilis Chamam
50 Louise Manifold
51 Neil Stewart
52 Andrew Smaldone
53 Yuko Noda McRae
54 Cindy Heuieun Hong
55 Andrew De Friez
56 Sagan Lee

**MA Fine Art Degree Show 2005
Central Saint Martins College of Art and Design**

Untitled
84 cm x 58 cm;
ink on watercolour paper;
ca. February 2005

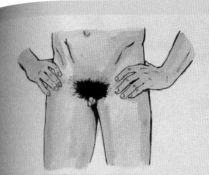

Untitled
5 cm x 53 cm;
ink on watercolour paper;
ca. January 2005

Untitled
2 cm x 81 cm;
ink on watercolour paper;
January – March 2005

Each image communicates the moment you are looking at it. It hooks you, draws you in. It represents the scouring of the mind, the desire for the Other, the lack of and search for something. I do not know what it is until I find it.
I scour the internet for images using words randomly. A void opens, a bizarre universe, but still so very familiar. When something catches my eye words vanish. It comes down to how compelling each image is. I make a choice and communicate it to you in the way I find most natural.

Ground floor

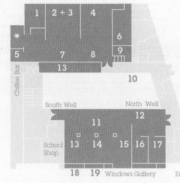

01 Talya N. Kozminsky
02 Daniel Greaney
03 Abigail Howe
04 Alexandros Mangos
✳ Eun Lee
05 Gali Timen
06 Theodore Mugkihuly
07 Sarah Hood
08 Sungsu Yu
09 Siu Hong Cheung

10 Adrian Holme
11 Lucille Power
12 Neva Elliott
13 Paul Caton
14 Rebecca Gould
15 Cece Wilden
16 Simon Reuben White
17 Stephen Connolly
18 Taisei Shioda
19 Elena Bajo

Mezzanine

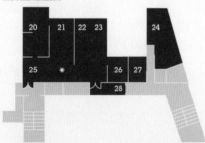

20 Johanna E. Laitanen
21 Birgitte Haahr Lund
22 Kleio Gikizeli
23 Toshiyuki Kobayashi
24 Peter Remke

25 Cherie-Marie Veiderveld
✳ Naniu El-Gammal
26 Mary Anstice
27 Gareth Polmeer
28 Ka Man Yip

a Chair
50 cm x 50 cm x 130 cm;
mild steel;
2005

08/Sungsu Yu

...ructure
...0 cm x 60 cm x 340 cm:
...ild steel,
...005

7th floor

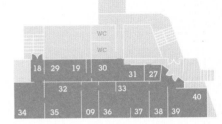

09 Siu Hong Cheung
18 Taisei Shioda
19 Elena Bajo
27 Gareth Polmeer
29 George Henry Longly
30 Matthew Smith
31 Jane Short
32 Stuart Elliott

33 Samah Hijawi
34 Emily Clay
35 Sue Leavett
36 Arin Sunaryo
37 Andrea Muendelein
38 Boris Kajmak
39 Jeremy Wood
40 Lalie Schewadron

8th floor

9th floor

10 Adrian Holme
28 Ka Man Yip
41 Sharon Wyper
42 Jane E Bentley-Taylor
43 Hrvoje Majer
44 Helgi Snaer Sigurdsson
45 Marina Kassianidou
46 R J Hinrichsen
47 Peter Hardy

48 Jennifer Jacobs
49 Vasilis Chamam
50 Louise Manifold
51 Neil Stewart
52 Andrew Smaldone
53 Yuko Noda McRae
54 Cindy Heuieun Hong
55 Andrew De Friez
56 Sagan Lee

Untitled
c-type print
2005

20/Johanna E. Laitanen

In the language of
an exhibition
smoke machine, timer,
2005

29 /George Henry Longly

Moscow Style Book
Client Booth-Clibborn Editions *Design* Conny Freyer, Eva Rucki, Sebastien Noel *Year* 2005
Moscow Style is the third in a series of books on cities featuring fashion, photography, graphics, architecture and art from some of the most innovative practitioners working in Russia today. Troika was comissioned for the complete art direction of the book. After a few trips to Moscow and many vodkas, we selected, edited, designed and managed the production of the book.

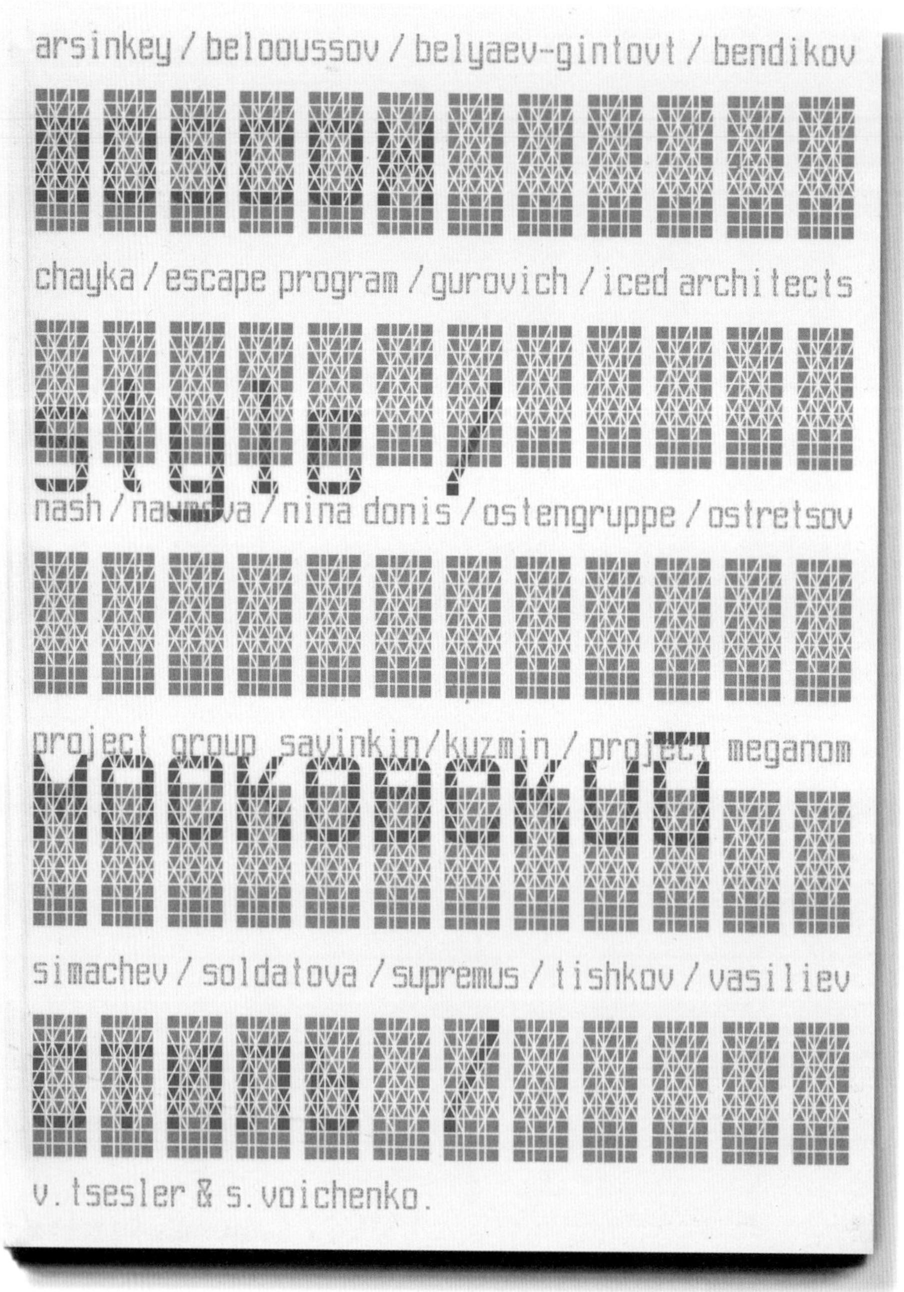

580

aes+f group /

Tatiana Arzamasova, Lev Evzovich, Evgeny Svyatsky, Vladimir Fridkes /

AES+F projects reflect a wide range of contemporary issues, spanning continents, civilizations, religions and political systems. Their work often shares a shocking visual quality, portraying the human body and its elements in bizarre contexts.

'Action Half Life' is a work in progress that questions heroism at a time when war, exploits, and pathos is just a part of a virtual show endlessly dissipating into mass circulation. The driving concept is an attempt to precipitate the "genome of heroism" out of today's world of grim reality. "Our heroes are teens carefully selected from more than 500 top applicants who had first been screened by the best modelling agencies. All of those young heroes are conquerors in the virtual world. Their enemy is absent, and pain and suffering are forbidden by the very nature of the game. They are so alienated that nothing, not even their common virtual battlefield, inhibits their giving themselves over to pure personal exploit, to securing victory over an enemy that does not exist."

With their series of projects entitled 'King of the Forest' (2001-2), AES+F explores the themes of child exploitation by corporate media.
"Like the children in these photographs, many artists today, including AES+F, are walking on a tight rope of glamour stereotype, since they feel this is the only way out of the abyss. Some balance dangerously, others fall brilliantly and catch the rope again; the point is to be on the edge." (Ekaterina Degot).

Their 'Islamic Project' started in 1996 as a series of installations and performances. The attempt is to create a social psychoanalysis of western society's fears and preconceptions about Islam. Set as performances, the fake 'AES travel agency to the Future' stages these visual anticipations of an Islamic-influenced world while selling hypothetical souvenirs and memorabilia such as postcards, posters, mugs, T-shirts, and even carpets.

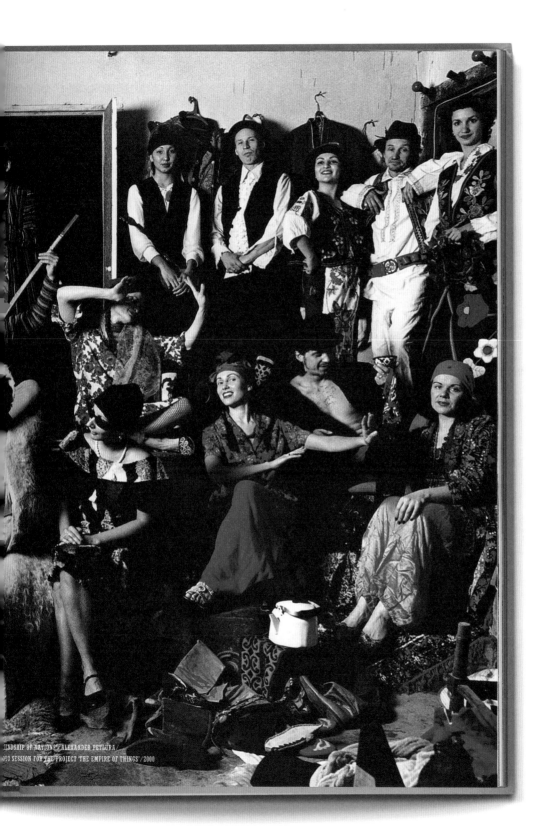

'FRIENDSHIP OF NATIONS'. ALEXANDER PETLURA /
PHOTO SESSION FOR THE PROJECT 'THE EMPIRE OF THINGS' / 2000

584

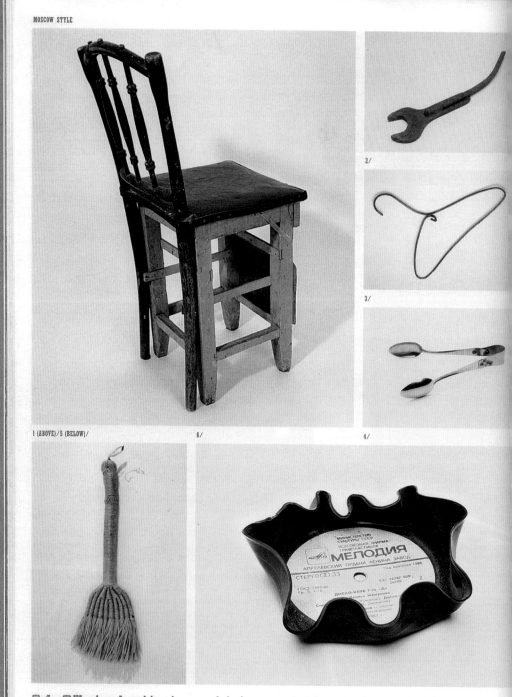

1 (ABOVE)/5 (BELOW)/   6/   4/

24,25 / vladimir arkhipov /   1/'CHAIR AND STOOL'/1995///2/'THE TRACTOR DRIVER'S KEY'/STEEL BAR/BEFORE 2(
3/'WELDER'S PEG'/STEEL, WIRE/1999////////////////////////////////

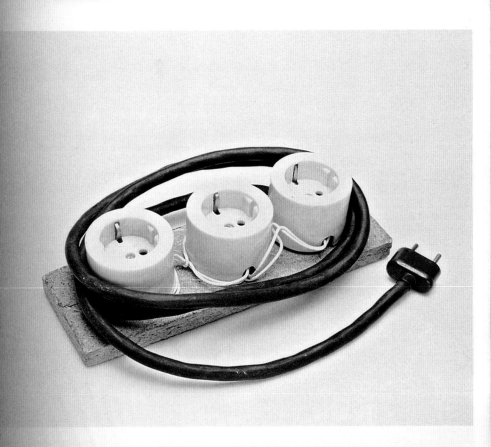

Home-made Forms of the World/ Since 1994 Arkhipov has been working with everyday objects. As spontaneous manifestations of indigenous culture, unaffected by fashion or 'world culture', these items have an independent, alternative existence. They have been brought into existence purely at the behest of the person who has made them for his or her own use. Each piece is entirely unique, and therefore a work of art despite the absence of aesthetic intent. Arkhipov documents everything about the object – who made it, where, when and why – through video interviews.

CHAIR AND STOOL/ 'A stool is a stool. You have to sit on it. So I buy a house but there's nothing to sit on. First I sit on a bucket, but then I say to myself "Surely I can make a stool?" I take some pieces of wood, and one, two, three – the stool is ready.' ANATOLI YAMANOV, SANITARY ENGINEER
WELDER'S PEG/ 'A peg is just a peg. There's nothing more to say about it. I just did it… what other form can it take? This is the only possible form… because I'm a welder.

The building site is full of wire, any wire. I took as much as was needed and wound it around. That's all. If someone steals it or it disappears, I won't regret it. I will make another one…' IVAN POGODIN, WELDER
BESOM/ 'What can I say? There are times when I have nothing to do, I don't have any money so I go and do these besoms little by little. I have to wind and wind. I have nothing more to add.' ALEXANDER ANTONOV, PENSIONER
FLOWER-POT STAND/ 'Near to us there's a school and they just put flower-pots into these things. It's waterproof and this small hole coincides exactly with what the pot itself has right in the middle. My wife did it. Just from an old disc. We didn't listen to it anymore.' HUSBAND OF SVETLANA, SCHOOL TEACHER
TRIPLE ADAPTER WITH A LONG FLEX/ 'It's just a triple adapter… I took three wall outlets from my previous apartment and made a triple adapter from them… You can of course buy such an adapter in a shop, but it's expensive. Why buy, if I can do it myself? I have all the "ingredients" I need at work. I mean my clients have. No one will notice if I take three pieces. It took me ten minutes to do this.' PETR ANISIMOV, BUILDER

4/'SPOON-TONGS'/'TEA-SPOONS, STAINLESS-STEEL STRIPS/BEFORE 1999///5/'BESOM'/SYNTHETIC CORD/1996///6/'FLOWER-POT STAND'/VINYL DISC/1997//////////////////////////
7/'TRIPLE ADAPTER WITH A LONG FLEX'/SOCKETS, FLEX, WOOD, SCREWS/1999//

Jose Pedro Cortes; Silence

Client Jose Pedro Cortes *Design* Conny Freyer, Eva Rucki, Sebastien Noel *Year* 2006

Pedro asked us to design the book to let people read it comfortably wherever they want - like on a park bench or waiting for the bus.

The format is therefore unusually small for a photography book, and we chose a thick cardboard cover to make it ruggedised. 19.5 × 16 cm, 112 pp.

590

BY AIR MAIL
par avion Royal Mail

Small Packet

& WEBB

London E2 8DD

16H Perseverance Works, 38 K

07739 7585

Webb&Webb
16H Perseverance Works
38 Kingsland Road
London E2 8DD
020 7739 7585

0887

BARCEL

SPAIN

Royal Mail

POSTAGE   PAID   UK
21/04/07   £5.07   IP18
158130   1-2220270-1

28, BAJOS

1TGES

A

Great Britain
Recommandé

R

Royal Mail   **signed**for
             international

RI 8151 2156 8GB   Sig req

RI 8151 2156 8GB   Sig req

RI 8151 2156 8GB
PRIORITY HANDLING & REGISTERED DELIVERY

Client Phaidon *Design* Brian Webb, James Webb, Dan Smith *Year* 2006
Large format book for Phaidon, designed as a scolarly work with general appeal as an up-market picture book.

592

PHAIDON

THE ARTS AND CRAFTS MOVEMENT
ROSALIND P BLAKESLEY

This elegant volume is a comprehensive survey of all
aspects of the popular Arts and Crafts Movement,
which was at its height between 1880 and 1910. The
movement was one of enormous intellectual and
artistic ambition and had a worldwide influence on
all areas of the decorative arts, architecture, cabinet
making and even garden design.

Inspired by critical thinkers in Victorian
England who opposed the dehumanizing nature of
industrialization, early practitioners campaigned for
a revival of craft techniques, for the elevation of the
applied arts and for honesty in design. This new study
charts the course of the movement in all media,
including painting, craft and architecture, and examines
the theory and philosophy behind a variety of seminal
pieces, including fine examples of work by Charles
Robert Ashbee, Edward Burne-Jones, Charles and
Henry Greene, Charles Rennie Mackintosh, William
Morris and Philip Webb, alongside lesser-known
examples from Scandinavia, Germany and Russia.

Featuring extensive archival material,
previously unpublished works and groundbreaking
new research, *The Arts and Crafts Movement* offers a
thorough overview of this highly popular intellectual
and artistic movement, which transformed the
expectations of architecture and design and spread
its ideas to places as diverse as Chicago and Budapest.

Top spread

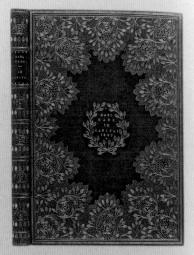

Thomas James Cobden-Sanderson
Binding of William Morris's Copy of Le Capital 1884 fig 53

CRAFT AND COMRADESHIP IN THE METROPOLIS

IN THE 1860s AND 1870s THE ARTS AND CRAFTS HAD BEEN CHARACTERIZED BY AN INTERLACING WEB OF THEMES. IN THE 1880s AND 1890s, HOWEVER, ONE STRAND CAME TO THE FORE – THAT OF FELLOWSHIP?

This was linked to the rise of socialism, with its agenda of shifting systems of power and means of production from private hands to the community as a whole. Many members of the Arts and Crafts Movement in Britain became committed socialists, its byword of social inclusion matching their concern to democratize the arts. Fellowship as a form of empowerment also developed in other walks of life, from welfare and science to education and philanthropy, and while some of the groups which resulted were little more than clubs for hard drinking and gluttonous dining, others, such as the Institution of Civil Engineers, were committed to a specific cause. There was a rise in the membership of Friendly Societies, a network of working-class clubs which stemmed from trade-related associations of the eighteenth century, and offered subsidies such as sickness and funeral benefit (by 1880, membership had reached approximately 2.2 million). From the middle of the century trade unionism was also on the increase, and in 1884 the Fabian Society was established with the aim of engaging in non-revolutionary reform along socialist lines. On a less political level, there was everything from the literary and philosophical societies, which increased rapidly from the 1820s, to the intriguing Society for the Suppression of Vice.

Whatever their size or purpose, these groups all shared a fundamental sense of community. This had featured strongly in the rhetoric of Pugin, Ruskin and Morris, and in the 1880s was to become a defining characteristic of the British Arts and Crafts Movement. As Morris asserted in his socialist story, A Dream of John Ball, which was published in instalments from 1886 to 1887: 'Fellowship is heaven, and lack of fellowship is hell; fellowship is life, and lack of fellowship is death.' Reflecting this sentiment, a succession of craft guilds, workshops and societies began to develop throughout Britain, in city centres and rural retreats, with formal manifestos or simple bonds of friendship, each relating to varying degrees the social, creative and, on occasion, philanthropic aims of the Arts and Crafts. It up until now, the Movement had been a set of ideas and aspirations shared by a few assertive and charismatic individuals; in the 1880s it acquired a wide support base, a coherent identity and, in 1887, a name, when the writer and bookbinder Thomas James Cobden-Sanderson (1840–1922) coined the phrase 'the Arts and Crafts'.

Some of the earliest craft associations of the period were run by women, for whom the applied arts had long been an acceptable form of activity. In 1879 Elizabeth Wardle,

51

Bottom spread

THE ARTS AND CRAFTS MOVEMENT

NORDIC IDENTITIES: SCANDINAVIA AND FINLAND

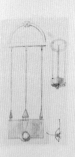

1902 Finch went on to work as the first ceramics teacher at the Central School of Applied Arts, and the Sparres bounced back with the Eva & Louis Sparre Design Bureau, whose products are often referred to as Iris work. With enviable energy and rude good health (Louis lived to the age of 101) the couple extended their repertoire to include book illustration, embroidery, weaving and metalwork. Sparre's patinated copper ceiling light of 1903, with its stylish construction of hooks and rings and its ingenious arrangement of light bulbs inside the circular drum (figs 181–2) exemplifies their continuing desire to create a modern design aesthetic, and other craftsmen shared this approach. Valle Rosenberg's compot bowl of 1910 (fig 206) is a case in point, its elegant form and stylized apples and pears on the handle of the spoon and at the top of the paired legs echoing the skilful understatement of Ashbee's designs.

The Friends of Finnish Handicraft and the Iris Workshops both made efforts to establish a Finnish style: the former's intention was to promote Finnish handicrafts and to refine them in a patriotic and artistic direction, and it and other applied art manufactures (the Nuutajärvi glass factory, for example) ran competitions for Finnish designs. Towards the end of the century Gallen-Kallela and the composer Jean

Sibelius were similarly credited with initiating a national idiom in their respective arts. Architecture, however, was thought not yet to have pulled its weight in the construction of a national culture, a concern which by the 1890s recurred in both the professional and the popular press. The architect Vilho Penttilä, for example, published several articles in Suomen Teollisuuslehti (The Industrial Magazine of Finland) in 1893–4 which considered the potential of Finnish wooden building traditions and lambasted the deficiencies of modern design. The principle that the exterior should always reflect the inner construction, and at the same time it should never try to hide the special character of the material used, too often remains unobserved,' Penttilä thundered. The question of what constituted 'Finnishness' in architecture was contentious, not least as Finland could not lay claim to any obvious historical precedent. The country boasted some splendid castles, but these had likely as not been built by Swedes, denying Finnish architects the native medieval example which had so captivated Arts and Crafts architects elsewhere.

In search of national models, a number of artists and architects began to travel to Karelia, where the roots of Finnish culture were supposed to be. The Sparres made their

182

Charles and Henry Greene
The Gamble House, 1908, in Pasadena, CA

Main Entrance, The Gamble House

they could be modified to suit any site. Interior renditions, for their part, exuded homely comfort, cultural accomplishment and tasteful restraint. Thus a design for a living room of 1905 (fig 235) includes an elegant lamp and runner and some well-chosen ceramics, while cultural pursuits are suggested by the piano and the books, which the inhabitant might read in the enticing Craftsman chair. The Craftsman published over 220 of these designs, complete sets of which were sold by mail order for do-it-yourself enthusiasts, and Stickley later issued them in book form as well. Accessible, adaptable and affordable, with Stickley setting their price range 'between two and fifteen thousand dollars', they initiated a vogue for unpretentious houses and bungalows, and in the process changed the face of American domestic design.

Until the First World War, the Craftsman empire appeared to be impregnable, with showrooms across the country, and Stickley seemed an invincible popularizer of the Craftsman ideal. In 1908, he began an ambitious, self-sufficient co-operative near Morris Plains in New Jersey. He also moved the editorial and administrative part of his business to prestigious offices in New York, expanding into the twelve-storey Craftsman Building in Manhattan, complete with showroom and restaurant, in 1913. Sadly, he had overextended his business, and financial rot set in, but such was the popularity of the Craftsman aesthetic that even Stickley's brothers emulated his success. As early as 1900 Leopold (1869–1957) and John George (1871–1921) set up a rival enterprise, the L & J G Stickley Company in Fayetteville, New York, which mass produced versions of their brothers' furniture. In a galling move, they also took over Gustav's Eastwood workshops after he filed for bankruptcy in 1915. Stickley's empire therefore came to a humiliating end, but his furniture, houses and The Craftsman had made simple, honest design accessible to a vast public, in the process establishing comfort and convenience as key to the modern American home.

The Craftsman was one of several periodicals which disseminated Arts and Crafts ideals. The Studio had been published in America as The International Studio since 1897, and the Ladies' Home Journal, with its plans for reasonably priced homes, was an important conduit of domestic architecture and design. Its contributors included Prairie School architects, Cram from Boston, and Will Bradley, who from 1901 to 1902 published a series of furniture designs and interiors known as the 'Bradley House', which featured

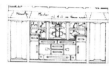

Charles Greene
Dining Room Sideboard, The Gamble House, 1908

230   231

Antonius Rumpe and Adhémar Letwé
Little Tour from Le Cottage, 1902
The Getty Research Institute, Los Angeles, CA

Antonius Rumpe and Adhémar Letwé
Hall, Little Tour from Le Cottage, 1902
Bibliothèque Royale de Belgique, Brussels

commissioned the pair to design a music salon for his Viennese mansion earlier that year. Inspired by what they had seen, the two Austrians resolved to create an island of tranquillity in their own country, which, amid the joyful hum of arts and crafts, would be welcome to anyone who professes faith in Ruskin and Morris. The result, the Wiener Werkstätte, opened in Vienna in 1903, financed by Wärndorfer and directed by Hoffmann and Moser, Hoffmann's friend from Secession days.

In the Wiener Werkstätte's first Work Programme of 1905, Hoffmann launched a splenetic invective against the trumpery of modern design: 'The boundless evil caused by shoddy mass-produced goods and by the uncritical imitation of earlier styles, is like a tidal wave sweeping across the world. [...] The machine has largely replaced the hand and the business-man has supplanted the craftsman.' To counteract this, the Werkstätte aimed to provide craftsmen with a forum in which to practise and publicize their skills, hoping in the process to re-establish the role of the craftsman in contemporary production, and to improve the standards and availability of good design. As Hoffmann explained, 'We wish to create an inner relationship linking public, designer and

worker and we want to produce good and simple articles of everyday use. Our guiding principle is function, utility our first condition, and our strength must lie in good proportions and the proper treatment of material.' True to his word, Hoffmann designed cutlery (fig 127) which is proud, strong and devoid of fuss, with a minimum of joints and details which might be weakened or damaged by the wear and tear of everyday use. His silver sugar pot with a simple fruit motif (fig 128), on the other hand, is a seductive exercise in truth to materials, its tactile curves exploiting the silver's polished sheen. Moser too flaunted good materials and skilled craftsmanship in pieces such as his music cupboard (fig 129), which was treated with white lead to enhance the natural grain of the oak. The stylized female figures on its chased silver plaques point to aesthetic considerations shared with the Glasgow Four, whose work was much admired in Vienna at the time.

The Wiener Werkstätte laid great emphasis on the well-being of its workers, even if this meant charging high prices. The inevitable result was that the Werkstätte found itself working for the moneyed elite and gradually moved into the luxury of Art Nouveau. In the Palais Stoclet (1905–11)

The Chevalier de Miramon de Beaufeu
Stoclet interior from Le Cottage, 1904
Bibliothèque Royale de Belgique, Brussels

128   129

598

222 Daniel Berkeley Updike, Robert Anning Bell
and Bertram Grosvenor Goodhue
Pages from *The Altar Book*, 1896.
Black and red ink on white paper.
35.5 x 28.3 cm (14 x 11 in.)

nt

Client Antique Collectors Club *Design* Brian Webb, Chris Gloster *Year* 2005
An introduction to the design work of two well known artists.

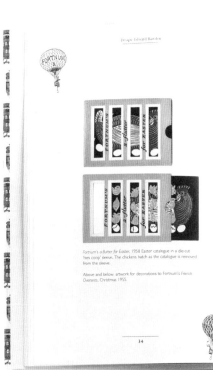

Fortnum's a-flutter for Easter, 1958 Easter catalogue in a die-cut 'hen coop' sleeve. The chickens hatch as the catalogue is removed from the sleeve.

Above and below, artwork for decorations to Fortnum's *French Oversees*, Christmas 1955.

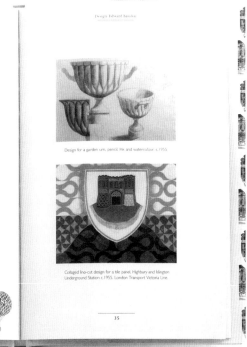

Design for a garden urn, pencil, ink and watercolour. c.1955.

Collaged lino-cut design for a tile panel, Highbury and Islington Underground Station c.1955. London Transport Victoria Line.

The engine used in Ealing Studio's *Titfield Thunderbolt* film was The Lion, made in Leeds in 1838. Bawden's poster, based on the engine, was produced in landscape and portrait formats, the artwork drawn in coloured crayons with added watercolour. The film, directed by Charles Crichton and written by TEB Clarke, tells the story of a village fighting the closure of its branch line. The poster and Christmas card below, were produced in 1953.

Cut-to-shape Easter Catalogues for Fortnum & Mason. c.1955.

Watercolour design for the proposed decimal currency introduced in 1971. Bawden's proposals, c.1962, illustrating national and traditional pence symbols were rejected.

Fortnum & Mason Christmas Catalogues, 1955, 1956 and 1958, commissioned by the advertising agents Colman Prentice and Varley. Father Christmas is illustrated in Bawden's favourite animal in the 1958

version which becomes a CATalogue with a title page poem ending The Christmas Cat perused each page and found new friends at every stage.

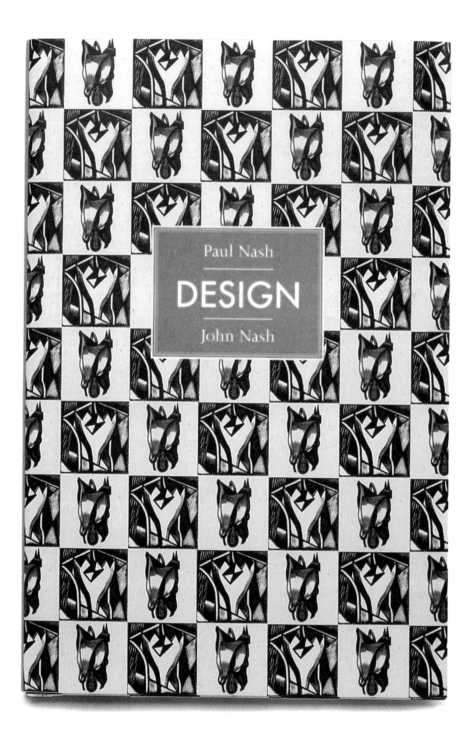

Desi

Design

Paul Nas
twentieth
Wars, he
awarenes
with felic
of the Ma
his myth
heir to Pa
contradict
which fou
unique, a
However,
full exper
ceramics,
Herbert R
of the love
He taught
Bawden, I

John Nash
career as a
draughtsm
but prefer
Marines, a
to conflict,
exploited a
Dangerou
He served
and in 19
work at th

This fasci
work of th
an expecte
reputation

The patter
engraving,
John Nash

Paul Nash, book jacket for Richard Aldington's *Roads to Glory*, 1930. Published by Chatto & Windus; printed at Curwen Press. Paul Nash had previously illustrated Aldington's *Death of a Hero* and asked that the cover of this book of war stories should be as 'dramatic as possible'.

Both Paul and John Nash saw active service in the Armed Forces and served as official war artists during the First World War, resulting in some of the most powerful and sardonic images of warfare.

Design
Paul Nash and John Nash

'The real thing is to get used to saying with a pencil what you want to say, until you instinctively think in lines and masses.'
(Gordon Bottomley to Paul Nash, 14 April, 1910)

Despite their closeness and the fact that, to a large degree, their careers followed similar paths, Paul and John Nash were very much individuals and disliked being lumped together as 'the Nash brothers', or 'the brothers Nash'. Paul, born 11 May 1889, was nearly four years older than John, born 11 April 1893; like their younger sister, Barbara, they were all born at the oddly named Ghuznee Lodge in Earl's Court, a gloomy, respectable, West London residential area dominated by blocks of red brick mansion flats. Paul was later to describe their birthplace as 'a pariah of a house', with an outlandish name and a pretentious conservatory where nothing would grow. The latter comment being particularly significant given the fact that both he and John were to become landscape painters of distinction, and that John was to excel as one of the twentieth-century's outstanding botanical draughtsmen. Plants, whether naturalistic or as elements of dream and 'fantasy', were also to play an important part in Paul's repertoire and imagery. William Nash, their father, was a moderately successful barrister and Recorder for Abingdon, but, to the detriment of his practice, he sold the London house in 1901 and moved his family to the country in the hope that the change would benefit his ailing wife Caroline. The move was only marginally beneficial; she died in a nursing home nine years later.

However, from the point of view of the two brothers, the move got them out of the city, which they disliked, into the

5

A Song About Tsar Ivan Vasilyevich, by Mikhail Lermontov, translated by John Cournos. Published by the Aquila press, 1929. Nash designed the text layout, and wood engravings in black and red and binding in red morocco inlaid with black and ivory niger.

Nash's pattern papers for the Curwen Press have been in constant use since their first printing, 1925-1928.

Journey
Client Royal Mail *Design* Brian Webb, Chris Gloster *Year* 2003
Small format, limited edition letterpress book.

Classic Chairs
Client Luke Hughes and Company *Design* Brian Webb, James Webb *Year* 2006
Small format, 120 page book of 'classic chairs' produced over a 20 year period by Luke Hughes & Co.

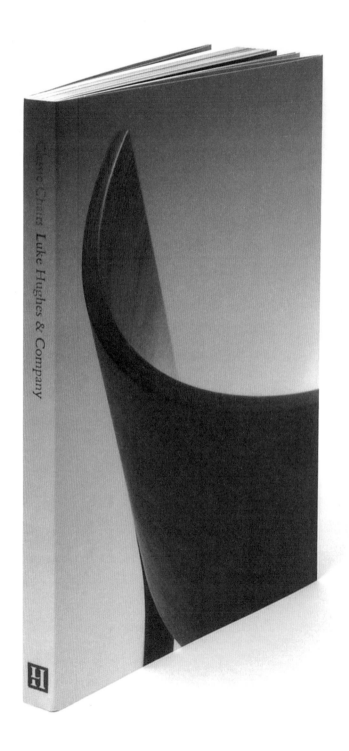

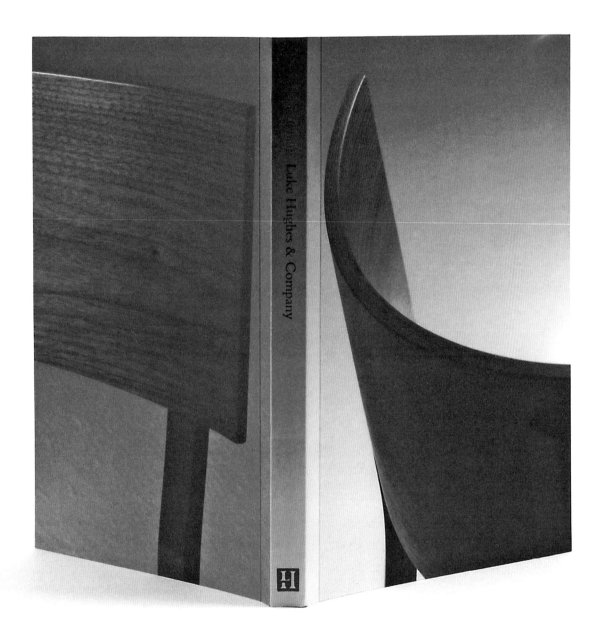

Luke Hughes & Company

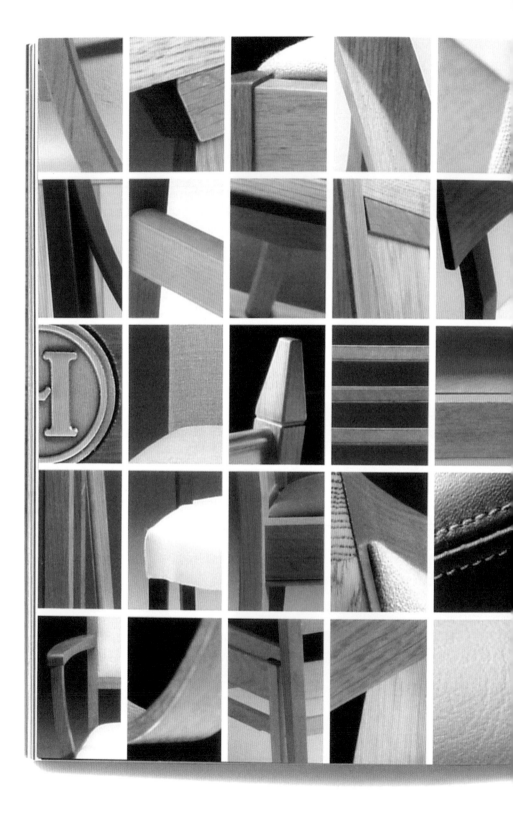

Downing

32|33

St Swithin's

88|89

In his marvellous fantasy fiction of 1930, Fattypuffs and
Thinifers (*Patapoufs et Filifers*), André Maurois described
a parallel universe divided between two rival societies. The
Fattypuffs live up to their name, their chairs are as rounded
as they are themselves, with ample upholstery and baroque
ornament. The Thinifers, on the other hand, prefer never
to sit at all if they can avoid it and even eat standing. What
furniture they possess is tall and spindly, like themselves.

Chairs in our world have similarly been divided according
to opposing belief systems. Upholstery may be a sin among
certain designers, and suffering in the name of good design
a means of redemption from some unnamed transgression.

In Maurois' book there is a war in the Kingdom of Undersea,
and the efficient Thinifers quickly conquer the slow and
unwarlike Fattypuffs. In the peace that follows, however,
Fattypuff culture begins to subvert these stern moralists,
establishing a tolerable balance between the two extremes.

Luke Hughes and Company has achieved a similar truce
in the war of the chairs, realising that comfort in the seat
is an asset to quality of life, but does not have to come at
the expense of practicalities. At the same time, they have
achieved a happy balance between plain and fancy, robust
architecture and fine design, industrial production and
delicate craftmanship. Alan Powers

Peter Blake Sculpture

Client The London Institute *Design* Brian Webb, Chris Gloster *Year* 2004
Book to accompany Sir Peter Blake's first exhibition of sculpture.

Above **At the AB Foundry, September 2003.** Left and centre **Peter Blake** supervises the making of the wax models of men and horses that will come together in his bronze sculptures 'Four Man Up' and 'Equestrian Act'. Right Blake watches the modelling of 'Endless Column', his homage to Brancusi.

Above **In the assembly area Blake's 'Family' of bronzes come together under the watchful eyes of** the artist and foundry manager Jerry Hughes. And meanwhile (for there's always a meanwhile) a tiny model of a Victorian dog and her puppies watch the fun from their cushion.

Sculpture Studio where Alice and the Mad Hatter peer from a window while Snow White, the Junior League of America and a cast of comic book characters are taking their places in the 'Parade for Saul Steinberg'. It's a world of riches and depths, a labyrinth of feints and allusions and echoes everywhere. It could, of course, be chaotic but thanks to Blake's curatorial genius everything appears to be occupying its allotted place. All of the time.

Although Peter Blake says he is not recognised for his sculpture, the work hasn't been without its influence. Indeed his sculpture has, in its own quiet way, exerted a considerable influence across the decades. His 'Captain Webb' work, for example, prefigured Warhol's interest in consumer packaging (exemplified by his 1964 series of Brillo boxes) and Damien Hirst's huge jemmied collecting box that recently graced Hoxton Square takes its cue, as Hirst has acknowledged, from Peter Blake's work.

And so in ending to return to the question of titles. Who else but Peter Blake could have dreamt up 'The Surrealist Shows Snow White His Garden', 'Man Selling Musical Instruments to Members of Minority Groups', 'Africans Looking at an Indian Sculpture' or 'Family Meeting a Leopard on a Japanese Bridge'. And so on and on. Asking what they mean or where they come from or which comes first isn't quite the point. They simply sum up the brilliant juxtapositions and connections that only Peter Blake can conjure. The elements from which the wizard weaves his magic. And that's the point. He alone knows the combination...
Michael Benson

Opposite In the sculpture studio again. This time accompanied by his pet rhinoceros, 'The Surrealist Shows Snow White His Garden'.

The London Institute Gallery

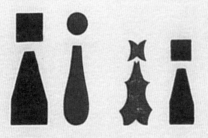

Weather
Client Royal Mail *Design* Brian Webb, Chris Gloster *Year* 2005
Small format, limited edition book, with stamp illustrations by Raymond Briggs.

Why do the Winds Blow?

Wind is moving air, which brings various kinds of weather with it, according to its source.

The air moves from places where the air pressure is high to places where it is lower, and we often find that the pressure is lower over hot regions that it is over cooler. That is why a breeze will blow from the cool sea to the much warmer land on a hot and otherwise calm day. This is the sea breeze, or onshore breeze. At night, when the sea is warmer than the land, the breeze blows the other way, from land sea. Air behaves in the same way as water and moves because of pressure differences. The greater the pressure – the faster the flow.

Mist and Fog

Mist, like cloud, is made of tiny droplets of water; but while clouds are formed by the cooling of rising air, mist forms when warm air is cooled by contact with cool air close to the ground. Mist occurs more frequently in river valleys, along streams or over lakes, because the air has become saturated with water vapour by evaporation. The mist we see round mountains, hills and high ground is really low cloud.

Fog is a thick mist and is formed in just the same way. In big towns water droplets form very easily round the particles of soot and dust which are present in the air, and this can result in a very thick and dirty fog.

VALUE → GIFT.

end

Contagious Magazine

Client Xtreme Information *Design* Why Not Associates *Year* 2005
Identity and design for quarterly magazine and dvd. Contagious is a subscription only title,
which reports on the most innovative work in marketing and advertising.

620

MAVI / New York / The US flagship for this Turkish jeans label uses display fixtures that educate and reference the history of the brand and the craft of making denim. 25% of the store is dedicated to displaying commissioned art installations and short films by new and innovative directors. The store targets the area's large student population and aims to provide a desirable meeting space. Design: Pompei AD (www.pompeiad.com) / Photography: Bruce Lee Berger

Drake Hotel / Toronto / This hotel is a platform for showcasing art pieces by local artists and encouraging creative participation from hotel guests. There is an Artist Residency Program and a Video Alliance where video artists meet to show and discuss new works. Guests can select and watch these art videos on the television systems installed in their rooms. Not a retail example but an important and influential concept. / Design: 3rdUncle (3rduncle.com)

This report was compiled by GDR Creative Intelligence, based in London, who provide clients with a unique insight into the creative industries that drive global design trends in retail, hospitality and leisure. GDR compile their global research into quarterly Retail Innovation Reports, featuring cutting-edge case studies sourced from designers and architects around the world. / www.gdruk.com

---

'Emotionally-sticky retailing' / **How retailers are building social programmes into their offer to create focal points for the community /**
We've seen 'retail theatre' but now it is time for something deeper, more genuinely connected to the community, more emotionally involving. We're talking about entertainment, education and the seamless splicing of commerce with culture.
The following selection of case studies illustrates how retailers on different continents are incorporating sociable spaces, community events and educational elements into the retail offer. The net effect is a form of 'emotionally sticky' retailing that builds deeper connections with the consumer, encouraging them to return to the brand or store time and time again
A report by GDR Creative Intelligence, London…

THE EMPIRE STRIKES BACK

CASE STUDY / McDONALD'S / THE EMPIRE STRIKES BACK / IT'S BEEN A TOUGH START TO THE NEW MILLENNIUM FOR McDONALD'S. THE BURGER BEHEMOTH HAS SEEN ITS STOCK PRICE SLIDE, FACED TUMULT IN THE BOARDROOM AND TAKEN FLAK FROM ANALYSTS, OBESITY WARRIORS AND THE ANTI-GLOBALIZATION LOBBY. BUT THE COMPANY IS FIGHTING BACK, WITH HEALTHIER MENU OPTIONS, BOLD INTERIOR DESIGN, A HIP HOP SIGNATURE TUNE, FORTHRIGHT PR STRATEGY AND A RADICAL COMMITMENT TO 'BRAND JOURNALISM' IN PLACE OF TRADITIONAL MARKETING TECHNIQUES.

LUCY AITKEN PROVIDES A UK PERSPECTIVE

624

guide to

ecstacity

nigel coates

Dangeging the two at different scales. Music is big, but it actually has a physical effect, it is inside your body. Likewise the city - it's big, but condenses into a kind of genie inside you.

You see everyone taking part in design. There's no point in designing an object that's stuck on the shelf to be admired. You should be able to grab it, be turned on by it, and claim it as your own. That's why you design things that contain the imprints of the person you hope will use it. And that's why you take on, and wear, the spirit of things that others have designed more than you do with your own.

Design democracy: We face a special moment: the one in which we face ourselves, instead of stifling or coveting our sensuality (as so much design does). Any style, from modernism to baroque, is a mask. As little more than a timid respite, style tries as hard to simplify a busy world. The ecstatic embraces complex responses to the urban environment, from its hardware through to the software of events and experiences, to the very fabric of the everyday achievements of work or p-leisure.

Now we know our bodies better, know what drives them and satisfies them. We are prepared to become what we really want to be: rather than squeezing into stereotypes like a badly fitting corset. To explore this process of becoming, we could wallow in vast technological fields. You could, like Barbarella, be persuaded to die from a surfeit of pleasure. You've put aside the pursuit of godliness for what Baudrillard ironically called the ecstacy of communication. He thinks that we are lost in a swirl of promiscuous information that borders on pornography, with no boundaries between public and private, and no distinction between the pure object of communication and its counterfeit reproductions. But increasingly both artists and the users of the Internet have learned that values do not necessarily come from authenticity. There is no reason why the artist's interpretation is necessarily better than the ad wiz

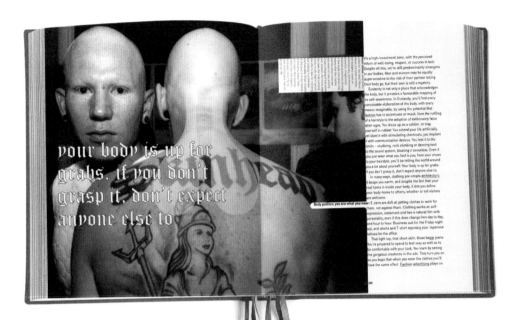

Making an angel

Client Booth-Clibborn Editions *Design* Why Not Associates *Year* 1998

Design of book documenting the creation of Antony Gormley's sculpture *The angel of the north.*

628

ISBN 1-86154-063-9

9 781861 540638

making
an
angel

an enlightened icarus

dr stephanie brown

The biggest single sculpture in Britain, made in the closing years not only of the century but of the millennium, Antony Gormley's *Angel of the North* inevitably seems to assume the status of a bold defining moment, a confidently conclusive sculptural statement. On this level it is in a class of its own - though it also relates to a climate of fin de siècle giganticism, evident in the Millennium Dome. The Angel is certainly of its time and cannot escape such associations; but it is also a work that has evolved from an established artist's practice which, in turn, consolidates distinctive strands in late twentieth-century sculpture. Is it possible, then, to view the Angel not as a freakish case for special pleading but as an ambitious and innovative development of Gormley's existing preoccupations, and an instructive pivotal point between modernist and postmodernist sculptural idioms?

The difficulty of comparing this work with other sculptural entities is compounded by its dual identity as figurative sculpture and landmark. Large-scale landmark sculpture of a progressive type is firmly associated with non-figurative, temporary interventions such as Christo's wrapping of existing landmarks and geographical features. Because of its scale, the Angel initially invites comparisons with colossal landmark statuary such as the Rio de Janeiro Christ and the Statue of Liberty rather than with central developments in modern sculpture. The two categories are not mutually exclusive, however, and the former has been used to succinctly illuminate the latter. In 1970 the American sculptor Carl Andre formulated an account of major shifts in twentieth-century sculpture through analogy with changing perceptions of the Statue of Liberty' and this offers a convenient frame within which to discuss the Angel's wider context.

Unveiled in 1886, a present from France to America celebrating both their revolutions, the statue of *Liberty Enlightening the World* was a symbolic personification of an abstract idea. Andre observes that interest was originally focused on the form of this personification and on the way the sculptor Frédéric-Auguste Bartholdi modelled the copper sheets which constituted the outer skin of the statue. Attention then switched to Gustave Eiffel's cast-iron interior structure with its girders and cantilevers; and finally to the place, Bedloe's Island, where the statue was sited. Andre thus proposes the history of twentieth-century sculpture as successively concentrating on form, structure and place. Since 1970, a fourth category, 'socio-cultural space', as opposed to physical locus, has been suggested as completing this metaphorical progression.² All these strands are amalgamated in the Angel, and can be loosely applied in relating it to key aspects of sculpture in Britain in the second half of the twentieth century.

The form of the Angel is that of a winged figure, whose fusion of human anatomy with geometric elements links it to sculptures of the 1950s which embodied what Herbert Read

termed the 'geometry of fear', expressing art's post-war alienation from technological society. Agitated figure sculptures externalised inner states, mainly anxiety and despair, and sculptors such as Lynn Chadwick and Kenneth Armitage (ill.), produced hybrid forms fusing the human figure with unwieldy geometric elements - most commonly wing-like extensions. The significance of this was explicit in works entitled *Icarus* - a subject treated repeatedly by Michael Ayrton - but the Icarian reference was implicit in almost all these works.³

The myth of Icarus focused disillusionment with technological progress, which had promised freedom but promoted the terrible efficiencies of Nazi extermination camps and American A-bombs. Icarus was figured as modern man, irrevocably bonded to wings which betray aspiration and accentuate the vulnerability of flesh. Speaking of the Gateshead Angel's direct predecessor, *A Case for an Angel* 1990 (ill. 2), Gormley remarked: 'It isn't a kind of Icarus - you know, little bird feathers.'⁴ Yet the wings of the fifties sculptures were not avian but constructed in form, and are formally and thematically closer to Gormley's angels than are the traditional bird-winged angels on funerary and war memorials.

The Gateshead Angel returns to the 'marriage of anatomy and technology', presenting it in optimistic rather than fearful terms.⁵ It also echoes the awkwardness of the fifties sculptures, though in a radically different, non-expressive way, and Gormley has stated, 'My version of an angel is a rather uncomfortable mixture between aeronautics and anatomy.'⁶ In this sense, the Angel, like all of Gormley's work, can be seen as an 'attempt to materialise uncertainty', and he draws attention to this in mentioning the 'tension between the angel's slight vulnerability and the toughness of the metal structure that will keep it standing'.⁷ Tension is also evident in the use of this particular type of structure both to describe a humanoid form and to ensure that it is rooted to the earth.

In the sixties, steel structures became the most important sculptural idiom - replacing the figure with abstract forms and dispensing with the plinth. Assemblages of steel plates and beams, pioneered by Anthony Caro and his followers from St Martins School of Art, demonstrated the possibility of an almost infinite extension of sculptural form. Caro was anxious to free sculpture of its totemic connotations and to introduce a greater emphasis on the horizontal. The Angel retains the former while stretching the latter to an unprecedented degree, not as a formalist demonstration of sculptural viability, but to maximise the meaning of the work. The result is a clear exposition of Gormley's central idea of a continuum between the body and spirit or consciousness, and between the earthly and heavenly realms. In this relationship the body, no matter how elevated, is finite; terminated by contact with the earth - that is, mortality. Although aspiration and infinity are traditionally represented by verticality, Gormley seems to invert this, using the horizontal

STEELWORK HEIGHT 20m
WINGSPAN 54m
WING HEIGHT AT BODY JUNCTION 6.2m
TOTAL WEIGHT 208 TONS
(EACH WING 50 TONS, BODY 108 TONS)
ANKLE CROSS-SECTION 780mm BY 1,400mm
(EQUIVALENT TO AN ORDINARY DOOR IN THE HOUSE)
3,153 PIECES OF STEEL ASSEMBLED
136 BOLTS NEEDED TO ATTACH WINGS TO BODY
(EACH 48mm DIAMETER)
22,000 MAN HOURS SPENT IN FABRICATION
(TWENTY MEN WORKING FULL-TIME FOR SIX MONTHS)
10km OF WELDING IN FABRICATION

DESIGN HORIZONTAL WIND FORCE ON WINGS 70 TONS
(EQUIVALENT TO THE ANGEL BOLTED TO A VERTICAL SURFACE
AND A 35-TON LORRY PARKED ON EACH WING)
450 TONS FORCE IN WING DIAPHRAGMS
1,200 TONS FORCE IN ANKLE RIBS
50 TONS FORCE IN EACH 50mm BOLT
(SO EACH BOLT COULD CARRY A LORRY AND A HALF)
2,500 MAN HOURS SPENT IN ENGINEERING DESIGN AND DRAWING
FOUNDATIONS **5000m³ OF SOIL EXCAVATED**
AND LATER REPLACED TO REFORM MOUND
100 TONS OF GROUT PUMPED INTO MINE WORKINGS
UP TO 33m BELOW GROUND
700 TONS OF CONCRETE AND 32 TONS OF REINFORCING STEEL
USED IN FOUNDATION EXTENDING 20m BELOW GROUND
52 BOLTS NEEDED TO HOLD ANGEL UPRIGHT IN WIND
(EACH 50mm DIAMETER AND 3m LONG)

Dean quinn

EMMa _louise.

christopher
DAniel

James Hall

634

michael nawthorney.

AMANDA.

Why Not Associates 2
Client Thames and Hudson *Design* Why Not Associates *Year* 2004
Book documenting a 5-year period of Why Not Associates design work.

636

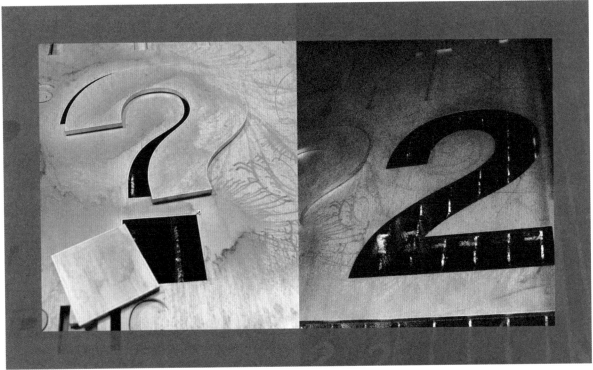

In 1525, the Archbishop of Glasgow, Gavin Dunbar, put the colourfully worded 'Mother of all Curses' on the Reivers, English and Scottish sheep rustlers and robbers who terrorized the border lands between the two countries. Priests read the curse to their congregations in every parish of the area – what is now Cumbria, Northumberland, the Borders and Dumfries and Galloway – in an attempt by the Catholic Church to stop cross-border violence and increase tax revenues by preventing smuggling. Despite these efforts, border reiving continued for another two hundred years.

Finding this mention inspired Carlisle-born artist Gordon Young to create the Cursing Stone and Reiver Pavement as part of his contribution to the city's millennium project. Young found the boulder for the project in Scotland; originally weighing fourteen tons, it took over twenty days to be carved and polished before the text was finally sandblasted onto its surface. The stone sits on an eighty-metre granite walkway that has surnames of Reiver families repeatedly sandblasted onto the surface.

Even before it was installed, there was an outcry from various members of the church, who saw the stone as 'a shrine for devil worship', and it eventually became blamed for the foot and mouth crisis! We think the project proves that you can only create really powerful graphics if you have strong content.

"As for the future of the stone and the curse it brings, they need to be broken, both literally and spiritually, for all time."
Reverend Kevin Davies

"Words can affect reality for good or ill and become even more powerful when they are written down."
Reverend Kevin Davies

"It has mocked God, and God will not be mocked."
Leslie Irving

"…I curse their face, their ene, their mouth, their nese, their toung, their teith, their crag, their schulderis, their breist, their hert, their stomok, their bak, their wame, their armes, their leggis, their handis, their feit, and everilk part of their body, frae the top of their heid to the soill of thair feit, befoir and behind, within and without…"

'a violent piece of spiritual language'

And, finally, I condemn thaim perpetualie to the deip pyt of hell, the remain with Lucifer and all his fellowis, and thair bodeis to the gallowis of the Burrow Mure, first to be hangit, syne revin and ruggit with doggis, swyne, and utheris wyld beistis, abhominabile to all the warld. And thair candillis gangis frae your sicht, as wes thair saulis gang fra the visage of God, and that thair name be put furth of the buke of lyfe, quhill thai forbeir thair oppin synnys foirsaidis and ryse frae this terribill cursing, and mak satisfaction and pennance.

'Apocalypse: Beauty and Horror in Contemporary Art' was conceived as part of the Royal Academy's own millennium project. The RA is not known for its presentation of radical art of the moment, but 'Apocalypse' was a follow-up exhibition to the very successful and controversial 1987 'Sensation: Young British Artists from the Saatchi Collection' for which Why Not designed the poster and advertising material (see Why Not, pp. 202–03).

In 'Apocalypse', thirteen contemporary artists were each given a gallery space in which to present work that addressed the powerful and dramatic issues of the time. Artists included: Jeff Koons, Jake and Dinos Chapman, Mariko Mori and Chris Cunningham, and the exhibition was curated by Norman Rosenthal and Max Wigram. As with 'Sensation', Why Not were asked to produce an original icon to represent the exhibition rather than taking the more traditional approach of using an image of detail from one of the featured works.

We were given a copy of the book of Revelation to read for inspiration, and, armed with that and the exhibition title, we began to design around the obvious images of doom and gloom: fire, death, volcanic eruptions, holocausts, and so on. In tandem with this, we bastardized the font Trade Gothic so all the counters were filled in black. It was immediately apparent that the word 'apocalypse' was very bold in this font and when juxtaposed against positive images, the overall effect was incredibly striking, making the viewer question the meaning of the piece.

We presented our preferred combination for use on the London Underground – the swimmers embracing in the water – which the Royal Academy liked, but they also asked to see alternatives and dutifully we suggested many (see opposite)! In the end, we returned to our favourite.

The Yorkshire Sculpture Park is one of
Europe's leading open-air art organizations
showing modern and contemporary work by
UK and international artists in five-hundred
acres of eighteenth-century landscaped
grounds and two indoor galleries. Gordon
Young and Why Not designed a one-
hundred-metre pathway to connect the car
park with the new visitor centre, designed
by Feilden Clegg Bradley. The pathway was
a fund-raising venture with the idea that
visitors would pay to have their name
inscribed in the path. Our initial tests used
sandblasted granite, but this immediately
appeared too funereal, so we experimented
with steel, which had to have a raised
chequered pattern to prevent people from
slipping. We redrew the stencil font
WaterTower so that no parts of any letter
were too thin in case they became rusty and
broke off. The use of steel, which changes
colour as it ages, and the stencil font allow
the path to sit comfortably with the modern
design of the centre.

The poet Simon Armitage wrote a poem for
the park specifically about the path.

Making a Name

Here is a name – it is your name for life.
Loop it around your ears and toes – it works
like puppet strings, like radio control.
Try it for sound – slide it between your teeth.

Stitch that name into your socks and vest.
Sketch the shape of your name with a felt-tip.
Will it float or fly, or should it be screwed
to an office door, propped on a desk?

Once we were known by our quirks and kinks,
known by our lazy-eyes, our hair-lips.
Once we were named by the knack of our hands:
we were fletchers, bakers, coopers and smiths.

Don't sell your name to a man in a bar!
Don't leave your name in a purse on the beach!
Don't wait for a blue plaque – get yourself known
with glitter and glue, in wrought ironwork;

sign your autograph with a laser-pen
on the face of the moon. Here is your name
and a lifetime only to make it your own.
Then the mason takes it, sets it in stone.

Simon Armitage © 2002

1999

Alexander Boxill
Unit 1
Providence Yard
Ezra street
London E2 7RJ
+44 (0)20 7729 0875
info@alexanderboxill.com
www.alexanderboxill.com

Aloof Design
5 Fisher Street
Lewes
East Sussex
BN7 2DG
+44 1273 470887
www.aloofdesign.com

Axis Graphic Design Limited
9 Silverdale Road, Manchester M21 0SH
England
www.axisgraphicdesign.co.uk

BB/Saunders
7Plough Yard
London
EC2A 3LP
+44 (0) 20 7422 9181
www.bbsaunders.com

Blueprint
6-14 Underwood Street
London , N1 7JQ
+44 (0) 20 7490 0049
www.blueprintmagazine.co.uk

Carter Wong Tomlin
29 Brook Mews North
London, W2 3BW
www.carterwongtomlin.com

CHK Design
8 Flitcroft Street
London WC2H 8 DL
+44 (0)20 7836 2007
info@chkdesign.com
www.chkdesign.com

Copy Fanzine
London
info@copymagazine.org
www.copymagazine.org

Crush
6 Gloucester Street
Brighton, BN1 4EW
+44 (0) 1273 606 058
info@crushed.co.uk
www.crushed.co.uk

David Pearson
info@davidpearson.com
+44 (0) 20 7790 2727

Deep
12ª Imperial Studios
3-11 Imperial road
London SW6 2AG
+44 (0) 20 7751 0824
deeper@deep.co.uk
www.deep.co.uk

Design Holborn
123 Aberdeen House
22-24 Highbury Grove
London, N5 2EA
+44 (0) 20 7288 7200
info@designholborn.co.uk
www.designholborn.co.uk

Eat Sleep Work/Play
332 Kingsland Road
London E8 4 DA
+44 (0) 79 5065 8097
www.eatsleepworkplay.com

EI8HT
1-5 Honduras Street
London, EC1Y 0TH
0207 253 8801
info@foto8.com
www.foto8.com

EMMI
Studio 17
310 Kingsland Road
E(4DB London
+44 77 5200 1311
hello@emmi.co.uk
www.emmi.co.uk

FL@33
59 Britton Street
London, EC1M 5UU
+44 (0) 20 7168 7990
contact@flat33.com
www.flat33.com

Fluid
12 Tenby Street
Birmingham B! 3AJ
+44 (0) 121 212 0121
drop@fluidesign.co.uk
www.fluidesign.co.uk

Form
47 Tabernacle Street
London EC2A 4AA
+44 (0) 20 7014 1430
studio@form.uk.com
www.form.uk.com

Hat-Trick
3rd Floor
3 Morocco Street
London SE1 3HB
+44(0) 20 7403 8926
info@hat-trickdesign.co.uk
www.hat-trickdesign.co.uk

HDR Visual Communication
Bradbourne House
East Malling
Kent ME19 6DZ
+44 (0)1732 875 200
mail@hdr-online.com
www.hdr-online.com

Hemisphere
Binks Building 30-32 Thomas Street
Northern Quarter
Manchester M4 1ER
+44 (0)161 907 3730
post@hemispheredmc.com
www.hemispheredmc.com

Hypetype Studio
Office 3, Cooks Court 62 High Street
Yarm TS15 9AH
+44 (0) 1642 888 633
info@hypetype.co.uk
www.hypetype.co.uk

John Brown
136-142 Bramley Road
London W10 6SR
020 7565 3000
info@johnbrowngroup.co.uk
www.johnbrowngroup.co.uk

Kasia Korczak
mail@kasia-korczak.com
www.kasia-korczak.com

Kerr/Noble
3-4 Hardwick Street
London EC1R 4RB
+44 (0)20 7833 7277
info@kerrnoble.com
www.kerrnoble.com

Laki 139
9 Ship Street, Shoreham by Sea
West Sussex BN43 5DH
+44(0) 7815 067643
info@laki139.com
www.laki139.com

Marcus Piper
www.marcuspiper.com

John Morgan Studio
Room B.225.   MacMillan House
Platform 1
Paddington Station
London W2 1 FT
+44 (0)20 7402 6622
info@morganstudio.co.uk
www.morganstudio.co.uk

NB Studio
4-8 Emerson Street
London SE1 9DU
+44(0)20 7633 9046
mail@nbstudio.co.uk
www.nbstudio.co.uk

Nick Bell Design
5.06 Tea Building
56 Shoreditch High Street
London E1 6JJ
+44 (0)20 7033 2991
studio@nickbelldesign.co.uk
www.nickbelldesign.co.uk

Pentagram
11 Needham Road
London W11 2RP
+44 (020)7229 3477
email@pentagram.co.uk
www.pentagram.co.uk

Plan-B Studio
Studio 12
25 Horsell Road
London N5 1XL
+44 (0) 207 700 1166
info@plan-bstudio.com
www.plan-bstudio.com

Roundel
7 Rosehart Mews
Westbourne Grove
London W11 3TY
+44 (0)20 7221 1951
info@roundel.com

Sampsonmay
4 Tanner Street
London SE1 3LD
+44 (0)20 7403 4099
studio@sampsonmay.com
www.sampsonmay.com

Saturday
Biscuit Building 3rd Floor 10 Redchurch Street
London E2
+44 (0)20 7749 4500
studio@saturday-london.com
www.saturday-london.com

Scott King
+44 207 359 2316
info@scottking.co.uk
www.scottking.co.uk

Sea Design
70 St John Street
London EC1M 4DT
020 7566 3100
info@seadesign.co.uk
www.seadesign.co.uk

Stephen Coates
Studio 6
The Lux Building 2-4
Hoxton Square
London N1 6NU

Studio8 Design
N°1 Sans Walk
London EC1R 0LT
020 7251 6430
info@studio8design.co.uk
www.studio8design.co.uk

The Cheese Room
37 Albert Road
Tamworth, Staffordshire
England B79 7JS
info@thecheeseroom.com
www.thecheeseroom.com

Troika
88ª Acre Lane - Unit 1
London SW2 5QN
+44 (0)2077372244
studio@troika.uk.com
www.troika.uk.com

Webb&Webb
16H Perseverance Works
38 Kingsland Road
London E2 8DD
020 7739 7585

Why Not Associates
22C Shepherdess Walk
London N1 7LB
+44 (0)20 7253 2244
info@whynotassociates.com
www.whynotassociates.com

Thank you all
studios for your
collaboration and...

... your patient.

648